International Organisation in
World Politics

International Organisation in World Politics

Third Edition

**DAVID ARMSTRONG,
LORNA LLOYD AND
JOHN REDMOND**

First edition published 1982 (David Armstrong: *The Rise of International Organisations: A Short History*)

Second edition published 1996 (David Armstrong, Lorna Lloyd and John Redmond: *From Versailles to Maastricht: International Organisation in the Twentieth Century*)

Third edition published 2004 by
PALGRAVE MACMILLAN
Houndmills, Basingstoke, Hampshire RG21 6XS and
175 Fifth Avenue, New York, N.Y. 10010
Companies and representatives throughout the world

PALGRAVE MACMILLAN is the global academic imprint of the Palgrave Macmillan division of St. Martin's Press LLC and of Palgrave Macmillan Ltd. Macmillan® is a registered trademark in the United States, United Kingdom and other countries. Palgrave is a registered trademark in the European Union and other countries.

ISBN 1–4039–0302–6 hardback
ISBN 1–4039–0303–4 paperback

This book is printed on paper suitable for recycling and made from fully managed and sustained forest sources.

A catalogue record for this book is available from the British Library.

A catalog record for this book is available from the Library of Congress.

10   9   8   7   6   5   4   3   2   1
13 12 11 10 09 08 07 06 05 04

Printed in China

To Alan, Carol and Maggie, with our love

Contents

List of Tables

List of Figures

List of Abbreviations

ACP	African, Caribbean and Pacific Countries
AEC	African Economic Community
AFRC	Armed Forces Revolutionary Council (Sierra Leone)
AFTA	ASEAN Free Trade Area
APEC	Asia Pacific Economic Cooperation
ARF	ASEAN Regional Forum
ASEAN	Association of Southeast Asian Nations
AU	African Union (replaced OAU in 2002)
BiH	Bosnia and Herzegovina
CACM	Central American Common Market
CAP	Common Agricultural Policy
CFP	Common Fisheries Policy
CFSP	Common Foreign and Security Policy
CIS	Commonwealth of Independent States
COREPER	Committee of Permanent Representatives
CTC	Security Council Counter-Terrorism Committee (2000–)
DPKO	UN Department of Peacekeeping Operations
DRC	Democratic Republic of the Congo
EAEC	European Atomic Energy Community *or* East Asian Economic Caucus
ECB	European Central Bank
ECOMOG	Economic Community of West African States Monitoring Group
ECOSOC	United Nations Economic and Social Council
ECOWAS	Economic Community of West African States
ECSC	European Coal and Steel Community
ECU	European Currency Unit
EDC	European Defence Community
EEA	European Economic Area
EEC	European Economic Community
EFTA	European Free Trade Area
EMS	European Monetary System
EMU	European Monetary Union

EPC	European Political Community
ERDF	European Regional Development Fund
ERM	Exchange Rate Mechanism
EU	European Union
FCO	(British) Foreign and Commonwealth Office
FTAA	Free Trade Area of the Americas
G7	Group of Seven
G-77	Group of 77
GAOR	General Assembly Official Records
GATT	General Agreement on Tariffs and Trade
GEF	Global Environmental Facility
GFAP	General Framework Agreement for Peace (Dayton peace agreement) for Bosnia-Herzegovina, 16 December 1995
IAEA	International Atomic Energy Authority
IBRD	International Bank for Reconstruction and Development (World Bank)
ICC	International Criminal Court
ICJ	International Court of Justice
ICRC	International Committee of the Red Cross
ICTR	International Criminal Tribunal for Rwanda
ICTY	International Criminal Tribunal for (the former) Yugoslavia
IGC	Intergovernmental Conference
IGO	International Governmental Organization
ILO	International Labour Organisation
IMF	International Monetary Fund
INGO	International Non-governmental Organisation
IPCC	Intergovernmental Panel on Climate Change
KLA	Kosovo Liberation Army
LAFTA	Latin American Free Trade Area
LAIA	Latin American Integration Association
MEP	Member of the European Parliament
MERCOSUR	Common Market of the South
NAFTA	North Atlantic Free Trade Area
NATO	North Atlantic Treaty Organisation
NEPAD	New Partnership for Africa's Development
NGO	Non-governmental organisation
NIEO	New International Economic Order
NPT	Non-proliferation Treaty
NWICO	New World Information and Communications Order
OAS	Organisation of American States
OAU	Organisation of African Unity (succeeded by AU in 2002)
ODECA	Organisation of Central American States
OECD	Organisation for Economic Cooperation Development
OEEC	Organisation for European Economic Cooperation
ONUC	UN Operation in the Congo
OPEC	Organisation of Petroleum Exporting Countries
OSCE	Organisation for Security and Cooperation in Europe

P5	The five permanent members of the Security Council (USA, Russia, France, the UK, China)
PHARE	Poland and Hungary Assistance for Restructuring their Economies
PRC	People's Republic of China
PTA	Preferential Trading Area
RIIA	Royal Institute for International Affairs
RPF	Rwandan Patriotic Front
RSK	Republic of Serbian Krajina
RUF	Revolutionary United Front (Sierra Leone)
SAARC	South Asian Association for Regional Cooperation
SADC	South African Development Community
SAP	Structural Adjustment Programme
SCR	Security Council Resolution
SEA	Single European Act
SEATO	Southeast Asia Treaty Organisation
SFRY	Socialist Federation of Yugoslavia
SMP	Single Market Programme
SRSG	Special Representative of the Secretary-General
TENs	trans-European networks
TEU	Treaty of European Union
TNC	Trans-national Corporation
UDI	Unilateral Declaration of Independence
UN	United Nations
UNCDF	UN Capital Development Fund
UNCIVIPOL	United Nations Civilian Police Force
UNCTAD	UN Conference on Trade and Development
UNEF	United Nations Emergency Force
UNESCO	United Nations Educational, Scientific and Cultural Organisation
UNFICYP	UN Force in Cyprus
UNHCHR	UN High Commissioner for Human Rights
UNHQ	United Nations Headquarters, New York
UNITA	National Union for the Total Independence of Angola
UNMOGIP	UN Military Observer Group in India and Pakistan
UNMOVIC	UN Monitoring, Verification and Inspection Commission (UNSCOM's sucessor)
UNOSOM	United Nations Operation in Somalia
UNPROFOR	UN Protection Force
UNSCOB	UN Special Committee on the Balkans (Monitored Greek border, 1947–52)
UNSCOM	UN Special Commission set up under SCR 687 (1991) to supervise Iraq's destruction of WMD and ballistic missiles with a range greater than 150 kilometres, together with related items and production facilities, and to ensure that the acquisition and production of prohibited items are not resumed. (The IAEA is responsible for nuclear aspects of SCR 687.)
UNTSO	UN Truce Supervision Organisation
UNUMA	United Nations Assistance Mission in Afghanistan

UPU	Universal Postal Union
VAT	Value Added Tax
WEU	Western European Union
WFC	World Food Council
WMD	weapons of mass destruction
WTO	World Trade Organisation

Preface

This book is a completely revised, expanded and updated version of the same authors' *From Versailles to Maastricht: International Organisation in the Twentieth Century* (Macmillan, 1996). Lorna Lloyd contributed the chapters on the United Nations (and also the tables and figures), John Redmond the chapters on the European Union, and David Armstrong the remainder. Although coverage of the League of Nations is slightly reduced from the earlier edition, all other subjects are dealt with at greater length, and there are new chapters on global governance, global civil society, and the new regionalism, as well as a new section on theoretical perspectives in the first chapter. All chapters make use of substantial original research as well as the available secondary literature. The result, we hope, is a historical overview of the most important international organisations of the last hundred years, that provides enough factual detail and analytical depth for it to be of value not just to students of the subject but to the general reader seeking to understand the complex story of the rise of the international organisation.

We would all like to thank past and present students at our various institutions for their many helpful comments. We also wish to thank our colleagues at the Universities of Birmingham, Exeter, Keele and elsewhere for freely dispensing of their time and expertise, although we naturally accept full responsibility for any errors of fact or judgement. Thanks are also due to the Palgrave editorial team, especially Terka Acton and Sonya Barker, and to Professor Geoff Berridge, Dr Ann Hughes and Dr Mike Young, the staffs of the UN Information Centre in London, the Hammarskjöld Library in New York and the Peace Palace Library at the Hague. Mr David Travers answered a string of queries and provided copies of his invaluable contributions to *The Annual Register*. Valuable comments and suggestions on the UN chapters were provided by Sir Brian Barder, Professor Alan James and another expert who has asked to remain anonymous. Most of all, our thanks are due to our long-suffering spouses, to whom this volume is dedicated.

The Rise of the International Organisation

THE DEVELOPMENT OF INTERNATIONAL ORGANISATIONS BEFORE 1919

The three essential conditions for an international governmental organisation (IGO) to exist are, first, independent political communities; secondly, rules agreed among such communities that purport to regulate their relations with each other; and thirdly, a formal structure to implement and enforce the rules. Without the first, a regulatory structure would be essentially imperial or hegemonial, if it was not actually part of a single polity. Without the second, orderly relations, where they existed, would be a random consequence of informal interaction among sovereign entities. Without the third, rule enforcement would depend on diplomacy and state-craft rather than at least some element of management by a standing body created for that purpose. Many schemes for classifying IGOs are possible – by membership or function, for example – but these three criteria define the essential qualities of an IGO as such.[1]

Analysts of IGOs have pointed to many precursors of contemporary institutions, like the UN, the WTO or the EU, that have played an increasingly significant part in the shaping of the modern world order. For some, the earliest IGO was the Amphi-ctyonic Council of ancient Greece but this existed primarily for the very limited purpose of enabling the Greek city states to engage in common religious observance and protect the shrine at Delphi. It was essentially a celebration of cultural unity amongst the Greeks rather than a means of managing the consequences of the sovereign independence of the city states. Its members were required to swear an oath designed to limit the harm they could do to each other in the event of war – the basis for the argument that the Council was an IGO – but this was generally ignored.[2] Similar points may be made about other ancient international societies. All had systems of rules that sought to establish some measure of order in areas such as trade, war, boundaries or water rights. In some cases, such as imperial China or Egypt, the rules were part of a hegemonial power structure – in theory if not always in practice – although the Egyptians also allowed for the possibility of trade agreements with independent foreign nations.[3] In others, such as India, relations amongst the independent and semi-independent Indian states were in principle governed by various rules and religious precepts deriving, as in the case of Greece, from a sense of a common cultural identity, but there was no standing body entrusted with administering these rules.

Medieval Christendom comes closer to our conception of an IGO, with its ecumenical councils, chivalric orders, and complex and far-reaching international legal structures including what amounted to courts of appeal and arbitration. It even had, in the form of the priesthood, what Martin Wight terms a 'massive international bureaucracy'.[4] However, the hypothetical unity of western Christendom as a complex authority structure presided over by the Pope raises questions about the validity of conceiving of it as a true association of independent political communities, as our definition requires.

It was not until the nineteenth century that IGOs, properly so called, begin to appear in conjunction with the industrial and technological revolutions of that time. The profound changes in the political, economic and social landscape during that period were instrumental both in establishing a favourable climate for the proliferation of IGOs and in determining their agenda. This is most obvious in the fields of trade and international communications. The massive increase in production sparked off by the Industrial Revolution led to an equally heavy growth in trade, and, with the arrival of steam, in the speed with which trade took place.

As more and more of the globe was penetrated by European imperialism, so a highly complex worldwide economic network emerged. This influenced the growth of international institutions in four distinct ways. First, the greater number of international transactions increased the risk of conflict arising out of some trivial dispute. This was one factor behind the growing tendency during the nineteenth century for states to accept international arbitration of various types of disputes where, as the standard formula ran, 'neither honour nor vital interests' were involved.[5]

Secondly, agreed regulations and common standards had to be determined for such purposes as patenting inventions, classifying goods for customs duties and deciding exchange rates between currencies. What were then termed 'public international unions' were established to deal with such matters, and by the end of the nineteenth century the movement towards international standardisation was beginning to affect less technical and more obviously political areas, such as the protection of workers and children.

Thirdly, the traditional insistence by states upon a rigid interpretation of their sovereign rights was emerging as a significant barrier to the efficient conduct of international business. The classic illustration of this concerned the transmission of postal items across frontiers. Before the establishment of the General Postal Union in 1875 and its successor, the Universal Postal Union (UPU) in 1878, international postal communication was governed by numerous bilateral treaties rather than by a single convention. The objective of each state was to ensure that the balance of financial advantage deriving from these treaties was in its favour, which led to extremely high foreign postage rates being charged by all. As charges were levied at each frontier, the cost of sending a postal item from one country to another varied according to the route taken, with a half-ounce letter from the United States to Australia costing anything from 5 cents to $1.02.[6] The UPU adopted procedures that are still quite radical amongst IGOs, including compulsory arbitration of disputes and majority voting.

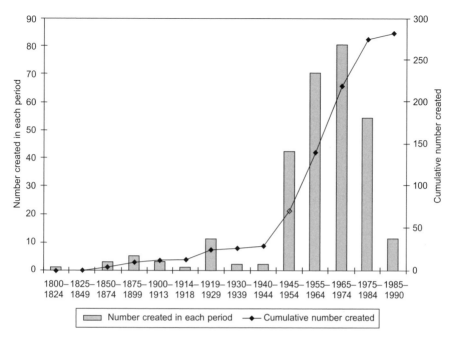

Figure 1.1 The rise in the number of intergovernmental organisations (IGOs), 1800–1990*

*Source: Union of International Associations, *The Yearbook of International Organizations, 1990–1991*, 27th edn (Munich, New York, London, Paris: K. G. Saur, 1990), pp. 1666–8.

Fourthly, the economies of the major powers were becoming increasingly interdependent, which provided them with certain mutual interests to set against their many rivalries.[7] The nineteenth century saw the first attempts to translate this interdependence into institutional form through the establishment of international commissions to regulate the trade in specific commodities, such as sugar.[8] Another effect of interdependence was that it helped to internationalise issues – to turn what would once have been purely national questions into matters of general concern. The control of disease was one such area, with several international unions set up in the nineteenth century, culminating in the Sanitary Convention of 1903 and the establishment of the International Office of Public Hygiene in 1907.[9]

It is important to note that none of these landmarks in the history of international organisation had an untroubled birth, nor did they hint at any prospect of more ambitious undertakings being successful. France, fearing possible financial losses, had delayed the formation of the postal union. Britain had resisted for many years any attempt to sign a sanitary convention on the grounds that this might harm its maritime interests. The sanitary councils had themselves been arenas for the conflicts of great power interests that went on throughout the nineteenth century. If such contention was so much in evidence in relatively minor matters, progress in areas regarded as affecting vital national interests such as security was inevitably much more limited. Yet it was not non-existent, as evidenced by two nineteenth-century developments: the creation of the Concert of Europe and the International Committee of the Red Cross.

THE CONCERT OF EUROPE

The Concert – the informal arrangement whereby the European powers consulted together at times of crisis – originated in the wartime alliance against Napoleon. Early ideas that the Concert should be a kind of international government with wide powers of intervention in the domestic affairs of states foundered on British insistence on the principle of non-intervention remaining the cornerstone of the international system. This was largely a consequence of different perceptions of national interest: the more ambitious proposals for the Concert emanating mainly from the conservative, dynastic empires which had most to lose from the principles of national self-determination and liberalism that had been propagated by the French Revolution. But the Concert system was none the less a significant factor behind the relative absence of conflict amongst the European powers for much of the hundred years after the end of the Napoleonic Wars, with the main exception being the period 1854–71. Its role should not be exaggerated: war weariness, the existence of a stable balance of power and the opportunities opening up for expansion outside Europe all played a part, but the central Concert emphasis on the need for consultation and diplomacy before resorting to force helped to prevent conflict up to the spectacular breakdown of the system in 1914.

Viewed as an international organisation, the Concert had far fewer legislative, administrative and executive organs than many of its successors, resting essentially on the Quadruple Alliance of Austria, Britain, Prussia and Russia (with France admitted in 1818 after a short probationary period) and on an agreement to meet in the event of any threat to the 'repose of Europe', by which was meant the territorial settlement that had been drawn up in 1814–15 with the aim of ensuring a durable balance of power. Its rules were equally informal – there is no constitutional document for the Concert like the League Covenant or the UN Charter. Yet it established a number of precedents for the League, and in particular for the United Nations. These included the assertion of special rights and responsibilities for the great powers. Although the status of 'great power' had long been recognised in European international relations, a complex – and disputed – system of diplomatic precedence had led to many minor conflicts and all European states guarded their formal positions as 'sovereign equals' very jealously.

What the four allies did, in effect, was to declare themselves the principal arbiters of Europe's affairs while simultaneously imposing a far simpler rule regarding precedence. The League Council and UN Security Council institutionalised this principle by granting the major powers permanent membership and the right of veto, albeit with the principle considerably diluted by enlarging the Councils to include smaller powers on a non-permanent basis. Secondly, the Concert took upon itself the right to confer international legitimacy on states: that is, to determine their very right to exist as states. By so doing it opened up the possibility that the international community, acting through its formal institutions, might broaden the concept of 'international legitimacy' so that this could apply to the conduct as well as the status of states.

Thirdly, the Concert laid down a number of general norms, some of which related to the internal as well as the external affairs of states. These ranged from the legal principles governing the navigation of international rivers to injunctions against the slave trade and assertions of the rights of religious minorities.

THE RED CROSS MOVEMENT

Humanitarian objections to the idea that a war, once commenced, should be waged with utmost ruthlessness had been heard since at least the Enlightenment.[10] But it was not until the 1860s that any systematic attempt was made to give formal, institutional substance to these objections through the creation of the Red Cross movement. Inspired by the memory of the suffering he had witnessed at the battle of Solferino in 1859, Henri Dunant brought together a committee of fellow Swiss humanitarians in 1863 that was later to be called the International Committee of the Red Cross (ICRC). This helped to promote the establishment of national Red Cross societies in other countries to bring relief to the wounded on battlefields, and also managed to summon a diplomatic conference in 1864 that agreed the first Geneva Convention for the Amelioration of the Condition of the Wounded in Armies in the Field. Further conventions followed, culminating in the adoption of four Geneva Conventions in 1949, covering treatment for the wounded at land and sea, prisoners of war, and civilians and neutrals. One of the many interesting aspects of these developments in the law of war was the major role played by an international non-governmental organisation (INGO), the ICRC, in both drafting the Conventions and obtaining the agreement of governments and military authorities to the norms and rules contained in them.[11] This was due in large part to the ICRC's constant sensitivity to the rights of states and to its own need to tread warily and discreetly whenever states might feel those rights to be under threat. Such was the trust placed in the ICRC by governments that it was even able to extend its protection to a limited extent to political prisoners, being permitted by many governments to bring some material aid to them.[12]

THE HAGUE CONFERENCES

One event at the end of the century promised to take even further the process begun by the Concert of Europe and the ICRC of subjecting states' resort to war, and conduct during war, to an institutionalised structure of normative constraints. This was the Hague Conference of 1899 and its successor in 1907. These originated from a proposal for a disarmament conference by Tsar Nicholas and marked the high point of international arbitration. They were also the most highly attended conferences to date, with delegates from Europe, North and South America, and Asia, their popularity being a clear response to the interdependence that many now felt to be a crucial factor in international relations. As the President of the first Conference put it: 'We perceive that there is a community of moral and material interests between nations which is constantly increasing. ... If a nation wished to remain isolated it could not. ... It is part of a single organism.'[13] The most important implication of this interdependence was, he felt, that 'when a dispute arises between two or more nations, the others, without being directly involved, are seriously affected'. This in turn meant, in his view, that further machinery needed to be developed for states to submit their disputes for mediation, conciliation or arbitration.[14]

Although many delegates echoed these sentiments, they found it more difficult to agree upon the concrete obligations their states would have to accept, if these principles were to be given substance. The discussions at the Conferences consisted of a curious amalgam of idealistic statements of purpose and careful disavowals by all that they were undertaking any binding commitments. Hence the specific achievements of the first Conference were few: a so-called Permanent Court of Arbitration[15] and some provision for the use of International Commissions of Inquiry in certain disputes. The second Conference revised the conventions that had been agreed by the first and added ten new ones, mostly concerned with the laws of war. No significant progress was made in the area of disarmament – the original occasion of the Conferences.

The Hague Conferences are sometimes portrayed as having been a major influence on the creation of the League of Nations, but this is not strictly accurate. At the Paris Peace Conference, which created the League, there were very few voices in favour of building on the Hague experience, with the two most important delegations, the American and British, arguing that the League needed to be free from any association with previous ventures.[16] None the less, some of the devices favoured by the Conferences – for example, the use of arbitration, mediation and commissions of inquiry as means of defusing conflicts – found a place in the League Covenant. More generally, the Conferences reflected both the increasingly urgent international problems, which clearly required some kind of collective solution, and the immense obstacles to securing such solutions in a world of states each of which saw its sovereign independence as its highest value.

THE CONSOLIDATION OF IGOs

This central dilemma of international society is no less in evidence in the new millennium than it was at the beginning of the last century, as evidenced, for example, in the refusal of the United States to join the new International Criminal Court or ratify the Kyoto Protocol on climate change. Yet, in an apparent paradox, states seem increasingly willing to join international organisations and subject themselves to more international obligations than ever. An earlier edition of this book, written in 1995, referred to the creation in that year of two important new IGOs: the Organisation for Security and Cooperation in Europe (OSCE, formerly the Conference on Security and Cooperation in Europe: CSCE) and the World Trade Organisation (WTO, formerly the General Agreement on Tariffs and Trade: GATT). In 2002, African nations replaced their main regional organisation, the Organisation of African Unity (OAU), with a new organisation, the African Union (AU), modelled on the European Union and with a much more extensive remit including monitoring human rights and good governance and creating a standby peacekeeping force. The EU itself embarked upon the momentous experiment of a common currency for most of its members. On the other hand the sharp divisions between the Americans and British on the one hand,

and the other permanent members of the Security Council on the other, over the Iraqi crisis during first few months of 2003 was seen by many as causing irreparable damage to the UN, and indeed major frictions within the EU and NATO as well.

IGOs also continue to exist, even to thrive, after their original purpose has disappeared or become far less relevant, as is the case, some would argue, of the North Atlantic Treaty Organisation (NATO) and the Commonwealth. NATO was established on 4 April 1949 in response to a series of threatening moves on the part of the Soviet Union, including the Berlin Blockade of 1948. Its *raison d'être*, therefore, was to resist Soviet aggression in Europe, leaving open the question of its purpose in the post-Cold War world. In practice NATO has been busier in many respects since 1989 than in its first forty years. Its first shots in anger were fired in the Balkans, first in Bosnia and then during the 1999 campaign in response to Serbian oppression of the largely Albanian Muslim population of Kosovo. It has been enlarged to include several former members of its cold war opposite number, the Warsaw Pact, and, after the attack on the United States on 11 September 2001, has cooperated increasingly closely with Russia itself, including signing an association agreement in 2002. In addition, 11 September witnessed the first ever invocation of the main collective security clause of the alliance. NATO has also adopted a broader conception of security, embracing terrorist threats and trans-national crime. It has not been free of internal tensions, particularly those deriving from the apprehensions of some NATO members, especially France, over American domination of the organisation, with the French calling for a European security organisation from which the USA would be excluded. For their part, the Americans have criticised what they see as European under-spending on defence, which in their view has obliged the US to undertake a disproportionate share of the defence burden. The Balkan crises exposed the degree to which European security depended on American airpower, while the Afghanistan campaign revealed the increasing technological gap between the United States and its allies. This, and the Iraqi crisis of 2003, brought renewed questioning of the purpose of the organisation from both sides of the Atlantic, but still no serious calls for its closure.

The Commonwealth is the only worldwide multi-functional international organisation apart from the UN itself. Originating in the pre-1945 British Commonwealth of Nations, the association binding Britain and some of its former colonies such as Australia and Canada, it reconstituted itself in 1965 as somewhat closer to a conventional IGO, when it established a Secretariat. It remains something of an anomaly in the world of IGOs, with its only real common denominator being former membership of the British Empire (except in the case of Mozambique, admitted in 1995 on the insistence of the South African leader Nelson Mandela), and it has no formal constitutive document. In common with most IGOs, the Commonwealth is relatively poorly funded, with only about half the budget of the French equivalent to the Commonwealth, *la Francophonie*, an organisation with less than half the Commonwealth's population. Similarly, with around a quarter of the membership of the UN, it has less than 1 per cent of the UN budget ($15 million as against $2.5 billion) and less than 400 staff compared with the UN's 13,500.[17] Yet it has acquired a modest niche for itself, with its meetings of Heads of Government enabling its diverse membership to meet in relatively informal settings – particularly valuable for the several micro-states represented in the Commonwealth.[18] It has also played a significant – if limited – role in promoting the values of 'good governance' amongst

Table 1.1 Types of international organisations*

As will be clear from the examples, the categories into which organisations are divided are not mutually exclusive

Type	Definition	Examples
1. Intergovernmental organisations (IGOs)		
Organisational structures set up by any number of sovereign states to deal with any kind of subject matter.		
A. Classified by parties		
(i) Universal	Membership includes all sovereign states.	None. But the UN comes very close, the Vatican City State being the only unambiguously sovereign state that does not belong. The UN is therefore sometimes described as quasi-universal.
(ii) Global	Worldwide membership.	League of Nations, United Nations, the Commonwealth
(iii) Regional	Membership based on geographical propinquity.	Organisation of American States, European Union, Association of Southeast Asian Nations, African Union
(iv) Multilateral	More than two members.	United Nations, North Atlantic Treaty Organisation, Arab League
(v) Bilateral	Two members.	North American Aerospace Defense Command, International Joint Commission (Canada/USA)
B. Classified by purpose		
(i) Multipurpose or general	Engaged in a range of activities.	United Nations, the Commonwealth, Organisation of American States
(ii) Specific	Devoted to a particular activity.	World Health Organisation, Worldwide Fund for Nature
(iii) Promotional	Devoted to promoting certain goals.	International Labour Organisation, United Nations, World Health Organisation
(iv) Allocative	Distributing certain goods.	United Nations, World Bank (IBRD), International Monetary Fund
(v) Regulatory	Regulating the operation of certain inter-state activities.	Universal Postal Union, International Maritime Consultative Organisation, International Telecommunications Union
(vi) Consultative	Discussing, rather than taking, decisions that bind the members in their extra-organisational behaviour.	League of Nations, the Commonwealth, Organisation of American States, Non-aligned Movement

C. Classified by powers

(i) Debating — Membership does not involve accepting legal obligations so far as extra-organisational behaviour is concerned. — The Commonwealth, Non-aligned Movement

(ii) Decentralised — Membership involves accepting certain legal obligations regarding extra-organisational behaviour, but it is up to each member to decide when circumstances activate such obligations. — League of Nations, North Atlantic Treaty Organisation

(iii) Deciding — Empowered to place legal obligations on members regarding extra-organisational behaviour. — Collective security (Chapter VII) provisions of the United Nations Charter

(iv) Supranational — Possessing legal power to place legal obligations directly upon natural and legal persons within member states. — Only one, the European Union

2. (International) non-governmental organisations ([I]NGOs)

Organisations made up not of states, but of individuals, companies, political parties or other groups from more than one state, for example, Amnesty International, Fédération Internationale de Football Associations (FIFA), OXFAM. They may be classified in any of the above ways other than by A(i) and C(iv) (which by definition are only open to states). They may also, on occasion, collaborate with IGOs.

*Thanks are due to Alan James for his valuable comments and suggestions.

its members since its Harare Declaration of 1991 affirmed these as 'the fundamental political values of the Commonwealth'.

IGOs are clearly highly durable animals. Some of the reasons for this are obviously specific to each organisation. NATO survives, for example, because most Europeans are fearful of a return to American isolationism, and the organisation is a means of retaining an American commitment to the continent, because Americans still see some value in NATO, notwithstanding some recent tendencies towards unilateralism since 11 September, and because, if global nuclear war is no longer a serious possibility, many complex threats remain, ranging from humanitarian emergencies, through internal wars, to possible terrorist use of weapons of mass destruction. The Commonwealth survives because disbanding it would involve admitting the failure of its high ideals, because it is a fairly low-cost IGO, and because it provides some added value to the universe of IGOs, whether through the advantages of its not being American dominated, or through its utility for its smallest members or because of its contribution to good governance.

There are also more general factors that explain not just the survival of IGOs but the continuing expansion in their numbers and functions: even in the 1980s, for example, when the UN was under great pressure to rationalise and reduce its activities, it established 173 new agencies, while disbanding only 73.[19] Part of the explanation remains the ever-increasing complexity and intensity of international transactions, particularly in the era of globalisation. All major powers claim the right to be involved in determining and administering any global regulation of such transactions that may be contemplated, while all states would claim the minimal right of being consulted, and IGOs facilitate both objectives. IGOs, in effect, provide a means of legitimising actions that powerful members of the international community may wish to take and of mobilising support for such actions. Only the United States at one end of the spectrum and hermit states like North Korea at the other could even contemplate ignoring all other states and going it alone in seeking their own individual solutions to the problems posed by globalisation, but North Korea has incurred a terrible economic cost from its aspirations towards self-sufficiency while the United States has, on balance, made the rational calculation that the costs of going it alone are greater than the costs of seeking collective solutions in multilateral frameworks like international organisations. As a generalisation, however, it remains true that IGOs are more valuable for their smaller members than their larger ones. In some cases, such as NAFTA and the AU, the apparent success of the European Union (EU) has prompted attempts both to emulate that success and to deal with the problems caused by the increasing regionalisation of trade. It is also true that IGOs, like any large institutions, develop a bureaucratic dynamic of their own. Governments have grown accustomed to setting up institutions, including international ones, as a response to new problems, while the bureaucracies of such organisations immediately acquire an interest in enhancing the importance and indispensability of their IGO.

THEORETICAL PERSPECTIVES ON IGOs

Our aim in this book is to provide a broad analytical history of international organisation and some of the central issues with which IGOs have been concerned. Our perspective is not, therefore, a theoretical one as such, although inevitably our discussion will at times both be informed by theoretical considerations and have implications for, or provide empirical data to support, various theoretical viewpoints. Hence, it is appropriate to conclude this introductory chapter with an overview of the main theories relating to IGOs.

Because the development of IGOs has been concerned with many, if not all, of the most important issues of international politics and economics, theoretical *inferences* relating to the processes of international organisation may be drawn from the entire body of international political and economic theory. A number of theories have also been *directly* devised to explain various aspects of international organisation. Both indirect and direct theoretical studies may be divided into four broad categories:

Theories of Integration

As the name implies, these are concerned with the processes through which the states that are members of a particular IGO come to merge their sovereignties in various ways so that, in certain crucial respects, they tend to develop towards becoming a *single* entity rather than several entirely *separate* ones. This is probably the body of theory that has been most directly related to IGOs, particularly the European Union, which has attracted a vast theoretical literature attempting to explain, interpret, classify and predict the complex progression of the EU towards its Treaty of Rome objective of 'ever closer union'.[20] As, in practice, the EU seems to defy precise theoretical categorisation, a bewildering array of distinct theories exists to account for the undoubted fact that the Union has become something more than the sum of its parts. Theories range from the earliest 'functionalist' ideas of David Mitrany to much more ambitious 'federalist' perspectives. Functionalism argued that the process of collaborating in narrow technical or functional areas will 'spill over' into other social and economic fields and eventually to more sensitive political areas.[21]

The 'neofunctionalist' refinement of this, associated with Ernst Haas, attempted to situate functionalism more fully within everyday political processes, arguing that transnational constituencies of advocates for closer integration would emerge in the course of functional collaboration, since these would tend increasingly to identify their interests from the point of view of the international institutions within which they worked.[22] With its emphasis on elite socialisation and social learning, neofunctionalism may be seen as an earlier variant (albeit in a very specific context) of the 'constructivist' theories that became increasingly influential in international relations from the late 1980s, and which drew attention to the influence of ideas and the ways in which they changed in the course of intersubjective interaction amongst international actors.

Federalism is less a distinctive body of explanatory and predictive theory in the way functionalism and neofunctionalism are than an ongoing intellectual enterprise whose starting point is a belief in the value of ultimate regional (and even global) union, and that seeks to identify ways within federal constitutions of reconciling local demands for full representation of their interests with the need for effective central government. European federalism has been strongly influenced by the example of the United States of America, although others prefer to stress the much looser American *confederation* as a model for European integration.[23]

Theories of Cooperation

Realist and neorealist thinking in international relations starts from the premise that states in a condition of international anarchy will inevitably be self-interested, power-seeking and competitive actors, with virtually no real prospect, therefore, of more than minimal, short-term collaboration or of IGOs developing in the kinds of ways envisaged by integration theorists.[24] The power of such arguments caused many scholars interested in international institutions, especially in the United States, to revise their thinking in ways that could accommodate Realist critiques of their work.[25] Rather than focusing upon the prospects for merging of sovereignty – which Realism discounts – 'neoliberal institutionalists', regime theorists and others accept the basic Realist portrayal of states as competing, self-interested 'rational actors' but seek to identify reasons why states might, none the less, cooperate in international institutions.[26] For example, pointing to the continued existence of important institutions even during periods of heightened inter-state antagonism, they argue that institutions help to provide a context that reduces states' fears that other states will cheat in various cooperative arrangements. They achieve this by reducing uncertainty, unpredictability and 'transaction costs', improving actors' information, both qualitatively and quantitatively and even enhancing the possibilities of enforcing state compliance with regimes – for instance, through disputes settlement procedures such as those created for the WTO.[27]

Although institutionalists accept that a strong 'hegemon', such as the United States, might be needed to uphold regimes in areas like trade and monetary relations, they argue that institutions may enable particular regimes to endure even if the hegemon's power declines. A noted application of institutionalist ideas to the European Union is Moravcsik's 'liberal intergovernmentalism', which depicts the EU as an 'intergovernmental' rather than emergent 'supranational' organisation and argues that the EU essentially provides a framework for more efficient inter-state bargaining.[28]

Theories of Governance

These attempt to break away from the dichotomy between Realists (including those liberal thinkers who try to present their more optimistic views of IGOs within a Realist framework) and Idealists (including some integration theorists), whose ideas tend to derive from a belief that absence of government is what makes world politics so conflictual and uncertain. The concept of 'governance' (discussed in more detail in Chapter 12) has become increasingly popular as a means of denoting a world order in which, even in the absence of formal *government*, enduring structures of rules, norms and institutions have emerged in many areas of international life in ways that do not quite fit any of the prevailing Realist or Liberal theories. Wolfgang H. Reinicke, for example, argues that the interaction amongst governments, nongovernmental organisations and IGOs has produced a regulatory network that enmeshes and constrains governments.[29] Similarly, others see the central Realist concept of power as far more problematic than Realists believe, arguing that in practice power 'is shared and negotiated among diverse forces and agencies at many levels, from the local to the global'.[30]

Theorists attempting to comprehend the most developed and complex governance structure, the EU, began to characterise it as an 'emerging polity', a term that aims to capture this notion of shared and negotiated power in a new kind of political context.[31] The term 'consociationalism' has been borrowed from seventeenth-century political theory to denote the processes through which the EU endeavours to reach consensual collective decisions that accommodate its members' separate national interests and identities.[32] Although no other IGO comes close to the range and depth of institutional authority vested in the EU, there have been significant developments in many areas, as discussed in Chapter 12.

Critical Theory

Three particular strands of what may, broadly speaking, be defined as 'critical theory' in International Relations (IR) can be identified. First, influenced by Habermas and earlier members of the Frankfurt School, Robert Cox, Andrew Linklater and other IR theorists have sought to shift the emphasis wiithin the academic study of IR from 'positivist' and empiricist perspectives that try to employ scientific methodologies (such as rational choice theory) to conceiving of theory in transformative and 'emancipatory' terms. Secondly, Marxists and neo-Marxists have focused on global capitalism as the principal international structure, rather than the international anarchy favoured by Realists, and on the oppressive and exploitative consequences to which they see this as giving rise. Finally, feminists, proceeding from the absence of any reference to gender in most IR literature, have argued that existing power structures and 'discursive practices' have produced unequal and hierarchical relationships that particularly affect women.[33]

There are clearly links between all three critical perspectives as well as differences between them and indeed within each approach and they are more generally applicable than the other three theories, which specifically relate to international organisation. However, to the degree that IGOs, quite literally in certain respects, 'institutionalise' established modes of thinking and the power structures these reflect, they may also incorporate and legitimise existing power relations together with the inequalities and oppressions these may embody. For example, the World Bank and IMF have internalised the dominant neoliberal economic ideas in promoting structural adjustment and other programmes that may have a severe effect on various disadvantaged groups.[34] Kelly-Kate S. Pease has usefully distinguished different theoretical interpretations, including Marxism and feminism, of a range of IGO-related issues.[35]

We have not adopted a specific theoretical approach in this book; indeed, for the most part we have refrained from engaging in explicitly theoretical argumentation. Insofar as we tend to see IGOs primarily as the creatures and instruments of states, and one of their more significant purposes as constraining and ordering what might otherwise be more destructive and self-defeating political and economic. interactions, we are probably closest to Realist perspectives. However, we are sceptical about the claims to science made by contemporary Realists, we accept that IGOs may acquire a dynamic of their own that certainly justifies their designation as actors in their own right, we believe both that ideas may at times exercise a strong influence upon events and that they can change and develop in ways that are independent of the material structures within which they exist, and we are aware of the many inequalities and oppressions of contemporary world politics and the degree to which

IGOs may sometimes be complicit in these. We would also suggest that it is as close to a self-evident truth as we are ever likely to get in the analysis of world affairs that the EU, with its single currency and other institutional developments, has advanced in ways that confound most Realist predictions, even if they do not necessarily confirm Idealist or integration theories. All this is to say is that the social world (including the activities of IGOs) is complex and beyond the comprehension of any single body of theory.

NOTES

1. The Union of International Associations has developed the most elaborate system of classification: www.uia.org
2. Henry Wheaton, *History of the Law of Nations* (New York: Gould, Banks, 1845), p. 15.
3. David Lorton, *The Juridical Terminology of International Relations in Egyptian Texts through Dyn. XVIII* (Baltimore and London: Johns Hopkins Press, 1974), pp. 82–93.
4. M. Wight, *Systems of States* (Leicester: Leicester University Press, 1977), p. 28.
5. About 200 disputes went to arbitration between 1815 and 1900.
6. P. S. Reinsch, *Public International Unions* (Boston: Ginn, 1911), p. 21.
7. See ibid., p. 6, for an early use of the term 'interdependence'.
8. L. S. Woolf, *International Government* (London: Fabian Society, 1916), pp. 102–4.
9. Ibid., p. 104.
10. Geoffrey Best, *Humanity in Warfare* (London: Weidenfeld and Nicolson, 1983), pp. 31–74.
11. Martha Finnemore, *National Interests in International Society* (Ithaca and London: Cornell University Press, 1996), pp. 69–88; D. P. Forsythe, *Humanitarian Politics: The International Committee of the Red Cross* (Baltimore: Johns Hopkins Press, 1977).
12. J. D. Armstrong, 'The International Committee of the Red Cross and Political Prisoners', *International Organization*, Autumn 1985.
13. *The Proceedings of the Hague Peace Conferences: The Conference of 1899* (New York: Carnegie Endowment for International Peace, 1920), pp. 18–19.
14. Ibid., pp. 18–19.
15. This was in reality little more than a list of arbitrators who were available to states that might wish to make use of their services.
16. F. Wilson, *The Origins of the League Covenant* (London: Association for International Understanding, 1928), pp. 18, 58. See also H. W. V. Temperley, *A History of the Peace Conference of Paris* (London: Institute of International Affairs, 1924), vol. IV, p. 24.
17. F. Sobhan, 'The Commonwealth at the Turn of the Century', *The Round Table*, 351 (July 1999), p. ii.
18. Thirty-two of the Commonwealth's 54 members have populations of less than five million, of which 23 have populations of less than one million. See David Armstrong, 'From International Community to International Organisation?', *Commonwealth and Comparative Politics*, vol. 39, no. 3 (November 2001), p. 40.
19. Jan Klabbers, 'The Changing Image of International Organizations', in Jean-Marc Coicaud and Veijo Heiskanen (eds), *The Legitimacy of International Organizations* (Tokyo: United Nations Universtiy Press, 2001), p. 223.

20. For an excellent recent overview, see Dimitris N. Chryssochoou, *Theorizing European Integration* (London: Sage Publications, 2001).

21. David Mitrany, *A Working Peace System* (Chicago: Quadrangle Books, 1966).

22. Ernst B. Haas, *Beyond the Nation-State: Functionalism and International Organization* (Stanford: Stanford University Press, 1964).

23. Chryssochoou, *Theorizing European Integration*, pp. 42–8, 67–71.

24. The seminal work here is Kenneth Waltz, *Theory of International Politics* (Reading, MA: Addison-Wesley, 1979).

25. Prominent among such writers was Robert Keohane, whose earlier 'liberal institutionalist' perspective argued that increasing international interdependence provided greater opportunities for IGOs to play more significant roles. See Robert O. Keohane and Joseph Nye, *Power and Interdependence: World Politics in Transition* (Boston, MA: Little Brown, Boston, 1977).

26. Robert O. Keohane, *After Hegemony: Cooperation and Discord in the World Political Economy* (Princeton, NJ: Princeton University Press, 1984); Arthur A. Stein, *Why Nations Cooperate: Circumstance and Choice in International Relations* (Ithaca and London: Cornell Univesrity Press, 1990). For a Realist critique of neoliberal institutionalism, see Joseph M. Grieco, *Cooperation Among Nations: Europe America and Non-Tariff Barriers to Trade* (Ithaca and London: Cornell University Press, 1990).

27. Robert O. Keohane, *International Institutions and State Power* (Boulder, CO: Westview Press, 1989), pp. 166–7.

28. A. Moravcsik, 'Preferences and Power in the European Community: a Liberal Intergovernmentalist Approach', *Journal of Common Market Studies*, 31, no. 4 (1993), p. 507.

29. Wolfgang H. Reinicke, *Global Public Policy: Governing Without Government* (Washington: Brookings Institution 1989).

30. David Held, 'Cosmopolitanism: Ideas, Realities and Deficits', in David Held and Anthony McGrew (eds), *Governing Globalization: Power, Authority and Global Governance* (Cambridge: Polity Press, 2002).

31. Chryssochoou, *Theorizing European Integration*, pp. 92–124.

32. Ibid., pp. 131–70.

33. See the chapters on 'Marxism' by Andrew Linklater, 'Critical Theory' by Richard Devetak and 'Feminism' by Jaquie True in Scott Burchill and Andrew Linklater (eds), *Theories of International Relations* (Basingstoke: Macmillan, 1996), pp. 119–44, 145–78 and 210–51 for useful overviews.

34. See Jill Steans, 'Global Governance: a Feminist Perspective', and Alex Callinicos, 'Marxism and Global Governance', in David Held and Anthony McGrew (eds), *Governing Globalization: Power, Authority and Global Governance* (Cambridge: Polity Press, 2002), pp. 87–108 and 249–66.

35. Kelly-Kate S. Pease, *International Organizations: Perspectives on Governance in the Twenty-First Century* (Englewood Cliffs, NJ: Prentice Hall, 2000).

2

The League of Nations

THE LEAGUE IDEA AND THE ROLE OF WOODROW WILSON

Schemes to replace the endemic anarchy of international relations by a system designed to ensure peace, security and order were not unique to the twentieth century, but the unparalleled destruction of the First World War meant that for the first time they had to be taken seriously by the practitioners as well as the theorists of politics. Not only was there a popular clamour for some new means of controlling international violence, which democratically elected statesmen could hardly ignore, but the old international order had been decisively swept away, and its only successors with clear-cut answers to everything were Lenin's Bolsheviks, who threatened to overthrow the domestic social and economic orders as well. The Western powers at Paris were well aware of this, and the first problem that faced them was how to translate into concrete form a bewildering array of ideas as to what the League should be, while ensuring that the resulting organisation offered a viable reformist alternative to the revolutionary vision of the Bolsheviks.

Numerous private groups of concerned citizens, such as the American League to Enforce Peace, had been pressing various schemes for a new world order throughout the war, but their impact was fairly limited. They helped to focus public opinion upon the idea of a new order and popularised the name 'League of Nations' but the League that was actually created owed little of substance to their efforts. The British Foreign Office officials responsible for drawing up an influential British draft for a possible League accepted some of their underlying ideas but dismissed as 'impracticable' their specific provisions.[1] More significantly, President Woodrow Wilson, regarded by many as the 'father' of the League, refused to associate himself with any of the unofficial schemes, privately referring to the members of organisations promoting them as 'woolgatherers'.[2]

Wilson's role in the genesis of the League is a complex one. It is clear that he was convinced from an early stage that a new international system was required, and that he saw in this the means of obtaining both personal glory, and power and prestige for his country. Later, in common with other statesmen, he came to pin a variety of additional aspirations upon the League, including resisting the Bolshevik threat, underwriting the peace treaties, democratising the world, establishing a new economic order (with a pre-eminent role for the United States) and ending the colonial system. However, he had few, if any, well-defined ideas as to the actual form of the new organisation that was to bring about this diplomatic revolution.

Even before the war, Wilson had shown some interest in novel means of securing peace. His first Secretary of State, Bryan, had promoted a series of bilateral treaties whose principal feature was an agreement that, should a dispute arise, the states involved would observe a moratorium of one year to permit investigation and attempts at arbitration before resorting to war.[3] This unlikely notion that a 'cooling off' period might lower temperatures sufficiently to prevent war was to reappear as Article 12 of the League Covenant. A more significant early influence was an abortive attempt by Wilson and his close adviser Colonel House to sponsor a Pan-American Treaty in which an important element would be an article committing all parties to 'a common and mutual guarantee of territorial integrity and of political independence under republican forms of government'.[4] A similar wording was used in Wilson's first public endorsement of the League of Nations on 27 May 1916 and in the last of his famous Fourteen Points on the peace settlement in January 1918.[5] However, Wilson had gone over his May 1916 speech shortly before delivering it and erased any reference to the possible use of physical force against transgressors, indicating his awareness of the constitutional difficulties of gaining acceptance for a blanket commitment to use American military power.[6]

The problem of translating his high-sounding rhetoric into substantial obligations is apparent in all of Wilson's deliberations on the League. For example, he resisted early British schemes for a League revolving around the idea of an institutionalised great power concert as well as House's first draft constitution of July 1918, which had similarly excluded smaller powers. Yet he continued to insist that the League should be 'virile' without seeming to appreciate that the presence of small states could be a source of impotence.[7] Sometimes he spoke as if the League's peacekeeping objective was to be achieved mainly by open diplomacy and the pressure of public opinion.[8] On other occasions his original emphasis on mutual guarantees (which was reiterated in Article 10 of the Covenant) was claimed to be the 'backbone' of the League, without which it 'could hardly be more than an influential debating society'.[9] He could still, however, claim to the American Senate that Article 10 was 'binding in conscience only, not in law', and just before the Peace Conference said privately that he expected economic sanctions to be the main weapon used against aggressors.[10] He was similarly unclear about what provisions should be made, under the League, for former enemy colonies. As late as 10 December 1918, in discussion with his expert advisers, he believed that it was possible for such colonies to become the common property of the League and to be administered by the smaller nations.[11] However, when South Africa's General Smuts published his detailed plan for a League, Wilson enthusiastically endorsed his basic idea of a mandates system, although Smuts excluded from this the former German colonies in the Pacific and Africa as being 'inhabited by barbarians', whereas Wilson was to argue at Paris that they should be amongst the League's mandated territories.[12] By the time of the Peace Conference the mandates question, which had started life as a peripheral issue, had become so important to Wilson that he could maintain in his arguments with the other major powers that the League 'would be a laughing stock if it were not invested with this quality of trusteeship'.[13]

Part of Wilson's problem was that he had come to distrust his own State Department and in particular his Secretary of State, Robert Lansing, whom he considered to be too cautious and legalistic in his approach to the League.[14] Lansing differed from the President, first in the importance each attached to the League – Lansing insisted that the prime necessity was to push for the democratisation of authoritarian countries[15] – and secondly in his conception of the League. Whereas Wilson's thinking, vague though it was, entailed a *positive* commitment by all League members to employ sanctions against aggressors, Lansing proposed a strengthening of existing diplomatic devices such as arbitration and commissions of inquiry, but only a *negative* commitment by states to refrain from the use of violence in settling their disputes.[16] The result of the growing acrimony between the two was that Wilson refused to consider any analyses of the League idea that emanated from the State Department. Hence, at the start of 1919, all that Wilson had at his disposal in the way of detailed guidance on the League was a brief draft covenant drawn up by House in July 1918 and an equally short revision of this by Wilson himself.[17] House's version was full of resonant phrases about 'honourable' and 'dishonourable' international behaviour and, while Wilson had resisted this temptation, his draft suffered from his inability to translate his ideas into precise terminology that could not be torn into shreds by the legal advisers of other governments. Despite the disdain felt by most of the British Cabinet towards the League idea, considerably more thought had been given in official British circles to its concrete implications, and several draft covenants existed by 1919, of which Smuts's was the most detailed. The French and Italians had also produced their own versions by then. The League Covenant that was eventually decided was the outcome of a lengthy bargaining process amongst these and other players. Wilson's chief contribution was not as the originator of the Covenant but rather lay in his insistence that some edifice bearing the title 'League of Nations' should be created, that the League should be the first item on the Paris agenda and that it should be an integral part of the peace treaty.[18]

THE COVENANT OF THE LEAGUE OF NATIONS

The Covenant consists of 26 Articles, as against the 111 Articles of the United Nations Charter, but despite its relative brevity it still contains several features that are of great importance in the history of international organisation. Almost every Article was the subject of intense negotiation, first between the British and Americans, who between them produced the 'Hurst–Miller draft', on which subsequent discussions were based, and then in the Paris meetings. The key principles of the Covenant may be summarised as follows.

Collective Security
Although this term was not used until much later, its central theme – deterring potential aggressors by agreeing in advance to oppose them with a united front of all other states – was present in all of the deliberations. The collective security idea had been discussed in earlier international conferences, such as those after the Napoleonic Wars, but its immediate origin lay in the belief that the First World War would have been prevented had Germany been aware beforehand of how extensive

the opposition to it would become. The League's key collective security provisions were contained in Articles 10 and 16. Article 10 stipulated that the League's members 'undertake to respect and preserve as against external aggression the territorial integrity and existing political independence of all Members of the League'. In 1919 this was by far the most controversial Article being debated and was a major factor behind the American Senate's refusal to accept the peace treaty. However, partly because of this, the commitment had been extensively watered down, with an original 'guarantee' being replaced by an 'undertaking' and with the League Council merely being required to 'advise upon the means by which this obligation shall be fulfilled'. Article 16 states that if a Member resorted to war without going through various prior steps stipulated in the Covenant to bring about a peaceful resolution of a dispute, it would '*ipso facto* be deemed to have committed an act of war against all other Members of the League': the core principle in any collective security system.

However, the only advance commitment all accepted under this Article was to sever economic and other relations with the offending state. The Council could merely 'recommend' what forces they should contribute to any subsequent military operation. Earlier proposals from the French for an international army with a permanent general staff failed to win support. Moreover, there were some who were sceptical from the start about the whole concept of collective security. As early as 1916, Sir Maurice Hankey, Secretary to the War Committee in Britain, argued strongly – and presciently – that the promise of security held out by such projects was 'wholly fictitious' and likely to foster dangerous illusions, especially in Britain.[19]

Crisis Management

Many believed that the war had escalated out of control from its origins in a relatively minor crisis. Article 12, requiring states to observe a three-month 'cooling off' period before resorting to war, and Article 15, setting out procedures under which the Council would investigate and report upon disputes, were intended to prevent a repetition of such escalations.

Disarmament

The Anglo-German naval arms race before the war was seen as another factor contributing to the slide towards conflict. States had different ideas, however, as to which aspects of arms control and disarmament should be stressed: the British favouring an end to conscription, the French mainly interested in securing German disarmament, and the Americans calling for the abolition of the private manufacture of weapons. Article 8 contained some relatively weak provisions on this matter, calling upon the Council to formulate arms reduction proposals and upon states to exchange full and frank information on the subject. The private manufacture of weapons was duly declared 'open to grave objection', the Council being merely required to advise 'how the evil effects attendant upon such manufacture can be prevented'.

Justiciable Disputes

The nineteenth century had witnessed a growth in international arbitration and other means of legal resolution of disputes. Such 'justiciable disputes' were defined by Smuts in his draft Covenant as 'those which concern matters of fact or which are capable of a legal or judicial handling'. The Preamble to the Covenant referred to 'the firm establishment of the understandings of international law as the actual rule of conduct among Governments'. Article 13 committed Members to submit to arbitration those disputes which they recognised to be suitable for arbitration, and which could not be settled by diplomacy; while Article 14 established a Permanent Court of International Justice. This could hear 'any dispute of an international character' referred to it by the parties, or give an advisory opinion if asked by the Council or Assembly.

Social and Economic Issues

Article 23 extended the range of League activities well beyond security questions. This was in part a response to the challenge that had been posed by the Bolshevik Revolution and its claim to represent the interests of the working class, regardless of nationality, and also Lenin's anti-imperialist message. Members undertook to secure and maintain fair and humane conditions of labour and just treatment for their colonial peoples, while they also entrusted the League with a range of tasks, including supervision and execution of agreements relating to the traffic in women and children and the drugs trade. However, a proposal from Wilson to include a reference to freedom of religion failed because Japan refused to support it unless there was an additional provision opposing discrimination against aliens on the grounds of their race. This was anathema to the Australians and other members of the British Empire delegation, who feared the implications of such a clause for their immigration policies, so both proposals had to be dropped.

Trusteeship

The former enemy colonies became mandates of the League under Article 22. This, however, was far from embodying the kind of anti-colonial principles that are implicit in the UN Charter, referring as it did to 'peoples not yet able to stand by themselves under the strenuous conditions of the modern world', whose tutelage was to be entrusted to 'advanced nations'. While some territories that had been part of the Turkish empire were deemed to have the potential for self-government in the short term, others were clearly seen as being far from that condition. The League mandatories (effectively the new colonial powers) were required to observe certain principles, such as freedom of conscience and religion, in governing these territories but otherwise were simply to provide an annual report to the new Mandates Commission of the League.

Organisational Principles

The League was to have three main organs to carry out its work. The most important of these was its Council, seen by the British and others as a kind of institutionalised great power concert. Although the British initially called for Council membership to be open only to the major powers, pressure from the smaller states, as well as from Wilson, led to the novel device in Article 4 of having both permanent great power and non-permanent small power members of the Council, the latter to be elected by the Assembly rather than appointed from time to time by the great powers, as in the original draft Covenant. The Council was to have primary responsibility for carrying out the League's security provisions but its powers in this regard were far less than those accorded its UN equivalent, the Security Council, as discussed above. Very little was said in the Covenant about the Assembly's nature or composition. In 1919 the British saw it as a talking shop that would meet very infrequently and would be composed either of parliamentarians or of representatives of the public drawn from women's groups, religious interests and the like.[20] In the end the Assembly functioned much like its UN equivalent, the General Assembly, with its members acting as the official delegates of their states, meeting annually and taking whatever powers they could, such as overall financial control of the League, a responsibility that had not been specifically allocated by the Covenant.[21] The institution of the Secretariat occasioned far less controversy, with the Secretary-General (given the grander title of 'Chancellor' in most early drafts) seen as essentially an administrator and coordinator of the activities of the League with those of other organisations. Article 6, establishing the Secretariat, was agreed after only eight minutes' discussion.[22]

As a legal document the Covenant had many defects. Some Articles were ambiguous or contradicted other Articles. The crucial provisions for collective security were full of loopholes. However, the criticisms of this nature that were made at the time, and are still occasionally repeated, were misguided. States did not operate within the confines of a fully developed legal order where, like tax avoiders, they were merely engaged in an unending search for legitimate ways of attaining their ends. The fact that the Covenant could be interpreted as permitting some kinds of aggression in certain sorts of circumstances was immaterial, although anyone witnessing the battles in Paris over the precise wording of some clause might be forgiven for thinking otherwise. The significance of weak or ambiguous formulations in the Covenant was not that these might permit wars which a stricter wording would have prevented, but that they mirrored the doubts felt by most states about committing their security to the new system.

Although in general the cautious and restrictive wording of the Covenant accurately reflected states' determination to protect their sovereign rights and privileges as well as their scepticism about collective security, it did represent two tentative points of departure in the history of international relations. First, notwithstanding the insistence in Article 15 (repeated in Article 2 of the UN Charter) that the League should not concern itself with matters within the domestic jurisdiction of states, the Covenant does venture beyond a strict interpretation of this principle in a number of respects. In particular, it embodied a limited consensus as to the existence of certain international standards of conduct that were to apply both to colonial peoples and to working conditions in member countries. Although lacking any mechanisms to enforce observance of these standards, this did imply a limited right for the League to concern itself with human rights – a subject that was to become increasingly important in the League's successors. Secondly, the Covenant was a clear acknowledgement of the increasing range of common interests shared by states outside the field of security, and the need for more effective centralised supervision of these.

THE LEAGUE AND INTERNATIONAL SECURITY

At one level, the history of the League is synonymous with the often-told story of the failure of the Western democracies to oppose the aggression of the fascist regimes and prevent world war. The international order established at Versailles was inherently unstable because the temporary weakness of Germany and Russia meant that the balance of power upon which it was founded was essentially artificial and would come under increasing strain as those two states regained their strength. With the United States keeping aloof from any role in maintaining international order after the Senate's rejection of the Versailles Treaty, only two of the remaining great powers, Britain and France, had any kind of commitment to the territorial *status quo* determined at Paris, and by the 1930s, with the impact of the Great Depression, only these two retained any kind of commitment to liberal democratic values, extremist political views having taken hold in Russia, Italy, Japan and Germany. Such circumstances would have imposed severe strains on any international organisation devoted to a collective security principle whose implicit assumption is that overwhelming power will always be in the hands of those prepared to resist the enemies of order and peace.

Many have argued that even in more favourable international circumstances than those that prevailed in the 1930s there are certain basic flaws in the collective security concept. It requires states to be united in their determination to resist aggression, yet if such unity of purpose were to exist, the reason for it would have vanished.[23] The principle assumes that it will always be perfectly clear that aggression has been committed and that a particular state is the guilty party, yet world politics are seldom if ever so unambiguous.[24] Only a collective security pact capable of bringing effective sanctions to bear could hope for success, yet states are unlikely to establish such an obvious threat to their own monopoly of power.[25] Indeed it is clear that the major powers themselves had strong reservations about collective security: even when they were devising the system, London, Washington and Paris were also agreeing to a separate tripartite system of alliances to guarantee French security. When these alliances proved abortive following the American failure to ratify the treaties, France continued to seek security outside the League framework.

Yet this is not the whole story of the League's involvement with security issues. Lord Balfour's comment in 1925, that conflicts amongst the major powers arising from 'deep-lying causes of hostility' were beyond the League's competence, reflects a more general constraint upon the capacities of IGOs in a sovereign state system.[26] In this regard, one complicating factor for the League was the continued existence, for several years after the war, of the allied Ambassadors' Conference, which sometimes seemed to be a rival (and intrinsically more powerful) agency for ordering post-war international relations. The issue of the League's legal competence to consider matters already on the agenda of the Ambassadors' Conference was raised in the case of Yugoslavia's incursion into Albania in 1920 and during the Greco-Italian crisis of 1923.[27]

Similarly, some of Europe's more tradition-minded diplomats were at first disinclined to grant the League any responsibilities that might, however remotely, imply a diminution of national sovereignty. In 1921, for instance, Lord Curzon reproved the Persian Foreign Minister for writing to reassure the League Secretary-General that a recent Anglo-Persian agreement was not incompatible with the Covenant. The only effect of such a letter, he maintained, would be to afford the League a pretext to sit in judgement on Persia's sovereign right to interpret its own treaty obligations in any way it chose.[28] In early 1920, the allied powers refused to refer the Adriatic question to the League Council, arguing that to do so would imply that there was complete dis-agreement among the allies which diplomacy was unable to overcome, and adding, ingeniously, that a reference to the League under Article 11 (which mentioned situations threatening war) would 'start rumours of war unnecessarily'.[29] Taken at face value these observations seemed to negate the whole purpose of the League, which had been set up as a centre for diplomacy and an alternative to war.

The withdrawal of the United States was followed by widespread moves in the Assembly to water down the crucial collective security provisions of Articles 10 and 16. The impact of these could be seen in a British Foreign Office memorandum in 1926 suggesting that, whenever the League Council had to determine the Article 10 obligations of League members, it should have due regard for the 'geographical situations and special conditions' of each state, and that members themselves were free to decide whether they could contribute to any military action under Article 10.[30] The provisions for automatic sanctions in Article 16 were similarly weakened by a number of Assembly resolutions interpreted by the Foreign Office to mean that sanctions were not obligatory, although states should 'co-operate loyally' in any collective action under the Article.[31] Conversely, efforts to strengthen the League's collective security provisions were generally doomed to failure. Britain's representa-tive, Lord Robert Cecil, was unable to secure the adoption of a Treaty of Mutual Assistance, which would have made collective security operate on a regional rather than a global basis, and would have ensured that sanctions under this system would be more effective.[32] In 1924 the 'Geneva Protocol', which would have provided for compulsory arbitration of disputes, also failed to be adopted, primarily because of British objections.[33]

If the League was hampered from the start in its aspirations towards collective security, this did not prevent it from playing other roles in the security area. As it came to be a more familiar fixture on the international landscape, so the powers began to make greater use of it for a vast range of purposes, although there were still some who, like Britain's Lloyd George, privately bewailed the results of this trend: 'It [the League] should have been much more informal, like the Supreme Council. As it was, it had weak links spreading everywhere and no grip anywhere.'[34] In general, however, after this initial wariness had diminished, the powers developed the habit of passing on for League consideration a range of disputes and other international problems which for various reasons they were unable or unwilling to resolve by normal diplomatic means. For instance, in 1920 London brought the dispute between Sweden and Finland over the Aaland Islands before the Council because it saw this as the safest way of dealing with an issue of some delicacy (given Soviet interest in the Islands) without causing dissension amongst the Western powers.[35] Here one concern was to use the League to give an aura of legitimacy to the territorial distribution which had resulted from the break-up of the Tsarist empire. The same aim was apparent in an attempt by the allies to place the short-lived breakaway state of Armenia under League protection, although on this occasion the League Council declined the allied request, arguing that the League did not have the resources to undertake tasks of this magnitude.[36]

Even Lloyd George discovered a use for the League in 1921, when he threatened Yugoslavia with League sanctions during a conflict between Yugoslavia and Albania.[37] Lord Balfour was later to claim that the peaceful settlement of this dispute had only been possible because both states could accept the disinterestedness of the League's bodies, including the Commission of Inquiry that was set up to investigate the matter.[38] This was a fairly typical example of the self-congratulatory tone that accompanied some of the League's successes in the 1920s, and which helped to create a popular faith in the League's efficacy that was, in fact, founded on illusion. In this case it had been a great power ultimatum to a smaller state which had forced a settlement, and one, moreover, in a situation where both sides had been genuinely anxious to reach a border demarcation.

Other issues were passed to the League by the Supreme Council or the Ambassadors' Conference: sometimes because the powers didn't want to spend time on them; sometimes because the questions involved were intractable, and handing them over to the League was a convenient and legitimate way of evading responsibility for them; occasionally because they were an unwanted source of friction amongst the powers themselves; and sometimes because they genuinely called for a lengthy process of impartial investigation. Numerous border disputes in eastern and central Europe, Anglo-French differences over Upper Silesia, the Saar Territory, and French nationality policies in Tunis, and the problems of stabilising the international economy, all ended up with the League Council for one or more of these reasons. Its normal workload also included countless smaller problems arising out of its peace treaty responsibilities for various minority populations.

The resolution of questions of this kind led Britain's Foreign Secretary, Austen Chamberlain, to declare in 1925 that his respect for the League had increased now that he had seen it at work, not 'on one of those great problems which excite most attention but on those little problems which if we do not settle them might be a great trouble in the world'.[39] This raises the difficult question of how to assess the value of much of the League's work in the 1920s. The League existed in part to prevent minor crises from escalating into major confrontations between the powers, but one can only speculate as to whether any of the crises of the 1920s contained the seeds of a larger conflict which the League could, therefore, be said to have averted. However the more ambitious claims made for the League during this period were probably unjustified. Sarajevo had led to war in 1914 because many circumstances had combined to produce an atmosphere of war-preparedness in Europe. In the 1920s almost the opposite conditions prevailed.

The Greco-Italian Dispute

Of the many small conflicts and crises where the League played a part in the 1920s, three illustrate clearly its ability to make a useful contribution as well as its limitations. The first occurred in 1923 when three Italian diplomats were assassinated in Greece, prompting Mussolini's government to send a bellicose ultimatum to Greece with a set of demands which included the payment of a 50 million lire indemnity within five days.[40] When the Greek government did not submit immediately, Italian troops occupied the Greek island of Corfu, whereupon Greece appealed to the League Council. To most objective eyes the injured party in this case was Greece, with Italy having clearly violated the Covenant by its immediate recourse to arms. However, France was at this time involved in action somewhat similar to Italy's, having occupied the Ruhr in an attempt to enforce payment of Germany's reparations bill, and was in any case in no mood to condemn a fellow great power in order to bolster some abstract principle of collective security. The Council therefore contented itself with passing the matter to a Commission of Inquiry, simultaneously prejudging the outcome by ordering Greece to deposit 50 million lire in a Swiss bank pending the Commission's findings.[41]

The Greco-Bulgarian Dispute

The contrast with the Council's handling of the Greco-Bulgarian affair two years later is instructive. This began in September 1925 when Greek troops crossed into Bulgaria after a shooting incident on the border. Strong diplomatic pressure from Britain and France, acting through the League Council, brought about a rapid ceasefire and a Commission of Inquiry was appointed to investigate the causes of the conflict and the amount of reparations which should be paid. In contrast to the Greco-Italian dispute, when the Council in effect determined in advance both Greece's responsibility and that Italy should receive the full indemnity demanded, the Council in 1925 declared that 'all necessary care and deliberation should be employed in ascertaining the facts and fixing the amount of reparations due'.[42] Moreover, whereas in the Corfu incident a legal commission went some way towards condoning Italy's premature resort to force, in the Greco-Bulgarian conflict Briand, then President of the Council, stated as a general principle that 'in the case of a territory violated without sufficient reason reparations are due, even if at the time of the event the party committing the violation believes that the circumstances justified his act'.[43]

However, although the outcome of this affair was hardly the triumph for collective security it was claimed at the time, it did illustrate the advantages of the existence of the League in a crisis involving two small states where the great powers had no vital interests and so could act in concert. The Bulgarian government was confident enough to be able to instruct its troops not to resist the Greek incursion once it knew that the League Council was taking up the matter. Even Greece, which could justifiably feel aggrieved at the double standards which seemed to apply to similar behaviour by great and small powers, was partially appeased when it received economic aid, arranged through League auspices.[44] Both Greece and Bulgaria benefited from the appointment of a small group of observers to arbitrate over any frontier dispute for two years after the ceasefire – a forerunner of contemporary UN peacekeeping operations.

The Bolivia-Paraguay War

The Bolivia–Paraguay conflict, which developed into a major war in the 1930s, revealed that the League's sphere of action was mainly limited to Europe and that it could do little in Latin America without the support of Washington. When the first fighting occurred, in 1928, the matter was placed before the Council by the League Secretary-General, Sir Eric Drummond, in a rare use of his personal initiative.[45] However, the Council merely reminded the two sides of their Covenant obligations and passed the issue to a Pan-American institution, which unsuccessfully attempted to resolve the dispute by arbitration.[46] When the conflict reached the level of full-scale war in 1933 – a war in which 100,000 were to die – the League was far more extensively, although equally ineffectually, involved. It sent out a Commission of Inquiry, attempted vainly to bring about conciliation, appointed a special Advisory Committee and tried to enforce a ceasefire by organising (with some success) an arms embargo, first against both sides, then against Paraguay alone after it had rejected Assembly proposals on the war.[47] Although the United States participated in the arms embargo, it refused to join either of the investigative bodies and it was clear to the disputants that these lacked credibility without an American presence.[48]

By the end of the 1920s the League had developed a number of techniques which it had used with varying degrees of success in several conflicts. There were established routines for investigating disputes, conciliating the parties and keeping the peace in the aftermath of the fighting. These had, on occasions, even been backed by the threat of sanctions. Yet, as the major crises of the 1930s unfolded, the League seemed increasingly irrelevant, to a point where such a momentous event as the loss of statehood by one of its own members, Austria, in 1938, could take place virtually without comment from the League. But in most cases it was not so much that the League did nothing – the 1930s witnessed the entire range of possible League responses to crises – but that what was done was always too little or too late.

The Manchurian Crisis

The limitations of the League were perhaps demonstrated most clearly in the first great crisis of the 1930s, when Japanese troops overran Manchuria in 1931.[49] Japan had a legitimate military presence in Manchuria to protect its interests in the South Manchurian Railway, and it was an explosion on the railway, allegedly detonated by Chinese soldiers, which sparked off the Japanese move into Manchuria. Although it was revealed much later that the whole incident had been manufactured by the Japanese army as a pretext for the invasion, blame at the time appeared to be more evenly divided. The League Council at first hoped to be able to deal with the issue in much the same way as it had handled the Greco-Bulgarian conflict – as an 'accidental' outbreak of fighting which both sides wanted to be peacefully resolved. China appealed to the League under Article 11 of the Covenant, rather than immediately resorting to the collective security and enforcement provisions of Articles 10, 15 and 16. The Council's first move was to call for a ceasefire and withdrawal of Japanese troops. When the Japanese did not withdraw and further Council meetings (attended for the first time by an invited American delegation) were fruitless, it was decided on 10 December to send a League Commission under Lord Lytton to investigate the dispute.

Meanwhile Japan's advance continued, and in January 1932 new fighting broke out in Shanghai. This led China to make a fresh approach to the League, this time invoking Articles 10 and 15 and appealing to the Assembly rather than the Council. The Shanghai affair proved to be merely a temporary episode but Japan, increasingly dominated by militarist elements, established a separate puppet state in Manchuria, 'Manchukuo', on 9 March. Nearly seven months later the report of the Lytton Commission was published. Although it refused to countenance international recognition of Manchukuo, it called for Manchuria to have autonomous status within China, with a significant Japanese influence over its administration. The report strove to maintain a similar even-handedness throughout, but its adoption by the Assembly on 24 February 1933 was followed on 27 March by Japan's withdrawal from the League.[50]

The Manchurian crisis brought into sharper focus than any previous conflict the range and complexity of the problems faced by collective security in general and the League in particular. The first area of confusion concerned whether Japan could be identified as a clear-cut aggressor. Throughout the crisis Japan was acknowledged to possess legitimate interests in Manchuria, and, especially in the early days, many were inclined to believe that the Chinese had brought the conflict upon them-selves[51] – a belief bolstered by the frequent Japanese assurances as to their limited intentions, which the Council had little option but to accept.[52]

Secondly, and inevitably in a crisis sparked off by a great power, a variety of larger political considerations outweighed the immediate issue for the other powers. Britain and France were anxious not to take any action that would be opposed by Washington, while in the United States the State Department was influenced by the possibility that League opposition to Japan might have an adverse effect on the delicate domestic balance of power in Japan between civil and military factions.[53] None of the powers was really willing to confront Japan, while, in accordance with a long tradition, one section of the British Foreign Office was more concerned lest French duplicity might enable Paris to gain some advantage over London in its relationship with Japan.[54]

A third problem, and one for which the institutionalised character of collective security was partly responsible, was the considerable delay in implementing the various stages of the League's consideration of the matter. Japan was able to use a variety of delaying tactics including legal quibbles throughout the crisis while the length of time taken for the Lytton Commission to be constituted and arrive in China occasioned bitter complaints from the Chinese.[55]

Finally, the crisis clearly revealed the Eurocentric nature of the League. Several influential British diplomats argued, in effect, that the fundamental principles on which the League was based were not applicable to this conflict because the Japanese had not yet 'assimilated the ideas of international relations which have guided British policy since the war',[56] and because, given Japan's special rights in Manchuria, 'the ordinary canons of international intercourse have no application in Manchuria'.[57]

The Ethiopian Crisis

Ominously, the League's disarmament Conference, which met from February 1932 until the end of 1934, failed to produce any results other than to confirm a 1925 agreement that poison gases should be prohibited in warfare. But the crisis which effectively broke the League as a force of any significance in the important political questions of the time was the Italian invasion of Ethiopia on 3 October 1935. Although Ethiopia was a sovereign member of the League, Mussolini's government had long seen it as occupying a special, quasi-colonial position in relation to Italy. As early as 1926 Ethiopia had had occasion to protest to the League because of an Anglo-Italian agreement over the exploitation of Ethiopia's economic resources. The 1935 crisis began with clashes between Italian and Ethiopian soldiers in the Wal-Wal region of Ethiopia in December 1934. Although Italy initially seemed prepared to accept a peaceful solution, Italian pressure continued with a build-up of troops in neighbouring Somaliland. On 16 March, Ethiopia appealed to the League under Article 15, which dealt specifically with disputes that had not proved amenable to arbitration or judicial settlement.

For France and Britain the crisis posed a number of genuine dilemmas, including the risk of pushing Mussolini into a great power conflict and possibly into the welcoming arms of the real danger in Europe: Hitler's Germany. On the other hand, should the prestige of the League be seriously damaged by inaction over Ethiopia this might have equally unfortunate consequences.

Mussolini was able, following the earlier example of Japan, to engage in a number of delaying tactics, and it was not until September 1935 that the League Council effectively took up the crisis, although Britain and France had in the meantime been involved in informal negotiations with Italy.[58] They had also begun to consider the prospects and likely consequences of applying military sanctions against Italy should Article 16 be invoked. French Prime Minister Laval and Sir Samuel Hoare, Britain's Foreign Secretary, privately agreed that sanctions should be limited to economic and financial measures, to be applied 'cautiously and in stages'.[59] But in public Hoare made a strong speech at the Assembly in the hope that this might deter Italy from the action it was so obviously contemplating. A League Commission of Inquiry into the Wal-Wal incident in effect exonerated both parties, while another League Committee (investigating one of Italy's pretexts for the legitimacy of its pressure on Ethiopia) recommended on 18 September that a League Commission should be appointed to promote internal reform in Ethiopia: a rare early instance of a global IGO concerning itself with the internal affairs of a member. But the futility of all such gestures of conciliation was demonstrated when Italy launched its invasion on 3 October. Four days later the Council decided that Italy had gone to war in violation of its Covenant obligations, and on 11 October the Assembly appointed a Committee to coordinate the imposition of sanctions.

From this point, the international response to the invasion proceeded at three different levels, which were not always in harmony with each other. At one level, the various League institutions and special Committees concentrated primarily on the sanctions question. At another, Britain and France, while also involved in organising sanctions, continued their behind-the-scenes efforts to obtain an agreed settlement, efforts whose course was critically influenced by important differences between the two powers.[60] At the third level, public opinion played an important though by no means always a helpful role, and one in which the different national publics, especially in Britain and France, did not speak with the same voice.

The principal economic sanctions imposed were an embargo on exports of war materials to Italy, a prohibition of all Italian exports and a ban on loans to Italy. Debate at Geneva came to focus on whether stronger sanctions were required, particularly prohibiting oil exports to Italy and closing the Suez Canal to Italian shipping. The second was never a real possibility: Britain and France, who controlled the Canal, both regarded this as clearly a military rather than an economic sanction and one that would very probably lead to war.[61] But an embargo on oil was another matter and came close to being imposed. Two problems were: first, fears that American producers might take advantage of an embargo, notwithstanding Washington's declared support for sanctions; and secondly worries that an oil embargo might provoke Mussolini into a 'mad dog act' – that is, a declaration of war.[62] Britain was also concerned that, should this happen, she might not be able to count on the support of France, which was going through a period of political turmoil and where public opinion, partly influenced by newspaper campaigns, appeared hostile both to Britain and to any idea of war with Italy.[63] It was largely these considerations, alongside the ever present apprehension that this would be the wrong war at the wrong time, given the rise of German power, that led to the abortive 'Hoare–Laval

Pact' in December, by which the two powers would have attempted to settle the crisis on terms favourable to Italy.[64]

However, opinion in Britain, which was strongly pro-Ethiopian, forced Hoare to resign when details of the Pact were revealed, and eventually at the end of February 1936, after a League committee of experts had concluded that a universally supported oil embargo would prove effective against Italy within three and a half months, Britain decided to support oil sanctions. This caused consternation in France, coming as it did at the same time as the developing crisis over Germany's remilitarisation of the Rhineland. But French apprehensions proved to be premature as resistance in Ethiopia quickly collapsed before oil sanctions could be introduced. On 10 May the Ethiopian emperor, Haile Selassie, cabled the League that he had decided to end the war, prompting, amongst many other responses, Guatemala's immediate withdrawal from the League because 'events have demonstrated the impossibility of putting into practice the high ideals aimed at when the League was founded'.[65]

At one level, the Ethiopian crisis may be seen as a case study of the inherent problems in collective security's requirement that states undertake a general and open-ended commitment to unite against any aggressor in a situation where action against one state could jeopardise the balance of power against another, far more dangerous aggressor. In the event the chief error of the powers lay in their inability to reach a clear-cut decision either for or against firm opposition to Italy. The best illustration of this does not involve sanctions but the other, less dangerous side of the coin: assistance to Ethiopia. In 1930 the League had passed a draft Convention agreeing to give financial support to states suffering aggression, but this had never come into force.[66] Ethiopia appealed for financial assistance on 1 November 1935, arguing that 'relying upon the guarantee of collective security embodied in the Covenant, the Ethiopian Government had created neither arsenals nor arms and munitions factories'.[67] Britain's ambassador to Ethiopia strongly urged the government to support the Ethiopian request, but Hoare replied that as the League as a whole (which was waiting for a lead from Britain) refused to agree to a collective loan, Britain would not do so unilaterally.[68] Ethiopian military resistance to Italy was, in fact, surprisingly effective for some months, and after the ceasefire Ethiopia's delegate to the League argued strongly that lack of financial support to purchase weapons and munitions had been the decisive factor in the Ethiopian defeat.[69]

Many explanations and excuses have been offered for the League's failure in the security field: it lacked universality, with the United States never a member and Germany, the Soviet Union, Japan, Italy and several Latin American states withdrawing at various points; it had to cope with crises of extraordinary magnitude and frequency at a time when the popular mood in the democracies was against war, and when the worldwide depression made even the cost of economic sanctions seem intolerable; the association of the League with the Versailles Treaty made it automatically unpopular in Germany; the Covenant was a flawed document from the start, with too many ambiguities and loopholes; or alternatively it was too ambitious and always impracticable in a world of sovereign states. From another perspective, to talk of the League's failure is meaningless when the true failure in the 1930s was of Anglo-French diplomacy and will in the face of relentless aggression, with the League merely one of the instruments available to the two powers. If so, it was never an instrument in which they seemed to invest much confidence: the combined annual budget of the League, the ILO and the Permanent Court was seldom greater than 6 million dollars – barely the cost of a single cruiser.

THE LEGAL, ECONOMIC AND SOCIAL FUNCTIONS OF THE LEAGUE

The League had extensive and growing functions apart from its collective security role. It attempted to carry out its peace treaty obligations to minorities by organising plebiscites or investigating disputes; its conferences tried to determine rules and guidelines to govern international economic relations or such matters as the refugee problem; it drew up international conventions on environmental and ecological questions, such as the regulation of whaling, or controlling the pollution of the seas by oil; it devised more comprehensive international regimes in areas like communications and transit, preventing the spread of epidemics, or controlling drug traffic.

It also had more formal legal responsibilities through the creation of the Permanent Court of International Justice. This consisted of eleven (later fifteen) judges selected by both the Council and Assembly, to 'represent the main forms of civilization and the principal legal systems of the world', in the words of Article 9 of its Statutes. The Court heard 66 cases between 1922 and 1939, of which 28 were requests for advisory opinions; 50 of the cases were filed before 1932. Many of the cases stemmed from friction arising out of the peace treaties, especially where Polish–German relations were concerned. Some created significant precedents, as when a 1928 advisory opinion on the courts of Danzig appeared to imply that individuals had rights under international law, thus rejecting the traditional doctrine which only accorded such rights to states.[70]

Danzig was also one of the League's two administrative responsibilities, having been established as a free city in order to meet Polish demands for access to the sea without actually ceding the city, with its mainly German population, to Poland. It was not directly governed by the League but placed under its protection, with a High Commissioner to act as mediator in disputes. The position of the High Commissioner became increasingly impossible with the Nazification of Danzig that commenced in 1933, and by 1937, the Council had effectively abandoned Danzig to its fate. The League's second administrative responsibility was for the Saar Territory, an economically important area on the Franco-German border that was claimed by both countries. The League governed it for 15 years, at the end of which it organised a plebiscite which, as expected, gave the Territory back to Germany, with a massive Nazi campaign making the result even more inevitable.

The League, in the shape of its Mandates Commission, also had more limited administrative functions with regard to the former enemy colonies. The different types of League mandate were listed as: C mandates (South-west Africa, and Germany's Pacific territories), which the new mandatory powers, South Africa and Australia, were able to govern virtually without constraint; B mandates (other African colonies of Germany), where several restrictions on the mandatory power were laid down; and A mandates (Palestine and Trans-Jordan, Syria and Lebanon, Iraq), which had a wide range of different provisions. The charter for Palestine, for example, included the requirement to put into practice the Balfour declaration, which had promised a Jewish national home there. The Iraq mandate stipulated that Iraq should be given its independence as soon as possible.[71] The Mandates Commission was given only marginal and indirect powers of supervision and in practice played little part other than reviewing the annual report mandatory powers were required to submit.

The true growth area in international organisation was in economic, social and humanitarian work, with more than 60 per cent of the League's budget going to these functions by 1939.[72] It enjoyed the least success in its economic role, notwithstanding some early triumphs when it undertook responsibilities for the financial reconstruction and stabilisation of Austria, Hungary, Bulgaria and Greece.[73] However, the more deep-seated problems of the world economy eluded all attempts at international solution, whether within or outside the League framework. The League was rather more successful in its other 'technical' activities. It established major institutions such as the Health Organisation and the Communications and Transit Organisation, as well as numerous committees on such matters as the drug trade, refugees, the traffic in women and children, and intellectual cooperation. The important non-members of the League, including Germany before it was admitted in 1926, participated in most of these activities from the start. Although the new technical organisations did not supplant all of the existing international unions, as had originally been intended, they did make a significant contribution to the development of international regimes in their respective fields. For example, the Health Organisation established new procedures for combating epidemics, sent out several large medical units to China, standardised a great number of medicines, stimulated interest in nutritional problems and initiated studies of child welfare, public health training and many other subjects. Similarly, the International Labour Organisation – the only significant part of the League structure to remain intact after 1945 – which the United States did join had a significant impact in promoting higher standards for working conditions.

THE STRUCTURAL FRAMEWORK OF THE LEAGUE

One aspect of the League which had, for better or worse, a lasting impact on future international organisations and on the wider conduct of diplomacy was the structure of its principal organs, the Council, Assembly and Secretariat. In each case the basic pattern set in the League was maintained in the UN as well as in several regional organisations.

The Council's prospects of becoming an institutionalised great power concert had vanished when the Peace Conference accepted the principle of four Council seats for smaller states on a non-permanent basis. Once this was conceded, it inevitably made the acquisition of such places a matter of prestige and even, for some states, a major foreign policy goal. The Assembly had decided in 1920 that the main criterion in the allocation of non-permanent places should be equitable geographical distribution.[74] This accentuated an already evident tendency towards the formation of regional blocs, as was evident in the crisis occasioned by Germany's admission to the League (and an automatic Council seat) in 1926, which led to claims for permanent Council membership from Brazil, Poland and Spain. An attempt was made to appease them by increasing to nine the number of non-permanent seats (which had already been increased in 1922 to six), to include a new category of three 'semi-permanent' seats, whose members could be re-elected by a two-thirds majority of the Assembly. This did not satisfy Brazil and Spain, who both resigned from the League, although Spain returned within two years.

The Assembly, despite being seen as by far the least important League body, had been allocated a number of functions by the Covenant, including, under Article 3, the capacity to deal with 'any matter within the sphere of the League or affecting the peace of the world'. But these formal provisions were far less important in establishing the Assembly's significance than a series of precedents set in the first Assembly, which opened on 15 November 1920. These included the decisions to meet every year, not every four years as originally envisaged, to assume overall financial control of the League, and to require the Council to present it with a report on its activities every year. On important political questions the requirement for Assembly votes to be unanimous sometimes prevented action, though nothing like as often as had once been feared.[75]

Only three disputes were referred directly to the Assembly, with results which in general did not suggest that such a large organisation could play a useful role where tact and diplomacy might be needed more than verbal belligerence. This was particularly the case with the first dispute, the fighting in Shanghai during the Manchurian crisis, where the highly nationalistic and sensitive government in Japan did not take kindly to criticism from smaller states. The Assembly debates were one of the factors leading to Japan's withdrawal from the League, as they were, also, in prompting Paraguay to withdraw after the Bolivia–Paraguay dispute had been referred to the Assembly. The third instance, the Soviet invasion of Finland at the end of 1939, came when the League was already virtually irrelevant, although its action in expelling the Soviet Union was likewise an expression of moral indignation rather than a well thought-out attempt to resolve the crisis.

The third part of the League's structure was its Secretariat. In the absence of clear guidelines in the Covenant, the first Secretary-General, Sir Eric Drummond, tried to establish the principle that League officials were responsible to the League rather than to their own countries, but, inevitably perhaps, practice did not always match the theory. Places on the Secretariat assumed a political significance from the outset as the major blocs in the League tried to ensure that their interests were well represented. For instance, when the Frenchman Joseph Avenol replaced Drummond in 1933, Italy, Germany and the smaller states as a group each demanded and received the 'compensation' of an additional place on the Secretariat.[76] Moreover, as Drummond's biographer notes: 'In a sense, Secretariat positions and places on temporary or permanent League bodies ... were a type of spoils system manipulated both to pay off political obligations as well as to assure the continual loyalty or assistance of a particular power.'[77] This was especially the case of the fascist states, but even Drummond maintained close links with the British Foreign Office, frequently informing London about his Secretariat business and sometimes about his dealings with other powers, and receiving access to confidential documents in return.[78]

In two respects the Secretariat demonstrated the value of having a permanent body of international officials. It frequently served as a useful and necessary channel of communication between the many parts of the League, including the national delegations. And over the years it became a repository of information and experience about the unique problems of international organisations. It may say something for the validity of the concept of the impartial international civil servant that many League officials later took up employment with the UN.

CONCLUSION

There are three main reasons why the failure of the League did not doom the whole process of international organisation. The first is that the obvious defects in the League Covenant could be amended, particularly with the United States as a member. Secondly, it was clearly going to be increasingly difficult for the major powers simply to ignore the voices of the smaller states in matters where the latter felt they had a significant interest, and a global IGO meeting continuously provided a means of giving all states a chance of making their opinions known. Finally, the League had been established as a response to several clearly perceived problems and these showed no sign of going away. Indeed, the tasks which seemed to require cooperative international solutions had grown in number, as even the briefest comparison of the Covenant with the UN Charter indicates. It was, therefore, possible to see the League not as having failed but as having made a start, if not an especially encouraging one.

NOTES

1. D. H. Miller, *The Drafting of the Covenant*, vol. I (New York, 1928), p. 4.
2. R. S. Baker, *Woodrow Wilson: Life and Letters* (London: Heinmann, 1939), vol. VIII, p. 65.
3. Bryan claimed that this idea originated in similar proposals that he had been advancing for some years as a means of resolving labour disputes. See *The Memoirs of William Jennings Bryan* (Washington, DC: Kennikat Press, 1925), pp. 384–5.
4. *Papers Relating to the Foreign Relations of the United States: The Paris Peace Conference* (hereafter *PPC*), vol. 1. (Washington Department of State, 1943), p. 23.
5. R. S. Baker and W. E. Dodd (eds), *The Public Papers of Woodrow Wilson*, vol. II (New York: Harper, 1927), pp. 184–8.
6. R. Lansing, *The Peace Negotiations: A Personal Narrative* (Boston, MA: Houghton Mifflin, 1921), p. 34.
7. Baker, *Woodrow Wilson: Life and Letters*, vol. VIII, pp. 340, 343.
8. Baker and Dodd (eds), *Public Papers*, vol. I, p. 330.
9. Ibid.
10. C. Seymour (ed.), *The Intimate Papers of Colonel House*, vol. IV (London: Benn, 1928), p. 292.
11. Ibid., p. 292.
12. Miller, *Drafting of the Covenant*, vol. II, p. 28. See also G. Curry, 'Woodrow Wilson, Jan Smuts and the Versailles Settlement', *American Historical Review*, LXVI, no. 4 (July 1961), pp. 968–86.

13. *PPC*, vol. III (1928), p. 766.
14. S. F. Beamis (ed.), *The American Secretaries of State and their Diplomacy*, vol. X (New York: Cooper Square Publishers, 1954), 154.
15. Letter from Lansing to House, 8 April 1918, in *Papers Relating to the Foreign Relations of the United States: The Lansing Papers, 1914–1920* (Washington, DC, 1940), pp. 118–20.
16. Lansing, *Peace Negotiations*, pp. 48–76.
17. Miller, *Drafting of the Covenant*, vol. II, pp. 7–15.
18. G. W. Egerton, *Great Britain and the Creation of the League of Nations* (London: Scolar Press, 1979), p. 83.
19. Cited in ibid., p. 114.
20. Miller, *Drafting of the Covenant*, vol. II, p. 300.
21. M. Burton, *The Assembly of the League of Nations* (New York: Howard Fertig, 1974), pp. 72–5.
22. Seymour (ed.), *Intimate Papers*, vol. IV, p. 47.
23. Cf. W. S. Schiffer, *The Legal Community of Mankind* (New York: Columbia University Press, 1954), pp. 199, 205.
24. I. L. Claude, *Power and International Relations* (New York: Random House, 1962), pp. 196–7.
25. F. H. Hinsley, *Power and the Pursuit of Peace* (Cambridge: Cambridge University Press, 1967), pp. 307–22.
26. A. Zimmern, *The League of Nations and the Rule of Law* (London: Macmillan, 1936), pp. 304–5.
27. D. Armstrong, L. Lloyd and J. Redmond, *From Versailles to Maastricht: International Organisation in the Twentieth Century* (Basingstoke: Macmillan, 1996), pp. 34–5.
28. *Documents on British Foreign Policy* (hereafter DBFP), 1st series, vol. XIII (London: HMSO, 1963), p. 489.
29. *DBFP*, vol. VII (London: HMSO, 1958), pp. 134–5.
30. *DBFP*, series 1A, vol. 1 (London: HMSO, 1966), p. 847.
31. Ibid., p. 848.
32. B. Dexter, *The Years of Opportunity: The League of Nations, 1920–1926* (New York: Viking Press, 1967), pp. 171–6.
33. *DBFP*, series 1A, vol. I, p. 7.
34. Notes of a conversation between Lloyd George and Briand, 5 January 1922, *DBFP*, vol. XIX (London: HMSO, 1974), p. 13.
35. *DBFP*, vol. XI (London: HMSO, 1961), pp. 335–7, 372–3.
36. *League of Nations Document A.37* (1920), p. 25.
37. For the text of Lloyd George's telegram to the League Secretary-General, see T. P. Conwell-Evans, *The League Council in Action* (London: Oxford University Press, 1929), p. 43.
38. 'Report to the 3rd Assembly', *League of Nations Document A.7* (1922), p. 31.
39. *League of Nations Official Journal* (hereafter LNOJ) (February 1925), p. 146.
40. For a comprehensive account of this affair, see J. Barros, *The Corfu Incident of 1923: Mussolini and the League of Nations* (Princeton, NJ: Princeton University Press, 1965).
41. 'Report to the 5th Assembly', *League of Nations Document A.8* (1924), p. 19.
42. 'Report to the 7th Assembly', *League of Nations Document A.6* (1926).
43. Cited in E. Bendiner, *A Time for Angels: The Tragicomic History of the League of Nations* (London: Weidenfeld and Nicolson, 1975), p. 218.

44. Dexter, *The Years of Opportunity*, p. 135.

45. J. Barros, *Office without Power: Secretary-General Sir Eric Drummond, 1919–1933* (Oxford: Clarendon Press, 1979), p. 252.

46. Ibid., pp. 253–7.

47. See J. Barros, *Betrayal from Within: Joseph Avenol, Secretary-General of the League of Nations, 1933–1940* (New Haven, CT: Yale University Press, 1969), pp. 47–51; and Bendiner, *A Time for Angels*, pp. 317–19; Zimmern, *The League of Nations*, pp. 424–30.

48. The United States did, however, join a separate 'mediatory group', see Zimmern, *The League of Nations*, p. 429.

49. The most comprehensive study of the Manchurian crisis is C. Thorne, *The Limits of Foreign Policy: The West, the League and the Far Eastern Crisis of 1931–1933* (London: Hamish Hamilton, 1972).

50. Japan's reasons for withdrawing from the League included an assertion of the 'just and equitable principle' that it was necessary for the operation of the Covenant to vary in accordance with the actual conditions prevailing in different regions of the world. *LNOJ* (May 1933), p. 657.

51. For one example out of many of this kind of thinking in the British Foreign Office, see *DBFP*, series 2, vol. VIII, pp. 681–2.

52. See F. P. Walters, *A History of the League of Nations*, vol. II (London: Oxford Universtity Press, 1952), p. 474.

53. *DBFP*, series 2, vol. VIII, pp. 679–80.

54. *DBFP*, series 2, vol. VIII, pp. 714–15.

55. Fifth meeting of the Council (28 January 1932), *LNOJ* (January 1932), pp. 327–8.

56. Telegram from the Tokyo Embassy, *DBFP*, series 2, vol. VIII, p. 700.

56. 'Foreign Office Memorandum', *DBFP*, series 2, vol. VIII, pp. 826–9.

58. Barros maintains that part of the responsibility for the League's non-involvement in the early stages of the Ethiopian crisis rested with the Secretary-General, Avenol, whose consistent advice was that the affair should be settled informally between the major powers. This may be crediting him with rather more influence than he actually possessed. See Barros, *Betrayal from Within*.

59. G. Warner, *Pierre Laval and the Eclipse of France* (London: Eyre and Spottiswoode, 1968), p. 106.

60. See *DBFP*, 2nd series, vol. XV, *passim*, for details of these differences.

61. 'Minute by Sir R. Vanittart on the Position of Sanctions and the Possibility of Closing the Suez Canal to Italian Shipping', *DBFP*, 2nd series, vol. XV, pp. 332–40.

62. Hoare and Eden Memorandum, *DBFP*, 2nd series, vol. XV, pp. 332–40.

63. See, for example, telegram dated 26 November 1935 from Hoare to the British Ambassador in Washington, *DBFP*, 2nd series, vol. XV, pp. 324–5.

64. Memorandum dated 15 December 1935 from the British Ambassador in Washington to Hoare, *DBFP*, 2nd series, vol. XV, pp. 480–2.

65. *LNOJ* (June 1936).

66. *LNOJ* (1930) Special Supplement no. 84.

67. *LNOJ* (January 1936), pp. 24–6.

68. *DBFP*, 2nd series, vol. XV, pp. 269, 274–5.

69. *LNOJ* (June 1936), p. 660.

70. Sir Hersch Lauterpacht, *The Development of International Law by the International Court* (London: Stevens, 1958), pp. 273–6.

71. For further details on the regulations for each type of mandate, see the League of Nations, *The Mandates System* (Geneva: League of Nations, 1945), pp. 24–32; and Q. Wright, *Mandates under the League of Nations* (Chicago: Chicago University Press, 1930), pp. 24–63.

72. *The Bruce Report on the Technical Work of the League*, Special Supplement to the Monthly Summary of the League of Nations (September 1939), p. 7.

73. Report to the 4th Assembly, *League of Nations Document A.10* (1923), pp. 49–59.

74. Report to the 2nd Assembly, *League of Nations Document A.9* (1921) p. 64.

75. Burton, *The Assembly of the League of Nations*, pp. 175–205.

76. Barros, *Betrayal from Within*, p. 12.

77. Barros, *Office without Power*, p. 395.

78. Ibid., pp. 54, 291.

chapter 3

The American-led, Cold War UN, 1945–60

THE CREATION OF THE UNITED NATIONS

Two things were clear in the minds of the wartime allied leaders: they would create a new collective security system and they would not build it on what was now seen as a discredited League structure.[1] Yet despite themselves, the framers of the Charter created an organisation that bore 'a most embarrassing resemblance' to the League.[2]

Significant elements of successful pre-existing international machinery, such as the International Labour Organisation, were adopted without fundamental alteration. The structure of the UN, with its Secretariat, Security Council and General Assembly, mirrored the equivalent organs of the League (see Figure 3.1). Both organisations were firmly based on the principle of sovereign equality (Article 2.1 of the Charter), and many of the commitments are virtually identical. But the immediate context in which the Charter was drafted was different in three ways.

First, the drafting of the Charter was much more professional and considered. Its general outline had been agreed by the end of the Moscow Conference in October 1943. Exceedingly complex negotiations between professional diplomats at Dumbarton Oaks in August–September 1944 worked out many of the details, but the sensitive issue of the Security Council veto was left to the top-level Yalta meeting in February 1945. There the 'big three' – the USA, USSR and UK – agreed that on all but procedural matters, each of the Security Council's permanent members would have a veto – that is, could prevent the adoption of a resolution by voting against it. They then imposed it on the San Francisco Conference of April–June 1945.[3]

Secondly, the UN was deliberately created before the end of the war. This was because the 'big three' wanted to cash in on wartime unity. They feared post-war disunity both at home (the Americans were worried about a resurgence of isolationism) and among the allies. They also wanted to avoid the 1919 mistake of linking the new organisation with the peace treaties.

Thirdly, and according to one of the drafters, '[n]othing … was so original in the Charter as the manner of its making'.[4] The San Francisco Conference, which was attended by fifty states, took place in an unprecedented glare of publicity. Some 1200 amendments were tabled and discussed, and important changes were made. The General Assembly's powers became more definite and it was given the right to

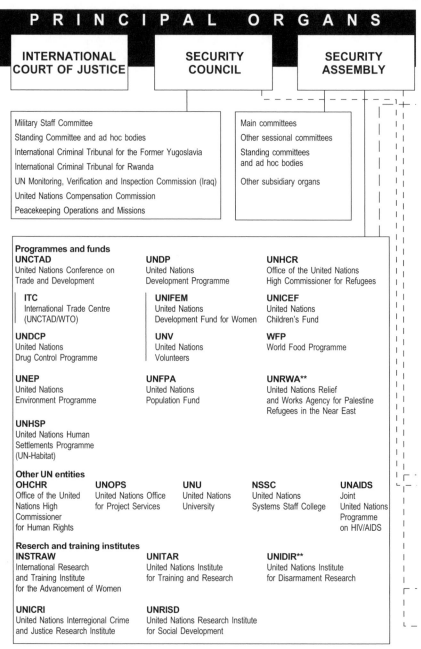

Figure 3.1 The United Nations system

O F   T H E   U N I T E D   N A T I O N S

ECONOMIC AND SOCIAL COUNCIL	TRUSTEESHIP COUNCIL	SECRETARIAT

Functional commissions
Commission for Social Development
Commission on Human Rights
Commission on Narcotic Drugs
Commission on Crime Prevention
  and Criminal Justice
Commission on Science and Technology
  for Development
Commission on Sustainable Development
Commission on the Status of Women
Commission on Population and
  Development
Statistical Commission

Regional Commissions
Economic Commission for Africa (ECA)
Economic Commission for Europe (ECE)
Economic Commission for Latin America
  and the Caribbean (ECLAC)
Economic and Social Commission for
  Asia and the Pacific (ESCAP)
Economic and Social Commission
  for Western Asia (ESCWA)

United Nations Forum on Forests

Sessional and Standing Committees
Expert, ad hoc and related bodies

Related Organisations

IAEA
International Atomic Energy Agency

WTO (trade)
World Trade Organization

WTO (tourism)
World Tourism Organization

CTBTO Prep.com
PrepCom for the Nuclear-Test-Ban-Treaty
Organization

OPCW
Organization for the Prohibition of
Chemical Weapons

Specialised Agencies*
ILO
International Labour Organization

FAO
Food and Agriculture Organization
of the United Nations

UNESCO
United Nations Educational, Scientific
and Cultural Organization

WHO
World Health Organization

World Bank Group
IBRD International Bank for Reconstruction
      and Development
IDA   International Development Association
IFC   International Finance Corporation
MIGA Multilateral Investment Guarantee Agency
ICSID International Centre for Settlement
      of Investment Disputes

IMF
International Monetary Fund

ICAO
International Civil Aviation Organization

IMO
International Maritime Organization

ITU
International Telecommunication Union

UPU
Universal Postal Union

WMO
World Meteorological Organization

WIPO
World Intellectual Property Organization

IFAD
International Fund for Agricultural Development

UNIDO
United Nations Industrial Development
Organization

OSG
Office of the Secretary-General
OIOS
Office of Internal Oversight Services
OLA
Office of Legal Affairs
DPA
Department of Political Affairs
DDA
Department for Disarmament Affairs
DPKO
Department of Peacekeeping Operations
OCHA
Office for the Coordination
of Humanitarian Affairs
DESA
Department of Economic
and Social Affairs
DGACM
Department of General Assembly
and Conference Management
DPI
Department of Public Information
DM
Department of Management
OIP
Office of the Iraq Programme
UNSECOORD
Office of the United Nations
Security Coordinator
OHRLLS
Office of the High Representative
for the Least Developed Countries,
Landlocked Developing Countries
and Small Island Developing States
ODC
Office on Drugs and Crime
UNOG
UN Office at Geneva
UNOV
UN Office at Vienna
UNON
UN Office at Nairobi

discuss and make recommendations on any matter affecting the peace of the world or the general welfare of nations.[5] The powers of the Economic and Social Council (ECOSOC) were significantly altered, and its dignity was enhanced by making it one of the UN's principal organs. The Conference added a Declaration Regarding Non-Self-Governing Territories (Chapter XI). It drafted two lengthy Chapters (XII and XIII) on trusteeship, which had not been discussed at Dumbarton Oaks, and in so doing strengthened the system that had been submitted by the sponsoring powers and France. It also established the Trusteeship Council as a major organ.

DIFFERENCES FROM THE LEAGUE

As mentioned, there were fundamental similarities between the UN and the League. But within these elements of continuity there were five significant differences of shape and emphasis.

The first was the veto. In the eyes of the 'big three', this was the greatest improvement over the League, in that – as the British Commentary on the Charter put it – 'the successful working of the United Nations depends on the preservation of the unanimity of the Great Powers. ... If this unanimity is seriously undermined no provision of the Charter is likely to be of much avail.'[6] Secondly, whereas the Covenant was more British than American, the Charter was the reverse. This largely accounted for the third difference: that the new organisation was given a greatly enlarged role in economic and social matters. There were several reasons for this: the immediate problems of postwar economic reconstruction; a widespread feeling that some international safeguards should be instituted to counter the blatant and extreme violations of human rights of the kind committed by the Nazis; and a suspicion that war might result from adverse economic conditions. Fourthly, the Charter has a different tone. The Covenant rather suggested that the League's major problem would be accidental and limited war, whereas the Charter seems to envisage large wars begun deliberately by wicked men. The final difference was that the UN marked several steps forward in terms of the expectations of states, as seen in the suggestions that economic, social and welfare issues might be considered internationally, that colonial powers had a responsibility 'to promote ... progressive development towards self-government or independence',[7] and that human rights were a matter for international concern. A clash soon developed between this last idea and Article 2.7 of the Charter (which forbids UN intervention in 'essentially ... domestic matters'), which in time resulted in some erosion of the non-intervention principle.

THE EARLY YEARS: COLD WAR DISPUTES AND THE COLLAPSE OF THE CHARTER SYSTEM

The cold war between the US-led West and the Soviet-led East was already perceptible by the time the Charter came into force in October 1945. Because of its tensions, the most important intended change from the League – that the Security Council should be something like a great power directorate – did not materialise, foundering on the shoals of superpower mistrust. The clearest manifestation of this was the 279 vetoes cast during the cold war. Most vetoes in the first period, 1945–60, were cast by the Soviet Union (see Table 3.1), reflecting her isolated position in the Council. Unsurprisingly, the USA made propagandistic use of the situation, arguing that it demonstrated Soviet obstructiveness and introducing resolutions that would patently elicit vetoes.

Table 3.1   Patterns in the use of the veto

Period	China*	France	UK	USA	Russia/ USSR**	Total
2002	0	0	0	2	0	2
2001	0	0	0	2	0	2
2000	0	0	0	0	0	0
1999	1	0	0	0	0	1
1998	0	0	0	0	0	0
1997	1	0	0	2	0	3
1996	0	0	0	0	0	0
1995	0	0	0	1	0	1
1994	0	0	0	0	1	1
1993	0	0	0	0	1	1
1992	0	0	0	0	0	0
1991	0	0	0	0	0	0
1990	0	0	0	2	0	2
1989	0	2	2	5	0	9
1988	0	0	1	6	0	7
1987	0	0	2	2	0	4
1986	0	1	3	8	0	12
1981–85	0	4	7	24	2	37
1976–80	0	5	4	10	4	23
1971–75	2	2	8	11	5	28
1966–70	0	0	2	1	1	4
1961–65	0	0	1	0	11	12
1956–60	0	2	2	0	15	19
1951–55	1	0	0	0	29	30
1946–50	0	2	0	0	51	53
Total	5	18	32	76	120	251

*Taiwan occupied China's seat until October 1971 when it was replaced by the People's Republic of China.
** In December 1991 the Russian Federation succeeded to the Soviet Union's seat.

Note:
Statistics derived from Sally Morphet, Research and Analysis Department Memorandum, *Table of Vetoed Draft Resolutions in the United Nations Security Council, 1946–1995* (Foreign and Commonwealth Office, International Research Unit, Research and Analysis Department, January 1996); and Celine Nahory, Giji Gya and Misaki Watanabe, *Subjects of UN Security Council Vetoes*, http://www.globalpolicy.org/security/membership/beto/vetosubj/htm.

In this climate it was impossible to create the envisaged UN machinery for the maintenance of international peace and security. Since East and West did not trust each other to carry out military action on behalf of the UN, the Military Staff Committee talks about the creation of a UN force broke down in 1948. The Security Council also played only a limited role in the pacific settlement of disputes.

THE KOREAN WAR AND THE QUESTION OF COLLECTIVE SECURITY

In the Korean War, the UN moved from being simply a forum for diplomatic pressure and propaganda to playing a forceful role in a way not envisaged by the drafters of the Charter. When North Korea invaded South Korea on 25 June 1950, the US immediately took the matter to the Security Council. Because the Soviets were boycotting the Council (over the failure to give China's seat to the new, Communist regime), the Council was able to adopt an American resolution calling on members to 'furnish such assistance to the Republic of Korea as may be necessary to repel the armed attack and restore international peace and security in the area'. By mid-September, 14 states had sent ground forces for the defence of South Korea.[8] However, the American force commander, General MacArthur, was carried away by virulent anti-communism and military success and provoked the entry of China into the war. The UN suffered near-disastrous reverses and, with the Soviets now back in the Security Council, the United States raised the issue in the General Assembly. Under the Uniting for Peace Resolution (Resolution 377), the Assembly authorised itself to consider any threat to the peace if the Security Council was blocked by the veto. The following year, at America's instigation, China was condemned as an aggressor. The war dragged on until July 1953 when an armistice agreement restored the *status quo ante.*

The American propaganda-machine portrayed Korea as a collective security operation. This claim is justified in three ways. First, the UN took strong action against aggression. Secondly, a UN-commanded force was established after the Security Council had condemned North Korea's invasion. Thirdly, although the Charter gives the Security Council primary responsibility for maintaining international peace and security, the General Assembly clearly has a secondary or residual role. It might not have been collective security as envisaged in the Charter, but it was pretty well in line with the League's conception that individual states would contribute as and when they individually recognised that aggression had been committed.

However, the operation in Korea was not collective security as envisaged in the Charter, but peace enforcement – partial and threatening action authorised by the UN. This was, firstly, because whereas the Charter-makers had assumed that all the great powers would participate in decisions about collective security, the US had swiftly taken advantage of a Soviet boycott of the Security Council to pass US-inspired resolutions.

Secondly, the Korean operation was overwhelmingly American. The US contributed 50 per cent and the South Koreans 40 per cent of the UN ground troops, to which only 16 out of 60 UN members contributed men. The US also provided most of the air and sea forces. The UN command was practically identical with the US

Far Eastern Command, sharing the same commanding officer and common head-quarters. Moreover, General MacArthur considered himself a US commander waging war on communism on behalf of the US. Nor were other members much consulted. The final armistice was negotiated on Washington's instructions and the Security Council played no role. Conversely, and contrary to the Charter's conception of collective security, North Korea was not isolated but received considerable assistance (chiefly from Beijing), and the Soviet Union staunchly opposed what the UN was doing.

Thirdly, there was little of the centralised decision making envisaged by the Charter. It was up to individual states to decide whether they wished to participate militarily in the war or in the economic embargo against China after the General Assembly had condemned it as an aggressor in February 1951.

Fourthly, after crossing the 38th parallel (dividing North and South Korea) in October 1950, the exercise was transformed into a campaign to unite Korea. Only military failure brought the UN back to its original aim of acting 'solely for the purpose of restoring the Republic of Korea to its status prior to the invasion from the north and of re-establishing the peace broken by that aggression'.[9]

Fifthly, the US would have acted anyway as the Korean War was in her interest: she ordered her armed forces to come to the aid of South Korea even before the crucial UN resolution. However, using the UN to legitimise US actions was not entirely straightforward, as to some extent the UN tied Washington's hands, and at crucial moments the General Assembly exercised a restraining influence.

CHINESE REPRESENTATION IN THE UN

An important legacy of the Korean War, and another consequence of US dominance of the cold war UN, was the travesty of Taiwan continuing to sit in China's Security Council seat for 22 years after the establishment of the (Communist) People's Republic of China (PRC) in 1949. The Korean War intensified already-strong American hostility to Beijing; and the General Assembly, prompted by the US, condemned the PRC as an aggressor. Selective sanctions were imposed against it. The United States then used her dominance in the General Assembly to prevent the discussion of the question of China's seat. As the General Assembly became dominated by the third world, and the US lost her assured, automatic majority, Washington resorted (in 1961) to having the question of Chinese representation declared an important question. This required a two-thirds majority and kept Taiwan in the UN for another decade. Only in 1969 did votes for the People's Republic start picking up, and in October 1971 Taiwan was replaced by the PRC.

THE RISE OF THE GENERAL ASSEMBLY

In the Uniting for Peace Resolution, America had sought to capitalise on her dominance in the General Assembly by trying to turn that organ into a body that could authorise collective security operations. This soon proved unfeasible and

Washington turned back to alliances such as NATO, for her security needs. None the less, the prestige of the General Assembly rose at the expense of the strife-ridden Security Council. This was because the US continued being more or less assured of voting majorities in that organ and because weaker states were keen to increase the authority of the Assembly. And so, while the Security Council lost work and went into decline, the General Assembly came to be seen as *the* important organ.

THE UN AND DISPUTES ARISING OUT OF THE ENDING OF COLONIALISM

Indonesia

The cold war did not prevent the UN playing a useful role in several disputes arising out of the end of colonialism. One of the earliest examples of UN mediation, which also indicated the UN's powerful anticolonial thrust, was in 1947 when the Dutch colonial authorities clashed with the *de facto* Indonesian republican government. In the first of many such claims by colonial powers, the Netherlands said it was a domestic matter, falling within Article 2.7 of the Charter. The Security Council successfully evaded this assertion and appointed a three-nation Good Offices Committee to try to conciliate the two parties. A truce was arranged but was quickly violated by the Dutch. The Council then upgraded the Committee into a Commission for Indonesia and gave it greater powers. After strong US pressure, the Netherlands agreed in March 1949 to grant speedy independence to Indonesia.

In this instance, the existence and character of the UN clearly influenced the behaviour of the two principal actors – the Netherlands and the USA – and also the eventual outcome. Washington did not want to upset or humiliate the Netherlands, but she was worried about communist influence in the region and was unwilling to allow Moscow the propaganda victory of being seen as the greatest friend of liberation movements. The mere fact of UN membership forced the USA to take a stance on a dispute she might otherwise have ignored. The Netherlands was affected by a rising tide of criticism, especially from Asian countries who were willing to organise sanctions. The UN played a valuable role in defusing and settling the crisis and, thanks to it, the Dutch government escaped from an uncomfortable situation in a face-saving way.

Palestine

The UN also played a part in bringing independence to the former Italian colonies in Africa – Libya, Somaliland and Eritrea – though in the latter's case, not until after a long armed conflict with Ethiopia. Two other disputes arising out of decolonisation also produced considerable and long-lasting strife: Palestine and Kashmir. In Palestine, Britain's attempts to maintain law and order were frustrated by American meddling, ruthless Zionist terrorism and the sheer costs of keeping a large portion of her war-weary army in that territory. With the Cabinet unable to think of a solution, Britain turned to the UN.

In August 1947, after three months' investigation, the majority of the members of a Special UN Committee thought that Palestine should be partitioned into an Arab state, a Jewish state and a UN-administered Jerusalem. (The minority recommended a federal state with Jerusalem as its capital.) The Jews welcomed the partition plan since the balance of advantage was in their favour. The Arabs, however, were implacably opposed to the creation of a Jewish state. Britain had earlier warned that she would not enforce a solution unacceptable to both sides. Believing the plan to be an inequitable recipe for disaster, and in the faint hope that announcing her imminent withdrawal might make the Arabs and Israelis reach a settlement, Britain declared she was abandoning the mandate. Thereafter she took no part in UN discussions on Palestine and sullenly let events run their course prior to her departure on 15 May 1948.

Thanks to strong-arm US tactics, the General Assembly approved the partition plan, and a UN Commission for Palestine was set up to implement it. However, the UN Commission never left New York and the Jewish community in Palestine declared the existence of Israel at midnight on 14 May 1948. A few minutes later President Truman granted immediate recognition without consulting or informing anyone. All the members of the Security Council were worried that the bloodletting that followed the creation of Israel might escalate dangerously. So the Security Council used tough words, demanding a four-week truce, which was obtained with the assistance of unarmed UN officers. When fighting broke out again a month later, the Security Council ordered an indefinite truce and brought in more officers to supervise it. The situation remained precarious. Peace treaties were impossible. The presence of international officers – later known as the UN Truce Supervision Organisation (UNTSO) – became a permanent fixture.[10] Several UN officials were killed during the 1948 fighting, including the UN mediator, Count Bernadotte of Sweden.

Kashmir

The problem of Kashmir was a legacy of Britain's hasty partition of India. Following Independence in August 1947, the situation became increasingly inflammable. A large force of Pathans crossed the border from Pakistan, leading the Hindu ruler of Muslim Kashmir to accede to India, who then provided military help. Finding her army confronting Pathan tribesmen, India protested to the Security Council that Pakistan was interfering in Kashmir. Pakistan protested that her hands were clean and that India was violating self-determination and oppressing Kashmiri Muslims. The Security Council despatched a Commission, which obtained the parties' agreement to a ceasefire (coming into operation on 1 January 1949) and used a small group of military officers to watch over the ceasefire and prevent minor incidents getting out of hand.

Since neither India nor Pakistan renounced their claim to the whole of Kashmir, the officers remained after the delineation of the ceasefire and became known as the UN Military Observer Group in India and Pakistan (UNMOGIP). A few dozen UNMOGIP soldiers were still there in 2003, monitoring the 500-mile partition line (which India claims is an international frontier) from the Pakistani side. Although there is frequent tension, and India and Pakistan have several times come to blows, neither party is constantly thirsting for war. India grudgingly accepts the presence of UNMOGIP (despite insisting since 1972 that it has no function) while Pakistan sees UNMOGIP as a symbol of her continuing grievance.

AN ALTERNATIVE APPROACH TO SECURITY: PEACEKEEPING

It was not until the late 1950s that it was recognised that the UN was engaging in a distinctive activity that, while not envisaged in the Charter, was immensely helpful in threatening situations. At the time, the Secretary-General Dag Hammarskjöld often referred to peacekeeping as 'preventive diplomacy'. This reflected his belief that peacekeeping was a diplomatic method whose purpose was chiefly to prevent the cold war seeping into conflicts. However, although peacekeeping did do this, it had a wider role. It referred 'to the international help which is sometimes sent to an immediate problem area' when conflicting parties 'wish, at least for the time being, to live in peace'.[11] In retrospect, it is clear that this was what the UN did in Indonesia, Palestine and Kashmir. Yet the concept of peacekeeping has always been misunderstood, partly because it is often confused with collective security and enforcement action. Peacekeeping's expanded role since the end of the cold war has also muddied the concept. However, the fourfold characteristics of traditional peacekeeping did not alter during the cold war years, and they are still relevant to a number of missions today.

The first of these characteristics is that such missions' operational personnel are drawn from armed services. Such people are usually available for immediate despatch to trouble spots; they are acceptable to the local military with whom they will have to deal; and they have the expertise which is generally needed. They are subject to tight discipline (important in sensitive spots on foreign soil), and the authoritative approach of the military can be very useful. Such peacekeepers are drawn from countries with no immediate interests in the dispute, and during the cold war they tended to come from the Nordic countries, Canada, India and Ireland.

The second, vital, characteristic of traditional peacekeeping is its values (or principles): the requirement that such bodies adopt a non-threatening and impartial approach. Peacekeepers are not in the business of using or threatening force. They are armed lightly (or, in the case of most observer groups, not at all), and may only use their weapons in self-defence and to assert freedom of movement. They do not take sides, whatever their private feelings or those of their states. Only thus are they likely to be trusted by all disputants.

Thirdly, traditional peacekeeping fulfils three functions. *Defusion* helps to reduce an immediate crisis by enabling disputants to withdraw in a face-saving way, by helping to avoid a crisis escalating to war, or by deterring third parties from intervening. Once in place, the force may help to settle future crises. UNTSO and UNMOGIP served this function. *Calming* activity helps to keep a potentially dangerous situation quiet, just as a bandage protects an open wound. Peacekeepers may also stop things getting worse by dispelling each side's anxiety about the other's intentions, and helping to prevent incidents. Sometimes, the wound is so deep that, as with UNMOGIP, peacekeepers are in for a long stay. Peacekeeping to *settle* or *resolve* disputes occurs when an impartial third party is required to ensure that each party honours its side of an agreement. For example, to maintain order during a plebiscite, to oversee a plan for national reconciliation, or to administer a disputed territory prior to handing it to one of the disputants without the other losing face.

The final characteristic of traditional peacekeeping refers to the context in which it operates. Its function is, in all key respects, one of cooperation. An authorising body such as the Security Council or General Assembly must agree on the establishment of the operation, determine its duration and, if need be, extend its mandate. States must supply resources and funds for the operation. And host states must give their consent and be willing either to settle their dispute or to desist from hostilities for the time being. If consent is withdrawn, the force must be removed, otherwise sovereignty would be infringed; contributing states would probably withdraw their troops; and the non-cooperation or hostility of the host state would quickly make peacekeeping untenable. Unless all the immediate parties to a dispute are willing to co-operate, peacekeeping cannot work. If just one side cooperates, peacekeepers may no longer be regarded as impartial, and much of the mission's *raison d'être* will be lost.

UNEF

The first UN Emergency Force (UNEF I), in the Sinai – often regarded as the beginning of peacekeeping – illustrates these characteristics. It began as a defusing operation when Britain and France invaded Egypt in 1956. Since British and French vetoes blocked Security Council action, the General Assembly used the Uniting for Peace procedure to discuss the Suez crisis. The majority supported a Canadian suggestion that a UN force should replace the British and French troops. But in order that all concerned could put their own interpretation on what had happened, the exact way of replacing the British and French was left vague. No-one was deceived that Britain and France were being forced out of Egypt, but they kept some dignity. After they and the Israelis had gone, UNEF's 6000 troops from ten countries sat on the Egyptian side of the Egypt–Israel border, Israel having rejected their presence. The force remained a calming presence until 1967 (diminishing in scope as the years went by), helping to prevent incidents and reducing anxiety.

The Congo

The UN operation in the Congo from 1960 to 1963 illustrates the way in which the cold war continued to dominate the UN in the security field. It also marked the culmination of the USA's manipulation of the cold war UN.

Having been thrust precipitously into statehood on 30 June 1960, the former Belgian Congo (now the Democratic Republic of the Congo) immediately disintegrated into bloodshed and chaos following a mutiny by the Congolese army. Without the permission of the Congolese government, Belgium began intervening to restore law and order. The Congolese government appealed to the UN for protection from Belgian aggression.

UNEF I had given a powerful impetus to the idea that despite the breakdown of collective security, the UN could play a significant role in the maintenance of international peace. The despatch of an observer group to the Lebanon in 1958 had further whetted this appetite. Thus the Security Council hardly batted an eyelid at despatching a 20,000-strong peacekeeping force to the Congo, although, by the peacekeeping standards of the day, it was huge and tremendously expensive. By September the UN Operation in the Congo (ONUC) had easily supervised the withdrawal of Belgian forces. But ONUC's more important purpose was to defuse a potential new area of cold war conflict by interposing a neutral, UN force that would isolate the country from superpower ambitions. Other than France (who sympathised with Belgium), the chief external powers all initially supported ONUC. For the superpowers, it was their first involvement in Black Africa and they invested considerable energy and prestige in it. Washington had long been a supporter of peacekeeping in principle, and using the UN seemed an ideal way to avoid the Congo becoming 'a kind of whirlpool of great power politics and conflicting world ideologies'.[12] Moscow, meanwhile, was keen to make political capital by having Belgium branded an aggressor, gaining a friendly Congolese government and preening her anticolonialist credentials. Unfortunately, the mercurial Congolese Prime Minister, Patrice Lumumba, leaned clumsily towards Moscow, encouraging Western fears of Soviet intervention. These worries were shared by the Secretary-General, Dag Hammarskjöld, who allowed ONUC to take a line that weakened Lumumba's position and led to his downfall and eventual death at the hands of his enemies. The West was not unhappy at this, but the Soviet Union was livid. Bitterly attacking Hammarskjöld for acting 'in the interests of the colonisers and in flagrant contradiction of the Charter',[13] the USSR refused to have any dealings with him and demanded the Secretary-General be replaced by a three-man *troika* consisting of representatives of the West, the East and the non-aligned.

A complication of the Congo crisis was the secession, at its start, of the copper-rich province of Katanga, which was very important to the Congolese economy. The Katangese had no overriding sense of loyalty to the Congolese state and were encouraged by Belgium in their greed to keep the profits of the copper mines. But this violated the principle of territorial integrity and, had it succeeded, would have offered a dangerous precedent for would-be secessionists elsewhere. It was also seen as a neocolonialist move by the Soviets and the non-aligned.

Because UN members were more interested in achieving political goals than adhering to peacekeeping principles, the Security Council authorised the use of force to end civil war and expel mercenaries, and it was used against Katanga several times before a decisive military action (at the end of 1962) brought the secession of the province to an end. By taking sides in a major domestic conflict the UN had moved from peacekeeping to peace enforcement: that is, it took partial and threatening action to achieve a settlement of a conflict.

The Congo episode was controversial in several ways. Additionally, it produced an unhappy fall-out for a number of years. It coloured Soviet attitudes to peacekeeping. It made African states apprehensive about playing host to peacekeepers. It made many states, and the Secretariat, very cautious about the UN getting involved within states in a law-and-order role (fearing that, as in the Congo, it could all too easily lead to political controversy). And it gave the UN severe financial problems. Until then peacekeeping costs came out of the regular budget. However, despite a ruling from the International Court of Justice, 32 states, including France and the Soviet Union, did not pay their shares of the costs of the Congo operation (and the Soviets also refused to pay for UNEF I). By 1964 arrears stood at $100 million and there was a major crisis since, under Article 19 of the Charter, a defaulter is at a certain stage deprived of its vote in the General Assembly. Had this been applied, the Soviet Union would probably have left the UN. This was averted by avoiding formal votes for a year. Then, in 1965, the US conceded that the General Assembly would not apply Article 19 on this occasion. According to one observer, America's retreat on the constitutional issue was 'the end of an era: the end of American hegemony within the UN'.[14]

THE RISE AND FALL OF TWO SECRETARIES-GENERAL

To discharge his office effectively, a Secretary-General (see Table 3.2) must be trusted by the UN's members, especially the most powerful. When national interests clash, he must walk a political tightrope between the claims of opposing sides. In the paranoid atmosphere of the cold war UN, the balancing act was particularly delicate – and not always successful.

Trygve Lie

The first Secretary-General was Trygve Lie of Norway. He was a dynamic man, full of initiative and very ambitious for his office and for the UN. He adopted an active role from the outset, declaring in September 1946 that under Article 99 it was his duty to inform the Council of threats to the peace, and, if the Council did not act, he must. By July 1948 he was exercising, unchallenged, the right to present his own amendments to resolutions before the Council. However, Lie offended the USA (in 1946 over Iran), and incurred British criticism (over the Berlin crisis in 1948), and Soviet enmity (over Korea). During his last few years in office, he was completely ignored by the Soviets in their official contacts with the UN and in its attendant social life.

When Lie's term expired in 1951, he did not seek reappointment, but the Western powers felt that, as a matter of principle, it was important to support Lie. The Soviets responded by vetoing Lie's reappointment and, after the Security Council had reported that it was unable to agree on a recommendation, the General Assembly re-elected Lie. However, the Soviet boycott meant that Lie could not effectively discharge his office and he resigned in November 1952.

Dag Hammarskjöld

Lie was not the best man for the job. He was too brash, hasty, didactic, tactless and, in his quest for the UN-inspired millennium, unrealistic. He left the organisation in a

Table 3.2 UN Secretaries-General

Trygve Lie	Norway	1 February 1946 to 10 April 1953
Dag Hammarskjöld	Sweden	10 April 1953 to 18 September 1961
U Thant	Myanmar (formerly Burma)	3 November 1961 to 30 November 1962 (Acting Secretary-General) 30 November 1962 to 31 December 1971 (Secretary-General)
Kurt Waldheim	Austria	1 January 1972 to 31 December 1981
Javier Pérez de Cuéllar	Peru	1 January 1982 to 31 December 1991
Boutros Boutros-Ghali	Egypt	1 January 1992 to 31 December 1996
Kofi Annan	Ghana	1 January 1997 –

poor shape. His successor was Dag Hammarskjöld of Sweden, who was expected to stick to administration and to be untroublesome and quiet. Hammarskjöld immediately reorganised the Secretariat; he was cautious, and he gained a reputation for being financially 'sound'. However, he had no more intention than Lie of taking a back seat. He also had tremendous gifts. He combined ingenuity, subtlety, tact, discretion and great intelligence with deft political skills.

Under Hammarskjöld, and apparently because of him, the UN seemed to flourish. Increasingly, the UN tended to 'leave it to Dag', who, seemingly, could perform marvels. In 1954 he arranged the release of US airmen who had been imprisoned in China during the Korean War. When the Soviets invaded Hungary in 1956, he was asked to 'take any initiative which he deemed helpful'. During the 1956 Suez crisis he played a very active and effective role, and was granted remarkable executive powers in respect of the peacekeeping force that the UN despatched to Egypt. In 1958 he expanded the UN presence in Jordan and Lebanon. In 1959 he took the initiative in visiting Laos after allegations that foreign troops had infringed the Laotian border. In 1960 he was granted considerable powers in controlling the UN's Congo operation. Hammarskjöld was able to achieve so much not just because of his genius, but because he took office at an ideal time: Stalin had died, Eisenhower had become US President, there was a ceasefire in Korea, and a slight thawing of cold war tension. Being relieved that the UN was making progress in a few areas despite the paralysis of the Security Council, the 'big five' allowed Hammarskjöld to act relatively independently.

However, Hammarskjöld broke his political back by being too independent. In seeing himself as a servant of the principles of the Charter, he ignored the vital importance of keeping the permanent members happy. By running the Congo operation as a pro-Western enterprise and giving a nod and a wink to Lumumba's removal, he incurred the wrath of the Soviets. They boycotted him and began touting their *troika* proposal. But he did not just offend Moscow. There was friction with the Eisenhower administration because of its attempts to bring down the regime in Guatemala; France was so incensed by Hammarskjöld's attitude towards French policy in Algeria and his role during the Bizerte crisis of 1961 that President de Gaulle did not send condolences when Hammarskjöld died; and there were rows with other leaders. Had Hammarskjöld not been killed in a plane crash in September 1961, the aura that surrounds his name would probably have dissolved.

THE 'NON-POLITICAL' UN

The UN must be distinguished from the wide range of institutions known as UN Specialised Agencies, which have been established to serve various functional ends. Collectively, the UN and the Agencies are often called the UN 'family' or the UN 'system'. However, each agency is an entirely separate international organisation. Some, like the Food and Agricultural Organisation, were established before the UN. Others were set up as part of the post-Second World War planning. Two of these, the International Monetary Fund and World Bank, effectively lead a life independent of mainstream UN activities.

Within the UN proper, however, there are also many functional commissions, *ad hoc* groups, 'programmes' and 'funds'. And two of what the UN refers to as its Principal Organs also have what may be seen as a 'non-political' focus: the Economic and Social Council (ECOSOC) and the International Court of Justice (ICJ). But this does not mean that attempts will not be made, as in the case of ECOSOC, to use such bodies for political ends; nor that even the most non-political body of all – the ICJ – is removed from the impact of major political phenomena such as the cold war.

ECOSOC

ECOSOC was intended to be the chief coordinator of the UN's economic and social activities and was given special responsibility to promote respect for, and observance of, human rights and fundamental freedoms. Unfortunately, ECOSOC grew into a sprawling and complex organisation. This was due to its broad terms of reference and multiplicity of functions, combined with the early decision to pursue 'every social and economic objective in sight, with an extravagant faith in the virtue of words and resolutions and in the value of proliferating committees and commissions'.[15] Subsidiary bodies include commissions, committees and working groups on a huge range of topics. Thanks to effective logrolling, a West European Economic Commission was followed by Asian and Latin American Commissions, nominally supervised by ECOSOC. Also formally under ECOSOC auspices, but in practice autonomous, are such bodies as the United Nations Children's Fund, the Office of the High Commissioner for Refugees, the Industrial Development Organisation, and the UN Development Programme.

In the cold war UN, the work done in some of these fields was relatively uncontroversial. But negotiating and proffering advice on important social and economic questions provided a wide opening for superpower tensions. Profound ideological divergences over economic doctrine deepened the rifts between states whose representatives had scant respect for the Charter – or reality – in airing antagonisms and prejudices as they sought to score debating points. Discussions of social questions, such as freedom of information or religious persecution, put the Soviet Union on the defensive. On the other hand, the Soviets courted Afro-Asian favour by holding the US up to ridicule on such questions as racial discrimination (which was still legally practised there in the early 1950s). The role of pro-American and pro-Soviet non-governmental organisations offered further complications.

The conflict between East and West robbed ECOSOC of the basis that would have made possible effective cooperation. In economic matters, the US had a profound impact since many development programmes were effectively dependent upon US financial support. However, as the UN became dominated by the third world, there was disenchantment with ECOSOC's acceptance of the Western view of a minimalist role for functional agencies. As will be seen in the next chapter, other fora became more important.

The International Court of Justice

Because the Permanent Court of International Justice (PCIJ) was regarded as one of the League's greatest achievements and successes, in 1945 its name was simply changed to the International Court of Justice (ICJ), and it was made one of the UN's principal organs. However, the cold war climate was unpropitious for the Court. From the beginning, and up to a point in contrast with the League, law played second fiddle to politics.

During the cold war, the ICJ languished. In its 24 years, the PCIJ delivered 32 judgements and 24 advisory opinions, all of which were accepted. By contrast, after 45 years, the ICJ had given only 33 judgements and 19 advisory opinions. Judgements and advisory opinions have been rejected by all the permanent members other than Britain, as well as by Bulgaria, Hungary, South Africa, Italy and West Germany.[16] In addition, far fewer states accepted the compulsory jurisdiction of the Court (under the system known as the Optional Clause), and those who did accept the Clause tended to attach very sweeping reservations.

This gave rise to a common perception that the ICJ was irrelevant. Yet there was nothing wrong with the Court. The position was simply that in a society marked by pessimism, divisiveness, high levels of tension and ideological rivalry (which extended to the content of international law), the Court could not play a significant role.

CONCLUSION

The UN was intended to be an improvement on the League, but its fate during the cold war is a reminder that it is not the machinery or constitution of an organisation that is crucial, but the attitude of its members and the international climate. All UN members sought to use the organisation to further their national interests, but the US was most successful because of its dominance in international society. The superpower quarrel prevented the creation of the intended security machinery, and permeated all aspects of the UN system. Still, the UN was able to play a useful role in some disputes, and the development of peacekeeping sometimes helped states to live at peace.

Meanwhile, the UN had quickly become a vital adjunct to diplomacy. As a club of sovereign states, the UN (unlike the League of Nations) was very much a going

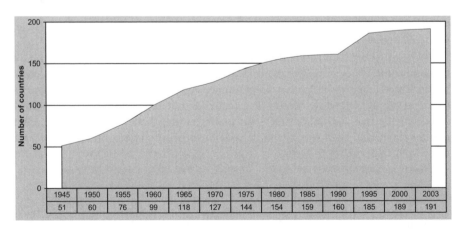

Figure 3.2 The growth in UN membership

concern after fifteen years (and still growing after more than fifty years, see Figure 3.2). In fact, one of the most notable things about the UN during this period is that despite the most acute international tension, states who were outvoted did not walk out of the UN. Evidently, the idea that the world should be equipped with an organisation that included all states was one whose time had come.

NOTES

1. David Armstrong kindly allowed me to make liberal use of his chapter on 'The United Nations in World Politics' in *The Rise of the International Organisation: A Short History* (London: Macmillan, 1982).
2. Sir Alexander Cadogan, 'The United Nations: a Balance Sheet', *The Year Book of World Affairs 1951* (London: Stevens, 1951), p. 2.
3. Smarting under recent insults to his pride, de Gaulle of France refused to be one of the sponsoring powers. At America's insistence, China was included in the rank of great powers, but it did not really count.
4. Charles Webster, 'The Making of the Charter', *History*, vol. 32 (March 1947), p. 16.
5. Articles 10, 13 and 14. Article 12, however, maintains the special position of the Security Council. The General Assembly can make recommendations on any matter unless the Security Council 'is exercising in respect of any dispute or situation the functions assigned to it in the present Charter'.
6. *A Commentary on the Charter of the United Nations*, Cmd 666 (London: HMSO, 1945), pp. 16–17. Cf. Inis Claude, 'The Security Council', in Evan Luard (ed.), *The Evolution of International Organizations* (London: Thames & Hudson, 1966), pp. 71–2.
7. Article 76.b of the Charter.
8. The number of contributing states rose to 16 by early 1951.
9. US Secretary of State, Dean Acheson, in *Department of State Bulletin*, vol. XXIII, no. 575 (10 July 1950), p. 46. Quoted in Leland M. Goodrich, 'Korea: Collective Measures against Aggression', *International Conciliation*, no. 494 (October 1953), pp. 172–3.
10. As of April 2003, UNTSO is still present in the area.
11. Alan James, *Peacekeeping in International Politics* (London: Macmillan, 1990), p. 1.
12. Interview with Francis D. Wilcox, 11 September 1960. CBS News, *The Collected Transcripts from the CBS Radio and Television Broadcasts*, vol. 6: *Face the Nation, 1960–1961* (New York, 1972), p. 299.
13. Quoted in Foreign & Commonwealth Office Background Brief, *UN Peacekeeping*, January 1987.
14. Max Jakobson, *The United Nations in the 1990s: A Second Chance?* (New York: UNITAR, 1993), p. 41.
15. H. G. Nicholas, *The United Nations as a Political Institution*, 5th edn (London, Oxford, New York: Oxford University Press, 1992), pp. 139–40.
16. However, it must be remembered that advisory opinions are not binding.

4

The Third World UN, 1960–80

THE THIRD WORLD AND THE UN

The decline in US dominance of the UN began in 1955 when America lost its 'automatic' two-thirds majority in the General Assembly. For in that year, after much superpower wrangling, sixteen new members were admitted. (Until then, Security Council vetoes or a lack of the required number of positive votes barred admission to any states expected to side with either superpower in the cold war.) Within a few years decolonisation had transformed the UN into a third world dominated organisation: out of 114 members in 1964, fifty-seven were Afro-Asians. In consequence, the UN of the mid-1960s would have been 'hardly recognisable' to those who were at San Francisco.[1]

Committees, commissions and working groups proliferated on issues that directly concerned the third world. The UN's agenda widened. Soon there were almost yearly conferences on development or development-related issues – for example, the 1974 Rome food conference, which produced an ambitious, long-term plan and led to the establishment of the World Food Council. The thrust of the third world UN was in the direction of economic activities. By the early 1980s, up to six times more was spent in this field than on international peace and security.

The Soviets courted the third world, but third world states voted with the Soviets only when their views coincided, and in the early 1960s the US won twice as much support as the Soviets on cold war issues. However, as the growth of non-alignment indicates, most new members did not see the cold war as 'their' concern. They had their own agenda and it did not coincide with that of the Soviets or the West. They wanted to change the largely Eurocentric vision prevailing in the UN, to expand the UN's institutions in the direction of development, and to make the organisation more 'democratic'.[2] The UN's Economic and Social Council (ECOSOC) and the Security Council became more representative: membership of the former grew from 18 to 27 in 1965, and from 27 to 54 in 1973. The Council expanded from 11 to 15 in 1965. But this did nothing to remove the international evils as perceived by new states. They had all the righteousness of the weak and only one trump card, their ability to speak out – loudly if necessary – and to pass General Assembly resolutions by overwhelming majorities. An increasingly strident Assembly became a third world campaigning body in which voting victories substituted for fundamental changes.

ANTICOLONIALISM

From the very beginning the UN had a strong anti-imperial flavour. Two of the 'big three' founder-members – the USA and USSR – were officially anti-imperial, and the UN's ranks were rapidly swollen by newly liberated states for whom decolonisation was a burning issue to be pursued whenever the opportunity arose. There was no dispute about the right of the General Assembly, acting through the Trusteeship Council, to exert influence in trust territories, whose administering powers were bound by individual trusteeship agreements. The Trusteeship Council collected annual reports from administering states, received petitions and despatched three-yearly missions to each territory. Its membership was equally divided between administering and non-administering powers. This rendered it insufficiently aggressive or critical for the anticolonials. Whenever possible, therefore, they used the General Assembly and bypassed the Trusteeship Council. The Assembly heard oral petitioners who had been refused a hearing by the Council, sent its own visiting missions to trust territories, made recommendations (not always in accord with those of the Council) directly to administering authorities, and tried to get the Trusteeship Council to take certain sorts of action. And so the Trusteeship Council declined in business and prestige.

Separately from its provisions about Trusteeship, the Charter had a section (Chapter XI) called the Declaration Regarding Non-Self-Governing Territories (that is, regarding straightforward colonies). Initially, the colonial powers disputed the General Assembly's right to discuss any information they transmitted to the UN under this Chapter. However, in 1946 the anticolonials succeeded in creating a temporary Special Committee on Information from Non-Self-Governing Territories. The Committee's mandate and functions were then repeatedly extended and in the 1950s it became the main focus of anticolonialism. During these years, the General Assembly decided that resolutions on non-self-governing territories did not require the two-thirds majority that had been taken for granted until 1953. The colonial powers' emphasis on the importance of 'progressive development' (Article 73.b) was criticised as too slow. And the Assembly utterly rejected Belgium's argument that overland empires (such as, so it was claimed, the Soviet Union) were similar to overseas empires.

In 1960 the admission of 17 former colonies gave a big boost to anticolonialism, and the Soviet Union seized the opportunity to curry friends and make trouble: it proposed a declaration demanding freedom for all colonies within a year. The 43 Afro-Asians took up the idea, modified it, and in December 1960 a draft resolution (the Declaration on Granting Independence to Colonial Countries and Peoples) was overwhelmingly passed as Resolution 1514. It demanded immediate independence and proclaimed the 'subjection of peoples to alien subjugation, domination and exploitation' to be 'a denial of fundamental human rights ... contrary to the Charter of the UN, and ... an impediment to ... world peace and co-operation'.[3]

In 1961, the effort to revoke the legitimacy of colonialism was pushed to an extreme when India 'liberated' Goa from Portuguese rule and the three Afro-Asians on the Security Council supported India, ignoring Article 2.4, which bans the use or threat of force. Then, in 1965, Resolution 2105 comprehensively condemned colonial rule as a threat to international peace and security and a crime against humanity.

Meanwhile, in 1963 the Committee on Information from Non-Self-Governing Territories[4] had been wound up because irked colonial powers would have nothing to do with it. By then, the anticolonials were pursuing their imperialist quarry in other fora: the Assembly's Fourth Committee and the predominantly Afro-Asian 'Committee of Twenty-Four', which was established in 1961. The latter committee collected information and received petitioners – providing they had the 'right' bias. (In 1967 it refused to circulate petitions in which Gibraltarians protested about Spain or residents of Aden complained about interference by the United Arab Republic [as Egypt was then called].) It despatched visiting missions where the colonial power would accept them and, when visits were denied, held meetings in the field, near to the territories. It also compiled its own list of colonial areas to which independence should be granted.

The Committee of Twenty-Four became increasingly extreme, partly because the fiercest anticolonials – the 38 sub-Saharan African states – were frustrated over the 'hard core' colonial areas remaining in Africa. By the end of the 1960s, however, there were few trust territories, and such colonies as remained were mostly very small. But the campaign continued. It resulted in irritated Western powers leaving the Committee of Twenty-Four. When Portugal recognised the independence of its former African colonies in 1974, the anticolonial spotlight focused almost exclusively on Southern Africa. Here the target was not just colonialism (in the shape of the white minority regime in Rhodesia, and South Africa's continuing control of South West Africa – Namibia), but the racist policies of Rhodesia and South Africa.

RACIAL DISCRIMINATION

South Africa

Racial discrimination had become an international issue in 1946 when the General Assembly criticised South Africa's treatment of people of Indian origin. Gradually the criticism broadened, and when South Africa introduced complete racial segregation in 1952, the General Assembly launched its onslaught. In 1961, apartheid was condemned as a flagrant violation of the Charter. In 1962, the General Assembly passed its first resolution calling for sanctions (only the Security Council can impose them), and institutionalised the anti-racist campaign by creating the Special Committee against Apartheid (as it was known from 1970). From 1966 onwards it was assisted by an anti-apartheid centre in the UN Secretariat.

The 11 members of the Special Committee against Apartheid were all from the third world or eastern bloc and they harried South Africa as vigorously as the Committee of Twenty-Four hounded imperialists. (The UN Council for Namibia acted similarly in respect of South Africa's occupation of Namibia.) South Africa was hounded out of the Food and Agriculture Organisation in 1963, and the International Labour Organisation in 1964. In 1963 the Security Council called on states to embargo arms sales to South Africa, and in 1965 the General Assembly passed the strongly-worded Declaration on the Elimination of All Forms of Racial Discrimination, Resolution 1904. By 1973, 12 per cent of all Assembly resolutions attacked South Africa. In 1974, South Africa suffered the humiliation of having her delegates' credentials rejected (which meant they could not appear in the General Assembly or on its committees). In 1976 the Assembly began advocating 'armed struggle'. By the early 1980s, South Africa was being verbally attacked in over half the plenary sessions and criticised in a fifth of Assembly resolutions. South Africa's trading partners were condemned for encouraging racist policies and the Security Council was unsuccessfully called on to apply comprehensive mandatory sanctions.[5]

Rhodesia

Rhodesia came before the General Assembly in 1961, and was one of the first territories tackled by the Committee of Twenty-Four. The latter castigated British colonialism, international monopolies and white settlers for being in league with one another. But it was Rhodesia's unilateral declaration of independence (UDI) in November 1965 that put it on the front burner. At Britain's behest, the Security Council immediately condemned the 'illegal, racist minority regime',[6] urged states to withhold recognition, called on Britain to end the rebellion, and asked other states to break off economic relations and apply an oil embargo. This fell short of what the Africans ardently desired and demanded: British military force to defeat the rebels. But Britain made it clear she would veto military sanctions, and the Security Council would go no further than was acceptable to London.

However, the Commonwealth (not the UN) persuaded Britain in December 1966 to sponsor a Security Council resolution that led to the first ever application of mandatory sanctions. Nine exports vital to the Rhodesian economy were embargoed on the grounds that the illegal regime constituted 'a threat to international peace and security' (this incantation being necessary for Chapter VII to be invoked). Almost a hundred states reported compliance with the resolution and Zambia, which was dependent on Rhodesia for 95 per cent of her transport, was given urgent Commonwealth aid and a British-sponsored airlift of oil. In 1968, at Britain's request, the Security Council approved a total trade ban on Rhodesia. The British navy patrolled the sea surrounding Beira (the port nearest to Rhodesia), but there was much sanctions busting, primarily by South Africa, which supplied Rhodesia with oil, and Portugal (which ruled neighbouring Mozambique). Moreover, in 1971 the US Congress lifted the ban on importing 'strategic and critical' materials from Rhodesia (chiefly chrome and nickel).

When Rhodesia declared itself a republic in 1970, it again came before the Security Council. The Afro-Asians insisted on voting on a resolution they knew Britain would veto. Having seen the Security Council's sanctions committee paralysed for months because of 'a silly little squabble about its membership', Washington responded to 'openly insincere manoeuvrings'[7] by casting its very first veto. But in the mid-1970s the political balance in Southern Africa changed with Angolan and Mozambican independence, and nationalist guerrillas gained an increasing military advantage. South Africa in effect told Rhodesia's leader Ian Smith to settle, and Smith reached an internal agreement in 1978. The world refused to recognise it. By then Rhodesia was taking up practically all Lord Carrington's (the British Foreign Secretary) time.

Significantly, it was not the UN that weighed most heavily in Britain's thinking but Commonwealth pressure; the political and economic costs of not settling; the views of Britain's European partners and the USA; and (in the eyes of some) the danger of the expansion of Russian influence. Building on his predecessor's negotiations, Lord Carrington chaired the Lancaster House talks that led to Rhodesia becoming Zimbabwe in May 1980. In this there was no role for the UN: it was a Commonwealth force that monitored the pre-independence elections.

THE 'NON-POLITICAL' UN

In the third world UN, the Western, liberal distinction between what was technical and political became blurred. Issue compartmentalisation broke down and everything became 'related to everything else'.[8] This is well illustrated by the events leading to the demand for what was called a 'New International Economic Order' (NIEO).

The New International Economic Order

President Kennedy's proclamation of the 1960s as a UN Development Decade has been described as being 'to economic development what the Declaration on Colonialism was to self-determination'.[9] Thereafter the 'north–south gap' was a major UN issue, which gained impetus from the influx of third world members and the arrival in 1961 of a Burmese Secretary-General, U Thant, who regarded the problem as 'the most serious source of tension in the world'.[10] In 1960 the UN created the International Development Association to provide loans on favourable terms to third world countries. And in 1962, ECOSOC endorsed Thant's proposals for action in such areas as development planning, mobilising human resources, international trade, development financing, technical cooperation and other aids to development. Meanwhile, the General Assembly passed numerous resolutions endorsing legal principles that would favour the interests of the third world in its dealings with foreign-owned businesses. But although there were some gains, the gap between rich and poor widened and, in terms of assistance and growth, 'the decade was a dismal failure'.[11]

By then the third world's expectations had markedly increased and, being disappointed with ECOSOC's conservative line, it had created bodies in which to challenge the whole American-inspired, liberal trading system: 1964 saw the creation of the United Nations Conference on Trade and Development (UNCTAD) and the emergence of the 'Group of 77' like-minded third world states.[12] By maintaining a united front under the leadership of UNCTAD's first Secretary-General, Raoul Prebisch, the developing states called attention to their trade problems and the way in which these were aggravated by the developed states, while successfully keeping attention away from reforms they could introduce themselves. In this way, they managed to change the terms of the debate and put the West on the defensive.

Seeing UNCTAD as 'a demand for everything by those who have nothing',[13] the West ignored such UNCTAD demands as more 'untied' aid, lower tariffs and stable prices for primary commodities. This prompted much name-calling and recrimination, especially against the USA, who acted as scapegoat for the West. But two developments in the early 1970s led the West to take a more constructive attitude towards the problem of development and admit the inequity of the existing international economy. First, there was the collapse of the Bretton Woods system, widespread harvest failures and a major international economic crisis. Secondly, the quadrupling of oil prices in the wake of the 1973 Middle East War had a tremendous psychological impact, raising doubts about the West's supply of raw materials from the South, on which it seemed increasingly dependent. Developing states felt greatly encouraged and the more radical, led by Algeria, saw the oil crisis as the first shot in a world economic revolution.

In April 1974, at the sixth special session of the General Assembly, Southern assertiveness blossomed into full-blown demands for a New International Economic Order (NIEO). Agreement on practical measures was well-nigh impossible, but two resolutions were adopted. The first, the Declaration on the Establishment of a New International Economic Order, combined 'features of a recitation of past evils, a salutation of present changes in the international economic power structure, and a manifestation of desired reforms in the system'.[14] The second resolution adopted a 'Programme of Action' for the NIEO. This had no substantive weight, being an enumeration – in emotive and value-laden words – of the aspirations of the developing states and the normative duties of the developed. Later that year, the regular Assembly session adopted a 'Charter of Economic Rights and Duties of States'. This contained stiff medicine for the rich. In the words of some Western wags, it was 'all developing state rights and developed state duties'.[15]

However desirable the NIEO might have been, it demanded more self-abnegation than the rich possessed. It achieved some modest economic gains, but had only limited impact on its targets, the Bretton Woods Institutions and the IMF, for the key states that were required to offer themselves as sacrificial lambs were those who voted against the Programme of Action. The South soon realised that there was little progress to be made in this confrontational direction. It therefore changed tack and began moderating its tone as early as the General Assembly's 1975 special session on the NIEO. As the 1970s wore on, the prospects of an NIEO vanished. The North came to feel less vulnerable. The oil countries were not willing to use their leverage on behalf of other developing countries. The poor could not create other cartels similar to OPEC. The South's solidarity crumbled in the face of non-complementary short-term interests and the success of the West in drawing in the *nouveaux riches*. The final crunch came in 1980 when there was an attempt to empower the General Assembly to bring all UN institutions into line with development doctrine and fundamentally to reform the IMF. The General Assembly's 1980 special session came to a dismal end 'and effectively derailed "global negotiations"' on an NIEO.[16]

Meanwhile, although there were troubles elsewhere in the UN system (as will be discussed below in respect of the International Labour Organisation), much valuable work was done. For example, the World Weather Watch, launched by the World Meteorological Organisation in 1967, was highly useful and successful and offered no scope for making political hay. Thanks to the World Health Organisation, the battle against malaria appeared to be making great progress, and smallpox was eradicated. The Food and Agriculture Organisation's support for the 'green revolution' was hailed for dramatically improving food supplies through the introduction of high-yielding cereals (although environmentalists were critical). Arguably, the UN system's contribution to eliminating poverty was a drop in the ocean. But at least something *was* happening. People benefited through having sewers and clear running water in villages. Children were saved from hunger and early death. Education, hospitals and roads were provided in developing states. Bridges were being built between the North and the South and there was emerging a global society that recognised the existence of a community of interest between interdependent states.

THE IMPACT OF THE GENERAL ASSEMBLY'S ACTIVITY

The General Assembly has two levels of activity. One is the private level. Virtually all member states have sent permanent missions to the UN, so that within the geographically-confined space of an area around the UN's headquarters there are high-ranking diplomatic posts from almost all the world's states. This is particularly important for third world states, who, being relatively poor, cannot afford many embassies. Representation at the UN, however, gives them the opportunity to make private face-to-face contact with diplomats from all members. It also provides access to representatives from the Vatican State (the only significant non-member since Switzerland joined the UN in 2002) and from non-governmental organisations, of which, by the 1990s, a thousand had consultative status with ECOSOC. As at most conferences, off-stage discussions can have as much importance, and, on particular issues, often more, than what goes on in public. A recent American delegate put it thus: 'Open meetings make good theater, but deals are cut in back rooms. ... For every one diplomat in the U.S. seat, playing by the rules, ten others should be working in the corridors.'[17]

The second level of the General Assembly's activity – its public face – is, of course, important. Here states can speak for the record, and mount their open diplomatic campaigns. Some of these campaigns have had little effect, or have even been counter-productive. Those who were on the receiving end of barracking in UN committees grew weary of discussions that were devoid of reality and in which they were continually having to resist attempts to expand the UN's authority. Thus the colonial powers withdrew from the Committee on Information from Non-Self-Governing Territories. Britain ceased participating in discussions on Rhodesia in the Committee of Twenty-Four. A 1964 attempt to broaden the membership of the Committee on Apartheid was unsuccessful, as opponents of sanctions refused to join. And in 1975 an anti-Israeli resolution equating Zionism with racism, which was interpreted as a thinly veiled attack on the United States, nourished America's growing disillusion with the UN.[18]

States did not alter their fundamental policies just because of General Assembly demands. For example, in addition to criticising the superpowers for discussing arms control outside the UN framework, the General Assembly designated the 1970s and 1980s as 'disarmament decades' and convened three special sessions on disarmament (in 1978, 1982 and 1988). But the main achievements were negotiated elsewhere. Britain did not speed up decolonisation because of the UN, though the anticolonialist campaign provided an added justification for her colonial disrobing. The UN did not fundamentally alter Britain's policy on Rhodesia or end racial discrimination in Southern Africa. States whose cooperation was necessary for stiffer sanctions against Rhodesia or South Africa did not change tack or give in to haranguing. Furthermore, one impact of sanctions can be to rally populations behind the target governments, and to make those governments more intransigent and anti-pathetic to anything connected with the UN. This happened in Rhodesia and South Africa. Thus Rhodesia's Ian Smith claimed that there was 'more justice where Satan reigns than where the United Nations wallows in its sanctimonious hypocrisy'.[19]

However, third world campaigns were by no means always fruitless. A variety of points should be noted. In the first place, as well as demonstrating the depth of moral commitment to a cause, fiery speeches are one way of releasing a real build-up of political steam. It is therefore possible that they may reduce the temptation actually to indulge in hot-headed action. Secondly, General Assembly campaigns provided a means whereby the dislike of certain situations could be effectively dramatised, and so be given increased prominence. Thus, such devices as walking out when South African representatives addressed the Assembly kept racial discrimination in South Africa in the public eye.

Thirdly, by repeatedly passing resolutions by large majorities, the third world campaigners not only achieved symbolic victories but also had some influence on that amorphous entity known as 'world public opinion'. General Assembly resolutions may be no more representative of world public opinion than, say, *The Times* or *Sun* is of British public opinion. But they do signal developments in the world's *diplomatic* climate, and that in turn helps to set the international agenda. Resolution 1514 and subsequent resolutions, for example, amounted to a *de facto* amendment of the Charter and the outlawing of colonialism, at least in political terms, and perhaps also in legal terms. At the same time, they serve a vital role in placing and keeping issues on the international agenda until the time is ripe for words to be put into action. This is what is meant when it is said that General Assembly resolutions represent something more than the sum of their parts. It also explains why such importance is regularly attached by member states to getting a majority in favour of their case, or to preventing their opponents from securing a majority. In this way the General Assembly has become an important element in international diplomacy.

A fourth consideration is that public discussion in the General Assembly may sometimes precipitate policy changes by individual states. A state that knows it is going to be attacked may occasionally trim its policy sails in the hope of being able to present a better defensive case. The knowledge that a delegate has to stand up and be counted on an issue that is of no direct concern to her or his state may move that state away from its initial inclination and in favour of the majority view, or at least towards abstaining on the vote. Courting unpopularity through a gratuitous display of one's personal sympathies may be judged to be not worth the diplomatic cost. This clearly seemed to happen over South Africa as the Assembly's anti-apartheid tempo heightened, for certain Western states came to opt for abstention on draft resolutions which called for sanctions, rather than allow themselves to be seen as providing comfort to an international pariah. Moreover, in the case of some states – those of Asia – hostility to South Africa seems genuinely to have increased as a result of regularly having to vote on the matter in the General Assembly. Through being forced to take a public position, their substantive position underwent change. And even when policy did not alter, it might have affected the way it was presented, and that, in turn, had the potential to influence actual policy.

Fifthly, it must also be borne in mind that states are always alert to the possibility, on issues which do not greatly interest them, of 'selling' their votes, or bartering them to achieve a desired result on another matter. And, sixthly, the General Assembly has been increasingly looked to to provide legitimacy for states' policies. The obverse of this aspect of the Assembly's activities is the diplomatic ploy of hiding behind a resolution of the General Assembly – claiming an inability to act because the Assembly has ruled it out or, where the Assembly is thought to have responded weakly, simply trying to shift the blame for not having acted for oneself to the world body.

What all this amounts to is the undoubted fact that the General Assembly has become a diplomatic forum of some significance. It is *not* a legislature. Nor do its votes necessarily have a high moral character. It is a diplomatic register which states have found it increasingly unwise to ignore, and which they have, when in the majority, tried to use to further their own policies. It is, therefore, the third world states who have benefited most from the General Assembly's public activities. But, naturally, states on the receiving end of the majority's censure were far from happy about this development. Above all, this was true of the world's most powerful state, the US.

AMERICAN DISILLUSIONMENT AND INCREASED USE OF THE SECURITY COUNCIL

American enthusiasm for the UN waned as the General Assembly became dominated by the third world. Although in the 1960s the great majority of resolutions were still supportive of America's position, disillusion began setting in when, in 1964, third world states would not back the USA over its intervention in the Congo. (America had done this to protect Western citizens.) America also felt aggrieved at being treated roughly by the Committee of Twenty-Four for her handling of her possessions in the Pacific and Caribbean. For example, although Puerto Rico had voted freely in 1948 in favour of a compact of association with the USA, in 1972 the Committee included Puerto Rico on its list of dependent territories and began demanding self-determination and independence in increasingly extreme and unwarranted terms.

The USA, together with Britain and France, retreated from the General Assembly to the Security Council and, in so doing, initiated its slow revival. The Security Council was not, however, a cosy, comfortable place, especially following the addition, in January 1965, of six more members. The West had lost its dominance in the Security Council and for the first time had to engage in genuine diplomacy on a broad, inter-caucus basis. There was also a growing tendency on the part of states who were not on the Security Council to demand that they be given a hearing at open (public) Security Council debates, where their interests were involved. This had begun in 1971, when liberation movements as well as states were invited. Not long afterwards invitations were extended to anyone the majority wanted to hear.

Symptomatic of America's declining leadership of, and support for, the UN was President Ford's warning in 1974 against the 'tyranny of the majority', and the appointment in 1975 of Patrick Moynihan as the United States' ambassador to the UN. A blunt, confrontational man, Moynihan believed that the UN was growing 'in a certain kind of ideological authority ... deployed on behalf of totalitarian principle and practice wholly at variance with its original purpose' and that it was time for

Americans to make themselves 'feared international forums for the truths [t]he[y] might tell'.[20] In the 1970s the General Assembly's tilt against Israel made things worse, and demands for an NIEO caused indignant outrage.

There was a new American indifference to UN appeals. Aid was cut, Rhodesian sanctions were violated to maintain chrome imports, and America's contribution to the budget was reduced from 31 to 25 per cent. President Carter, who took office in 1977, sought to restore the UN's place in American foreign policy and won African favour by appointing a veteran civil rights leader, Andrew Young, as US ambassador to the UN. But the UN was now an organisation of the underdogs and Carter could not outweigh powerful internal opposition to what was regarded as an unholy Soviet/third world alliance in the International Labour Organisation (ILO).

The International Labour Organisation

The 1970s had begun with Congress withholding US budget payments to the ILO because a Soviet citizen was appointed to a senior position. In 1974, and without proper prior investigation, the ILO conference passed a resolution condemning Israel's labour practices in the occupied territories. The same meeting failed to adopt an Expert Committee's report containing several specific condemnations of the Soviet Union. The final straw was when the 1975 ILO conference granted observer status to the Palestine Liberation Organisation. That November, Washington gave notice of withdrawal because the ILO had 'become increasingly and excessively involved in political issues which are quite beyond the competence and mandate of the organisation'; had shown 'appallingly selective concern' in respect of human rights'; increasingly demonstrated 'utter disregard' of 'due process' in condemning states without following the correct procedures; and its unique tripartite structure – granting representation to employers, workers and states – had been eroded because some employers and workers were under the thumbs of their governments.[21]

The ILO continued causing offence while America worked out its two years' notice. First the conference blocked a US nomination for vice-president. Then it rejected an American proposal to ensure the observation of due process before states were attacked. And thirdly, it displayed 'double standards' in not adopting a report critical of Argentina, Chile, Ethiopia and Uganda, while damning Israel by refusing to accept data on labour conditions in the West Bank. Despite pressure from close allies and the State Department, Carter reluctantly withdrew because the ILO had not taken 'corrective measures ... to restore that organisation's commitment to its original purposes'.[22]

The ILO survived the loss of America's 25 per cent of the budget by additional voluntary contributions and financial economies. But it wanted Washington back and introduced significant changes. Noticeably less rhetoric flew around the conference hall. The agenda became markedly 'non-political'. There were no anti-Israeli resolutions. The ILO tackled the problem of human rights in the Soviet satellites in Eastern Europe by condemning Czechoslovakia and investigating trades union policies in Czechoslovakia and Poland. Moreover, the adoption of a secret ballot for some votes enabled individuals to vote according to conscience rather than the dictates of their governments. Satisfied, the USA rejoined the ILO in February 1980.

The Security Council

In 1965 the enlargement of the Security Council from eleven to fifteen members shifted the balance away from the P5 (five permanent members). The latter could now be outvoted by non-permanent members who constituted a majority that could block a resolution with seven abstentions. Non-permanent members, who now tended to see themselves as representatives of their regional group, began inviting, and giving a hearing to, non-members of the Security Council, thereby contributing to a certain amount of 'irrelevancies and invective'.[23] The USA found herself increasingly isolated and, in consequence, resorted to the veto.

None the less, the Security Council remained a relative haven to which both superpowers retreated from an awkward and unbiddable General Assembly. This contributed to an increase in the Council's authority, as did four other developments. First, the 1962 Cuban missile crisis made the superpowers recognise that they needed to cooperate, and this ushered in the relaxation of tension generally known as *détente*. It also brought home to the P5 the desirability of agreeing amongst themselves and engaging in genuine diplomacy on a broad, inter-caucus basis. Secondly, this process was further encouraged by the 1967 and 1973 Middle East wars, which reminded all the P5, especially the USA, that they shared a *common* interest in avoiding war and that the UN could be useful in this. Thirdly, Richard Nixon, who was elected US President in 1968, was inclined to acknowledge Soviet strategic parity and talk the language of the balance of power. Fourthly, the trend towards the Security Council was strengthened when the People's Republic of China, who favoured the Security Council as a place for conducting business, replaced Taiwan in 1971, at a time of markedly improved American–Chinese relations. Apart from the 1971 India–Pakistan war – when Chinese, Soviet and American interests diverged sharply – the Security Council became a forum for action as opposed to expressions of opinion.

As a result, limited collegiality emerged and the P5 began having private meetings and consultations. These had originally been limited to deliberations on the appointment of a Secretary-General. But in the late 1960s regular discussions began to be held on substantive issues. By the early 1970s, the Council was also holding 'informal consultations of the whole': off-the-record meetings (governed neither by the Charter nor by rules of procedure) at which representatives could speak freely without committing their states. A commodious and well-provided consultation room was built adjacent to the Council chamber, thereby making consultations a symbolically separate replica of formal Council meetings.

THE UN AND THE MAINTENANCE OF INTERNATIONAL PEACE AND SECURITY

The third world UN had little impact on the maintenance of peace and security, for notwithstanding the fact that many disputes arose in the third world, they almost all had a cold war dimension and so limited the UN's ability to act. And on direct cold war issues the UN continued to be of little relevance. However, although the UN was shunted to the margins when the superpowers clashed, it could be still valuable. During the 1962 Cuban missile crisis, the USA used the Security Council to embarrass the USSR with photographic evidence of the Soviet missile sites. Off-stage corridor diplomacy and the Secretary-General's mediation assisted in resolving the crisis. Yielding to U Thant rather than to President Kennedy's ultimatum enabled Khrushchev to save face. But the US looked to the Organisation of American States to legitimise its naval 'quarantine' of Cuba, and Fidel Castro's blank refusal to allow the UN to dismantle the missile sites was a reminder of the need to take account of the pride and views of smaller states.

The USSR vetoed a resolution condemning its invasion of Czechoslovakia in August 1968, and had the newly installed, puppet Czechoslovak government remove the item from the UN's agenda. Since the Soviets had no intention of backing down, there was nothing practical the UN could do. But because of the UN, the Soviets were put in a very uncomfortable position. The Soviet ambassador was 'weary, uneasy and embarrassed',[24] and gave the impression 'that he was reading out texts which even he could not believe'.[25] Although the Soviet veto of a condemnatory resolution was a foregone conclusion, desperate filibustering revealed the want of a convincing justification. The fact that ten out of fifteen Council members voted for the resolution clearly recorded the weight of opinion – as did many speeches in the subsequent General Assembly.

Over Vietnam, the organisation was quite helpless. This was not just because Washington would only allow the UN to act as a sounding-board for its claims to be an aggrieved party and tireless seeker after peace. Hanoi also rejected the UN's competence in what it considered to be an internal conflict, and Hanoi's friends followed her lead. The Secretary-General tried to mediate but all efforts were rebuffed. Almost all states regarded the 1967–70 Nigerian civil war as a strictly internal matter – the line adopted by the Organisation of African Unity. Since no state ever took it to the UN, the world body had no role.

The India–Pakistan War of 1971

The birth of Bangladesh in the 1971 India–Pakistan war vividly indicated the UN's impotence when permanent members' interests were at stake. By June 1971, millions of refugees were flooding into India from East Pakistan and cholera had broken out in Calcutta. But the Soviet Union was protector of India, the Peoples' Republic of China was Pakistan's patron, and the USA was reluctant to take a strong stand that might damage *détente* with Moscow and *rapprochement* with Beijing. Because of this, they 'did not even discuss the problem privately'.[26] U Thant's 'pleas and warnings to the Security Council, both privately and publicly, fell on deaf ears'.[27] Only when war commenced, on 3 December, did the Security Council meet, but it was blocked by vetoes and passed the matter over to the General Assembly under the Uniting for Peace procedure. The Assembly called for a ceasefire and withdrawal of forces, two weeks before the Security Council did likewise (though without taking a vote). But by then Indian troops had achieved their objectives and Pakistani capitulation was almost complete.

Cyprus

However, while the UN could do nothing when the superpowers fell out, its peacekeeping activities continued making a valuable secondary contribution to peace –

with the support not just of the major powers but also of the third world states. The UN Force in Cyprus (UNFICYP) – which, unusually, contained troops from a permanent member, Britain – was despatched in 1964 to try to prevent fighting between Greek and Turkish Cypriots, to maintain order, and to assist in restoring normal conditions. During the next ten years UNFICYP did much humanitarian work but, in the face of considerable intercommunal tension, could do no more than interpose itself on the *de facto* front lines between the communities, patrol sensitive areas and generally try to keep things calm.

A bungled coup attempt in 1974 led to a Turkish invasion and, later, to the creation of the Turkish Republic of Northern Cyprus (the Republic being recognised only by Turkey). UNFICYP could do nothing about this for it was neither intended nor equipped to resist an army on the march. But it helped defuse the crisis, marginally stemmed the barbarity of the fighting, helped firm-up ceasefire lines and established Nicosia airport as a UN-protected area. Since then the force has acted as a buffer on the divided island.

Kashmir, 1965

Peacekeeping had also proved useful in 1965 when India and Pakistan came to blows. With the help of the Secretary-General they were able to end fighting over, and (in due course) agree on ownership of, a desolate, uninhabited salt marsh, the Rann of Kutch. But they ignored Security Council calls for a ceasefire in Kashmir, and in a rare show of unanimity that reflected the perceived seriousness of the threat, the Council despatched U Thant to the sub-continent. The intransigence of both sides forced Thant to proclaim his 'helplessness' to the Security Council, which symbolically underlined its support for him by going, as a body, to the airport to welcome him back. After several days' deadlock, both sides found acceptable a Security Council resolution demanding a ceasefire and withdrawal of troops to the positions held before fighting began. Thant set up a new, short-term observer group that assisted the existing peacekeeping mission on the India–Pakistan border in the vital task of calming things down and supervising the ceasefire. It was not the Security Council that was decisive in obtaining the ceasefire and withdrawal. It was the Soviet Prime Minister, Alexei Kosygin, who negotiated the Tashkent declaration, signed by the two parties in December 1965.

War in the Middle East, 1967 and 1973

In Egypt, the First UN Emergency Force (UNEF I) had an unanticipatedly long life. While the Soviets grumbled, the United States, other Western powers and a number of smaller states welcomed the idea that UNEF I should play a calming role in this dangerous region. For its part, Egypt found it advantageous to have an international buffer between her and her stronger neighbour. As long as Israel and Egypt were willing to live at peace, UNEF I helped them to maintain it. But Arab–Israeli tensions rose dangerously high in the spring of 1967 and, following an Egyptian request for UNEF I to get out of the way in a certain area, it was completely (and controversially) withdrawn by the UN Secretary-General. This was at a time of Security Council paralysis; the first 1967 Council meeting was held in late May but it adjourned after propaganda and mud-slinging. When war broke out on 5 June, neither Israel nor Egypt called a Security Council meeting. However, it quickly became clear that Israel would massively triumph over Egypt, Syria and Jordan. Leonid Brezhnev, the Soviet leader, wanted to save his allies from worse humiliation, and, as he told President Lyndon Johnson on the hot-line, Moscow desired no part in a Middle East war. So the Soviets backed down from insisting that Israel be condemned as an aggressor and the Security Council called for a ceasefire. After six days, Israel had achieved its objectives and the Security Council supported Thant's proposal to send observers to restore a UN presence. Officers from the peacekeeping force that had been based in Jerusalem since 1949 – the UN Truce Supervision Organisation (UNTSO) – were therefore despatched to the Golan Heights between Israel and Syria, and later to the Suez Canal between Israel and Egypt. But although in November 1967 the Security Council unanimously agreed a framework for the comprehensive settlement of the Middle East conflict (Resolution 242), no settlement could be reached. Arabs and Israelis continued living in a state of war, with frequent acts of violence on both sides. UNTSO suffered casualties and the Secretary-General seriously contemplated its withdrawal. Still, it was a useful buffer as long as the parties did not want fighting to escalate.

The second most dangerous post-1945 crisis occurred when war broke out in the same region, in 1973. After over a week of inertness, the immediate danger of confrontation jolted the superpowers into 'an impressive and rare display of statesmanship and great power unanimity'.[28] Through the Security Council they called for a ceasefire. Fighting broke out again and ominous Soviet troop movements prompted the USA to move its forces and put them on nuclear alert. The mere agreement to send a second UN Emergency Force (UNEF II) to Sinai defused the superpower crisis, but UNEF II's really vital role was in bolstering the fragile ceasefire and defusing tensions on the ground. It then monitored the withdrawal of troops and established a buffer zone in the Sinai. Since both Egypt and Israel wanted to maintain stability, they both cooperated with UNEF II, which helped ensure calm until the Camp David Agreement of 1978 and the Egyptian–Israeli Peace Treaty of the following year. Mindful of her Arab clientele's condemnation of these developments, the Soviet Union then announced it would veto an extension of UNEF II's mandate. The force was therefore quietly withdrawn. Inspectors from a US-manned Sinai Support Mission acted as observers until 1982 when a non-UN Multinational Force and Observers took over and Israel finally quit Egyptian territory.

Meanwhile, at the end of May 1974, gruelling shuttle-diplomacy by the US Secretary of State, Henry Kissinger, produced an Israeli–Syrian agreement to disengage their forces under the supervision of the UN Disengagement Observer Force (UNDOF), which would then patrol a buffer zone between them. The superpowers jointly sponsored UNDOF's creation as they wanted to limit the possibilities of confrontation via their Syrian and Israeli clients. In less than a month, UNDOF had defused a very hostile situation and, by its continuing presence, helped to prevent accidental conflict on a very dangerous border. (It should be noted that another peacekeeping force was despatched to Lebanon in 1978. It engaged in valuable humanitarian work but was helpless to prevent Israeli incursions and was stuck behind Israeli lines for three years after the Israeli invasion of Lebanon in 1982.)

THE ROLE OF THE SECRETARY-GENERAL: U THANT

The choice of U Thant of Burma to fill out the remainder of Hammarskjöld's term of office directly reflected the added prominence of new Afro-Asian states. Thant took over when the UN was going through dire days. It was in financial straits, peace-keeping activities were under challenge and Moscow was pushing for a three-man *troika*. Thant's courageous and skilful handling of the 1962 Cuban missile crisis defused the *troika* campaign. On his own initiative he provided Khrushchev and Castro with acceptable ways of backing down, and he engaged in toilsome post-crisis negotiations while the Council remained inactive. In November 1962 no-one challenged Thant's election to a full, five-year term of office and he was able to insist on, and obtain, the same authority as previous Secretaries-General. He reluctantly accepted a second term (to begin in 1967) when the P5 'promised him every consideration and virtually pleaded with him from a kneeling position'.[29]

Yet when Thant left office there was a widespread sigh of relief. One reason was the myth that, compared with Hammarskjöld, Thant was inactive, ineffective and lacked character and leadership qualities. The two men's personalities were unalike. They were from very different parts of the world and whereas Hammarskjöld operated in a bustle, Thant moved quietly. But perhaps Hammarskjöld had *too much* personality. He nearly wrecked the Secretary-Generalship; Thant strengthened the office and demonstrated its capacities.

Thant was not lacking in backbone. He made no secret of his views and would not be moved against his will. He spoke out against the Vietnam war, told the Soviet public on Moscow Radio that they were misinformed about the Congo, and not only denounced the Soviet invasion of Czechoslovakia but urged the despairing Czechoslovak ambassador to speak out in the Security Council. But Thant was attacked for timorousness when Western powers needed to blame someone for the outbreak of the Six-Day Middle East War in 1967.

Thant presided over the UN when it was in the political doldrums. The development of sophisticated methods of crisis management between the superpowers robbed him of the space to manoeuvre that had existed for his predecessor. It also made the world less anxious about small wars escalating into superpower confrontations. None the less, Thant probably acted more independently than any other Secretary-General.

He went beyond Hammarskjöld in authorising first the use of force and then decisive military action to end Katanga's secession from the Congo. Despite French and Soviet wariness and criticism, he extended the Secretary-General's responsibilities for the maintenance of peace. He took the initiative in the 1962 agreement transferring West New Guinea from the Netherlands to Indonesia and the associated despatch of a UN mission (the UN Temporary Executive Authority – UNTEA) to the territory, enabling them to avoid handing it over directly to Indonesia. Dutch recognition that time was not on her side, and US diplomatic pressure, were important in resolving this dangerous crisis, but Thant's role was also valuable.

In 1963 he helped work out a disengagement agreement in the Yemeni civil war and obtained the Security Council's blessing for UN observers being posted between Yemen and Saudi Arabia. In 1963 he also persuaded the relevant parties to allow a team of UN observers to determine whether the peoples of North Borneo and Sarawak wanted union with Malaysia rather than Indonesia or the Philippines.[30] The Security Council approved Thant's proposal to despatch the UN India–Pakistan Observation Mission (UNIPOM) in 1965, and in 1970 he mediated on the future of Bahrain, thereby enabling Iran to relinquish its claim and Britain to withdraw from the Gulf. Thant got away with things because he was more circumspect than Hammarskjöld and avoided unnecessary confrontation. When Thant failed, it was because of the parties' attitudes – for example, in 1971 when his warnings of fratricidal strife in East Pakistan were ignored.

Withdrawing UNEF I in 1967 earned Thant much criticism. However, failing to accede to President Nasser's demand would have violated the key peacekeeping principle of consent, and few states would have been willing to accept peacekeepers in future. The UN had no right to do what it liked with volunteers who had temporarily donned blue berets; and in any case two contributors had made it clear that, given Egypt's request, they would withdraw their troops. In the view of one of his close advisers, Thant has been 'grossly underestimated' and his scapegoating over the withdrawal of UNEF I was a 'monstrous case of historical injustice'.[31]

THE ROLE OF THE SECRETARY-GENERAL: KURT WALDHEIM

Thant was not, however, an administrator and the Security Council sought a successor who could put the Secretariat in order and tackle the UN's financial problems. After much difficulty, and at the eleventh hour, the Security Council chose Kurt Waldheim of Austria. Ironically, in view of the fact that he was later discredited because of wartime service in the Nazi armed forces, Waldheim's main recommendation was said to be his uncontroversial record.[32] A senior Secretariat official later described him as 'an energetic, ambitious mediocrity', who possessed 'determination and, on occasion, courage' but 'lacked the qualities of vision, integrity, inspiration, and leadership'.[33] None the less, he 'gave satisfaction'[34] and fared better than his predecessors.

This was, first, because Waldheim was spared the types of controversies that faced Lie and Hammarskjöld, and he encountered fewer potential banana skins. The continued improvement of the international climate, and the unwillingness of parties to use the UN in important conflicts, limited his scope. Meanwhile, the entry of the People's Republic of China into the UN in 1971 added a powerful supporter of Franco-Soviet determination to keep the Secretary-General on a short lead.

The second reason why Waldheim was less criticised was that states had come to realise that a diplomat's pragmatic, quiet, unshowy approach was best for the job. Waldheim was safe. He did not hector. He was nervous about offending members, and conflicted with governments only three times: by speaking out over US bombing of North Vietnamese dykes in 1972; by putting terrorism on the 1972 Assembly agenda (against the wishes of several important states); and in 1976 by publicly calling for a ceasefire in Lebanon and its maintenance as a unified state.

A third reason why Waldheim fared better was because his predecessors had firmly established the office of Secretary-General. They had won the right to address the Security Council, to take charge of peacekeeping operations (under the authority of the Council), to engage in fact-finding and good offices on their own initiative and to initiate peacemaking. Although the Council kept a tight rein on Waldheim, he adjusted UNTSO's observation arrangements following the 1973 Middle East War. When UNEF II took over most of UNTSO's tasks on the Egyptian–Israeli border he put peacekeeping on a sounder financial footing by proposing that UNEF II's costs be treated as part of the expenses of the UN.[35] When Turkey invaded Cyprus in 1974, he asked the President of the Security Council to call a meeting so that he could report on information received from his representative and the UN Force Commander. And with the division of Cyprus, Waldheim turned UNFICYP from a law-and-order force into a barrier force.

Britain sharply rebuked Waldheim in 1972 when he tried to involve his office in the Northern Ireland conflict, and he also failed to negotiate Vietnamese withdrawal from Kampuchea (Cambodia). But he organised a highly successful conference aimed at helping Kampuchean refugees. A 1979 meeting on Vietnamese refugees and displaced persons doubled the number of resettlement places, produced $190 million in new funds for resettlement centres, and persuaded the head of the Vietnamese delegation to stop forced departures (then running at 65,000 a month). By working quietly and discreetly, Waldheim claimed to have often 'save[d] a human life, even free[d] whole groups of people from persecution'.[36] The most dramatic instance was when he flew with eight French hostages to Paris in 1977 after arranging their release from the Western Sahara.

Only after Waldheim ceased being Secretary-General did it come to light that, instead of spending the greater part of the Second World War in Vienna writing a short, unimpressive thesis (as he had claimed), Waldheim had been in the Balkans as a junior staff officer with German army units that committed atrocities. He claimed he knew nothing of the atrocities, and there was no evidence to link him to them directly. Whatever the truth, Waldheim's twists and turns – initially suppressing the truth, then trying to deny it, and admitting at each stage only what could be proved against him – raised serious question marks about his fitness ever to have held high office.

CONCLUSION

International society was transformed by the emergence of the third world, but the underlying realities of the game between sovereign states remained unchanged. The main impact of the third world was in shifting the UN's priorities and significantly altering the international agenda by anathematising colonialism, racial discrimination and the North–South gap. The majoritarian impulse and outspokenness of the South made life increasingly uncomfortable for the West (in itself an indication of the significance of the UN). It also contributed to the P5's retreat to the Security Council and that organ's gradual rehabilitation. But the cold war continued to prevent the Council playing a leading role in many international disputes and the UN 'shared in the slump of idealism that Vietnam induced'.[37] By 1980 the slump was turning into crisis.

NOTES

1. Lawrence S. Finkelstein, 'The United Nations: Then and Now', *International Organization*, vol. 19, no. 3 (1965), pp. 368–9.
2. Whether and how democracy can apply to an inter-state body is a large and controversial question.
3. The voting was 89 to none, with nine abstentions. Abstainers included Britain, Belgium, France, Portugal and the USA.
4. In 1952 the word 'special' was dropped.
5. Under increasing internal and this external pressure, President de Klerk signalled capitulation in 1990 by repudiating apartheid and releasing Nelson Mandela from prison. The dismantling of apartheid led to sanctions being lifted and in April 1994 a multiracial government was elected under President Mandela.
6. SCR 216 (1965).
7. Andrew Boyd, *Fifteen Men on a Powder Keg: A History of the UN Security Council* (London: Methuen, 1971), p. 262.
8. Robert W. Gregg, 'The Politics of International Economic Cooperation and Development', in Lawrence S. Finkelstein, *Politics in the United Nations System* (Durham and London: Duke University Press, 1988), p. 109.
9. Ibid., p. 130.
10. U Thant, *View from the UN* (Newton Abbot: David & Charles, 1978) p. 441.
11. Ibid., p. 447.
12. Despite its growth (to 133 members in 2003), the G-77 retains its original name.
13. Fred Hirsch, 'Is there a New International Economic Order?' *International Organization*, vol. 31, no. 4 (1977), p. 524.
14. Gillian White, 'A New International Economic Order?', *Virginia Journal of International Law*, vol. 16, no 2 (1976), p. 336.
15. Gregg, 'The Politics of International Economic Cooperation and Development', p. 141.
16. Ibid., p. 139.
17. Suzanne Nossel, 'Retail Diplomacy: The Edifying Story of UN Dues Reform', *The National Interest*, Winter 2001–2, pp. 97–8.
18. The voting on Resolution 3379 was 72 to 35, with 32 abstentions. It was annulled in 1991 by Assembly Resolution 46/86.
19. Quoted in Boyd, *Fifteen Men on a Powder Keg*, p. 226.
20. Daniel Patrick Moynihan (with Suzanne Weaver), *A Dangerous Place* (London: Secker & Warburg, 1979), pp. 36, 11.
21. Henry Kissinger to the Director-General of the ILO, 6 November 1975.
22. Statement by President Carter, 1 November 1977.
23. Sir Colin Crowe, 'Some Observations on the Operation of the Security Council, including the Use of the Veto', quoted in Geoff Berridge, *Return to the UN: UN Diplomacy in Regional Conflicts* (London: Macmillan, 1990), p. 5.
24. Thant, *View from the UN*, p. 382.
25. Boyd, *Fifteen Men on a Powder Keg*, p. 306.
26. Thant, *View from the UN*, p. 424.

27. Ibid., p. 436.

28. Brian Urquhart, *A Life in Peace and War* (London: Weidenfeld & Nicolson, 1987) p. 238.

29. Boyd, *Fifteen Men on a Powder Keg*, p. 356.

30. This, however, prompted Indonesia's three-year confrontation with Malaysia and, indirectly, her brief departure from the UN.

31. Brian Urquhart interview, 1 June 1984, New York, UN Library, UNST DPI Oral History (02).

32. H. G. Nicholas, *The United Nations as a Political Institution*, 5th edn (London, Oxford, New York: Oxford University Press, 1992), p. 73.

33. Urquhart, *A Life in Peace and War*, p. 228.

34. Alan James, 'Kurt Waldheim: Diplomats' Diplomat', *The Year Book of World Affairs, 1983* (London: Stevens, 1983), p. 92.

35. By a special allocation for this and subsequent peacekeeping operations, costs were allocated on a different basis from that which is operative for the UN's general budget: the permanent members paid proportionately more, the least well-off proportionately less.

36. Kurt Waldheim, *The Challenge of Peace* (London: Weidenfeld & Nicolson, 1980), p. 1.

37. Nicholas, *The United Nations as a Political Institution*, p. 203.

5

A Period of Crisis: the UN in the 1980s

As the seventies turned into the eighties, the international climate changed unfavourably for the UN, making it unable to play a role in many conflicts because of the unwillingness of disputants. The revolutionary Iranian government that seized power in February 1979 ignored appeals from the Security Council and an ICJ ruling demanding the release of American diplomats who had been taken hostage in Iran. There was fighting between China and Vietnam (whose patron was the USSR). Israel and the Palestine Liberation Organisation were locked in conflict in Lebanon. Central America was suffering from social strife and insurgency. In December 1979 the cold war flared up, with the USSR's invasion of Afghanistan. When the Iran–Iraq war began in September 1980, the Security Council idly watched two 'troublesome' states slaughtering each other. During his first term of office as Secretary-General, Javier Pérez de Cuéllar could not identify a single conflict that had been resolved because of the UN's efforts.

These unpropitious conditions were reflected in the 'largely immobilized' Security Council.[1] UN diplomats regarded it as the least successful UN organ and, in his first annual report, de Cuéllar expressed concern about the world being 'perilously close to a new international anarchy ... embarked on an exceedingly dangerous course, one symptom of which is the crisis in the multilateral approach in international affairs and the concomitant erosion of the authority and status of world and regional intergovernmental institutions'.[2] However, it was the US–UN relationship that demanded de Cuéllar's greatest attention and was his biggest concern during his first term as Secretary-General.[3]

THE US–UN CONFLICT IN THE GENERAL ASSEMBLY

In the United States, the election of Ronald Reagan as President in November 1980 compounded 'a mood of widespread disenchantment' with the UN. The organisation was 'attacked on the grounds that it produces more rhetoric than action, that it is ineffective and often ignored, and that the one-nation, one vote system allows the Third World to dominate decision making – divorcing voting power from the ability to act'.[4]

The USA still found the UN useful, especially for letting the Secretary-General try to solve seemingly intractable problems like Afghanistan or Cyprus. And America's disastrous experience in 1982–4 with the Multinational Peacekeeping Force in Beirut was a sharp reminder of the value of leaving peacekeeping to the UN. (Both Jeane Kirkpatrick – Reagan's ambassador to the UN – and Reagan acknowledged the UN's past peacemaking and peacekeeping successes.) The Security Council was also the obvious – and safest – place to denounce the shooting down of a Korean Airlines jumbo jet that had strayed hundreds of miles off course over a strategic Soviet submarine base.

But America's patience with the snapping and snarling underdogs in the General Assembly had run out. In 1982 she was on the losing side in 24 out of 157 resolutions. In nineteen of them, the US was entirely alone or joined only by Israel. Further offence was given by the UN's refusal to endorse America's interventions in Central America. And so the Reagan administration tended to regard the UN as 'a troublesome sideshow', a place where Kirkpatrick and her associates were 'embattled defenders of the faith, venturing out from their fortress in the U.S. Mission mostly to do battle with the infidel, to chastise offenders, and to worry about the loyalty of putative allies'.[5] Meanwhile, the right-wing Heritage Foundation thought 'a world without the United Nations would be a better world'.[6] Former American envoys wished the UN would 'be towed off into the sunset' and maintained that the Security Council had 'become the captive of a Soviet/Third World working majority and of that bloc's political agenda: anti-Israel, anti-West, anti-US'.[7]

This picture of the US as the victim (in voting terms) of all but their close friends was not an entirely accurate representation of reality. The General Assembly did not operate on clear-cut bloc lines. Even America's European allies did not support her intervention in Grenada in 1983, for which she was condemned by the General Assembly. On the other hand, and notwithstanding the general cohesiveness of the Soviet bloc, Poland sided with the US more often than Mexico. Among African states, Zimbabwe (a large recipient of US aid) voted with the US less often than Libya. Moreover, the General Assembly condemned the Soviet presence in Afghanistan, called for the immediate withdrawal of Vietnamese troops from Kampuchea (Cambodia) in 1979, and rejected Cuban efforts to designate Puerto Rico as a US colonial territory. In the Security Council in 1978, six non-aligned states voted with the United States on Namibian independence, and the US continued to pursue the multilateral path in Southern Africa, regarding Security Council resolutions as 'the basis and pivot for a settlement' and as providing 'indispensable credibility'.[8]

However, what counted were the perceptions of the Reagan administration, and these led it to brush aside careful Secretariat analyses demonstrating that the majority of states voted with the USA on more than half of the resolutions passed by the General Assembly. They also encouraged the bypassing of the UN in the hope that the US would thereby be more likely to dominate negotiations, avoid embarrassing criticism and exclude the Soviet Union from international settlements.

Meanwhile, the supposed profligacy of the Secretariat and the UN system generally offered a means of wreaking vengeance on the UN. The UN's long-standing financial difficulties had become acute by the 1980s. This was partly because the UN's burgeoning budget had defied all attempts at reduction, partly because of the failure of many states to pay their dues on time, and partly because some (like the USA) were withholding part of their dues. Hustled by the Heritage Foundation, Congress passed the Kassebaum Amendment in 1985, requiring America's UN contribution to be reduced from 25 to 20 per cent of the budget unless the UN adopted weighted voting on budgetary matters. Because additional Congressional legislation cut federal spending, in 1986 the US paid only about 12 per cent of the budget. No-one else could – or would – meet the shortfall. (Most states paid between 0.01 and 0.02 per cent of the budget.) With the USA accounting for over 80 per cent of the UN's indebtedness, the UN was in trouble.

Instead of focusing on world problems, the Secretary-General had to waste precious time chasing money and keeping the organisation afloat. Conferences were cancelled, staff expenditure was slashed, and the 1986 General Assembly was reduced from 13 to 10 weeks. At the beginning of 1987 there was less than a week's cash in hand and the year's end saw the Secretary-General forecasting imminent insolvency. America's European allies made clear their disapproval of US financial delinquency, as did Japan, who wanted a permanent Council seat in a viable UN. Other defaulters shamed Washington by announcing they would remit what they owed: China intended to repay nearly $4.4 million, the Soviet Union offered $18 million, and France (who owed $4.35 million) said she would start paying her full assessed contribution.

These varying pressures gradually produced results. Kirkpatrick found debates and resolutions becoming more constructive. At the 1986 special Assembly session on Africa, self-criticism was more apparent than attacks on 'imperialism'. An '18-Member Group' of the Assembly bowed to America by, in effect, proposing cuts in the Secretariat, recommending weighted voting on the UN budget, and curbing General Assembly extravagance. The proposals were accepted in 1986 with quiet Soviet support. (The USSR shared America's desire to keep the reins firmly in great-power hands.) Applauding the decision, the American delegate promised to recommend to the President and Congress that the US meet her full assessed contribution and pay off outstanding debts, and the State Department duly invited Congress to modify the Kassebaum Amendment. However, as we shall see, the reduction in American indebtedness was partial and short-lived.

THE ROLE OF THE SECRETARY-GENERAL: JAVIER PÉREZ DE CUÉLLAR

In 1981, Kurt Waldheim was nearing the end of his second term of office as Secretary-General. He aspired to a third term, but was blackballed by China, and after six weeks' discussion and sixteen secret ballots, the Security Council despaired of agreeing on a Secretary-General, let alone a good one. Eventually, however, Javier Pérez de Cuéllar of Peru emerged as a compromise candidate who was acceptable to everyone. A former diplomat with considerable UN experience, de Cuéllar was cast in the Waldheim mould. But his qualities were superior to those of his predecessor. By steering a middle course between the models of Hammarskjöld and Thant, de Cuéllar won the high opinion of all, even those who did not think well of the UN. He was unafraid of sticking out his neck, but although critical of the big powers in general, he avoided giving serious offence to them individually. In 1986 there was no dispute over giving him a second term of office.

Like his predecessors, Pérez de Cuéllar inherited problems in the Secretariat, which was 'fat and flabby' with '[t]too many top-level officials, political appointments, rotten boroughs and pointless programs'.[9] In 1986 the General Assembly agreed that cuts were needed. Within twelve months, senior staff had been reduced by almost a third, and over the next few years there was a 13 per cent overall cut in the size of the Secretariat. But de Cuéllar was uninterested in administration and did not take advantage of these developments by reducing the budget and improving the Secretariat's administrative functioning. Morale suffered.

On the political front, Pérez de Cuéllar inherited an office that had considerable influence, which he protected by maintaining his impartiality. Up to a point his position was also enhanced by the revival of the cold war, and by the power struggle between the USA and the General Assembly. No eyebrows were raised when he took independent initiatives over the brewing dispute between Venezuela and Guyana; in promoting a regional peace process in Central America; in the 1982 Falklands War; and in sending fact-finding missions and establishing political offices in Kabul, Islamabad, Teheran and Baghdad. He also successfully expanded his mediatory role to include disputes between members within the UN itself when he warded off a potentially damaging Arab proposal to challenge the credentials of the Israeli delegation. And his appointment as formal arbitrator in the *Rainbow Warrior* affair testified to his and the UN's high standing.

Pérez de Cuéllar was criticised for failing to stir the Security Council into action in advance of the expected Israeli invasion of Lebanon in 1982. The only time he directly invoked Article 99 (over Lebanon in 1989) it had an unsatisfactory outcome. However, indirect use of this article is usually more effective. For example, the Secretary-General can produce a confidential memorandum; drop hints in the right quarters; ask the Council President to call a meeting so that he can make a report; or, during a meeting, draw the Council's attention to new information and remind it of his responsibilities and the gravity of the situation. This reflects the fact that the Secretary-General has influence rather than power, and that many of his most useful actions take place behind the scenes. It was therefore misplaced to complain that de Cuéllar's 'face, voice and style seemed incapable of expressing anything beyond clause 36 of subsection D of UN Resolution 1001'.[10] One who was in a good position to judge described him as 'a man of rare talents' who achieved much 'because he went about his business by stealth'.[11]

NON-POLITICAL ORGANS

US dissatisfaction with what she regarded as mismanagement, inefficiency, extravagance and, above all, the spread of politics like an 'infection'[12] from the General Assembly to the specialised agencies, led her to throw the UN Educational, Scientific and Cultural Organisation (UNESCO) into crisis. America's commitment to internationalism had always tended to be defined in terms of the American way of life, and it seemed UNESCO was opposing 'the very principles'[13] upon which the US had built the specialised agencies. Since UNESCO was considered marginal to US interests, it bore the brunt of Washington's wrath and was used to fire a warning shot to the UN system as a whole.

The UNESCO Crisis

UNESCO 'is the intellectual arm of the United Nations system', seeking to 'build peace in the minds of men and to do this through education, science, culture and communication'.[14] Most of its activities are uncontroversial. These include preserving endangered cultural monuments (most famously, the Nubian temples threatened by Egypt's Aswan Dam), scientific collaboration (for example, research into the environment and preventing desertification), and teacher training and literacy programmes (for example, providing education for refugees). However, by virtue of UNESCO's mandate,[15] its other activities make it the 'most political' agency. 'It's unpleasant. It's inevitable, and you have to keep it below the toxic level,' said a former senior official.[16]

Politicisation crept in during the 1970s, when Britain and America tended to neglect UNESCO while third world states used it to pursue 'explicitly political' matters 'in the guise of debates on UNESCO-type issues'.[17] Serious trouble began with anti-Israeli moves in 1974. It continued in 1975 when Western delegates walked out after the Arabs asked UNESCO to endorse a General Assembly resolution defining Zionism as a form of racism. It came to a head over the proposed New World Information and Communications Order (NWICO), which was ostensibly aimed at countering Western, 'imperialist' control of news reporting.

There were three dimensions to the NWICO campaign. First, NWICO reflected the developing states' resentment that Western news agencies, which provide most international reporting, produced a one-way flow of communication that gave 'a false and distorted' image of developing states.[18] The West responded to this by helping third world countries to improve their communications and information systems. Secondly, NWICO had a significant cold war dimension. The USSR was its prime mover and much of the debate about 'decolonising' information was clothed in Marxist rhetoric. Thirdly, NWICO would have stringently limited the free flow of information by government 'licensing' of journalists, and making governments answerable to one another for unfriendly press reports. This would, of course, have been to the benefit of the Soviet Union and other undemocratic regimes. A raw American nerve was touched. What UNESCO described as 'an essential objective for the world community, on a level with the new international economic order',[19] the US saw as a call to 'war', in which it was 'not the future of press freedom which is at stake, but the future of UNESCO'.[20]

Dissatisfaction with NWICO moved on to resentment that the eight states who paid 60 per cent of UNESCO's budget were 'insulted and ... vilified with anti-colonialist propaganda'.[21] Not only that, but UNESCO (and some other specialised agencies) had 'lost touch with economic reality' and indulged in 'too much travel, too many conferences, too much misuse of resources and too little cutting off of dead wood'.[22] Believing that bilateral programmes might give better value for money, in July 1983 the Reagan administration ordered a thorough review of US participation in UNESCO. This had an immediate salutary effect. That year's annual conference avoided ideological confrontation. Several contentious resolutions were neutralised. Britain obtained consensus support for a flexible description of NWICO as an 'evolving and continuous process'. And the budget was trimmed (though not enough for the USA and ten other states, who abstained when it was voted on).

Meanwhile, however, anti-UNESCO propaganda had gained the upper hand in the USA. Congress prohibited the support of any organisation that threatened freedom of the press. The powerful, right-wing Heritage Foundation insisted that UNESCO's activities were inimical to American interests and values. And even the normally supportive *New York Times* said UNESCO had become 'a babel of words notable for their muddiness and dishonesty' and that its every meeting had become 'an anti-Western rally'.[23] It was not surprising that, in December 1983, the USA gave notice of withdrawal from UNESCO because of its 'politicisation' of virtually every subject, its 'hostility' towards free institutions, its 'unrestrained budgetary expansion' and its wasteful management methods.[24]

Britain, too, believed UNESCO was a 'corrupt and useless body',[25] and this was emphasised in influential press reports of its 'always misguided and corrupt goings-on'.[26] In April 1982 the UK demanded several specific reforms, including: a budgetary standstill, greater priority being given to practical activities in the field (especially education, science and culture); better control by the governing bodies; improved management and personnel arrangements; and proper attention to evaluation.

Vilification of UNESCO came to focus on the Senegalese Director General, Amadou M'Bow, not least because he responded to Anglo-American criticism by waging a 'private war' against them. It was observed that his long absences from Paris, combined with a reluctance to delegate, made for erratic management; and that 'autocratic, vindictive and conflict-seeking'[27] bureaucratic procedures tended to 'stifle initiative, delay decisions and risked setting up paperwork barriers with the real world'.[28] In short, M'Bow had 'created an immense mess'.[29] (This was not altogether fair, as UNESCO had problems before he took office and his dictatorial predecessor had done 'little to suppress the clouds of jobbery and political nonsense which flowed steadily through the portals of the Paris headquarters'.)[30]

UNESCO's Executive Board and M'Bow set up a committee and working groups to consider reform. But Washington demanded fundamental constitutional change (to give 'minority' – or Western – opinion an effective veto power) in an impossibly short space of time. America left in December 1984. A year later, despite considerable success in securing changes, and arguments that she benefited from membership, the UK also withdrew. (In December 1985, Singapore was another to leave, because of unhappiness over her assessed contribution.)

With the departure of Britain and America, UNESCO's budget was cut by almost a third. After a struggle and, crucially, the loss of Soviet support, M'Bow was dethroned in 1987. His successor, Professor Federico Mayor, from Spain, at once set about making reforms. NWICO was dropped and by 1991 a quarter of the budget was being devoted to eradicating illiteracy. Dr Mayor admitted having 'failed in one-fourteenth of the objectives' he had set himself,[31] But although he turned UNESCO into a well-run agency with the lowest staff costs in the UN system, Britain and the USA were not enthusiastic about re-joining.

The Food and Agriculture Organisation

Another agency that had fallen on hard times was the Food and Agriculture Organisation (FAO) under Edouard Saouma of Lebanon. It 'functioned relatively efficiently, in its own terms: but the terms were the wrong ones'.[32] Self-sufficiency in food production was pushed without adequate consideration of whether it was the best all-round policy and of the ecological costs. Speaking anonymously, a senior official spoke of ruinous policies, saying

> [M]y children will look back and say that we, the new colonials, ruined Africa with food aid, ensuring that in the next century it will be a totally dependent basket case. Why do we push it? It buys governments' votes. We are in the power business, not the business of food.[33]

Other demoralised civil servants also spoke frankly to the press, so that the FAO's public relations staff spent much of Saouma's 18-year reign complaining about hostile articles. Centralised concentration of power and petty controls were the order of the day. 'The author of a path-breaking FAO survey on the carrying capacity of land, published in 1985, said that it took him twenty years – "sixteen to get permission to start, four to carry it out"'.[34] Yet Saouma was easily re-elected for a third term, defeating a Western-supported African candidate.

The International Labour Organisation

The experience of the International Labour Organisation (ILO) in the 1980s contrasts sharply with that of UNESCO. At the same time as narrowly approving an anti-Israeli resolution at the beginning of the decade, the ILO conference failed to adopt a report citing East European violations of relevant international law. Then the wheel turned full circle. Poland withdrew in 1984, complaining that critical reports constituted interference in her internal affairs. Other Soviet bloc countries supported Poland, alleging that 'the ILO is being turned into an arena for political manoeuvres to serve the interests of certain circles'.[35] And in 1985 the Soviets considered withholding contributions to 'inappropriate' ILO projects, and protested about a pro-Western bias. However, Soviet foreign policy was about to be transformed by Mikhail Gorbachev, and the dispute vanished.

CONCLUSION

The outlook for the international community and the United Nations often seemed bleak in the 1980s. The inclement international climate did not encourage states to turn to the UN to resolve their differences instead of using it as another forum in which to act them out. In addition, after years of being on the receiving end of abuse, the major contributor to the UN – the United States – decided that enough was enough. It was time for the piper to call the tune; time to bring to heel the baying third world (and its perceived Soviet pack leader). But this was achieved at a cost of tipping the UN into crisis and it did not allay the hostility towards the UN that had grown up in important quarters in the USA.

Yet the decade was to end with dramatic, profound and stunningly swift changes. The cold war ended and there emerged a period of increased commonality of interests between states. This contributed to the development of collegiality in the Security Council and a very active UN role in the maintenance of international peace and security. But while this accorded with the role envisaged for the UN when the Charter was drawn up, it was not matched by adequate resources being made available to the Organisation to meet the different kind of turmoil that was unleashed. It is to these challenges that we will now turn.

NOTES

1. Javier Pérez de Cuéllar, *Pilgrimage for Peace: A Secretary-General's Memoir* (New York: St Martin's Press, 1997) p. 7.
2. Report of the Secretary-General on the Work of the Organization, September 1982, UN document A/37/1.
3. de Cuéllar, *Pilgrimage for Peace*, p. 9.
4. Kurt Waldheim, 'The United Nations: the Tarnished Image', *Foreign Affairs*, vol. 63 (Fall 1984), p. 93.
5. Brian Urquhart, *A Life in Peace and War* (London: Weidenfeld & Nicolson, 1987). p. 327.
6. Quoted in Robert C. Johansen, 'The Reagan Administration and the UN: the Costs of Unilateralism', *World Policy Journal*, vol. 3 (1986), p. 603.
7. *Independent*, 28 August 1993; Johansen, 'The Reagan Administration and the UN', p. 603.
8. Chester Crocker, quoted in Sally Morphet, 'State Groups at the UN', in Paul Taylor and A. J. R. Groom, *The United Nations at the Millennium: The Principal Organs* (London, New York: Continuum, 2000), p. 252.
9. Urquhart, *A Life in Peace and War*, pp. 230, 352.
10. Richard Dowden, 'Too Blunt for his Own Good', *Independent*, 31 October 1994.
11. Sir Crispin Tickell, in House of Commons, Foreign Affairs Committee, Third Report: *The Expanding Role of the United Nations and its Implications for United Kingdom Policy*, vol. 2: *Minutes of Evidence and Appendices* (HCP 235-II) (London, 1993), pp. 360, 168.
12. Elliot Abrams (Assistant Secretary of State for International Organisation Affairs), Address to a meeting of the United States Association of the USA (UNA–USA), 5 June 1981.
13. Ibid.
14. Professor Federico Mayor (Director General of UNESCO), in House of Commons, Foreign Affairs Committee, Fifth Report, *Membership of UNESCO* (London, 1993), p. 18. (Subsequently referred to as *Membership of UNESCO*.)
15. According to its Constitution, 'real' peace rests 'upon the intellectual and moral solidarity of mankind'. '[T]he wide diffusion of culture, and the education of humanity for justice and liberty and peace' are 'indispensable to the dignity of man and constitute a sacred duty'.
16. Richard Hoggart, *The Times*, 4 November 1977.
17. Richard Hoggart, *An Idea and its Servants: UNESCO from Within* (London: Chatto & Windus, 1978), p. 81.
18. Quoted in Richard Hoggart, 'The Mass Media: a New Colonialism?', the Eighth Standard Telephones and Cables Communication Lecture (1978), p. 1.
19. UNESCO, *UNESCO: What It Is, What It Does, How It Works* (Paris: UNESCO, 1980).
20. Abrams, Address to UNA–USA, 5 June 1981.
21. *The Times*, 22 August 1983. The eight were the USA, Japan, West Germany, the Soviet Union, France, Britain, Denmark and New Zealand; 68 states paid 0.01 per cent of the budget.
22. Abrams, Address to UNA–USA, 5 June 1981. UNESCO's budget was $48 million in 1964–5; ten years later it was $156 million; and ten years later again, $382 million.

23. Quoted in *The Times*, 30 December 1983.
24. 'World Information and Communication', FCO background brief; *The Times*, 30 December 1983.
25. Max Beloff to the author, November 1994.
26. Max Beloff, 'Utopia Undone', *The Times Literary Supplement*, 26 January 1996.
27. *The Times Higher Education Supplement*, 7 November 1986.
28. *The Times*, 6 August 1981.
29. *The Times Higher Education Supplement*, 7 November 1986.
30. Letter from Professor Julius Gould, *The Times*, 10 November 1984. Cf. Nicholas A. Sims, 'Servants of an Idea: Hoggart's UNESCO and the Problem of International Loyalty', *Millennium: The Journal of International Studies*, vol. 11, no. 1 (1982), p. 66.
31. This was the continued concentration of UNESCO's expenditure and personnel at its Paris headquarters. Federico Mayor, in *Membership of UNESCO*, pp. viii, 31.
32. Rosemary Righter, *Utopia Lost: The United Nations and World Order* (New York: Twentieth Century Fund, 1995), p. 176.
33. Quoted in ibid., p. 180.
34. Ibid., p. 180.
35. UN, Press Release, ILO/2194, 7 December 1984. Quoted in Mark F. Imber, *The USA, ILO, UNESCO and IAEA: Politicization and Withdrawal in the Specialized Agencies* (Basingstoke: Macmillan, 1989), pp. 68–9.

The New World Disorder: the UN and the Maintenance of International Peace

The 1990s was a decade of transformation in international relations. The cold war ended. There was a big rise in UN members. Apartheid vanished from South Africa. Iraq was expelled from Kuwait amidst much talk of a 'new world order'. The number of democracies nearly doubled and there were three times as many peace agreements signed as in the previous three decades. But there was also considerable turbulence: volatility and strife in the former Soviet bloc; ethnic and religious turdmoil; humanitarian disasters and emergencies in developing states where civil disorder was out of control and security severely lacking; and more wars and open conflicts than at any time in the preceding half-century. The rigid certainties of the cold war had been lost.

It is noteworthy that states turned to the UN to try to tackle these problems. In consequence, the UN experienced great triumphs (as in the 1991 expulsion of Iraq from Kuwait) and also dreadful failures (as in its failure to prevent genocide in Rwanda and Bosnia). But if unrealistically high expectations of the UN were dashed, much was achieved. The suffering of many victims of conflict was relieved, and the concepts of peace and security and of peacekeeping were fruitfully extended in an endeavour to go further towards dealing with the underlying causes of war and creating conditions in which formerly conflicting groups could learn to live at peace.

COLLECTIVE SECURITY REVISITED: IRAQ'S INVASION OF KUWAIT

The collective security scheme of the UN Charter is inherently ill-suited for a world of sovereign states who naturally insist on retaining control of their own armed forces. It is also almost impossible for it to work where the major powers are deeply distrustful of each other. Thus until the 1990s the UN only once even approached putting collective security into practice – in the unusual situation of the Korean War. But with the ending of the cold war this obstacle to the implementation of the Charter's scheme was removed. And almost immediately a case arose which led to what many regard as being as good an instance of traditional collective security as the world is likely to see.

Having huge debts from his war with Iran, an eye to the main chance, and troubled relations with wealthy Kuwait, Iraq's ruthless ruler Saddam Hussein invaded and proclaimed the annexation of the latter in August 1990. The Security Council speedily condemned his action and passed a Chapter VII resolution (Security Council Resolution [SCR] 661) imposing mandatory economic sanctions. But although sanctions were almost universally applied, they dented neither Saddam's will nor his powerful military machine. Accordingly, the Security Council demanded (in SCR 678) that Iraq either withdraw by 15 January 1991 or face the might of a United States-led coalition. As compliance was not forthcoming the coalition attacked on 17 January (the operation being called Desert Storm), and Iraq capitulated on 3 March. On 3 April the Security Council determined the terms of a peace settlement. Other resolutions condemned the repression of the Iraqi population, and established an observer mission to monitor the Iraq–Kuwait border.

Although the liberation of Kuwait encouraged much optimism about the UN's role as world policeman, critics of Desert Storm contended that the UN merely legitimised US action. The argument ran as follows. The US (and hence the UN) acted because of America's strategic and oil interests in the Middle East and because America twisted arms to get what she wanted. Thus the Council delegated the leadership of the anti-Iraq coalition to the United States (authorising it in SCR 678 to use 'all necessary means'). An American general was in day-to-day charge. The Council received written and oral reports, but it did not formally discuss them. The ending of the campaign (in which national flags, not the UN's, were flown) was in American hands.

The Gulf War was clearly in the national interest of the USA, and from a foreign policy perspective, it was a typical national interest/balance of power operation. But the fact that it suited America does not preclude it from *also* serving the interests of other states and the international community. In several respects, indeed, the episode met the criteria for collective security as set out in the Charter.

First, there was clear-cut aggression, Iraq having attempted the annexation of another state. Secondly, Iraq was almost unanimously condemned. Thirdly, there was powerful resolve in all important quarters to right this wrong. In consequence, the Security Council was deeply involved, passing twelve resolutions before Desert Storm was launched. The operation was supported militarily by twenty-nine allies, financially by Japan and Germany, and morally by the vast majority of states. Even Libya, Yemen and Jordan participated in economic sanctions. SCR 678 could hardly have been more authoritative since almost all Council members were represented by foreign ministers at the meeting that passed it. Fourthly, even if a permanent UN force had existed, it would not have been capable of dealing with a threat from the then fourth largest armed force in the world. The 'hired gun approach' was 'unavoidable'.[1] And, fifthly, at the end of the war, the five permanent members of the Security Council (P5) all contributed troops to the peacekeeping force sent to monitor the Iraq–Kuwait border (the first time this had happened in a UN peacekeeping mission).

Not much more can be expected from collective security than was achieved by the UN in 1991. That the UN responded as it did was due to the uniqueness of the events that precipitated action and the chance combination of a number of factors: the importance of oil, Kuwait's strategic position, Iraq's unpopularity, the end of the cold war, the change in Soviet foreign policy, and the USA's ability to act.

Perhaps Washington would have acted similarly without UN support, but the lengths to which the USA went to get UN votes underlines the importance of the UN's legitimising role. The UN endorsed the propriety of what the coalition did; it helped keep states in political line; and it was a means of generating diplomatic and general public support for the war on Iraq. Conversely, not going through the UN would have had very high foreign policy costs: considerable Arab discontent; possibly continuing close Iraqi–Soviet relations; and Chinese unhappiness. Working through the UN also emphasised the Organisation's importance, helped to constrain US proponents of tougher action, and expanded the UN's credibility.

THE REVIVAL OF PEACEKEEPING

Expansion

Peacekeeping was relatively uncommon before the end of the cold war, only thirteen missions being established between 1945 and 1987. However, the activity began to come into its own in the late 1980s (see Table 6.1). Missions proliferated and a

Table 6.1   The expansion of peacekeeping

	Peacekeeping missions in being at year's end	Total number of peacekeepers (based on highest month each year)	Annual cost (in millions of US $)
1985	5	12,500	141
1986	5	12,500	242
1987	5	12,500	240
1988	7	13,000	266
1989	10	17,900	635
1990	8	13,700	464
1991	11	15,300	490
1992	13	52,200	1767
1993	16	78,500	3059
1994	17	76,500	3342
1995	16	68,900	3364
1996	17	29,100	1522
1997	15	25,000	1226
1998	16	14,600	907
1999	19	18,400	1100
2000	16	38,500	1500
2001	16	47,800	2800
2002	15	46,799	2740
2003	13	45,732	2810

Source: United Nations documents and two tables on the Global Policy Forum website (www.globalpolicy.org) by Michael Renner, 'Peacekeeping Expenditures: 1947–2001' and Michael Renner and Christian Kaufholz, 'Size of UN Peacekeeping Forces: 1947–2001'.

confusing plethora of acronyms were coined for the 42 UN operations established between 1988 and the beginning of 2003. At the beginning of 2003, there were 15 ongoing peacekeeping operations, plus an additional 13 political and peacebuilding missions. The operations ranged in strength from a handful of international and local staff, to thousands of military, police and civilian peacekeepers (see Tables 6.2 and 6.3).

Immediately at the end of the cold war, peacekeeping proved useful in winding down two high-profile international conflicts: overseeing Namibia's transition to independence in 1989–1990 and confirming the withdrawal of Cuban (and South African) troops from Angola in 1989–91. Another mission enabled the Soviet Union to extricate itself from Afghanistan (1988–89), although it was less successful in its other task of trying to end Afghanistan's civil war (in which the USSR and Pakistan continued to intervene). A fourth mission supported the ceasefire and supervised the withdrawal of forces in 1988 when the long-running Iran–Iraq war came to an end.

In these ways, a hitherto poorly understood, obscure and relatively uncommon device attracted much attention, especially after UN peacekeeping forces won the 1988 Nobel Peace Prize. The ensuing exponential rise in the number of peacekeeping missions had four notable consequences. First, there was a huge rise in the number of peacekeepers, reaching a peak of 75,000 in 1993. Secondly, there was a correspondingly large increase in the peacekeeping bill. In 1987 only $183 million was spent on peacekeeping; by the mid-1990s the cost had risen to $3 billion. Peacekeeping expenditure then dropped, but it was back to $3 billion by the start of the twenty-first century. The third consequence was a large increase in the number of states that provided peacekeepers. In 1995, a total of 77 states had contributed peacekeeping personnel; in 2000 the number was 123. In 2002, 90 states contributed uniformed personnel – including states in receipt of peacekeeping assistance. Moreover, after 1990 it was no longer the case that generally the P5 did not contribute peacekeepers. The fourth consequence of the tumult of demands was that the UN began cooperating with regional organisations in peacekeeping and peacebuilding. This started in 1993 when the observer mission in Liberia became 'the first peacekeeping mission undertaken by the United Nations in cooperation with a peacekeeping mission already set up by another organization',[2] the Economic Community of West African States (ECOWAS). In the former Yugoslavia, the UN collaborated with three organisations: the Organisation for Security and Cooperation in Europe (OSCE), the European Union (EU) and the North Atlantic Treaty Organisation (NATO). Other peacekeeping missions conducted outside the UN are listed in Table 6.4.

Meanwhile, it was becoming clear that something in the nature of a metamorphosis in peacekeeping was under way. In contrast to the cold war era, the vast majority of operations now took place within (as distinct from between) states, and peacekeepers were sometimes being given a much larger range of tasks, leading to greater variety in their personnel. By no means all operations reflected this second development, and a few continued to be established in an inter-state context. But both the overall nature and the public image of peacekeeping were undergoing a significant change. As Kofi Annan (the Secretary-General and former head of UN peacekeeping) put it, peacekeeping missions now provide 'assistance to local authorities in a wide range of areas ... humanitarian relief and mine action [*sic*];

Table 6.2 Past UN peacekeeping and peacebuilding operations

Name and location	Duration	Function
DOMREP Mission of the Representative of the Secretary-General in the Dominican Republic	May 1965–October 1966	Monitor ceasefire
MINUGUA United Nations Verification Mission in Guatemala	January–May 1997	Verify ceasefire and demobilisation of combatants
MINURCA United Nations Mission in the Central African Republic	April 1998–February 2000	Help restore climate of stability and security as well as dialogue among political actors; supporting role in presidential elections
MIPONUH United Nations Civilian Police Mission in Haiti (succeeded by MICAH)	December 1997–March 2000	Assist in professionalising police force
MONUA United Nations Observer Mission in Angola (succeeded UNAVEM III)	June 1997–February 1999	Assist in consolidating peace and national reconciliation, enhancing confidence-building, and creating stable and democratic environment
ONUC United Nations Operation in the Congo	June 1960–June 1964	Monitor Belgian withdrawal, end Katangese secession, restore law and order, provide technical assistance
ONUCA United Nations Observer Group in Central America (Costa Rica, El Salvador, Guatemala, Honduras and Nicaragua)	November 1989–January 1992	Verify compliance with disarmament agreement and neutralise irregular forces in the region
ONUMOZ United Nations Operation in Mozambique	December 1992–December 1994	Facilitate and monitor implementation of peace accord, monitor withdrawal of foreign forces and provide security, establish non-partisan army, supervise elections, humanitarian relief and technical assistance

Name and location	Duration	Function
ONUSAL United Nations Observer Mission in El Salvador	July 1991–April 1995	Monitor ceasefire and human rights agreements
UNAMET United Nations Mission in East Timor (succeeded by UNTAET)	June 1999–November 1999	Organise and conduct 'popular consultation' to determine whether East Timor would become independent of Indonesia
UNAMIC United Nations Advance Mission in Cambodia (succeeded by UNTAC)	October 1991–March 1992	Assist in observation of ceasefire agreement
UNAMIR United Nations Assistance Mission for Rwanda	October 1993–March 1996	Protect humanitarian assistance efforts, encourage stability
UNASOG United Nations Aouzou Strip Observer Group (Chad–Libya)	May–June 1994	Verify withdrawal of Libyan forces
UNAVEM I United Nations Angola Verification Mission I (succeeded by UNAVEM II)	January 1999–June 1991	Verify withdrawal of Cuban troops
UNAVEM II United Nations Angola Verification Mission II (succeeded by UNAVEM III)	June 1991–February 1995	Monitor ceasefire agreement, and observe and verify elections
UNAVEM III United Nations Angola Verification Mission III (succeeded by MONUA)	February 1995–June 1997	Help restore peace and achieve national reconciliation
UNCRO United Nations Confidence Restoration Organization in Croatia	March 1995–January 1996	Implement and monitor ceasefire agreements
UNEF I First United Nations Emergency Force (Suez Canal sector, Sinai and Gaza)	November 1956–June 1967	Supervise cessation of hostilities and act as buffer between Israeli and Egyptian forces

Table 6.2 (*continued*)

Name and location	Duration	Function
UNEF II Second United Nations Emergency Force (Suez Canal sector and Sinai)	October 1973–July 1979	Supervise ceasefire and Arab–Israeli truce
UNFICYP United Nations Peacekeeping Force in Cyprus	March 1964–	Supervise truce in Cyprus and avert outside intervention
UNGOMAP United Nations Good Offices Mission in Afghanistan and Pakistan	April 1988–March 1990	Assist in observation of non-intervention agreement, and supervise Soviet withdrawal
UNIIMOG United Nations Iran–Iraq Military Observer Group	August 1988–February 1991	Supervise ceasefire and withdrawal of forces
UNIPOM United Nations India–Pakistan Observation Mission	September 1965–March 1966	Monitor India–Pakistan truce (except in Kashmir where UNMOGIP is based)
UNMIBH United Nations Mission in Bosnia and Herzegovina	December 1995–December 2002	Law enforcement and police reform via UN International Police Task Force (IPTF), and coordinating other UN activities relating to humanitarian relief and refugees, de-landmining, human rights, elections and postwar reconstruction
UNMIH United Nations Mission in Haiti (succeeded by UNSMIH)	September 1993–June 1996	Help modernise the armed forces; establish a new police force; establish secure, stable and democratic conditions; protect international and key installations
UNMOP United Nations Mission of Observers in Prevlaka (Croatia)	January 1996–December 2002	Monitor demilitarisation of strategic Prevlaka peninsula
UNMOT United Nations Mission of Observers in Tajikistan	December 1994–May 2000	Monitor ceasefire

Name and location	Duration	Function
UNOGIL United Nations Observation Group in Lebanon	June–December 1958	Monitor Lebanon–Syria border (Syria and Egypt were joined together as the United Arab Republic February 1958–September 1961)
UNOMIL United Nations Observer Mission in Liberia	September 1993–September 1997	Implement ceasefire agreements
UNOMSIL United Nations Observer Mission in Sierra Leone (succeeded by UNAMSIL)	July 1998–October 1999	Monitor military and security situation; disarm and demobilise former combatants; monitor respect for international humanitarian law
UNOMUR United Nations Observer Mission Uganda–Rwanda	June 1993–September 1994	Monitor the border. Unable fully to implement mandate because of Rwandan genocide
UNOSOM I United Nations Operation in Somalia (succeeded by US-led UNITAF)	April 1992–March 1993	Monitor ceasefire; protect shipment of humanitarian relief
UNOSOM II United Nations Operation in Somalia II	March 1993–March 1995	Protect relief work and discourage violence
UNPREDEP United Nations Preventive Deployment Force (former Yugoslav Republic of Macedonia)	March 1995–February 1999	Monitor borders with Albania and Federal Republic of Yugoslavia; ad hoc community services and humanitarian assistance in cooperation with civilian agencies
UNPROFOR United Nations Protection Force (Croatia, Bosnia–Herzegovina, borders of former Yugoslav Republic of Macedonia and Federal Republic of Yugoslavia) (succeeded by UNPREDEP, NATO-led IFOR and UNCRO)	March 1992–December 1995	Initially demilitarisation of designated areas in Croatia; mandate later extended to Bosnia–Herzegovina to support delivery of humanitarian relief and monitor 'no-fly zones' and 'safe havens'; mandate later extended to Macedonia's borders with the Federal Republic of Yugoslavia and Albania

Table 6.2   (*continued*)

Name and location	Duration	Function
UNPSG United Nations Civilian Police Support Group (Eastern Slavonia, Baranja and Western Sirmium [Danube region of Croatia])	January 1998–October 1998	Took over policing tasks from UNTAES in monitoring the performance of the Croatian police
UNSF* United Nations Security Force in West New Guinea (West Irian)	October 1962–April 1963	Observe implementation of ceasefire and act as 'police arm' of UNTEA and uphold its authority
UNSMIH United Nations Support Mission in Haiti (succeeded by UNTMIH)	July 1996–July 1997	Assist in professionalising police and maintaining secure and stable environment
UNTAC United Nations Transitional Authority in Cambodia	March 1992–September 1993	Demobilise armed forces of Cambodian factions; supervise interim government; maintain law and order; repatriation and resettlement of refugees and displaced persons; rehabilitate Cambodian infrastructure; organise democratic elections
UNTAES United Nations Transitional Administration in Eastern Slovenia, Baranja and Western Sirmium (Danube region of Croatia)	January 1996–January 1998	Replaced portion of UNCRO left in Eastern Slovenia; supervise and assist demilitarisation and territory's peaceful reintegration into Croatia
UNTAET United Nations Transitional Administration in East Timor (succeeded by UNMISET)	October 1999–May 2002	Provide humanitarian relief and run East Timor, preparing it for independence (preceded by UN Mission in East Timor [UNAMET] [June–November 1999]), which organised and conducted 'popular consultation' to determine whether East Timor would become independent of Indonesia

Name and location	Duration	Function
UNTAG United Nations Transition Assistance Group (Namibia)	April 1989–March 1990	Organise and supervise democratic elections leading to independence
UNTEA† United Nations Temporary Executive Authority (West New Guinea/West Irian)	October 1962– April 1963	Administer territory and maintain law and order during transfer of authority from Netherlands to Indonesia
UNTMIH United Nations Transition Mission in Haiti (succeeded by MIPONUH)	August–November 1997	Contribute to professionalising police force
UNYOM United Nations Yemen Observation Mission	July 1963– September 1964	Monitor Yemen–Saudi Arabia– Egypt truce

Source: This table is heavily indebted to the UN Department of Peacekeeping web pages (www.un.org/Depts/dpko/dpko/home.shtml); the appendix to Robert C. Johansen, 'Enhancing United Nations Peacekeeping', in Chadwick F. Alger (ed.), *The Future of the United Nations System: Potential for the Twenty-First Century* (Tokyo, New York, Paris: United Nations University Press, 1998); Alan James, *Peacekeeping in International Politics* (Basingstoke: Macmillan, 1990); and United Nations Department of Public Information, *The Blue Berets*, 2nd edn (New York: United Nations, 1990).
* See also UNTEA.
† See also UNSF.

disarmament, demobilization and integration of combatants; training of the police and judiciary; monitoring human rights; providing electoral assistance and strengthening national institutions', and even running states.[3] The ranks of peacekeepers included police, lawyers, judges, city administrators and experts in customs, fiscal management, public utilities, health, education, sanitation and agriculture.

For example, in the 1990s approximately 3500 civilian police officers were involved in the UN's Cambodian operation, and an extensive police reform and reconstruction mission was undertaken in Bosnia and Herzegovina. Electoral assistance has also been a fast-growing area. It began at the end of the 1980s in Namibia and Nicaragua; continued ambitiously in Cambodia in the early 1990s; and by the end of the decade the UN had helped to organise, supervise and verify 70 elections.

Namibia

South Africa's presence in Namibia in defiance of the General Assembly, the Security Council and the International Court of Justice had been one of the sharpest thorns in the UN's flesh. Determined efforts in the 1970s had produced an agreement in principle for a UN peacekeeping force to supervise pre-independence elections.

Table 6.3   Ongoing UN peacekeeping missions (January 2003)

Name and location	Starting date	Type of mission	Strength*	Annual costs†	Fatalities
MINURSO United Nations Mission for the Referendum in Western Sahara	April 1991	To oversee referendum over whether Western Sahara becomes independent or is integrated with Morocco	217 M 25 P 167 ICS	434.4	10
MONUC United Nations Organization Mission in the Democratic Republic of the Congo	November 1999	Monitor ceasefire and help implement ceasefire agreement	4371 M 49 P 559 ICS	608.3	12
UNAMSIL UN Assistance Mission in Sierra Leone	October 1999	Help to restore law, order and stability, and promote a disarm-ament, demobilisation and reintegration programme leading to democratic elections	16042 M 44 P 298 ICS	699.8	99
UNDOF UN Disengagement Observer Force (Syria)	June 1974	Supervise Israel–Syria truce in the Golan Heights	1043 M 39 ICS	40.8	40
UNFICYP UN Peacekeeping Force in Cyprus	March 1964	Supervise truce in Cyprus	1211 M 35 P 42 ICS	45.6	170
UNIFIL UN Interim Force in Lebanon	March 1978	Monitor truce in South Lebanon; assist Lebanese government	2077 M 116 ICS	117.1	246

Mission	Started	Purpose	Personnel*	Budget†	
UNIKOM UN Iraq–Kuwait Observer Mission	April 1991	Monitor demilitarised zone along Iraq–Kuwait border	1105 M 63 ICS	52.9	17
UNMEE United Nations Mission in Ethiopia and Eritrea	July 2000	Monitor ceasefire and help ensure observance of security commitments	4034 M 227 ICS	230.9	3
UNMIK United Nations Interim Administration Mission in Kosovo (in collaboration with OSCE and EU)	June 1999	Administer Kosovo while helping it to develop into a democratic society	4446 P 39 M 1022 ICS	345	20
UNMISET UN Mission of Support in East Timor (Succeeded UNTAET)	May 2002	Help promote stability, democracy and justice, and assist in running East Timor and providing security until all operational responsibilities are fully devolved to East Timor authorities	3853 M 730 P 895 ICS	305.2	5
UNMOGIP UN Military Observer Group in India and Pakistan	Jan 1949	Monitor India–Pakistan truce in Kashmir	44 M 24 ICS	9.2	9
UNOMIG UN Observer Mission in Georgia	August 1993	Monitor ceasefire and CIS force	117 M 91 ICS	33.1	7
UNTSO UN Truce Supervision Organisation	June 1948	Supervise Arab–Israeli truces	154 M 101 ICS	25.9	38

*M = military, P = civilian police, ICS = International Civil Servants. Excludes locally recruited staff.

† i.e. approved budget, July 2002–June 2003, millions of US dollars.

Table 6.4 Non-UN peacekeeping missions

Name and location	Duration
ECOMOG ECOWAS Ceasefire Monitoring Group (a) Liberia (Nigerian-led) (b) Sierra Leone	 August 1990– 1997–2000
IFOR Implementation Force (Bosnia) (Nato-led) (succeeded by SFOR)	 December 1995–December 1996
INTERFET International Force in East Timor (Australian-led)	 September 1999–February 2000
ISAF International Security Assistance Force (Afghanistan)	 December 2001–
KFOR Kosovo Force (Nato-led, complementary to UNMIK)	 June 1999–
MISAB Inter-African Force to Monitor the Implementation of the Bangui Agreements	 February 1997
MFO Multinational Force and Observers (Sinai) (US-led)	 April 1982–
MNF I Multinational Force (Beirut, Lebanon) (US-led)	 August–September 1982
MNF II Multinational Force (Beirut, Lebanon) (US-led)	 September 1982–February 1984
SFOR Stabilisation Force (Bosnia) (Nato-led)	 December 1996–
UNITAF Unified Task Force (Somali) (US-led) (Also known as Operation Restore Hope) (succeeded by UNOSOM II)	 December 1992–May 1993

However, South Africa stubbornly stayed put until the changed international climate and military defeats forced her hand. The consequential UN Transitional Assistance Group (UNTAG) in Namibia was a huge operation, costing as much as roughly half the UN's regular budget. It monitored the 1989 elections, oversaw the virtual demilitarisation of Namibia, kept law and order during the election process, engaged in humanitarian work and endeavoured to insulate Namibia from external influences.

Thanks to UNTAG, 97 per cent of registered voters participated in free and fair elections, which brought to an end a twenty-year armed struggle and introduced another member to the UN.

Cambodia

The elections in Cambodia were part of an ambitious and wide-ranging attempt at national reconciliation, during which the UN's Transitional Authority (UNTAC) in effect ran the country for a year. After bitter civil conflict followed by a decade of occupation by Soviet-backed Vietnam (China was backing the other main group), the occupying forces were withdrawn at the end of the cold war. Tortuous negotiations ensued, eventually resulting in the four Cambodian factions agreeing that the UN should mount a multifaceted peacekeeping operation. The culminating point of this enterprise was meant to be a government whose legitimacy was accepted on all internal sides. Things did not go smoothly. UNTAC had some sizable internal problems of its own; one of the main Cambodian factions withdrew its cooperation; and the others complied less than fully with what had been agreed. But the elections went ahead, the turnout was surprisingly high, and a government emerged in which power was shared by several of the factions. This enabled the UN to withdraw its 22,000-strong mission (three-quarters of whom were soldiers, and one-sixth police) at the end of 1993. Australia's Foreign Minister (who had been closely involved in the negotiation of the agreement) claimed that the operation was a 'flawed ... success'.[4] But trouble lay ahead (see below).

Former Yugoslavia

In the case of the UN Protection Force (UNPROFOR) that was sent to ex-Yugoslavia, the operation itself was frequently in grave difficulty, albeit in only one of the three successor states in which it operated. A small number of its personnel sat on the borders of the former Yugoslav Republic of Macedonia and the Federal Republic of Yugoslavia, being transformed in March 1995 into a 'preventive deployment' force (UNPREDEP). The problem there stemmed from the fact that about one-third of Macedonia's population were ethnic Albanians; that the neighbouring Serbian province of Kosovo was overwhelmingly Albanian; but that Serbia was anxious to retain a Serbian imprint on Kosovo because it is very dear to the Serbs on historical grounds. Clearly this presented a potential problem (which, as will be mentioned later, flared up in 1999). The UN hailed UNPREDEP as an innovative instance of 'preventive deployment' although, in fact, preventive missions are not novel, much traditional peacekeeping being an attempt to prevent something (though usually that something is a second round of fighting).

In the new state of Croatia, three large Serbian enclaves resisted Croatian rule. There was savage fighting, the Serb enclaves proclaimed the Republic of Serbian Krajina in December 1991, and (following EU recognition of Croatia) UNPROFOR was sent to the state in February 1992. Its job was to patrol the borders of the enclaves and watch over the behaviour within them of the Serbs, in the hope of discouraging further ethnic cleansing. It was replaced in March 1995 by a 'confidence restoration' mission to help execute a ceasefire arrangement and facilitate the reintegration of Serb-controlled areas. In one region, Eastern Slovenia, this involved establishing a transitional administration, but by the end of 1998 it had followed Western Slavonia and Krajina in being re-integrated into Croatia, and the Organisation for Security and Cooperation in Europe (OSCE) had taken over the task of monitoring the performance of the Croatian police.

By far the biggest part of UNPROFOR (and it became a very big force) was in Bosnia-Herzegovina. Almost half the population was Muslim, but the other half was divided roughly in a 2:1 ratio between Orthodox Serbs and Catholic Croats. After it declared independence from the Socialist Federation of Yugoslavia in March 1992 it was swept by violence. In the ensuing savage war, the Muslims were 'cleansed' by Serbs from the areas in which the latter were in a majority. This prompted increasingly strong revisions of UNPROFOR's mandate, including invocations of Chapter VII of the Charter, in conjunction with which the Security Council banned all military flights in the state's air space; asserted the right to ensure compliance with the ban; established six 'safe areas' (or 'safe havens') that were to be free from armed attacks; authorised certain measures to protect their civilian inhabitants; and demanded a nationwide ceasefire. On the ground, tough measures were sometimes taken in response to considerable provocation and promise breaking. NATO's planes were called in, and a 'rapid reaction force' was brought in on the ground, bringing a heavy Anglo-French battle group into the vicinity of Sarajevo. At that point UNPROFOR handed over to a heavily armed, 60,000-strong NATO-led force which, for a year, monitored the implementation of the 1995 Dayton agreement and which had the authority to use its arms, to enforce the military aspects of the peace agreement. After a year, another, smaller NATO-led force took up the next task of stabilising the peace – and at the time of writing (April 2003), NATO is still much involved in Bosnia, and a UN High Representative is present to keep an eye on things.

East Timor

East Timor is another territory which has attracted international attention – with, eventually, a much more favourable result. In 1999 a UN-supervised plebiscite was held to determine the future of this poverty-stricken former Portuguese colony, which had been snatched by Indonesia in 1975. Despite considerable intimidation, 98 per cent of the registered voters wanted independence. Elements of the Indonesian military administration and police force then orchestrated an orgy of murder, arson, looting and forced deportation in which 80 per cent of East Timor's buildings were destroyed, about a thousand people were killed, and three-quarters of the 890,000 East Timorese displaced. Given Indonesia's political and military weight, there was little enthusiasm for armed intervention. However, Australia felt unable to stand aside and, after much arm-twisting, Indonesia renounced its claim to East Timor and an Australian-led international force restored law and order and oversaw Indonesian withdrawal. East Timor then came under UN administration for two and a half years while its infrastructure was built up to enable it to stand on its own. In May 2002, Kofi Annan transferred power to the newly-elected President, who, in a warmly-applauded gesture of reconciliation, travelled to the ceremony in the company of the Indonesian President. The new sovereign state of Timor-Leste had been born.

The multifaceted nature of peacekeeping operations since the Cold War have often reflected the wish to get closer to tackling the roots of conflict. Instead of just trying to keep the peace, the UN was consciously expanding its peacemaking and peacebuilding activities to promote and consolidate democracy, and to provide more equitable and effective governance by strengthening civil society (see Table 6.5). For example, the observer group in Central America from 1989 to 1992 was integral to the winding up of a bitter dispute in Nicaragua in which the US had been the leading

Table 6.5 Ongoing political and peacebuilding missions (January 2003)

Acronym	Name	Duration	Strength*
BONUCA	UN Peacebuilding Office in the Central African Republic	February 2000–	19 ICS 5 MA 6 P
	Office of the Special Representative of the Secretary-General for the Great Lakes Region	December 1997–	7 ICS
	Office of the Special Representative of the Secretary-General for West Africa	March 2002	5 ICS
MINUGUA	UN Verification Mission in Guatemala	September 1994–	60 ICS 6 P
UNAMA	UN Assistance Mission in Afghanistan	March 2002–	166 ICS 4 MA 4 P
UNMA	UN mission in Angola	October 1999– February 2002	48 ICS 8 MA
UNPOB	UN Political Office in Bougainville (Papua New Guinea)	June 1998–	4 ICS 1 MA
UNOB	UN Office in Burundi	October 1993	28 ICS 1 MA
UNOGBIS	UN Peacebuilding Support Office in Guinea-Bissau	March 1999–	13 ICS 2 MA 1 P
UNOL	UN Peacebuilding Support Office in Liberia	November 1997–	10 ICS
UNPOS	UN Political Office for Somalia	April 1995	5 ICS
UNSCO	Office of the UN Special Coordinator for the Middle East	October 1999–	23 ICS
UNTOP	UN Tajikistan Office of Peacebuilding	June 2000	10 ICS 1 P

* ICS = international civil servants, MA = military advisers, P = police. Excludes locally recruited staff and volunteers.

external antagonist. In 1993–94, peacekeepers in Mozambique oversaw the de-mobilisation of a rebel army and its transformation into a legitimate political party competing in free and fair internationally-supervised elections, helping to consoli-date democratic arrangements as part of the settlement of internal conflict. And from 1998 to 2000 the UN contributed to the restoration of a climate of stability and security as well as dialogue among political actors in the Central African Republic. Furthermore, when peacekeeping missions were closed down in states that had undergone war, the UN in 1997 began experimentally leaving behind small peace-building support offices to reinforce the peace process and promote human rights, democracy and the rule of law. The work is sometimes dangerous and frequently very difficult; but it means that the UN has people on the ground, monitoring events, working to keep open crucial channels of communication between factions, and finding creative ways of assisting in recovery.

OVERSTRETCH

All this activity sometimes resulted in the UN overstretching itself, in terms of both its resources and its hopes. And because too much was expected of peacekeeping, there were unwise decisions that tarnished the UN's reputation and led to peace-keeping's golden age ending almost as soon as it began.

What went wrong? Moral outrage combined with humanitarian impulses de-manded that efforts be made to dampen down conflicts and alleviate the vast suffering they entailed – especially when they were taken up by the media. But since no-one wanted to dig deep into their pockets, the UN had to engage in bargain-basement peacekeeping. It was bargain-basement inasmuch as some missions were too small to execute their mandates. In Angola in 1992, 400 peacekeepers were given the impossible task of observing and verifying elections in a country the size of France, Germany and Spain combined. The Rwandan mission was almost half its recommended size and the Secretary-General was asked to suggest how it might be cut before it was even despatched. In Bosnia, a task force of around 1500 to 2000 police was asked to perform more extensive tasks than many thousands more heavily armed NATO soldiers.

Secondly, peacekeeping was bargain-basement in terms of the quality of some of the peacekeepers. Peacekeeping had expanded at a time when Western states were cutting back on defence expenditure and they had fewer troops to offer. Although the range of contributors grew, too many peacekeepers were badly trained, badly equipped and ill-prepared. In Rwanda, the UN 'had to take what we could get' in the way of troops, and there were large differences between the equipment of the 26 peacekeeping contingents, some of which turned up 'bare-assed', demanding 'that the United Nations suit them up'.[5] Many UN police in Cambodia lacked adequate training and were unready for the complexities of the mission. Some had had no prior policework experience at home, did not speak French or English (let alone Khmer), lacked equipment, could not drive police vehicles, and 'were corrupt and even criminal in their behaviour'.[6] Only half the estimated personnel required were deployed in some districts, and some UN police had no supplies or desks or files at their headquarters for many months. Still, its modest successes showed that, properly prepared, police could make a valuable contribution to peacekeeping.[7]

The third consequence of trying to run peacekeeping on a shoestring was that the Department of Peacekeeping Operations (DPKO) at UN headquarters was overwhelmed. Missions were ill-prepared. When General Dallaire first went to Rwanda, all he knew of the country was what he had found in a public library encyclopaedia. In 2000, the staff of the DPKO were still 'stretched to the bone'. For example, 12,000 UN troops in Sierra Leone were serviced by five DPKO staff with insufficient technical expertise.[8]

So far as the UN's hopes were concerned, overstretch was sometimes reflected, either during or after an operation, in the organisation's failure or inability to establish the social and political foundations which are required for an internally peaceful and smoothly operating state. The hugely expensive operation in Cambodia (costing $2 billion) departed 'as UN missions do . . . long before essential civil institutions had had a chance to grow'.[9] Nothing was done when, in 1997, the elected Prime Minister was ousted amidst heavy fighting; the elections that were held in 1998 were conducted in an atmosphere of intimidation and murder; and the country remained 'rife with corruption and cronyism, with continued illegal logging, drug trafficking, gem mining and rampant prostitution'.[10] Being preoccupied elsewhere and suffering 'diplomatic fatigue', the West had 'decided to abandon' the 'always . . . elusive dream' of democracy in Cambodia.[11] Six and a half years after the Dayton agreement, Bosnia remained 'a political and economic wasteland'.[12] Progress in protecting human rights in El Salvador and Haiti (where six missions were sent) was limited. Part of the reason for this stemmed from problems with the missions. But, importantly, it was also due to economic and social conditions, a 'difficult and tense political context . . . [and] an insufficient determination within the country to strengthen [the] institutions' of justice and human rights.[13]

These instances are a salutary reminder that the UN cannot on its own solve a political problem. Despatching peacekeepers is akin to applying a bandage to a wound, with a view to allowing it to heal. The greater the wound, the longer and more difficult is the healing process. Sometimes it can take many years. Sometimes the wound is too raw and too deep for any healing. For just as war may be a form of revolution, transforming a war-based society into a peaceful and open society is something of a revolutionary process. The long, complex and difficult task can try the patience of former combatants, especially in impoverished states that are emerging from civil wars, and that lack enough resources to establish peaceful democracies.

Indeed, in some states to which peacekeeping missions were sent, civil wars were still in full swing. In that context, where the rewards of success were high – the seat of government, with all its perks, prestige, and power – and the consequences of failure were perhaps dire, it is not surprising that the peacekeepers were viewed instrumentally. If their work was such that a government, faction or group was likely to benefit from it, cooperation would be extended to them; but if it looked as if the process of peacekeeping stood in the way of a group's ambitions, then there was little chance of the group showing them much respect. In Western Sahara, for example, Morocco has stalled for more than a decade on the intended UN-supervised referendum. In Angola, the losing side in the 1992 UN-supervised elections resumed military hostilities, which only ended a decade later when the rebel leader was killed.

In Liberia fighting continued despite peace accords. A false dawning of peace in the Democratic Republic of Congo (DRC) in 1999 saw peacekeepers sent into a country the size of western Europe during a four-year war that at one stage involved seven states and cost around two million lives. Not surprisingly, the mission experienced serious problems.

These experiences highlight the fundamental point that the success of traditional, non-forceful peacekeeping depends on consent. Disputants must be willing to cooperate with peacekeepers and wish to live at peace, at least for the time being. If they do not want, or fear, an adverse settlement, they may fail to cooperate with a mission. If they want to fight, only two things will stop them: removing the cause of the conflict or applying superior force, neither of which is provided by traditional peacekeeping.

DISASTER

However, the feeling that something – preferably low cost – ought to be done about deadly conflicts sometimes led politicians to fling traditional peacekeeping missions into inappropriate situations. Especially was this so in respect of conflicts that attracted considerable media attention. In a couple of cases it led to peacekeepers becoming 'bystanders to genocide'.[14]

Rwanda

In 1993 a small, traditional-type peacekeeping mission (UNAMIR) was sent to Rwanda to help implement a peace agreement between the Hutu government and Tutsi rebels (the Rwandan Patriotic Front – RPF). Then, however, in April 1994, the shooting down of the Rwandan President's plane as it came in to land at Kigali was the signal for Hutu extremists to seize power and embark on 'the fastest, most efficient killing spree of the twentieth century'.[15] In the course of a hundred days, about 800,000 people were systematically slaughtered, including roughly three-quarters of the Rwandan Tutsi population and many politically moderate Hutu.

During this time UNAMIR was almost paralysed. The first reason was because peacekeepers were only allowed to use force in self-defence. Secondly, UNAMIR was hugely under-resourced in men and ammunition. And thirdly, after the slaughter began, the Canadian commander, General Dallaire, was not in effective control of all his troops. The mission was on the verge of disintegrating when its Belgian members were withdrawn (after ten of them had been tortured and murdered) and Bangladesh intimated it might follow suit. Soon Dallaire lost every line of communication to the countryside and had only a single satellite phone link to the outside world.

Dallaire believed that UNAMIR could have made a marked difference if he had had 5000 soldiers. Others thought the same, and there were occasions when a handful of courageous peacekeepers saved many Rwandan lives. However, when the Secretariat sounded out a hundred states about strengthening the force, only one state responded positively: clearly the international community was disinclined to send troops and equipment into the Rwandan vortex. The USA, whose attitude was crucial, had other crises on its mind and, after its recent experience in Somalia, wanted no more African peacekeeping. And so the Security Council responded to Dallaire's appeal for reinforcements by cutting UNAMIR down to a token 270.

In May – a month after the killing had begun – outraged non-permanent members of the Security Council forced a reversal of the decision to downgrade UNAMIR, and the Council authorised its increase to 5500. But it took nearly six months to find the troops. The first reinforcements only arrived in August. By then the RPF had ended the genocide and formed a government of national unity. Meanwhile, France, which had been close to the ousted Hutu government, had obtained grudging Security Council approval for the despatch of 2330 of her soldiers (plus a token 32 Senegalese) to create a 'safe zone' for Hutus in the south-west (and in the process, gave safe haven to the murderous Interhamwe militia and other forces behind the genocide).[16] They stayed until August when the first UNAMIR II reinforcements took over the French-controlled areas.

Rwanda was 'a turning point in United Nations peacekeeping. It came to symbolize a lack of will to commit to peacekeeping, and above all, to take risks in the field.'[17] The readiness of the French to act independently in pursuit of their own interests only underlined the point. In the longer run, the genocide destabilised the Democratic Republic of the Congo, where the presence of Interhamwe rebels, combined with ethnic tensions and the opportunity for plunder, led in 1998 to a Rwandan–Ugandan invasion and war.

Srebrenica

When the Security Council created safe havens in Bosnia-Herzegovina in 1993 (see above), it did not check whether the parties on the ground (whose cooperation was essential) agreed about the idea. Nor did it change UNPROFOR's mandate or provide additional troops to secure the safe areas. Thus the Serb leaders could spit with impunity in the face of the UN and NATO. UNPROFOR's lightly armed peacekeepers did sterling humanitarian work but they were in an impossible situation, without a peace to keep and unable to prevent the worst atrocity in Europe since 1945 – when General Mladic and his Serb troops overran the so-called safe haven of Srebrenica and hauled off up to 8000 men and boys, whom they then slaughtered. The (mostly female) survivors became refugees.

There was a huge outcry at the passivity of the battalion of 110 Dutch peacekeepers in Srebrenica, who had been ordered not to fight. Critics spoke of dishonour and pointed to occasions when force had been successfully used against Serbs (while conveniently ignoring the times force had backfired). In the Netherlands the scars ran deep: in 2002 the government fell and the head of the army resigned after the release of a detailed report that criticised the government, the peacekeepers and the UN.

But as the Secretary-General had warned at the outset, conditions in Bosnia were entirely unsuitable for traditional, non-forceful peacekeeping. Until the Srebrenica massacre, and despite various references to Chapter VII in the relevant Security Council resolutions, UNPROFOR was in effect regarded as a traditional mission. One reason was the USA's unwillingness or inability to provide the necessary leadership, dollars or troops for tough action, and it was essentially Western states without troops in Bosnia who wanted strong measures. It is easy to be brave with someone else's men and money. Secondly, wrongs were being done on all sides. Thirdly, the lessons of history apparently argued against forceful action: one commander referred to the danger of crossing 'the Mogadishu line' (and ending up fighting, like UNOSOM in Somalia in 1993), and Boutros-Ghali worried about Bosnia turning into 'the UN's Vietnam'. Fourthly, the UNPROFOR presence in Srebrenica was only token. Dutch peacekeepers in Srebrenica were inadequately trained, cut off from supplies and support, hopelessly outnumbered, and outgunned by the Serbs, who threatened to kill Dutch captives. Fifthly, UNPROFOR's commander refused Dutch calls for air support because he feared it might compromise the international community's undoubtedly valuable humanitarian work. In other words, he was thinking of UNPROFOR as a traditional peacekeeping operation, for which impartiality was essential. That he thought this way reflects the conceptual muddiness of the Bosnian operation and its blurring of the distinctions between peacekeeping and peace enforcement.

SANCTIONS

Events such as these resulted in a gradual recognition that in some circumstances it might be desirable to go beyond traditional peacekeeping to an appreciably tougher stance. Closer attention began to be paid to the potential of the Charter's Chapter VII, in part with an eye to the possibility of non-military sanctions. Before 1990, the UN had imposed them only twice – on Rhodesia and South Africa. By the end of 2002 it had done so in one form or another 12 more times, and all UN military interventions between 1990 and 2000 were accompanied by such sanctions.

Thus comprehensive trade, financial and transportation restrictions were applied against Iraq, Haiti, and the former Yugoslavia. Other states faced selective sanctions. Libya was subject to an embargo on the export of arms, aircraft and components as well as a limited assets freeze and a ban on air links; Sudan faced diplomatic sanctions; arms embargoes were imposed on Ethiopia and Eritrea, Somalia, Liberia, the UNITA movement in Angola, Rwanda, the Taleban regime in Afghanistan and Al-Qaeda (supplemented by a flight and travel ban, a freeze on financial assets, and diplomatic sanctions), and on the Armed Forces Revolutionary Council junta and the Revolutionary United Front in Sierra Leone (supplemented by an oil embargo and travel restrictions). In respect of UNITA, Sierra Leone and Rwanda there was also a ban on the trade in 'conflict diamonds' – illegally exported rough diamonds that fuelled insurrections. After 1997, UNITA was also subject to travel restrictions and a freeze of funds affecting senior officials and their families, as well as limited import and export bans affecting territory under their control.

If sanctions are judged by their ability to alter behaviour, the record is dismal: Iraq did not become more tractable and Serbia's rulers made fortunes out of controlling the resulting illegal trade. Sanctions are also blunt instruments that cause suffering to innocent people and states. Many states resent the selective and inconsistent application of sanctions. There was manifest dissatisfaction with the prolongation of sanctions against Iraq and Libya and they were widely, if not totally, disregarded in Angola.

But how else can the UN deal with defiant and potentially dangerous states that flout accepted rules of conduct and display scant regard for the authority of the UN?

In such circumstances, economic sanctions can play an important symbolic role, offering a handy and relatively inexpensive means of expressing disapproval of unacceptable behaviour that threatens international peace and security. They may also be a prelude to the use of military pressure.

THE EMERGENCE OF 'PEACE ENFORCEMENT'

Chapter VII of the UN Charter is often called the enforcement Chapter. The activity that it authorises is clearly of that kind, and elsewhere in the Charter (in Article 2.7) reference is made to 'enforcement measures' being taken under it. But, as was seen earlier, the envisaged measures related to inter-state aggression – that is, collective security. In the mid-1990s, however, the revived focus on Chapter VII had chiefly to do with the possibility of tough measures being taken in response to serious problems occurring within states. Such action became known as 'peace enforcement'.

We have seen that in 1961 and 1962 UN peacekeepers used military force in (eventually successful) attempts to end Katanga's secession from the Congo. For years the lesson derived from that politically harrowing experience was the importance of the principle of peacekeepers being lightly armed and only using weapons in self-defence. No-one wanted 'another Congo'. Until the end of the cold war, that continued to hold true. But then, partly in response to genocide in Srebrenica and Rwanda, there was a move towards authorising missions to protect civilians under imminent threat of physical violence. This led, by the mid-1990s, to a recognition that peacekeeping doctrine needed revision, to take account of situations where peacekeepers could expect to encounter armed resistance. Hence the emergence of the idea of peace enforcement. It envisaged the possibility of a mission being given authority under Chapter VII to use force to ensure compliance with the terms of its mandate where that mandate is to restore or maintain international peace and security.

Peace enforcement differs from collective security inasmuch as the latter applies force *partially* – against an identified aggressor. By contrast, peace enforcement continues to emphasise the key peacekeeping principle of impartiality, but, in so doing, shifts the emphasis from impartiality towards disputants, towards impartiality in the execution of the mandate. In other words, traditional peacekeepers act even-handedly towards all parties to a dispute, whereas peace enforcers act against any party that may threaten to overturn a peace agreement or prevent the mission achieving its aims. This is justified on the ground that to do otherwise can result in ineffectiveness and amount to complicity with evil.

Peace enforcement may also abandon another key principle of traditional peace-keeping – consent. In some cases of enforcement (Iraq, the former Yugoslavia, Rwanda), intervention occurred against the wishes of the government. In others 'consent was controversial and of little practical meaning' (Liberia, Haiti, Sierra Leone), and although consent was obtained in respect of Somalia, it has been described as 'irrelevant'.[18]

As Table 6.6 indicates, most peace enforcement operations have been outside the UN. One reason for this was the debilitating effect on the USA of its UN-related experience in Somalia in 1993. Another reason is that it is not easy for UN members

Table 6.6   The differences between peacekeeping, peace enforcement and collective security[19]

Peacekeeping	Peace enforcement	Collective security
Impartial towards all disputants	Impartial in executing mandate	Partial against identified aggressor
Consent essential	Consent desirable but not necessary	Consent irrelevant
Lightly armed	Armed	Fully armed
Force used only in self-defence	Force used for self-defence and to ensure execution of mandate	Full use of force against aggressor
Mostly UN operations	Mostly non-UN operations; authority delegated to states, coalitions of states, regional organisations or alliances	In theory conducted by UN army under direction of Military Staff Committee. So far, invariably non-UN operations, but with authority delegated by the UN to the group of states making up the force

to agree what action to take in complex and fast-moving situations. Moreover, intervening in violent chaos calls for the swift despatch of a first-class, well-equipped force with a clear plan and rules of engagement, and a readiness to look and act tough. Because the UN lacks operational capacity, it has had to delegate (or acquiesce in) enforcement action being taken by states or regional organisations. This pattern is unlikely to change.

WIDENING THE CONCEPT OF 'THREATS TO' AND 'BREACHES OF' INTERNATIONAL PEACE AND SECURITY

In necessary conjunction with the development of peace enforcement, the concept of 'threats to' and 'breaches of' international peace and security has been interpreted in a much wider way than was envisaged when the Charter was drafted. This interpretative evolution has been steadily occurring throughout the UN's life, most recently to include personal freedoms, socio-economic factors, and even HIV/AIDS. More dramatically, however, in the 1990s the UN was ready to make formal determinations that civil war and internal strife were threats to international peace and security (something that was hardly conceivable during the cold war), and even to locate such a threat within a rebel movement – for example, UNITA in Angola. Such findings permitted the UN to authorise or use force under Chapter VII – that is, to engage in peace enforcement.

This sometimes occurred in situations where secession was an issue. As we have seen, forceful action in this context was not new, since armed force had been used to bring Katanga back into the Congo in 1962. In 1995, NATO took tough action against the Serbs (after the Srebrenica massacre) to prevent the break-up of Bosnia – although the Dayton peace agreement that autumn took account of the realities on the ground to the extent of accepting Serb demands for a separate Republica Srpska within a weak Bosnian framework.

Peace enforcement was also used in a secessionist context in the Serbian province of Kosovo. Only about one-tenth of its population of 2 million were Serbs, the rest being ethnic Albanians, many of whom sought independence or union with Albania. In March 1999, violence escalated when peace talks failed between the hardline secessionists and the Serb government. Since Russia and China would have vetoed any resolution authorising NATO to use force against the Serbs, NATO did not seek prior UN authorisation before it applied air power in order to prevent a humanitarian tragedy. The result was the opposite of what was intended: thousands were killed and more than a million ethnic Albanians were driven from their homes. But 78 days of bombing brought the Serbs to the negotiating table and produced a peace settlement. Serb forces withdrew, and the province was placed under UN administration. This, like the subsequent UN administration in East Timor, represented a significant extension of UN peacebuilding activity. A NATO-led force was also established to ensure Kosovo's security, one of its first duties being the disarmament of the secessionists' army.

The concept of international peace and security has also been extended to justify what has come to be called 'humanitarian intervention'. This began during the 1991 Gulf War when 2 million Kurds of Northern Iraq fled, virtually overnight, from attacks by Iraqi troops. The Security Council responded by, for the first time, declaring a safe haven (the area in Iraq north of the 36th parallel), where the Iraqi government was to cease all military activity so that humanitarian relief could be delivered unimpeded and Kurdish refugees could not be attacked. In this way, the Council signalled that it now regarded substantial flows of refugees and the gross abuse of human rights as a ground for action.

Since then, humanitarian considerations have been used as a basis (or a partial basis) for several instances of peace enforcement, including (the just discussed) Kosovo and (the soon to be discussed) Somalia. This does not mean that humanitarian motives were necessarily paramount in all such cases: security concerns were dominant in Liberia, and the nature of the regime was important in Haiti, where the Security Council broke new ground by treating an internal political crisis as a threat to international peace and security. However, there was always evidence of responding to people's needs. Nor did the spectacular failures of the UN in Rwanda and Srebrenica detract from the significance of this development. As the new century dawned, the Secretary-General echoed the feelings of many when he said that 'no legal principle –not even sovereignty – can ever shield crimes against humanity', and that the Security Council 'has a moral duty to act on behalf of the international community' to halt them.[20] In all circumstances, however, peace enforcement is likely to involve a plunge into turmoil. This will be illustrated by focusing on two such episodes.

Somalia

The first is the UN's missions to Somalia. In 1992, when the UN Operation in Somalia (UNOSOM) failed to safeguard the delivery of humanitarian assistance in a complex and ever-changing civil war, it was replaced by 31,000 US troops, who were authorised by the Security Council to use force to protect and distribute emergency aid. UNOSOM II took over from the USA in May 1993. It was a huge, very expensive operation (costing on average $3 million a day) and did valuable humanitarian work. However, when it began trying to disarm Somali factions it ran into trouble and there was serious fighting. The death of twenty-five Pakistani peacekeepers led to a futile, sometimes farcical, UN-authorised hunt for the Somali leader, General Aideed. It also led to the failed raid in Mogadishu that resulted in the death of nineteen peace-keepers (eighteen American and one Malaysian) and about a thousand Somalis. America's humiliation was compounded by television pictures of an interview with a trembling, disoriented American pilot and of the bodies of American soldiers being dragged through the streets of Mogadishu. By the end of March 1994, American troops had been withdrawn from UNOSOM II, and the peacekeeping mission was withdrawn from Somalia at the beginning of 1995, having failed to achieve many of its objectives. The feeling was that the Somalis had 'had their chance',[21] and for years the country remained 'the epitome of a failed state, essentially without a functioning central government and a breakaway quasi-independent Somaliland to the North'.[22]

The ramifications of the Somali débâcle were huge. Someone had to get the blame, and the USA (unfairly) blamed the UN, even though the US contingent remained under effective American control throughout, and UN commanders were not warned in advance about the raid against General Aideed. The USA also reconsidered its whole attitude to peacekeeping. President Clinton's May 1994 Presidential Decision Directive 25 (an executive instrument establishing US policy) adopted a cautious, constrained and selective approach to humanitarian intervention and peacekeeping. For its part, the UN Secretariat also decided it must be more cautious about taking risks.

Sierra Leone

The second peace enforcement episode – which can be considered a provisional success – was in Sierra Leone in 2000. In the 1990s, Sierra Leone descended into in-stability, military coups, an eight-year armed revolt by the Revolutionary United Front (RUF), and widespread and gross abuses of human rights. These included the forcible recruitment of 'child soldiers' (another addition to the UN agenda), who were made to commit atrocities on relatives. Tens of thousands lost their lives. Many more were maimed and the state became desperately poor and miserable. Each attempt to get the country back on its feet was followed by greater chaos and instability.

In the mid-1990s, a South African mercenary group restored order, and inter-nationally-supervised, democratic elections were held in March 1996. However, fol-lowing the mercenaries' departure, a combined force of RUF rebels and rogue soldiers overthrew President Ahmed Tijan Kabbah in May 1997 and took power as the Armed Forces Revolutionary Council (AFRC).

A number of factors would have made UN inaction unsurprising: the Organisa-tion's recent peacekeeping failures; Sierra Leone's strategic insignificance; ignorance of what was going on; and weaknesses in the West African policies of the three major outside powers. Yet not only was there universal condemnation of the AFRC, but the Security Council President issued a rebuke; the Organisation of African Unity, unusually, abandoned strict adherence to non-intervention by calling on the Economic Community of West African States (ECOWAS) to help restore constitutional order; and there was a UN embargo on oil and arms.

This led to Nigerian intervention, followed by a Nigerian-led ECOWAS monitoring group forcibly restoring President Kabbah in 1998, at which time a small UN observer mission, the UN Assistance Mission in Sierra Leone (UNAMSIL), was sent to monitor the situation and to help disarm combatants and restructure the security forces. However, Kabbah's authority did not extend far beyond Freetown and there was continuing violence, which climaxed at the end of the year when the RUF overran Freetown. Much blood was shed before the African monitoring group regained control of the city.

In July 1999, under pressure from the British, Americans 'and other powers intent on a quick fix',[23] Kabbah negotiated a power-sharing peace agreement with the psychopathic, brutal and corrupt RUF leader, Foday Sankoh. Under the agreement the observer mission was replaced by a significantly larger, 6000-strong assistance mission with a robust mandate that permitted armed force being used 'to afford protection to civilians under imminent threat of physical violence'.[24] It was intended to help implement the peace and to supervise the demobilisation and re-education of thousands of rebel fighters. But as the peace agreement was slapdash, 'bad and stupid', and as Sankoh did not want peace, Sierra Leone was soon 'setting new standards in duplicity and atrocity' and the peacekeeping operation began turning into a fiasco.[25]

For example, in January 2000 peacekeepers from Guinea (who had orders not to fight) were robbed of their weapons and armoured personnel carriers, and Kenyans were also stripped of their weapons. In February the mission was enlarged and given an expanded Chapter VII mandate, but this was not translated into action on the ground because the Indian force commander, General Jetley, insisted that UNAMSIL was a traditional-type peacekeeping force and was not there to fight. Very soon, however, UNAMSIL came into open conflict when the RUF reneged on the peace deal, attacked UN demobilisation camps, and captured over 500 peacekeepers and their equipment. The UN again enlarged UNAMSIL (to 13,000, making it the largest peacekeeping force then in being)[26] and went on to impose an ineffective ban on the trade in conflict diamonds.

UNAMSIL was now engaged in peace enforcement rather than peacekeeping, but had been found wanting when confronted by determined and very brutal rebels. The mission itself had fallen into a 'morass of politics and suspicion, lethargy and lack of direction',[27] and Jetley (who had fallen out with his Nigerian deputy) was accusing Nigeria of trading in conflict diamonds and appointing stooges to sabotage the mission. (Nigeria naturally demanded Jetley's removal and this was diplomatically arranged.) Meanwhile, the situation in Sierra Leone was very grim.

Yet strong and determined British intervention demonstrated that peace enforcement could work even in such unpromising circumstances. Britain had committed herself very heavily to restoring democracy in her former colony and clearly this was not going to be achieved by UNAMSIL. Britain therefore decided to act independently and sent 700 paratroopers to Sierra Leone to prevent UNAMSIL disintegrating, stabilise the situation, and facilitate the arrival of UNAMSIL reinforcements.

According to a UN official, the paratroopers 'stiffened the spines of everyone around by coming in, taking charge and simply stating that the RUF would not be allowed to succeed'.[28]

Thanks to Britain's robust intervention, UNAMSIL was able to deploy troops throughout the country and provide crucial assistance in restoring peace and promoting human rights, permitting a level of security not seen in Sierra Leone for many years. In January 2002, a special ceremony celebrated the successful disarmament of over 45,000 fighters, and a few months later President Kabbah was returned to power in peaceful and orderly elections. Democracy was fragile but there was a good chance of the decade-long nightmare being over.

It is, however, important to note that this satisfactory outcome was far from certain when the paratroopers were deployed. Conditions were dangerous (as demonstrated when eleven British soldiers were captured, and one of them lost his life) and there were strongly expressed fears of 'mission creep' and 'a return of the "Somalia syndrome"'.[29] Nor were other states keen to assist, and the UN had to scratch around for replacements when Jordan, Egypt and India decided to withdraw their peacekeepers. As the mission wobbled, Britain had to reverse the scaling down of her troops and send in more soldiers to help train the army and support it in repelling the rebels, to restore peace and to help rebuild the country.

EXPANDING PEACE ENFORCEMENT

War against the Taleban and Terrorism

The concept of international peace and security has been further extended as a means of justifying peace enforcement in two additional contexts. The first relates to international terrorism. Thus in 2001 a UN resolution was invoked by the US as authorising it to lead a coalition against the Taleban regime in Afghanistan because the latter refused to root out terrorism based on its soil. This occurred in the immediate wake of the 11 September 2001 attacks on the World Trade Centre's twin towers in New York and on the Pentagon in Washington, DC. (These events are often spoken of as '9/11', from the style Americans use for writing dates.) Within twenty-four hours the General Assembly and Security Council had passed unopposed, hard-hitting resolutions, and, in an unprecedented gesture of solidarity, the Council stood up to vote for SCR 1368 (which condemned those responsible and called on all states to help bring them to justice). Three weeks later, the Security Council passed a very far-reaching resolution (SCR 1373) banning all forms of support for terrorism; obliging states to cooperate in eliminating the terrorist threat; and establishing a Security Council Counter-Terrorism Committee to monitor the implementation of the resolution. SCR 1373 was generally deemed to give a legal endorsement to armed action against the perceived perpetrators of these and earlier anti-American terrorist acts (Osama bin Laden and his al-Qaeda network), and against the Taleban regime in Afghanistan when it refused to give them up.

This last campaign – Operation Enduring Freedom – was launched on 7 October 2001. It was an essentially American campaign in which only Britain participated militarily in the first wave of attacks. However, after the fall of the Taleban regime in

November, the UN returned to centre-stage. It sponsored the Bonn talks that paved the way for the return to consensual government in Afghanistan. Together with other aid agencies, it delivered massive humanitarian relief to the people of Afghanistan. The UN was also charged with, amongst other things, assisting the Afghans in creating a new constitution and a central bank, and with strengthening the civil service and improving human rights – the work of its agencies being consolidated, in March 2002, into the United Nations Assistance Mission in Afghanistan. In addition, the UN authorised the despatch of a 5000-strong International Security Assistance Force to Kabul and its surrounding areas in order to foster a secure environment for the political transition in Afghanistan. In this way, 2 million Afghan refugees were able to return from exile, the largest repatriation of refugees in three decades.

The war against the Taleban has sometimes been seen as a collective security operation. It was collective in the sense that there was widespread support for action, it being generally felt that with the events of 9/11, 'an unacceptable line had been crossed'.[30] Moreover, the New York attacks occurred only about four miles away from UN headquarters, where security scares heightened the psychological impact on world leaders who had arrived for the General Assembly, loved New York, and did not want to be on the receiving end of similar assaults. The relevant Security Council resolutions were unanimously endorsed, and during a week-long General Assembly debate on measures to eliminate international terrorism, an unprecedented 167 member states and four observers participated. America's NATO, OAS and ANZUS (Australia, New Zealand and United States) partners quickly invoked their treaty obligations to support the United States; ten states offered the use of ground forces in Afghanistan; another 130 states offered a diverse range of military assistance; and leading states such as China, Egypt, Mexico and Russia announced support for the US campaign.

Nevertheless, the war against the Taleban was not collective security. This was, first, because Operation Enduring Freedom was initially waged by just two states.[31] Secondly, the attacks on the USA did not come from a state. And thirdly, they were totally unrelated to annexation. Nor did the Security Council explicitly authorise action against the Taleban although the key resolutions (SCRs 1368 and 1373) affirmed – in the context of 9/11 – the inherent right of individual and collective self-defence, and the need to 'combat by all means' the 'threats to international peace and security caused by terrorist acts'. Thus the case is better seen as one of peace enforcement.

Iraq, 2002–3

The economic sanctions imposed on Iraq in the build-up to the 1991 Gulf war remained in force pending the fulfilment of the terms of that year's ceasefire resolution (SCR 687), particularly the demand which it and other resolutions made for the elimination of Iraq's (supposed) weapons of mass destruction (WMD). Because, however, sanctions appeared to cause great hardship to the weak, the poor and the vulnerable, the UN instituted a unique 'oil for food programme' in December 1996. It permitted the proceeds of controlled sales of petroleum to be used for purchasing items such as food and medicine; for UN-administered assistance to Kurds in the north; for meeting claims against Iraq; and for the costs of operating an observer mission on the Iraq–Kuwait border and a UN Special Commission (UNSCOM) that was charged (together with the International Atomic Energy Agency) with overseeing the dismantling of Iraq's WMD.

Meanwhile, however, Saddam was using some of Iraq's earnings for his own purposes, and defying Security Council resolutions in a cat and mouse game of 'cheat and retreat'.[32] He would lie about Iraqi weapons until he was caught out, at which point the threat of an imminent American attack to enforce compliance with UN resolutions would produce promises of cooperation with UNSCOM. In time, coalition fatigue set in and attention shifted to conflicts elsewhere. By 1997 a number of states, including three of the P5 (China, France and Russia), had had enough. They were tired of sanctions, of UNSCOM, of America's periodic use of cruise missiles to punish Saddam for trying to thwart UNSCOM, and of Anglo-American enforcement of the (legally contentious) 'no-fly zones'. (These zones had been established to protect the Kurds and others in the north and the Shia Muslims and Marsh Arabs of the south from Iraqi government attacks.)[33]

This enabled Saddam to drive a wedge between UNSCOM and the Security Council, implying it was UNSCOM that was the problem, not his alleged determination to have WMD. Deteriorating relations between Iraq and UNSCOM eventually led, at the end of 1998, to its withdrawal and the unleashing of US and British bombers over Iraq at the same time as the Security Council was considering the matter. There was much criticism of Britain and America, and Saddam refused to accept UNSCOM's designated successor, the UN Monitoring, Verification and Inspection Commission (UNMOVIC).

One of the effects of the terrorist attacks of 9/11 on America was that they made President George W. Bush determined on a showdown with the Iraqi regime, and military preparations for its removal were set in train. Only Britain's Prime Minister, Tony Blair, unambiguously supported him, most of the rest of the world expressing considerable disquiet. Britain and America contended that Saddam's flouting of UN Security Council resolutions[34] permitted the overthrow of a brutal and aggressive dictator who had shown no compunction about using chemical weapons during the Iran–Iraq war and against the Kurds of northern Iraq. Critics insisted that force should not be used without explicit Security Council authorisation, and condemned President Bush's vendetta against Saddam as arrogant, improper, unwise, vengeful and unjustifiable. It was, they claimed, especially foolish to set about overthrowing a government at a time when other Middle East passions were also inflamed.

In September 2002, it seemed that President Bush had been won round to the multilateral route, as he told the General Assembly that the USA was going to 'work with the UN Security Council for the necessary resolutions'. There followed almost eight weeks of bargaining and delicate negotiations, leading to a unanimous Security Council resolution (SCR 1441). It led to the return of weapons inspectors in November and gave Iraq 'a final opportunity to comply with its disarmament obligations' or face 'serious consequences'.[35] SCR 1441's indirect and tortuous wording reflected the deep divisions within the Council. France, Russia and China (plus, probably, a majority of the rest of the Council, including Germany) wanted the inspectors to produce firm evidence of a 'smoking gun' before countenancing the use of force. This proved elusive. In its absence a final, legitimising, Security Council resolution was unlikely, as France was threatening to veto any such proposal. In mid-March 2003, therefore (by which time military preparations were complete), President Bush abandoned the UN route. He would have liked to have the UN's endorsement, but was not going to be held back by its absence. The United States, and those who could still be mustered, would go ahead on their own.[36]

Thus the UN had no role in the war that led to Saddam's downfall, beyond making adjustments to the 'oil for food' programme and providing humanitarian relief. And, at the war's end, it was to be the USA, not the UN, that administered Iraq. However, continuing difficulties in Iraq led the US to begin to look favourably on a possible UN role in the transition to a 'new' Iraq.

The events leading to the overthrow of the Saddam regime demonstrate two cardinal points about the UN. One is that so far as matters that need economic or military resources are concerned, it is the sovereign state, and not the UN, that is still on top. States may be willing to work through the UN, even to use it as their cat's-paw; but if the UN is not agreeable to that, determined states can act without its blessing. There may, as in the Iraqi case, be diplomatic costs for so doing. But the capability for independent action is undoubtedly there. This, however, draws attention to the second point: that, as the Iraqi crisis showed, the idea that only the UN confers legitimacy on military action has, since the end of the cold war, taken deep root. Many states, and also millions of people throughout the world (including many Americans and Britons), made it clear that they opposed the war because the Security Council did not expressly sanction it. Furthermore, considerable media coverage was given to the UN Secretary-General's statements and to the Council's debates (four of which were at foreign minister level during the run-up to war). Hence (and despite the fact that some American policy makers, such as the Vice-President and the Secretary of Defense, were throughout impatient and dismissive of the UN), Washington and London put great effort into explaining, justifying and seeking support for their line. They did not satisfy their fellow UN members. But if the UN and the values it stood for did not matter, they would hardly have engaged in such extensive activity.

While, therefore, the bypassing of the UN undoubtedly dealt a blow to its standing, there is no reason to suppose that it was either substantial or permanent. Provided there is no return to a cold war type of confrontation between the major powers, the UN is likely, in matters of war and peace, to retain a high profile.

PLANNING FOR THE FUTURE

During the 1990s the UN spent some time evaluating contemporary developments. Governments cautiously welcomed Boutros-Ghali's recommendations in his 1992 *Agenda for Peace*[37] and his follow-up 1994 report on *Improving the Capacity of the United Nations for Peacekeeping* (both written at the Security Council's request).[38] Not many of Boutros-Ghali's proposals were implemented, but the Srebrenica and Rwanda bloodbaths prompted a further major examination of peacekeeping. At the Secretary-General's invitation, a panel of experts under Lakhdar Brahimi (a former Algerian Foreign Minister) frankly assessed the shortcomings of the existing system, and drew up recommendations for the UN's future efforts to maintain international peace and security.

The Brahimi Report pointed out in its very first paragraph that 'over the last decade, the United Nations has repeatedly failed to meet the challenge' of protecting people from war, 'and it can do no better today'. While confirming that the traditional tenets of peacekeeping (consent, impartiality and use of force only in self-defence) should remain the bedrock of this endeavour, the Report also emphasised the need to avoid 'complicity with evil' by being prepared to switch to enforcement, giving peacekeepers 'robust rules of engagement' so they can defend themselves *and their mandate* 'against those who renege on commitments to a peace accord or otherwise seek to undermine it by violence'.[39] The Report also recommended that peacekeeping should no longer be regarded as *ad hoc* but should be recognised as a core UN activity (and therefore funded from the regular budget).[40] Meanwhile various improvements could be made in the management, organisation and deployment of peacekeeping operations, and states should designate stand-by military and civilian personnel who could be trained to work together and deployed at short notice.

The Brahimi Report was well received at the special heads of state and government Millennium Summit in September 2000 and led to 'an intense and constructive debate'.[41] Resources improved; useful changes were made to the Organisation's structure, systems and procedures; and effort was put into establishing an effective support structure for peace operations. But as Kofi Annan and his predecessor had repeatedly emphasised, the success or failure of peacekeeping operations depended, above all, on the attitudes of the disputants and the willingness of other UN members 'to use this invaluable instrument wisely and well. ... [A] peacekeeping operation cannot succeed if there is no peace to keep, if it lacks an appropriate mandate, or if it is not given the necessary material and political support in a timely fashion'.[42]

It would be splendid if states were willing to provide the funds to improve the running of peacekeeping operations; designate well trained and equipped stand-by battalions that could be plunged into nightmare scenarios; and generally contribute whatever is needed. But just how difficult that is in a world of sovereign states (who naturally pay close regard to their own conception of their interests) and hesitant great power leadership was underlined a few months after the Brahimi Report appeared: when the mission in Sierra Leone ran into difficulties that threatened 'the UN's reputation in Africa and the credibility of all UN peacekeeping operations'.[43] States paid lip-service to enhancing the UN's rapid deployment capability, but dawdled in responding to Secretariat requests: in December 2001, only nine states had provided the information essential for establishing a system of stand-by arrangements. The likelihood of going back to the Charter and giving the UN its own permanent force is even more remote.

CONCLUSION

The turbulence of the 1990s, combined with a widening interpretation of threats to peace, meant that the post-cold war UN was more active than ever before. It is true that the Organisation was sidelined during the three-week assault on Iraq in 2003, and that earlier there was disillusion following its failures in Somalia, Rwanda and Bosnia; but on the whole the UN was active and innovative in responding to the challenges of the day. Peacekeepers continued engaging in such traditional activities as monitoring ceasefires – as witnessed by the continued existence of the missions in Kashmir and Cyprus. But they also started engaging systematically in more extensive and complex activities than hitherto, and they began cooperating with regional bodies, non-governmental organisations and the private sector.

The fact that the UN tries to maintain the peace in often difficult circumstances, and that its efforts in this direction have expanded in recent years, reflects the extent to which the idea has taken hold that the world organisation has a responsibility not only to try to stop the fighting and relieve human suffering, but also to attack the underlying causes of strife. Now it is time to move on from the naive idealism and cynical despondency of the 1990s and recognise the 'immense worth' of international peacekeeping. As Alan James pointed out at the beginning of the post-cold war era, 'In relation to the control of international conflict, it is one of the more fruitful developments of the twentieth century.'[44]

NOTES

1. Report of the Secretary-General on the work of the Organisation, 1991, UN document DPI/1168 4023.
2. Final Report of the Secretary-General on the United Nations Observer Mission in Liberia, 12 September 1997, UN document S/1997/712.
3. Report of the Secretary-General on the work of the organisation, 6 September 2001, UN document, A/56/1.
4. Gareth Evans, 'The Comprehensive Political Settlement to the Cambodian Conflict: An Exercise in Cooperating for Peace', in Hugh Smith (ed.), *International Peacekeeping: Building on the Cambodian Experience* (Canberra: Australian Defence Studies Centre, 1994), p. 12.
5. General Dallaire, quoted in Samantha Power, ' "Bystanders to Genocide": Why the United States Let the Rwandan Tragedy Happen', *Atlantic Monthly*, September 2001, www.theatlantic.com/issues/2001/09/power.htm. Cf. Report of the Independent Inquiry into the Actions of the United Nations during the 1994 Genocide in Rwanda, 15 December 1999, UN document S/1999/1257. (Subsequently referred to as 'Independent Inquiry into Rwanda Genocide'.)
6. Steven R. Ratner, quoted in Robert C. Johansen, 'Overlooked and Underutilized: International Enforcement by United Nations Civilian Police', paper presented at the International Studies Association annual convention, Minneapolis, March 1998.
7. Michael W. Doyle, quoted in ibid.
8. Richard Holbrooke (former US ambassador to the UN), quoted in Alan Bullion, 'India in Sierra Leone: a Case of Muscular Peacekeeping', *International Peacekeeping*, vol. 8, no. 4 (Winter 2001), p. 86.
9. Brian Urquhart, 'In the Name of Humanity', *New York Review of Books*, 27 April 2000.
10. *The Times*, 31 July 1998.
11. *The Times*, 5 September 1997.
12. Misha Glenny, 'Star Witness's Next Challenge is to Rebuild Lawless Wastes', *The Times*, 16 March 2002.

13. Report of the Secretary-General, 'International Civilian Support Mission in Haiti', 19 April 2001, UN document A/55/905.

14. See Power, 'Bystanders to genocide'.

15. Ibid.

16. Rwanda's population at the beginning of 1994 had been approximately 7.6 million, of whom 800,000 were slaughtered, 3 million were internally displaced, and over 2 million fled to neighbouring countries.

17. 'Independent Inquiry into Rwanda Genocide'.

18. 'Interventions After the Cold War', in supplementary volume to the Report of the International Commission on Intervention and State Sovereignty, *The Responsibility to Protect* (Ottawa: International Development Research Centre, 2001), p. 79. (Subsequently referred to as *The Responsibility to Protect*.)

19. This chart is based on one drawn up by Jane Boulden in *Peace Enforcement: The UN Experience in Congo, Somalia and Bosnia* (London: Praeger, 2001) and reproduced in Yumi Narita, 'UN Peacekeeping Operation in Bosnia-Herzegovina and its Problems', unpublished MA dissertation, Keele University, 2002, p. 16.

20. Kofi A. Annan, *'We the Peoples': The Role of the United Nations in the Twenty-first Century* (New York: United Nations Department of Public Information, 2000), p. 48.

21. *Independent*, 29 October 1994.

22. 'Interventions After the Cold War', in *The Responsibility to Protect*, p. 97.

23. Stephen Ellis, 'Warlords and Criminals Fill the Power Vacuum', *The Times*, 9 May 2000.

24. SCR 1289 (2000), 7 February 2000.

25. Editorial, 'Somalia Revisited', *The Times*, 9 May 2000.

26. In March 2001 it was enlarged again, to 17,500.

27. Bullion, 'India in Sierra Leone', p. 80.

28. Quoted in 'Interventions After the Cold War', in *The Responsibility to Protect*, p. 109.

29. Editorial, 'In Sierra Leone', *The Times*, 10 May 2000; 'Setback for Peace Missions in Africa', *The Times*, May 2000.

30. Sir Jeremy Greenstock (British ambassador to the UN), 'Annual review of the UN, 2001', 18 January 2002, www.fco.gov.uk.

31. This reflected doubts about whether agreement could have been reached on sending a UN force, or whether such a force would have been militarily successful.

32. Lawrence Freedman, 'Cheat and Retreat', *The Times Literary Supplement*, 12 January 2001.

33. Two days after the declaration of a safe haven for the Kurds on 8 April 1991, the UN ordered Iraq to end all military action in the area, including air force flights. This was the first 'no-fly zone'. On 26 August 1992 the USA declared a 'no-fly zone' below the 32nd parallel in the south of Iraq. This was justified by reference to SCR 688 (1991), which established the Kurdish safe haven, but SCR 668 did not specifically mention the south. On 3 September 1996 the southern 'no-fly zone' was extended to the 33rd parallel, just south of Baghdad. American and British aircraft patrolled the zones and struck against any violations and provocations from Iraqi air defences. Many states and observers contested the legality of this enforcement effort. The 'no-fly zones' were lifted in April 2003 at the end of the war against Iraq.

34. According to the FCO, Iraq had only partially complied with two provisions out of nine resolutions, putting it in breach of 23 out of 27 separate obligations under Chapter VII

of the UN Charter. See www.fco.gov.uk/servlet/Front?pagename=OpenMarket/Xcel; Jack Straw speech, 'A Challenge We Must Confront', 11 February 2003; US White House background paper, 'A Decade of Deception and Defiance', 12 September 2002, http://usinfo.state.gov/regional/nea/iraq/text/0912wthsbkgd.htm#defiance.

35. SCR 1441, 8 November 2002.

36. Out of America's proclaimed 45 coalition partners, only Britain and, to a much lesser extent, Australia gave active military support.

37. These included 'the importance of precise mandates, periodic review of these mandates, prior agreement of the government and the parties concerned, impartiality in carrying out the mandates, the authority of the Council to authorize all means necessary for UN forces to carry out their mandate, the exercise, if necessary, by UN forces of the inherent right of self-defence, and the urgent need for political settlement and the avoidance of indefinite peacekeeping operations'. See Juergen Dedring, 'The Security Council', in Paul Taylor and A. J. R. Groom, *The United Nations at the Millennium: The Principal Organs* (London, New York: Continuum, 2000), p. 87.

38. The latter should be distinguished from the report which he produced in January 1995: Supplement to an Agenda for Peace: Position Paper of the Secretary-General on the Occasion of the Fiftieth Anniversary of the United Nations (UN document S/1995/1).

39. Report of the Panel on UN Peacekeeping Operations, 17 August 2000, UN document A/55/305, S/2000/809,10.

40. In his Millennium Report, Kofi Annan wrote: 'Our system for launching operations has sometimes been compared to a volunteer fire department, but that description is too generous. Every time there is a fire we must first find fire engines and the funds to run them before we can start dousing any flames. The present system relies almost entirely on last minute, ad hoc arrangements, that guarantee delay, with respect to the provision of civilian personnel even more so than military'. See *We the Peoples*, p. 49.

41. Report of the Secretary-General, 'Implementation of the Recommendations of the Special Committee on Peacekeeping Operations and the Panel on United Nations Peace Operations', 21 December 2001, A/56/732.

42. Ibid., cf. Daily Press Briefing of the Office of the Spokesman for the Secretary-General, 23 October 2000.

43. Editorial, 'Somalia Revisited', *The Times*, 9 May 2000.

44. Alan James, *Peacekeeping in International Politics* (London: Macmillan, 1990), p. 370.

chapter 7

The Post-Cold War UN

The record of the post-cold war United Nations has been mixed. There have been two dynamic Secretaries-General, one of whom was widely seen as having fallen from grace while the other shared the Nobel Peace Prize with the Organisation. The General Assembly was more pragmatic and less confrontational, but this made it less exciting than in the past and it was somewhat upstaged by the UN conferences and summits that proliferated in the 1990s. The Assembly was also eclipsed by the Security Council, which was back in business with a vengeance. The international climate enabled the International Court at last to flourish. Human rights and humanitarianism were frequently violated, but important steps were taken by the UN: the position of UN High Commissioner for Human Rights emerged and the creation of war crimes tribunals presaged the establishment of a permanent International Criminal Court (see Chapter 12).

But while the UN's performance has often been positive, important elements in the United States viewed it through acutely sensitive and hostile eyes. To them it seemed that there was still a lot wrong with the world body, and that their country was paying too much for it. This had two damaging consequences. First, the USA continued to withhold funding, which meant that the ongoing financial crisis deepened. Secondly, the USA exercised its financial and political muscle against those individuals and aspects of the UN's work that it did not like. Not surprisingly this aroused fierce resentment, and America was accused of arrogance by those who were piqued at its dominance of the UN.

RETURN TO THE CHARTER: THE REJUVENATION OF THE SECURITY COUNCIL

At the beginning of the 1980s a rejuvenation of the Security Council was under way. Although this was far from evident at the time we can see clearly, in retrospect, that the five permanent members (P5) were developing a collegiate attitude, the non-aligned were working together more closely, and (with the assistance of the Secretary-General, Pérez de Cuéllar) the Council was moving towards better working practices and the adoption of common policies.

By the mid-1980s, decisions were being taken in 'informal consultations of the whole' – unofficial, off-the-record meetings held next door to the Council Chamber. Formal meetings turned into occasions for speeches for the record and rubber-stamping consensuses that had been achieved in private, particularly by the P5. Voting patterns reflected this development. From 1980 onwards the Council achieved unanimity more often than not, and between 1980 and 1985 the P5 voted together on 75 out of 119 resolutions, and just 29 resolutions were vetoed.

In the second half of the 1980s, there was even greater harmony, largely because the new leader of the USSR, Mikhail Gorbachev, had turned to the UN to try to protect his crumbling Soviet empire, giving it pride of place in his 'new thinking' about Soviet foreign policy. The Council's voting figures give a striking indication of this. Between 1986 and July 1990 the P5 voted together on 68 out of the 79 resolutions adopted; the non-aligned nearly always agreed; and both groups agreed more than they differed. The July 1987 Security Council resolution (SCR) demanding a ceasefire in the Iran–Iraq war was an instance of the increased harmony, signalling the emergence of a P5 concert. When Iran eventually accepted the resolution a year later, the superpowers displayed new-found amity by jointly providing transport for the peacekeeping mission despatched to supervise the war's ending.

Figure 7.1 demonstrates the extent of the Security Council's activity. After the end of the cold war in December1989, the Security Council went into almost constant session, often using lengthy informal consultations for substantive discussions, and

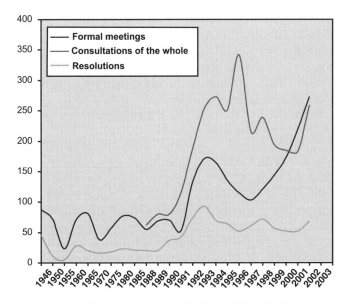

Figure 7.1   Security Council Activity*

*Sources: Reports of the Security Council to the General Assembly, 1994–2002; Michael J. R. Young, 'The Impact of a Changing International Environment on the Decisions and Practices of the United Nations Security Council: 1946–1995', unpublished PhD thesis, Keele University, 2001. The UN has no record of consultations of the whole of the Security Council before 1988.

brief, formal meetings to pass (numerous) resolutions that had already been privately agreed. Between August 1990 and the end of 1999 it approved 625 SCRs (almost twice as many as in the whole of the UN's preceding 44 years), and it did so with a considerable degree of consensus. Only seven vetoes were cast.

As we have seen, the Council was notably active in passing resolutions under Chapter VII of the Charter (the section dealing with enforcement measures). During the 1990s there were 158 Chapter VII resolutions (123 of them unanimous). By contrast, only 17 Chapter VII resolutions were passed between 1946 and 1989.

These developments reflected not only the existence of a new 'concert of powers', but also the UN's central role in international relations and an important twentieth-century development that lay at the heart of the Charter: the belief that great powers had responsibility for maintaining international order and that they should exercise their power through the world organisation. However, the success of the Security Council was accompanied by underdog suspicion and envy, and a countervailing twentieth-century doctrine – the democratic ideal – was invoked to justify reforming the Security Council so that more states would have a say in its deliberations.

REFORM OF THE SECURITY COUNCIL

The 'Question of equitable representation and increase in the membership of the Security Council' was inscribed on the General Assembly agenda in 1979. However, it did not become a pressing issue until the early 1990s when the Security Council began acting as envisaged by the Charter. This brought to the fore the inherent jealousy, antipathy and distrust felt towards the Security Council by states that rarely stood a chance of being elected, and that were indignant about so much work being done in unaccountable, secret, informal consultations. The exclusionary nature of the Security Council's sanctions and monitoring committees (which replicate the membership of the Security Council and conduct their business by consensus and *in camera*) heightened feelings of alienation. So did perceptions of a Western-dictated agenda and the application of double standards.

Five responses can be made to complaints about the Security Council's functioning since the end of the cold war. First, closed sessions were not novel and, anyway, what goes on in the Security Council is seldom secret for long. Secondly, Western dominance is not new. Thirdly, selectivity in invoking and applying sanctions under Chapter VII is inevitable. This is because the Security Council is a political organ with a limited and unbalanced membership; because, although the Security Council does not ignore international norms, its decisions are based on the perceived national interests of its members and are the outcome of bargaining and bartering over votes; and because the veto also plays a part in determining what can, and cannot, be done. Fourthly, in practice there has generally been widespread agreement on broad issues, but its expression in Chapter VII resolutions may produce a mutinous response outside the Council chamber. For example, there was unanimous condemnation of terrorism after the events of 11 September 2001, but fierce complaints about the binding and far-reaching anti-terrorism resolutions that were subsequently passed by the Security Council. And, fifthly, the Security Council's agenda is far from being dominated by issues that only matter to the West. At the end of the twentieth century, conflicts in Africa occupied three-quarters of the Security Council's time, and treating HIV/AIDS as a threat to international peace and security (so that it might be discussed) was a move in a direction of particular concern to many third world states, especially in Africa.

But it was not just the busyness of the Security Council that gave rise to calls for reform. American demands for changes in the UN system encouraged such talk. And, by insisting on such changes before it paid off its huge debts to the Organisation, the USA invited questions about its own position. Reform was also in the air because of a strong desire that the Organisation should play a significant and effective humanitarian role. Meanwhile, as the international system shook off the rigidity of cold war constraints, those who were likely to gain from any restructuring became vocal in asserting their claims. They condemned the existing structure for being Eurocentric and rooted in an outdated 1945 balance of power. Such complaints gained added weight when the Russian Federation succeeded to the Soviet Union's Security Council seat in December 1991, while Germany and Japan were still not included among the permanent members. The UN's fiftieth anniversary in 1995 encouraged further discussion about the Organisation's future.

Complaints about the Council's working methods, and demands that it operate more transparently, were the easiest to deal with. A good number of 'small but efficient improvements' (such as more frequent open meetings, making draft resolutions available, and providing better, more timely and more informative reports to the General Assembly) contributed to 'a more cordial overall atmosphere'[1] and made the Security Council's proceedings more open and more transparent. Moreover, the so-called 'Arria formula' (which draws a distinction between meetings of *members of the Council* and meetings of the Council *per se*) made it possible to open the Council up to outside viewpoints and influences by holding informal, frank briefing sessions with invited experts, and later on, with non-governmental organisations (such as Oxfam, Médecins sans Frontières, CARE, Amnesty International and the International Peace Academy).[2] In 2000 another step forward was taken when the Council met the Chairman of the US Senate Committee on Foreign Relations, Jesse Helms. (At Arria formula 'meetings of members of the Council', non-Council members are permitted to attend in a silent capacity.)

All this is not a satisfactory substitute for tackling the main problem: the need to restructure the Council. But that has proved utterly elusive. Some changes are relatively uncontroversial, such as increasing the size of the Security Council, though enlarging the Council to, say, 24 or 30 members might lead to a loss of the cordial relationship and intimate atmosphere that facilitates swift and effective action. Nor does there seem to be any significant criticism of the Council's power to take binding decisions. But the criteria for having a permanent seat and a veto, the ratio between permanent and non-permanent members, and whether the veto should be limited to Chapters VI and VII of the Charter, are controversial.

It has often been suggested that any additional permanent seats should be allocated on a regional basis. However, jostling African, Asian and Latin American states have been unable to agree on a single candidate for each of their proposed veto-wielding permanent seats (or, in Africa's case, the two which it claims on the ground that it is the largest regional group). On the other hand, by putting emphasis on 'the principle on which the Charter is based ... that power must be commensurate with responsibility',[3] Japan and Germany (respectively the second and third largest financial contributors to the UN) would be obvious candidates. But adding Germany would give the Security Council an even heavier European weighting. Hence the proposal to evict Britain and France and create a single, European Union (EU) seat.

However, the notion of an EU seat has four flaws: Britain and France can veto it; despite their decline, Britain and France still carry weight in international relations and play a significant role in the maintenance of international peace and security; as the UN is an organisation of sovereign states it is odd to suggest that a permanent seat be given to a regional organisation (why not NATO instead of the EU?); and the EU has not yet demonstrated the degree of commonality in foreign policy which would be necessary for it to act effectively on the Council. All told, as a close observer has said, 'it is inconceivable that an accord can be engineered that would satisfy the ambitions of the status-seekers in the race for permanent seats in an enlarged Council'.[4]

The widely held belief that that veto is anachronistic and undemocratic is a useful political rallying-cry. But notions about democracy in the conduct of international relations are flawed. They ignore the extent to which democracy is not practised within states, and wrongly imply that international society is analogous to domestic society. In any case, if the veto were removed, the USA would surely quit the UN, other powerful states might follow suit, and the Organisation would no doubt become as enfeebled as the League of Nations.

Thus none of the proposed formulae for reforming the Security Council have been able to reconcile the conflicting requirements of representativeness, legitimacy, authority and effectiveness. Until states resolve the key questions of who shall have permanent seats and who a veto, the debate about Security Council reform will continue to be sterile. Even in the unlikely event of agreement being reached, the outcome is likely to be a disappointment and those who are dissatisfied might make sure that it is a very long time before the General Assembly has enough positive votes (a two-thirds majority) to begin the process of amending the Charter.

THE US–UN SAGA

As we have seen in previous chapters, multilateralism does not come easily to the USA. One reason is that its constitutional arrangements permit domestic politics to impinge significantly on America's relations with multilateral institutions. Another is that the US has a fierce determination to protect its independence. In addition, there is a strong idealistic streak; a tendency to equate what is best for America with what is best for the world; and a sense of possessiveness towards the UN that is derived from a vivid awareness that the USA was its chief creator. Americans therefore tend to assume that they are uniquely qualified to pronounce on what should and should not be done[5] and to use American muscle accordingly. Moreover, as the world's greatest power, the USA does not incline towards, or feel the need of, compromise and accommodation to any great extent. Nor has it found it very comfortable in the UN to encounter unwelcome and unpleasant international realities that draw attention to the limitations of American values, power, and freedom of manoeuvre. The

UN also comes low in American foreign policy priorities, as is indicated by recurring delays in despatching ambassadors to New York.

There was a brief flirtation with the UN following the end of the cold war and the expulsion of Iraq from Kuwait; but the USA was still out of tune with many other UN members, as can be seen from its negative votes in the General Assembly. Under President George Bush, in 1992 it voted against 61 per cent of adopted resolutions, a record 'unmatched even by Israel, the second most "nonaccommodating" member, which had a record of voting against the majority ... 45 per cent of the time'. There was only a slight dip the following year when, under President Bill Clinton, the USA voted against the majority 56.7 per cent of the time.[6]

Clinton had, in fact, initially adopted a pro-UN policy, but this was stymied when the 1993 Somalia débâcle gave neo-isolationist, conservative Americans the opportunity they sought to attack the Organisation. A combination of electoral considerations, Republican domination of Congress after the mid-term 1994 elections, and the strong anti-UN sentiments of the powerful Chair of the Senate Foreign Relations Committee, Jesse Helms, meant that Clinton had to step warily. He blew cool on the UN, followed a vacillating policy, and tended to back down quickly and let the Organisation be blamed for things that went wrong. American hostility to, and distrust of, the President also rubbed off on the UN. Hence the return of fraught US–UN relations.

American opponents of the UN capitalised on widespread ignorance about the Organisation, exaggerating its weaknesses and American generosity, giving credibility to fantastic lies, and turning multilateralism into a 'dirty word'.[7] For example, the UN was wrongly said to owe money to the USA for peacekeeping, and to have exercised authority over US peacekeepers engaged in 'US' peacekeeping missions! Designating US landmarks (such as the Yellowstone National Park and Statue of Liberty) as World Heritage sites and/or Biosphere Reserves allegedly subverted US sovereignty. There were even rumours of mysterious 'little black helicopters' engaged in UN missions on US territory. As will be discussed below, the USA also came into conflict with the Secretary-General, Boutros Boutros-Ghali, and this made things worse. The Clinton administration leaked 'nasty' stories about him, and the 1996 Republican presidential candidate Robert Dole earned cheap campaign cheers by disparagingly referring to the Secretary-General as 'Boootrus Boootrus'-Ghali.[8]

The most high-profile feature of the difficult US–UN relationship, and one that was especially important because of its all-round adverse effects, was the UN's financing.

FINANCIAL WOES

The UN is not very expensive. In 2000 the budget for the UN's key functions – the Secretariat in New York, Geneva, Vienna, Nairobi and five regional commissions – was just $1.25 billion a year. That is, 4 per cent of New York City's annual budget, and nearly a billion dollars less than the annual costs of running Tokyo's fire department. The cost of two days of Operation Desert Storm against Iraq in 1991 – about $2 billion – would easily have covered all the UN's expenses, including peacekeeping and emergency operations, for a whole year.

But in the mid-1990s the UN's financial position was even worse than a decade earlier. There were four reasons for this. First, there had been a spectacular rise in the peacekeeping budget, which is assessed separately from the UN's regular expenses. Secondly, most states were chronically late in paying their UN contributions. Thirdly, in the early 1990s some governments, such as the Russian Federation and Ukraine, could not afford to pay contributions that had been calculated according to out-of-date Soviet economic statistics. Fourthly, states may withhold payments for political reasons. The greatest of these was the major contributor, the USA.

In 1990 Washington had returned to paying its UN contributions in full, and by the end of 1992 US debts had been considerably reduced. However, as the anti-UN campaign took off in the mid-1990s, and with the USA following a policy of zero budgetary growth, America returned to financial delinquency in a big way. Although Congress was generous in making voluntary contributions to many UN activities, it had come to believe that America was paying too much. In addition, the UN budget was a handy symbolic stick with which to beat the President and micromanage his foreign policy. In the mid-1990s the USA paid only roughly half its assessed contributions to the regular budget and peacekeeping operations; legislation that came into force in 1995 unilaterally cut America's share of the costs of each peacekeeping operation from 31 to 25 per cent; and specific conditions were attached to the payment of arrears. As unpaid US dues grew towards a quarter of the total, in 1996 it was (for the first time) voted off the influential Advisory Committee on Administrative and Budgetary Questions, a calculated snub that did not improve America's disposition towards the Organisation.

The United Nations tottered from one financial crisis to the next. The budget was slashed. The Secretary-General issued dire warnings of insolvency and cuts in services. Morale in the Secretariat sank as hundreds of officials were made redundant. Contributors to peacekeeping were left out of pocket.

There were many pleas for America to pay up, but it was the danger of automatically losing its General Assembly vote under Article 19 of the Charter that persuaded Congress to release funds.[9] In 1999, therefore, the USA made a payment of almost 50 per cent of its annual contribution to the regular budget. Meanwhile, more states began paying in full and on time. But the financial picture remained worrying because, first, the USA still owed huge sums. Secondly, UN expenditure had risen thanks to an expansion in peacekeeping and the increased cost of international criminal tribunals. Thirdly, years of negotiations between the President and Congress had resulted in the 1999 'Helms–Biden' law, which linked the payment of nearly $1 billion of US arrears to a cut in US contributions and the implementation of certain reforms. The accompanying threats to quit the UN if American demands were not met caused deep resentment amongst other members.

The US–UN financial conflict now turned into an increasingly acrimonious war about the scale of assessments, and the US ambassador was engaged in the stormiest and toughest negotiations of his career. So difficult were they that Senators Helms and Biden were stunned when American demands were met, and the Senate Foreign Relations Committee greeted the news with 'a historic standing ovation'.[10] Yet the deadlock was broken only at the last minute thanks to CNN's Ted Turner pledging $34 million to the UN. This was to cover the costs, for one year, of lowering American contributions to the regular budget from 25 to 22 per cent (thereby postponing the impact of consequential rate increases for other states). At the same time, 18 states shamed the USA by voluntarily increasing their share of the budget, and the P5 agreed to pay a larger share of peacekeeping costs. In this way, for the first time, the special responsibility of the P5 for the maintenance of peace was reflected in a financial premium.

Things did not run smoothly. Congress first stalled on paying arrears and then angrily withheld some of the money after America was (for the first time) voted off the Human Rights Commission while Libya and Sudan were elected.[11] However, the terrorist attacks on America on 11 September 2001 (9/11), and the remarkable outpouring of support manifested at the UN, had a remarkable effect. America's 2001 assessment, together with a huge chunk of the peacekeeping arrears, were swiftly forthcoming and Congress rushed to approve Bush's nominee as ambassador to the UN.[12]

Nevertheless, President George W. Bush's unilateralist inclinations were still very evident: he pulled out of the 1997 Kyoto Protocol on Global Warming; took a tough line in the Security Council over Iraq and Israel; refused to sign the 1997 Ottawa Agreement on Landmines and the 1989 Convention on the Rights of the Child; withdrew from the 1972 Anti-Ballistic Missile Treaty; and adopted a stony face towards the creation of an International Criminal Court.

THE GENERAL ASSEMBLY AND THE GROWTH IN UN MEMBERSHIP

The General Assembly's glory days of the 1960s and 1970s ended in disillusion. The campaign for a New International Economic Order failed amidst emerging divisions within the South, and these were exacerbated by the debt crisis and international public aid crisis (which also shifted attention away from the General Assembly towards the World Bank and the International Monetary Fund). The collapse of cold war rivalry removed a factor that had fostered coalitions and enabled the third world to some extent to play off the United States against the Soviet Union. And the rejuvenation of the Security Council was at the expense of the General Assembly, the proceedings of which became less dramatic and had a softer tenor.

Each year the General Assembly agenda is crowded; its meetings extend well past the traditional December closing date; and it approves hundreds of resolutions and decisions. However, not all this effort is well spent. Attempts at streamlining and rationalising General Assembly activities, so as to make it and its programmes more targeted and efficient, have had little impact. There is wastage and duplication of effort, and representatives from states with few resources are overwhelmed.

Yet the General Assembly of the twenty-first century has three considerable strengths. First, as indicated above, it is more workmanlike and down-to-earth than in the 1970s. This was reflected in the Millennium Declaration adopted at a special, three-day Millennium Summit of world leaders (held to coincide with the opening of the September 2000 Assembly). This agreed fifteen-year targets for tackling specific, key problems. These included halving extreme poverty, hunger and the number of people without access to safe drinking water; achieving universal primary education and gender equality; considerably reducing child and maternal mortality; reversing the spread of HIV/AIDS; tackling third world debt; ensuring environmental sustainability; promoting the use of information and communications technology for development; and putting an end to the use of child-soldiers. So far, states have not demonstrated much determination to turn the vision into reality, but setting the goals and commissioning annual progress reports thereon constitutes a new north–south 'global deal' that could influence international cooperation.

The General Assembly's second strength is that, as demonstrated by an influx of additional members, the UN is a prestigious organisation. The growth in UN numbers was most obviously due to the collapse of the Soviet empire, the dismemberment of Yugoslavia, and the tail end of decolonisation elsewhere. It also reflected the triumph of universalism over the notion that tiny states (such as San Marino) lack the capacity to assume the obligations of UN membership. Universalism also won out over Switzerland's fears that the Charter's collective security provisions were incompatible with Switzerland's traditionally neutral posture. Thus, by the end of 2002, the UN had 191 members. The Vatican State is now the only indisputably sovereign state outside the world body.

The General Assembly's third strength is that it is now a more representative organ as well as being the most important multilateral diplomatic meeting-place in the world. In 2002, for example, participants in the opening debate included 33 heads of state, 14 heads of government, 14 deputy prime ministers and 110 foreign ministers.[13] The Fiftieth Anniversary Assembly, in 1995, attracted about 140 world leaders. The Millennium Summit was the largest gathering of world leaders in history, with over 150 presidents, prime ministers and princes in attendance.

SPECIAL SESSIONS, SUMMITS AND CONFERENCES

Article 20 of the Charter allows the General Assembly to convene special sessions (see Table 7.1). It did this in connection with development and the New International Economic Order in 1975 and 1980, and disarmament in 1978, 1982 and 1988. In all, twenty-seven special sessions were held between 1947 and the end of 2002. In the same period it also used the 1950 'Uniting for Peace' procedure to hold ten emergency special sessions, just over half of them relating to the Middle East.

Meanwhile, the General Assembly and ECOSOC had also convened special, *ad hoc* conferences on specific questions whose interdisciplinary objectives seemed best suited to such a format (see Table 7.2). The first such major conference, on the environment, was held in Stockholm in 1972. Meetings of this kind became annual, and increased in frequency, number and size thanks to changing circumstances and developments not envisaged when the Charter was drawn up, as well as to the increased ease of transport and communication. Nearly 47,000 people attended the Earth Summit at Rio de Janeiro in 1992; nearly 50,000 went to the Beijing special summit on women in 1995; and 60,000 were at the Johannesburg Earth Summit in 2002. In 1990, 71 presidents and prime ministers were present at the child summit in New York; over a hundred went to the 2002 Johannesburg gathering.

The number of non-governmental organisations (NGOs) has mushroomed since 1945, and they have played a much greater role in the UN than was originally envisaged. Governments have sometimes resisted this, but NGOs have contributed

Table 7.1 General Assembly special sessions, 1945–2002*

Special session	Topic and document	Date of session	Requested or convened by
1st	Palestine	28 April to to 15 May 1947	United Kingdom
2nd	Palestine	16 April to 14 May 1948	Security Council
1st emergency	Middle East	1–10 September 1956	Security Council
2nd emergency	Hungary	4–10 November 1956	Security Council
3rd emergency	Middle East	8–24 August 1958	Security Council
4th emergency	Congo question	17–19 September 1960	Security Council
3rd	Tunisia	21–5 August 1961	38 Member States
4th	Financial situation of the UN	14 May to 27 June 1963	General Assembly
5th	South West Africa (Namibia)	21 April to 13 June 1967	General Assembly
5th emergency	Middle East	17 June to 18 September 1967	USSR
6th	Raw materials and development	9 April to 2 May 1974	Algeria
7th	Development and international economic cooperation	1–16 September 1975	General Assembly
8th	Financing of the UN Interim Force in Lebanon	20–1 April 1978	General Assembly
9th	Namibia	24 April to 3 May 1978	General Assembly
10th	Disarmament	23 May to 1 July 1978	General Assembly
6th emergency	Afghanistan	10–14 January 1980	Security Council
7th emergency	Palestine	22–9 July 1980, 20–8 April 1982, 25–6 June 1982, 16–19 August 1982, 24 September 1982	Senegal (Chairman, Palestinian Rights Committee)

Table 7.1 (*continued*)

Special session	Topic and document	Date of session	Requested or convened by
11th	New international economic order	25 August to 15 September 1980	General Assembly
8th emergency	Namibia	3–14 September 1981	Zimbabwe
9th emergency	Occupied Arab territories	29 January to 5 February 1982	Security Council
12th	Disarmament	7 June to 10 July 1982	General Assembly
13th	Africa	27 May to 1 June 1986	General Assembly
14th	Namibia	17 to 20 September 1986	General Assembly
15th	Disarmament	31 May to 25 June 1988	General Assembly
16th	Apartheid	12–14 December 1989	General Assembly
17th	Drug abuse	20–3 February 1990	General Assembly
18th	International economic cooperation	23–7 April 1990	General Assembly
10th emergency	Occupied East Jerusalem and the rest of the Occupied Palestinian territory	24–5 April 1997, 15 July 1997, 13 November 1997, 17 March 1998, 5, 8 and 9 February 1999, 18 and 20 October 2000, 20 December 2001, 7 May 2002, 5 August 2002	Qatar
19th	Earth summit + 5	23–7 June 1997	General Assembly
20th	World drug problem	8–10 June 1998	General Assembly
21st	Population and development (ICPD + 5)	30 June to 2 July 1999	General Assembly
22nd	Small island developing states	27–8 September 1999	General Assembly

Special session	Topic and document	Date of session	Requested or convened by
23rd	Women 2000: gender equality, development and peace for the twenty-first century (Beijing + 5 review)	5–9 June 2000	General Assembly
24th	World summit for social development and beyond: achieving social development for all in a globalised world	26–30 June 2000	General Assembly
25th	Implementation of the outcome of the United Nations Conference on Human Settlements (Habitat II)	June 2001	General Assembly
26th	Problem of human immunodeficiency virus/acquired immunodeficiency syndrome (HIV/AIDS) in all its aspects	25–7 June 2001	General Assembly
27th	Children	8–10 May 2002	General Assembly

* Article 20 of the Charter provides for the General Assembly to hold special sessions 'as occasion may require'. The Secretary-General convokes them at the request of the Security Council or a majority of UN members. Emergency special sessions are convened under the 1950 Uniting for Peace procedure.
Sources: www.un.org/ga/documents/lispss.htm, www.un.org/events/conferences.htm.

usefully and innovatively to UN conferences. They have been important in putting new issues on the international agenda; provided valuable, accessible, knowledge bases; and acted as the conscience of the world in respect of human rights. As the UN puts it, their participation in official and unofficial meetings has 'turned these conferences into true "global forums"'.[14] Business is another international actor whose collaboration has come to be regarded as important. Hence about 700 companies were represented at the 2002 Johannesburg Earth Summit, and business leaders were heavily involved in its debates.

UN conferences and summits have served a variety of purposes. They have helped develop new ideas; drawn attention to changing needs by redefining old problems and giving prominence to new, or increasingly salient, issues – such as children's rights and the environment; focused attention on matters that might otherwise be

Table 7.2 Selected UN conferences and world summits since 1964*

Date	Subject	Venue
March–June 1964	First UN conference on trade and development (UNCTAD I)	Geneva, Switzerland
August–September 1965	Population	Belgrade, Yugoslavia
April–May 1968	Human rights	Teheran, Iran
August 1968	Exploration and peaceful uses of outer space (UNISPACE I)	Vienna, Austria
May 1969	Tourism	Sofia, Bulgaria
September 1971	Peaceful uses of atomic energy	Geneva, Switzerland
June 1972	Human environment	Stockholm, Sweden
August 1974	Population	Bucharest, Romania
November 1974	Food	Rome, Italy
July 1975	International women's year	Mexico City, Mexico
May–June 1976	Human settlements (HABITAT I)	Vancouver, Canada
March 1977	Water	Mar del Plata, Argentina
September 1977	Desertification	Nairobi, Kenya
August 1978	Racism and racial discrimination	Geneva, Switzerland
September 1978	Technical cooperation among developing countries	Buenos Aires, Brazil
August 1979	Science and technology for development	Vienna, Austria
July 1980	Decade for women	Copenhagen, Denmark
August 1981	New and renewable sources of energy	Nairobi, Kenya
September 1981	Least developed countries	Paris, France
August 1982	Aging	Vienna, Austria
August 1982	Exploration and peaceful uses of outer space (UNISPACE II)	Vienna, Austria
August 1983	Racism and racial discrimination	Geneva, Switzerland
August 1984	Population	Mexico City, Mexico
July 1985	Conclusion of decade for women	Nairobi, Kenya
July 1987	Drug abuse and trafficking	Vienna, Austria
September 1987	Social welfare for development	Vienna, Austria
August–September 1987	Disarmament and development	New York
1987	Peaceful uses of nuclear energy	Geneva, Switzerland
September 1990	Least developed countries	Paris, France
September 1990	Children's summit	New York

Date	Subject	Venue
January 1992	Water and development	Dublin, Ireland
June 1992	Environment and development (Earth summit)	Rio de Janeiro, Brazil
June 1993	Human rights	Vienna, Austria
May 1994	Natural disaster prevention	Yokohama, Japan
September 1994	Population and development	Cairo, Egypt
March 1995	Social development	Copenhagen, Denmark
April–May 1995	Sustainable development of small island countries	Barbados
September 1995	Women and development	Beijing, China
June 1996	Human settlements (HABITAT II)	Istanbul, Turkey
November, 1996	Food summit	Rome, Italy
July 1999	Exploration and peaceful uses of outer space [UNISPACE III]	Vienna, Austria
April 2000	Crime and justice	Vienna, Austria
September 2000	Millennium summit: 'The role of the United Nations in the 21st century'	New York
May 2001	Least developed countries	Brussels, Belgium
July 2001	Illicit trade in small arms and light weapons	New York
August–September 2001	Racism, racial discrimination, xenophobia and related intolerance	Durban, South Africa
March 2002	Financing for development	Monterrey, Mexico
April 2002	Aging	Madrid, Spain
June 2002	Food	Rome, Italy
August September 2002	Sustainable development	Johannesburg, South Africa

* Article 20 of the Charter provides for the General Assembly to hold special sessions 'as occasion may require'. The Secretary-General convokes them at the request of the Security Council or a majority of UN members. Emergency special sessions are convened under the 1950 Uniting for Peace procedure.

Source: United Nations, Peter R. Baehr and Leon Gordenker, *The United Nations at the End of the 1990s*, 3rd edn (New York: St Martin's Press, 1999); Jacques Fomerand, 'UN Conferences: Media Events or Genuine Diplomacy?', *Global Governance*, vol. 2, no. 3 (September–December 1996); Peter Willetts, 'The Pattern of Conferences', in Paul Taylor and A. J. R. Groom, *Global Issues in the United Nations' Framework* (London: Macmillan, 1989).

neglected; helped to change international priorities; facilitated collaboration between different parts of the UN system and experts in different fields; created new international structures (such as the UN Conference on Trade and Development, the World Food Council, the UN Environment Programme, and the UN High Commissioner for Human Rights); set standards; codified international law; and catalysed political commitment behind draft conventions and programmes of action. Even if world leaders only put in fleeting appearances at such gatherings, they are forced to think about the issues arising and say something for the record about their states' policies.

The 1997 Kyoto Protocol to the UN Framework Convention on Climate Change offers a good example of the possibilities and limits of a standard-setting conference. By stating in a treaty the acceptable level of emissions of greenhouse gases, the weight of law is thrust behind individual commitments, and non-adherents will face added pressure to sign up to internationally agreed standards. The process had taken off in 1992 at the Rio (de Janeiro) Earth Summit (on the environment and development), where a 'Framework' Convention on Climate Change was signed (President Bush doing so in a last-minute dash to Rio). However, it was soon decided that the Framework Convention needed strengthening, and this was done in 1997 at a conference in Japan that adopted the Kyoto Protocol. A follow-up summit in Buenos Aires in 1998 negotiated the implementation of the treaty.

However, in 2001 President George W. Bush announced that he had decided against ratifying the Protocol, which President Clinton had signed but not submitted to the Senate for ratification. This produced a rift with many of America's closest partners and struck a body blow at the likely effectiveness of the instrument given that the USA (with just 6 per cent of the world's population) produced 25 per cent the world's emissions of carbon monoxide (one of the major greenhouse gasses). None the less, as a hundred states had ratified the Kyoto Protocol at the end of 2002, the treaty has clearly set an international standard for greenhouse emissions, and the USA and other non-signatories will be under continuing pressure to meet it.

The problem of persuading a superpower to comply with the product of UN conferences is just one of the misgivings that have been expressed about them. There have been other criticisms: their over-ambitiousness, frequency and cost; their duplication of work; their tendency to avoid or redefine problems and produce tediously ambiguous texts on which everyone can agree; their failure to make any significant progress in tackling particular problems; and the inclination towards inaction once the fanfare is over. Yet the object of UN jamborees is not to take authoritative decisions. Like General Assembly resolutions, they are political events aimed at attracting attention to issues and expressing approval or disapproval of competing claims. They may also fall foul of political disagreement, as illustrated by two recent conferences: the 2001 Durban Conference against Racism and the 2002 Johannesburg Earth Summit.

The omens for the Durban conference were not good and it ended in tatters. This was because of the pervading 'atmosphere of mistrust and ambush',[15] in which Arab and Asian delegates battled to have Israel's treatment of Palestinians deemed 'a new kind of apartheid'; insisted that there had been many holocausts, not just one; and demanded that Israel 'pay full compensation' to Palestinians (who were described as 'living under a foreign military occupying power').[16] There were also calls for former slave-holding nations to apologise and pay reparations for slavery. Eventually, the Americans and Israelis walked out, complaining that the conference had been taken over by Islamic extremists, and the European Union states said they would cease participating.

The Johannesburg Earth Summit was two years in the making and the largest UN conference ever. But it was an unhappy occasion. To industrialised states, it looked as if the poor states had compiled 'a shopping list' with a view to extracting subsidies.[17] The agreement that emerged from the conference was a feeble affair. Apart from proposing to halve the number of people without access to sanitation, and to set up an international network of marine reserves, the seventy-page final document consisted of 'a combination of warm words, rehashed promises or targets that are so vague or aspirational that they are in any practical sense meaningless'.[18]

It had also been produced in a rancorous atmosphere in which the Zimbabwean and Namibian leaders openly attacked Britain's Prime Minister for being a colonialist and there was fury at the USA's scornful attitude. The proceedings dismally ended 'in farce and disgrace', with the US Secretary of State being interrupted by jeering, slow hand-clapping, heckling and disorderly behaviour, and a mass walk-out.

Expectations at Johannesburg had been 'too high and the very concept of a grand meeting raised concerns about second-rate showmanship by Third World bullies'.[19] Hence Kofi Annan's warning about 'summit fatigue' and the advisability of reversing the trend towards a dramatic rise in the number of UN meetings. Smaller, more specific conferences of experts are also less likely than mega-summits to be 'hijacked by activists and dictators alike to bolster their own standing at Earth's expense'.[20]

NON-POLITICAL ORGANS

Unlike the Security Council, the 'non-political' organs of the UN proper (as distinct from its specialised agencies) were not revivified by the end of the cold war. Indeed, a harsher spotlight was thrown on their deficiencies. As Boutros-Ghali had pointed out at the beginning of the 1990s, piecemeal measures, establishing bureaucracies 'as substitutes for problem-solving and . . . in some cases, to camouflage problems rather than expose them to serious attention', had led to chaos. Duplication was 'widespread; coordination [wa]s often nominal; bureaucratic battles aimed at monopolizing a particular subject [we]re rife, and organizational objectives [we]re sometimes in conflict'.[21] Some organs continued to discuss contentious political issues which were by no means directly relevant to their activities. It could even be said that a few of these bodies seemed to be sustained solely by the vested interests of bureaucrats and member states, and no longer did useful work even if they had once done so. The Secretary-General recommended introducing a flexible, high-level mechanism to enable ECOSOC to respond in a continuous and timely way to new developments. But he had no power to bang heads together.

However, the lessening desire to score political goals in the General Assembly and ECOSOC had produced a more pragmatic and goal-oriented supervision of agencies, and an emphasis on 'proper monitoring and evaluation'. As Nigel White put it, the General Assembly 'is trying to manage the system instead of treating agencies as entirely separate'.[22] The reforms Kofi Annan has been making have also been beneficial. They have led to a more dynamic and proactive approach towards coordination between departments, funds and programmes; less overlap and duplication; and the introduction of coordination mechanisms for UN bodies in the field. Agencies that have not always worked together in the past have begun collaborating and working with governments, foundations and the private sector.

One agency whose fortunes have improved has been UNESCO. Britain re-joined as soon as a Labour government was elected in 1997, even though Federico Mayor had allegedly failed during his term as Director to do away with 'financial indiscipline, nepotism, cronyism and, even more ominously, irrelevance'. Management was expensive, 'top heavy and inefficient', and programmes were 'stuffed with old baggage, activities too small and ill-designed to make an impact'.[23] The election of Mayor's successor, the former Japanese ambassador to France, Koichiro Matsuura, was an unhappy affair in which the Japanese were said to have engaged in 'chicanery, influence-buying and ruthless diplomatic deception'.[24] However, the Bush White House was satisfied with Matsuura's dramatic reform of UNESCO's management structure and the organisation's new dedication to freedom of the press. In 2003 the USA rejoined UNESCO.

Meanwhile, the World Health Organisation (WHO) had continued to attract unfavourable publicity. Once it had had high prestige and was considered the 'best-managed' specialised agency; now it had fallen by the wayside because of poor management and financial practices. In 1993 inspectors described the overall picture of its technical programmes as one of 'organizational fragmentation verging on disintegration'.[25] The blame for this fell on the Director-General, Dr Hiroshi Nakajima, who lacked management and communication skills and was generally not up to the job. Yet in 1993 he was re-elected to a second term of office – albeit amidst allegations of attempts to buy votes. The controversy over Nakajima's reappointment crystallised and publicised a longer-standing underlying malaise about the WHO's role, structure and effectiveness.

'Eight years of corruption and scandal' under Nakajima ended in 1998 when he was replaced by the former Norwegian Prime Minister, Gro Harlem Brundtland. Brundtland promised to review the WHO's management style and was said to have certainly shaken it up.[26] But despite some notable successes, and the WHO's crucial role in international cooperation to promote health and combat illness and disease, it remained 'a heavily corroded bureaucracy ... a weak partner in initiatives that influence global health'.[27]

The office of UN High Commissioner for Human Rights (UNHCHR) was created by the General Assembly in 1993. Its mandate is huge: promoting and protecting human rights for all, and integrating the UN's far-flung human rights activities. But, as the former Irish President Mary Robinson discovered when she was UNHCHR (from 1997 to 2002), the office is a poisoned chalice. Robinson's resources were skimpy and she had to spend a lot of time lobbying governments for money. At the same time, she regarded it as her duty to speak out without fear or favour, and to stand up to bullies. In so doing, she turned her job into one of the most high-profile in the UN. She said China had a 'very significant way to go' in meeting international human rights standards;[28] an outraged President Putin refused to meet her following criticisms of Moscow's record in war-torn Chechnya; and she spoke sharply about NATO's 1999 bombing campaign in Yugoslavia. Above all, she offended the USA by criticising aspects of its war on terror and the execution of a 17-year-old; by her stands on Middle East issues (though she criticised both Israelis and Palestinians); and by endorsing the outcome of the Durban Summit against Racism. There were tales of an American anti-Robinson campaign (and there was also criticism of her management skills) but she stood down before there were any attempts to remove her.

It might, of course, be suggested that human rights is a particularly sensitive subject, that states react badly to public condemnation, and that far more can be achieved behind the scenes. This is true. But, as the next two examples underline, it is dangerous for the head of any organ to offend the USA .

The Intergovernmental Panel on Climate Change (IPCC) is an independent scientific body established to assess the degree of climate change and the contribution made by human activities such as burning fossil fuels. In April 2002, after a secret ballot in Geneva, Robert Watson (an outspoken American physicist who had chaired the IPCC for six years) was removed after pressure from the US government. Watson had enjoyed the confidence of many European governments and was an efficient manger; but the USA allegedly considered him too effective in mobilising international opinion over climate change. Hence his downfall.

The Organisation for the Prevention of Chemical Weapons (OPCW) was set up in 1997 to verify compliance with the Chemical Weapons Convention. Its director was a Brazilian, José Bustani. The USA had co-sponsored his 2001 reappointment (by consensus) for a second term of office. However, the Bush administration resented the restrictions of the Chemical Weapons Convention and the attempt by the independent-minded director of the OPCW to bring Iraq into the organisation, which would possibly complicate an attack on Baghdad. Accordingly, it called on Bustani to resign, accusing him of: mismanagement; advocating inappropriate roles for the Organisation; engaging in 'confrontational, abrasive, and inappropriate conduct';[29] not consulting member states; threatening punitive inspections of chemical industries in states (like the US) that wanted greater financial discipline and more rigorous inspections; and trying to placate America by offering to appoint an American to a senior position. Bustani refused to resign but he was ousted in April 2002 after a stormy, two-day debate at an emergency meeting.

Never before had the head of any international organisation been dismissed during his term of office and there were serious questions about the legality of so doing. Bustani passionately defended himself, and at an earlier meeting the American delegate had been booed when he failed to produce the promised evidence against Bustani. However, the OPCW was deeply in debt and was dependent on the USA for a fifth of its budget (half of which the USA had threatened to withhold until Bustani was removed). After much arm-twisting, most members of the OPCW decided that the Organisation's survival was more important than its director and the vote went America's way.

THE ROLE OF THE SECRETARY-GENERAL: BOUTROS BOUTROS-GHALI

A successful candidate for the Secretary-Generalship of the UN must satisfy the political requirements of the P5. In 1992 a 69-year-old former professor of International

Law and Foreign Minister of Egypt, Boutros Boutros-Ghali, met their needs. He was from Africa, whose 'turn' it was to fill the office and whose leaders he had courted. He spoke French (essential to avoid a French veto). He was a Christian married to a Jew. He was admired in the Egyptian foreign ministry for his intellect and courage. And he was widely respected as one of the architects of the 1978 Camp David agreements (which paved the way for an Egyptian–Israeli peace treaty).

Reform of the Secretariat was long overdue and Boutros-Ghali immediately set about the process in a draconian way, reflecting his belief that a bureaucracy could best be run by 'stealth and sudden violence'.[30] He cut recruitment and trimmed the number of senior advisers (while avoiding P5 discontent by keeping their nationals); rejigged offices and departments; and set about rooting out corruption and waste. However, political jobbery and the operation of a quota system (to ensure geographical balance) made the Secretariat resistant to change. It remained a 'monster of unwieldy centralism that stifles initiative, rewards mediocrity, encourages featherbedding, and bedevils any effort at intelligent recruitment'.[31]

In the early 1990s, when the UN was riding high on the post-cold war wave of 'assertive multilateralism',[32] Boutros-Ghali had a central role on the world stage. He despatched fact-finding missions; set up 'interim offices' (combining political information and humanitarian functions) in some former Soviet republics; took initiatives to limit conflicts and try to anticipate possible flows of refugees and displaced persons; and he was asked by the Security Council's first summit-level meeting in January 1992 – attended by presidents, kings and prime ministers – to produce a forward-looking report. *An Agenda for Peace* was the outcome, which was cautiously welcomed by the 1992 General Assembly.

All this suited Boutros-Ghali very well as he was ambitious for his office, which he equated with that of a head of state. Like Hammarskjöld he was keen to extend his authority and exercise his independent judgement. But like Lie, he sometimes lacked a realistic appreciation of what the UN can do. He was also vainglorious and had an unfortunate manner, conveying arrogance. He neglected the P5 and challenged the priorities of the Security Council, which he treated in an off-hand way (except at the ministerial level). And, fatally for him, he clashed loudly and severely with US representatives, particularly Madeleine Albright (whom he was said to regard as an 'East European peasant with American crassness')[33] and Warren Christopher (the Secretary of State).

In the autumn of 1995, Albright launched an all-out campaign to remove him on account of his alleged incompetence and arrogance, a move that Boutros-Ghali interpreted as intended to ensure her appointment as Secretary of State. Over the next year, the Americans followed a twin-pronged strategy of denigrating the Secretary-General while also trying to tempt him to stand down by offering him a year's extension of office (without Security Council authorisation), and then the headship of a non-existent foundation (coupled with hefty perks and the title of 'Secretary-General Emeritus'). Boutros-Ghali courageously refused to bow the knee. Even after the USA cast its long-heralded veto against Boutros-Ghali's reappointment (the other 14 votes were in his favour) it was over a fortnight before he admitted defeat and moved on to head La Francophonie.

THE ROLE OF THE SECRETARY-GENERAL: KOFI ANNAN

Kofi Annan's appointment as Secretary-General was, above all, due to two factors. First, as Secretaries-General normally serve two terms, an African was indicated for what would have been Boutros-Ghali's second term. Annan is Ghanaian. Secondly, as in 1961, the search was on for someone who would be 'more secretary than general',[34] who would adopt a low profile and a primarily managerial approach to the job. Annan was a career secretariat official who had so impressed the Americans that they had asked that he be made UN envoy in Bosnia when UN peacekeepers handed over to a NATO-led force.

Annan brought dignity and high polish to the job. Handsome, quietly-spoken, eloquent and assured, he became very popular. 'He is captivating in the best sense of the word', said the former German Chancellor Helmut Kohl: 'When he approaches you ... it is not possible to keep up any barriers.'[35] Not only does he keep calm in crises, '[h]e radiates calm. He is a very difficult man to quarrel with, despite the fact that he deals with people all the time who are extremely quarrelsome.'[36] People want to say 'yes' to him.

Annan's degrees in economics and management made him well placed to set in motion a 'quiet revolution',[37] introducing widespread reforms to make the UN a leaner, flexible, more effective, 'more people-oriented' organisation. The budget was kept down. Another thousand posts were cut (bringing numbers down to 8900 in August 2000 as compared with 12,000 in the mid-1980s), and other jobs were held vacant. Management procedures were streamlined, resources shifted from administration to development work, cabinet-style management was introduced, and there was greatly improved coordination among the far-flung members of the United Nations family. A Deputy Secretary-General was appointed (Louise Fréchette of Canada) to take charge of the Secretariat during Annan's absences from headquarters, to spearhead efforts to raise finance for development, and to 'ensure the coherence of the Organization's cross-sectoral activities'.[38] (In the process, greater stress was put on working with business to promote development and responsible social policies – by early 1999 the UN Development Programme was cooperating with 16 international companies.) Annan has introduced major proposals for reform and has claimed significant results in the areas within his remit: managerial, structural, coordination and operational. However, attempts at reform have been a regularly recurring feature of the UN since the late 1940s and the change that is most needed is the least likely: that UN members stop treating the Organisation as 'a sort of global trade union (and source of sinecures)'.[39]

Annan was markedly successful in improving US–UN relations. An American ambassador called him 'the best Secretary-General in the history of the UN',[40] and other P5 states were enthusiastic. Also, Annan's vision of where the UN should be going was firmly endorsed by UN members when it approved his special report to the September 2000 Millennium Summit. Entitled, *We the Peoples*, the Millennium Report put the betterment of individual 'human beings at the centre of everything ... from conflict prevention to development to human rights'.[41] Amongst other things, this meant focusing global attention on Africa's conflicts; on poverty, famine and the HIV/AIDS epidemic; on allaying African discontent about the UN's perceived failure to address its concerns; and on teasing money out of rich nations to address the threat from HIV/AIDS. In addition, Annan has promoted the idea of public–private partnerships to draw in new skills, and a 'global compact' with businesses – aimed at 'installing civic virtue in the global marketplace'.[42] He supported the idea of humanitarian intervention and more robustly professional peacekeeping, and won respect for not trying to hide his own failures as head of the UN's peacekeeping department. Instead, he commissioned frank, thorough, authoritative and independent reports into the genocide that occurred in Rwanda and Srebrenica, and in so doing made an important breakthrough in institutional accountability.

Like his predecessors, Annan has seen his role as encompassing the right to act independently. For example, he visited Tripoli to speak to Muammar Gadaffi about surrendering for trial two Libyans suspected of blowing up, over Lockerbie in Scotland, an American civil aeroplane travelling from Britain to the USA in 1988. In February 1998, during a crisis over weapons inspections in Iraq, he courageously invested much political capital in a risky trip to Baghdad in the face of strong opposition from Albright, who was by then Secretary of State.[43] But his circumscribed role was evident when Israel withdrew its agreement to a UN fact-finding mission into the bloodletting in the Jenin refugee camp in April 2002. Annan had first suggested the despatch of a large peacekeeping force with robust powers to oversee the withdrawal of Israeli troops, but Israel, NATO and the USA rejected this. A fact-finding mission then emerged as a means of avoiding the tabling (in the Security Council) of a tough, Arab-sponsored resolution condemning the actions of Israeli soldiers. When the Israelis refused to accept even this, Annan had no option but to abandon the idea.

Annan's remarkable blend of realistic idealism and finely honed political skills resulted in his re-election – by acclamation – for a second term of office six months early. Hence, too, his sharing the 2001 Nobel Peace Prize with the UN Organisation.[44]

THE INTERNATIONAL COURT OF JUSTICE

One very important non-political organ of the UN benefited hugely from the post-cold war climate: the International Court of Justice (ICJ). With the end of the cold war, the decline of the Optional Clause – whereby states agree in advance that they can be taken to the Court – began to go into reverse. Adhesions grew from 50 in 1989 to 63 in February 2003, and some former reservations to adhesions have been withdrawn. But because of the growth in the number of sovereign states, the percentage of Optional Clause signatories has only risen from 31% to just under 33%.

Meanwhile, the ICJ has been back in business with a vengeance. By 1990 it had issued just 33 judgements and 19 advisory opinions. By January 2003 the figures had leapt to 76 judgements and 24 advisory opinions. In 1999 a record 17 new cases had been submitted, bringing the total number of cases before the ICJ up to 29; and at the start of 2003 it was dealing with 24 cases. Not only was the ICJ busier than ever, it was hugely busier than its predecessor (the Permanent Court of International Justice [PCIJ]) ever was.

Additionally, the Court's post-cold war cases included ones related to major international crises: hostilities in Kosovo and the Congo; the destruction of an American passenger plane over Lockerbie in Scotland; allegations by both Bosnia-Herzegovina and Yugoslavia that the other had promoted genocide; and similar Croatian allegations against Yugoslavia. It gave an advisory opinion on the *Legality of the Threat or Use of Nuclear Weapons*, and dealt with a very complicated boundary dispute between Honduras and El Salvador that dated back to 1839 and had led to the four-day 'soccer war' in 1969 in which thousands died. Even allowing for numerous cases brought by Yugoslavia and the Congo, the increase in the amount of international judicial business is remarkable.

The parties appearing before the ICJ are as diverse as the disputes. The third world has cast off its earlier distrust of the Court and, in contrast to the Eurocentric PCIJ, the ICJ 'is universal in its clientele ... universal in its composition'.[45] The wide use of the ICJ is indicated by the fact that Libya has appeared before it 6 times, Iran 4 times, the Democratic Republic of Congo 4 times, the United States 21 times, and Yugoslavia 12 times.

CONCLUSION

The UN has at almost every turn confounded expectations, developing a momentum and a life of its own in response to political developments. What it is depends upon the members and the nature of relations between them. Good relations are reflected in a greater ease of cooperation through the UN system; poor relations may be ameliorated with the help of the UN; bad relations may exclude the UN from playing any role beyond serving as a means of scoring points.

Like all human organisations it is far from perfect, having many weaknesses and with some parts badly needing – but so far defying – major reform. That the United States feels able to do as it wishes, without worrying too much about UN approval, also demonstrates its limitations. Yet the fact that the greatest power in the world not only bothers about, but also pays as much attention to the UN as it does, is a remarkable testimony to the UN's central role in international relations. For almost six decades, the states that comprise the UN have come to value and need the Organisation. Through it they can pursue their interests, conduct diplomacy, debate and cooperate – to the extent they feel able – in achieving the purposes set out in Article 1 of the Charter. For, as Kofi Annan pointed out in his Millennium Report, the UN is 'the only global institution with the legitimacy and scope that derive from universal membership, and a mandate that encompasses development, security and human rights as well as the environment. In this sense the United Nations is unique in world affairs.'[46]

NOTES

1. Juergen Dedring, 'The Security Council', in Paul Taylor and A. J. R. Groom, *The United Nations at the Millennium: The Principal Organs* (London, New York: Continuum, 2000), p. 88.

2. The Arria formula is named after a Venezuelan, Diego Arria, who, in 1993, circumvented the long-standing rule that private individuals could not speak at regular Security Council meetings and consultations. This was by inviting co-Council members to tea in the delegates' lounge so that they could hear the testimony of a Bosnian priest. Arria formula meetings became regular and well attended.
3. *A Commentary on the Charter of the United Nations*, House of Commons, Cmd 6666 (London: HMSO, Miscellaneous no. 9, 1945).
4. Dedring, 'The Security Council', p. 90.
5. See John L. Washburn, 'United Nations Relations with the United States: the UN must Look Out for Itself', *Global Governance*, vol. 2, no. 1 (January–April 1996), p. 83.
6. Steven Holloway, 'US Unilateralism at the UN: Why Great Powers do not make Great Multilateralists', *Global Governance*, vol. 6, no. 3 (July–September 2000; on-line version).
7. Bruce Jentleson, quoted in Margaret P. Karns and Karen Mingst, 'The United States and the United Nations: a Case of Ambivalent Multilateralism', paper presented at the annual meeting of the International Studies Association, Chicago, February 2001.
8. Boutros Boutros-Ghali, *Unvanquished: A US–UN Saga* (London, New York: I. B. Tauris, 1999), pp. 267–8.
9. According to Article 19, a state shall be deprived of its vote in the General Assembly 'if the amount of its arrears equals or exceeds the amount of the contributions due from it for the preceding two full years' unless 'the failure to pay is due to conditions beyond the control of the Member'.
10. Suzanne Nossel, 'Retail Diplomacy: the Edifying Story of UN Dues Reform', *The National Interest* (Winter 2001–2), p. 96.
11. In fact, the USA had not been in competition with Libya and Sudan but with West Europeans for a Western-designated seat as elections are on a regional basis. It was re-elected in 2002.
12. In September 2002 Congress approved payment of the third, and final, Helms–Biden payment of arrears.
13. It may also be noted that Palestine – which (as the PLO) was granted observer status in 1994 – was permitted to co-sponsor resolutions on Palestinian and Middle East issues and speak on non-regional issues after the last registered member state. A PLO representative spoke for the first time in the general debate in 1998.
14. 'UN Conferences: What have they accomplished', www.un.org/news/facts/confercs.htm.
15. James Lamont, 'Racism Summit Ends in Rancour', *Financial Times*, 8–9 September 2001.
16. Victoria Brittain, 'UN Conference Loses its Bite, but Not its Bark', *Guardian*, 29 August 2001.
17. Editorial, 'Fail to Succeed', *The Times*, 24 August 2002.
18. Anthony Brown, 'Lip Service to a Plan that Won't Hold Water', *The Times*, 4 September 2002.
19. Editorial, 'Earthbound', *The Times*, 5 September 2002.
20. Ibid.
21. Boutros Boutros-Ghali, 'Empowering the United Nations', *Foreign Affairs*, vol. 75, no. 5 (1992), p. 100.

22. Nigel D. White, *The United Nations System* (Boulder, London: Lynne Reinner, 2002), p. 102.

23. Editorial, 'UNESCO's Choice', *The Times*, 14 October 1999.

24. 'Japanese "Trickery" Won Top UNESCO Job', *The Times*, 8 August 2000.

25. Cited in Yves Beigbeder, 'The Controversial Re-election of the WHO Director-General and its Consequences: Reform Proposals', paper delivered to ISA convention, Washington, DC, 28 March to 1 April 1994.

26. Editorial, 'Unhealthy Ambition', *The Times*, 15 May 2000.

27. Richard Horton (editor, *The Lancet*), letter, *The Times*, 10 December 2002.

28. 'UN–China Rift on Human Rights', BBC News, 21 November 2000.

29. Michael Binyon, 'US Tries to Oust UN's Weapons Control Chief', *The Times*, 20 April 2002.

30. Quoted in Brian Urquhart, 'The Making of a Scapegoat', *New York Review of Books*, 12 August 1999.

31. Rosemary Righter, *Utopia Lost: The United Nations and World Order* (New York: Twentieth-Century Fund), p. 280.

32. The phrase is attributed to Madeleine Albright. See Urquhart, 'The Making of a Scapegoat'.

33. James Bone, 'Heroine of the Hawks Flies Higher', *The Times*, 6 December 1996.

34. Quentin Peel and Carola Hoyos, 'A Cool Head', *Financial Times*, 13–14 October 2001.

35. Quoted in Joshua Cooper Ramo, 'The Five Virtues of Kofi Annan', *Time* Pacific, no. 41 (4 September 2000), www.time.com/time/pacific/magazine/20000904/cover1.html.

36. Lord Hannay, former British ambassador to the UN, quoted in Peel and Hoyos, 'A Cool Head'.

37. Kofi Annan, July 1997, unveiling his reform plan, *Renewing the United Nations*. This was his first major initiative as Secretary-General.

38. Secretary-General Statement to the Special Meeting of the General Assembly on Reform, 16 July 1997, www.UN.org/reform/track2/sgstatemn.htm.

39. Editorial, 'Cloudy up there', *The Times*, 6 September 2000.

40. Greg Barrow, 'Annan: Master of "Consensus Diplomacy"', BBC News, 28 June 2001. President Bush was one of the first leaders to endorse his candidacy for a second term.

41. Kofi Annan, Nobel lecture, December 2001. According to the 'Annan doctrine', 'The demands we face ... reflect a growing consensus that collective security can no longer be narrowly defined as the absence of armed conflict, be it between or within States. Gross abuses of human rights, the large-scale displacement of civilian populations, international terrorism, the AIDS pandemic, drug and arms trafficking and environmental disasters present a direct threat to human security, forcing us to adopt a much more coordinated approach to a range of issues. Such an approach ... compels us to think creatively. It requires us, above all, to understand that the various elements that contribute to human security must be addressed in a comprehensive way if we are to sustain durable peace in the future.' See United Nations, *Report of the Secretary-General on the Work of the Organization*, 30 August 2000, GAOR, 55th Session, Supplement no. 1 (A/55/1).

42. Report of the Secretary-General, 'Strengthening the United Nations: an Agenda for Further Change', 9 September 2002, UN document A/57/387.

43. Ramo, 'The Five Virtues of Kofi Annan'. The episode did not stop Albright regarding him as a brilliant Secretary-General.

44. Dag Hammarskjöld was awarded the prize posthumously in 1961. According to the Chairman of the 2001 Nobel Committee, there were 136 candidates and many were qualified. But 'in the end it was quite easy'. See *Financial Times*, 13–14 October 2001.
45. Address by Judge Schwebel (ICJ President) to the General Assembly, 26 October 1999, www.icj-cij.org/icj;www/ipresscom/SPEECHES/iSpeechPresidentGA54_19991026. htm.
46. Annan, *We the Peoples: The Role of the United Nations in the Twenty-first Century* (New York: UN Department of Public Information, 2000), p. 68.

chapter

The European Community, 1945-69: Origins and Beginnings

PRECEDENTS AND THE AFTERMATH OF THE SECOND WORLD WAR

The idea of European integration in various forms is a very old one but it was not until the latter half of the twentieth century that cooperative European integration began to take place on a significant scale. It is true that this was preceded by a flurry of activity in the interwar years – most notably, the establishment of the Belgo-Luxembourg customs union (1922), the Briand Memorandum[1] (1930) and the activities of Coudenhove-Kalergi's Pan-European Community, which advocated a European federation.[2] However, it was to take a second world war before European integration and a 'community' of European nation states could begin to become a reality. European integration was now an idea whose time had (finally) come. The aftermath of the war created a unique situation which made cooperation in (western) Europe essential, although its form and extent were, and still, are subject to extensive debate.

The war had left Europe weak and exhausted, and with an overwhelming desire for peace and a return to normality (and prosperity). The objective of preventing further intra-European war was a powerful influence on the shaping of a regenerated Europe. Many concluded that European integration offered the best way of containing Germany and providing a peaceful framework within which Europe could be rebuilt. Indeed, many were even more specific and agreed with the conclusion reached by the resistance leaders in 1944 (before the war had even ended): 'Only a Federal Community will allow the German people to participate in the life of Europe without being a danger for the rest.'[3] On the economic front, the Second World War had brought Europe to the brink of ruin and there was an obvious need for mutual cooperation to promote reconstruction, recovery and growth. Indeed, this was actively encouraged by the Americans when Marshall aid was distributed.[4] However, the geopolitical configuration of the continent after the Second World War meant that only western Europe could press forward with its plans at this time. Indeed, the shadow of the Soviet Union created very real fears of Soviet intervention, either directly or indirectly through Moscow's influence over the Communist parties in France and Italy which seemed close to power in this period.

141

In fact, there was a sense in (western) Europe of being caught between the two superpowers, but whilst the threat from the east was political and military, that from the west was more economic in nature; increasing reliance on American technology, the power of the dollar and the rise of the American multinationals were all sources of growing European apprehension. However, the United States actively encouraged European unity, and indeed, the view that the 'US role in this matter should not ... [simply] be one of passive encouragement'[5] was clearly stated in a speech by John Foster Dulles, delivered in January 1947, which explicitly advocated a federal Europe[6] and more concretely suggested that (friendly) US pressure might be applied in that direction.

The late 1940s witnessed a number of initiatives designed to integrate (western) Europe more closely although these largely fell short of their objectives; a major reason for this failure was British reluctance to countenance more than loose consultative arrangements which in no sense involved a transfer of sovereignty to a central authority. In March 1948, the Brussels Treaty linked Britain, France and the Benelux countries in a defensive pact. A month later, the Organisation for European Economic Cooperation (OEEC)[7] was established by sixteen European states as part of their attempt to meet the Marshall Aid requirements of greater European economic cooperation. Potentially the most important venture was the Council of Europe, set up in May 1949 with the general objectives of promoting unity in various fields and of protecting human rights. After functioning as little more than an ineffectual debating society for several years, the Council gradually began to acquire a significant role in regard to human rights, although early ideas that members would 'merge certain of their sovereign rights' vanished in the face of stubborn resistance from Britain,[8] reflecting its strong preference for intergovernmental cooperation. In the end it was economic rather than political forces which led to the beginnings of what is now the European Union, arising from a developing crisis during 1948–9 over the allied dismantling of German heavy industry; essentially, in the face of growing apprehension about the Soviet Union, the Americans sought to reverse their policy of dismantling the German steel industry and to impose this volte-face on the reluctant French.[9] The European Coal and Steel Community (ECSC) was an imaginative way of reconciling these differences.

THE FIRST PHASE: FROM COAL AND STEEL TO ECONOMIC COMMUNITY

The European Coal and Steel Community

On 9 May 1950, Robert Schuman, the French Foreign Minister, announced a proposal to pool, and administer jointly, national coal and steel resources in western Europe.[10] The Schuman Plan, drafted by Jean Monnet, was the blueprint for the Treaty of Paris, signed on 18 April 1951 by France, (West) Germany, Italy, Belgium, the Netherlands and Luxembourg (the 'Six'), which created the European Coal and Steel Community (ECSC). The ECSC was the first of three European Communities – the others being the EEC and the EAEC[11] – which were all eventually amalgamated in 1967. The stated purpose of the ECSC was to set up a common market for coal and steel but it was rather more than a simple economic exercise. It marked a major step in Franco-German *rapprochement* by providing a framework within which the German industrial heartlands in the Ruhr could be revived in a way that made 'war between France and Germany ... not merely unthinkable but materially impossible'.[12] But it was also more generally politically driven since it was widely hoped that the 'pooling of coal and steel production should ... provide for ... a first step in the federation of Europe'.[13]

Equally importantly, the ECSC established the institutional structure for European integration: (supranational) Commission, Council of (national) Ministers, European Parliament and Court of Justice, although two of these had different names in the Treaty of Paris (the Commission was the 'High Authority' and the Parliament was the 'Common Assembly', as indeed it was in the Treaty of Rome, which set up the EEC, only adopting the somewhat grander 'Parliament' at a later date). The Court of Justice and the High Authority were particularly innovative. The former was the first international court to have its judgements binding upon national governments, companies and the ECSC's institutions alike. The High Authority was even more pathbreaking because it combined administrative and political (decision-making) functions. It was charged with representing the 'general interest of the Community', and it was given considerable discretion to make ECSC policy in such important areas as determining the levy on coal and steel firms which financed the ECSC, although its powers over certain matters were limited by the need to obtain approval from the Council of Ministers and by the restraining powers of the Common Assembly.

The attitude of the UK towards the creation of the ECSC was distinctly unenthusiastic. Whilst the British also clearly desired peace, prosperity and the containment of Germany, they did not feel threatened to the same extent as continental Europe. After all, Britain had emerged from the war victorious over Germany (again) and still considered itself the equal of the United States and the Soviet Union; in any case, it had a 'special relationship' with the former and was geopolitically sufficiently distant from the latter to make the Soviet threat appear much less significant. In fact, in this particular case, any attempt by the British to hijack the ECSC and steer it onto firmly intergovernmental ground, as it had done with the OEEC and the Council of Europe, were scuppered by the French negotiating ploy of making the acceptance of the principle of supranationality in advance of negotiations a pre-condition of participation. Thus, the pattern was set and the ideological breach between Britain and continental Europe was now open: Britain was for intergovernmental cooperation in Europe and against supranationality, and this was to underpin the British government's official policy towards European integration for the next ten years and much of non-governmental opinion for rather longer.

The record of the ECSC until it ceased to exist as a separate entity in 1967 is somewhat mixed. It did make some progress on the economic front, although its efforts to create a common market in coal and steel were considerably assisted by the earlier activities of the OEEC and the Benelux customs union. Moreover, despite some early success in its efforts to flex its muscles against governments, the High Authority was overruled by the Council during the first real crisis in 1959 (caused by the over-production of coal) which was met by separate national measures rather than a Community wide plan.[14] Furthermore, the ECSC did not act as an immediate catalyst for political integration and, indeed, as the European Defence and Political Communities failed, was arguably unsuccessful in political terms. However, it

did initiate the process of European integration and clearly contributed to the creation of the European Economic Community (EEC) and Euratom later in the 1950s,
although the element of supranationality in these organisations was rather muted
compared with the ECSC.

If the ECSC represented a success, then what immediately followed on was a
failure. Moreover, it also seemed to undermine the functionalist theory[15] favoured
by Monnet and other federalists. The ECSC was supposed to be only the first sector to
be integrated in Europe; others were to follow, one by one, until a European political
union was finally created. The key mechanism for achieving this process was 'spillover'. In one sense, spillover meant that once one economic sector was integrated,
the interdependence of this sector with others would force them to follow and also
integrate. Another version was the concept of political spillover, whereby integration
in one (economic) sector causes pressure groups to operate at that (i.e. the European)
political level to exert influence; in time these groups would begin to see the value of
operating in this way and would support further integration in other sectors. Whilst
the European Defence Community was perhaps a harsh and not entirely appropriate
test of the theory, it did at least suggest that the spillover process would be a much
slower and more painful process than the federalists had hoped.

The European Defence Community

Although, there was a rather sterile discussion in various quarters about the possibility of extending integration into various sectors – particularly transport, agriculture, health, postal services and communications[16] – the next sector for debate was
forced onto the agenda by events rather than choice; when the Americans began
to press for (West) German rearmament to fill a gap in (west) European defences
effectively caused by American involvement in the Korean War from 1950, the
French put forward a proposal for a European Defence Community (EDC), the Plevin
Plan. The Plevin Plan was essentially a proposal for a European army and followed
the Schuman Plan in outline but with two significant differences: first, it was relatively less supranational and proposed more power for the Council of Ministers; and
secondly, the Germans were treated differently from other members in that all
German armed forces had to be part of the European army whereas the other five
members were allowed to keep some of their military resources under purely national
command. It was immediately obvious that the EDC was incompatible with wholly
independent national foreign policies, and logic implied that it should be accompanied with political integration. Consequently, an ambitious plan for a European
Political Community (EPC) was developed; it proposed the subordination of the ECSC
and EDC within a unified organisation with a single 'High Authority/Commission',
Council of Ministers and Court of Justice and a two-chamber European Parliament.

However, although it had clearly much wider implications than a mere defence
community, the EPC never got further than the draft treaty stage and it was on the
success of the EDC that both Communities stood or fell. In fact, the French never
really felt comfortable with the EDC, even though they were its initiators, for the
fundamental reason that they did not really want German rearmament in any form.
Consequently, successive French governments delayed putting the EDC before the
French Assembly for over two years (until August 1954). To no-one's great surprise
it was eventually rejected by 319 votes to 264.[17] Thus, in the early 1950s, the

opportunity to move to a level of political integration beyond that envisaged by the (Maastricht) Treaty of European Community (TEU) nearly thirty years later was not taken. Instead, the British stepped in and the 1948 Brussels Treaty Organisation, a mutual defence arrangement between Britain, France and the Benelux countries, was extended to include Germany (and Italy) and became the Western European Community (WEU).[18] This was a firmly intergovernmental organisation, which essentially withered quietly away (until it was reactivated as the embryonic defence arm of the European Community by the TEU in 1991).

Towards the European Community

In fact, the failure of the EDC and the EPC proved to be only a temporary delay; extending integration beyond coal and steel in the economic sphere had always remained on the agenda[19] and now took centre-stage. In 1955, representatives of the Six met at Messina on 1-2 June to 'initiate a new phase on the path of constructing Europe',[20] and agreed to pursue integration in the following areas:

- atomic energy;
- transport;
- the harmonisation of social policies;
- the establishment of an investment bank;
- the creation of a common market (to be preceded by a customs union).

They further agreed to establish a committee which became known as the Spaak Committee after its chairman, the Belgian Foreign Minister. A British representative did participate in the early meetings but was withdrawn in November as the British view hardened from 'one of indifference to one of opposition'.[21] The Spaak Committee soon chose to focus on nuclear energy and the common market proposal, although the latter eventually emerged as the centrepiece of the European Economic Community (EEC), which in fact incorporated the rest of what had been agreed at Messina. The Spaak Report was approved in May 1956, appropriate treaties were drafted, and in March 1957 two treaties were signed in Rome, one establishing the European Atomic Energy Community (EAEC or, more commonly, Euratom), and the second, the European Economic Community (EEC).[22] The treaties were ratified by national parliaments and became effective on 1 January 1958. The building of the European Union had begun in earnest.

THE TREATY OF ROME AND THE EUROPEAN ECONOMIC COMMUNITY

The Treaty of Rome (EEC) is an extensive, multifaceted document with 248 articles, 4 annexes, 13 protocols, 4 conventions and 9 declarations. It is wide-ranging and potentially expandable, as it includes an article (235) which essentially states that cooperation can be extended into any area provided all the member states agree, and it remains in force for 'an unlimited period'. Superficially, it is a simple economic agreement that creates a common market and some related common economic policies, but the element of supranationality and the underlying political agenda make it rather more (and potentially much, much more) than this. The range of the Treaty is such as to make summarising it very difficult but, broadly speaking, it has two components: first, the creation of a common market and related measures, and secondly, measures to make the EEC more than a common market.

Another approach which produces the same division would be to divide the contents of the Treaty into elements concerned with 'negative' integration (the removal of internal barriers or, more simply, agreeing not to do something) and 'positive' integration (the creation of common policies requiring actual agreement to take joint action). The former group includes the removal of tariffs and quantitative restrictions (creating a free trade area), the common external tariff (converting the free trade area into a customs union), measures to facilitate the free movement of people and capital, and a competition policy (to allow the common market created by the other measures). The policies involving going beyond a common market include the Common Agricultural Policy, the common transport policy, the European Social Fund, and the European Investment Bank. In general, those parts of the Treaty dealing with 'negative' integration are specified in some detail but those sections covering 'positive' integration are more vague and provide direction rather than detail. Thus, the timetable for establishing the customs union is clear but the articles relating to the Common Agricultural Policy (CAP) specify its objectives but leave the precise shape of the policy designed to achieve them for later negotiations.

In addition to these two broad categories of economic integration, the Treaty had various (implicitly long-term) objectives of more general economic integration that are perhaps best summarised in Article 2, which indicates that 'the aim of the Community, by ... progressively approximating the economic policies of the Member States ... [is] to promote throughout the Community a harmonious development of economic activities, a continuous and balanced expansion, an increased stability, an accelerated raising of the standard of living and closer relations between its Member States'. Finally, the Treaty also has an external dimension contained within it[23] and a number of 'escape clauses' triggered by economic difficulties or on the grounds of national security.

However, it was the institutional framework that aroused most interest as it was unique amongst international organisations and, indeed, remains so despite various subsequent attempts to imitate European integration in many parts of the world.[24] There were four principal institutions created:

- *The European Commission*, based in Brussels, had two members from each of the three larger member states and one from each of the smaller; it was the equivalent of the ECSC's High Authority. It was to represent the 'Community interest' and Commissioners had to take an oath to this effect. It had three functions: first, it was the guardian of the Treaties, ensuring that their provisions were observed; secondly, it was charged with implementing and administering Community policy; finally, and uniquely for a supranational body, it was to initiate policy.
- *The Council of Ministers* represented the interests of the member states and was the principal decision-making body, taking decisions on the basis of the Commission's proposals. It consisted of the member states' Foreign Ministers (General Council), or, if a specific policy area was being discussed, then the appropriate ministers in that field – for example, the Agricultural Council consisted of the Agricultural

Ministers. Most decisions were to be taken unanimously, although there was some provision for qualified majority voting[25] (and even, in six very trivial cases, a simple majority).

- *The Parliamentary Assembly*, which was to become the European Parliament, was originally not an elected body but rather its 142 members were nominated by the governments of the member states. Its principal function was to monitor the work of the Commission and Council and it had to be consulted on Commission proposals before the Council took a decision. Consequently, its powers were limited to an advisory rather than a legislative role, although it was required to discharge the budget and had the rather draconian (though never used) power of dismissing the Commission (by a two-thirds majority).

- *The Court of Justice*, based in Luxembourg, was the unglamorous, but extremely important, fourth major institution. It had two functions: first, it provided guidance and interpretation of the Treaties; and, second, it had to settle disputes relating to points of Community law, which might involve Community institutions, member states, companies or citizens.

The key relationship was between the Commission and the Council. The clear intention of those who drafted the Treaty of Rome was that the Commission should play a pivotal role: its function as the sole initiator of all Community policies and the fact that the Council could only amend a Commission proposal by unanimous vote gave it potentially enormous powers without any checks and balances, in the eyes of some observers.[26] However, it was the Council that took the decisions, and, of course, the Commission did not devise new policies in Olympian isolation. It engaged in a process of consultation with interested parties, including the Council, so that its proposals already commanded some degree of consensus by the time they reached the Council. Indeed, many who favoured integration saw this as producing a wholly novel 'Community method' of decision-making through a permanent dialogue between the Commission and the Council, a method that would oblige states increasingly to view problems within a Community, rather than a national, framework.[27]

There were also a number of more minor institutions: the European Investment Bank is a non-profitmaking provider of loans (at subsidised rates) to promote the economic development of the Community; the Economic and Social Committee (ECOSOC) is an advisory body drawn from three groups: employers, trade unions and the 'general interest'; and there is a Court of Auditors, which ensures the legality and sound financial management of the Community budget. Finally, there is another quite important body which, although not actually mentioned in the Treaty, was quickly found to be necessary and so was created. This is the Committee of Permanent Representatives (COREPER), which consists of national delegations of ambassadors and civil servants and prepares the work of the Council of Ministers. In fact, it takes some decisions, because it divides the agenda of the Council into relatively low-level issues, which are decided in COREPER and formally approved by the Council without further discussion (Agenda A), and more substantive issues, which do require full discussion and decision in the Council (Agenda B).

Finally, although the principal focus of this section has quite rightly been on the EEC, it is interesting to note that, initially, the proposal for an atomic energy community was deemed the most important, particularly by Monnet and his followers, partly because a sector-by-sector approach was suggested by the concept of spillover.[28] It did also play a significant role in that there was, to some extent, a trade-off between the EEC and Euratom. The French were very keen on the latter but much less so on the former, whereas the opposite was true of Germany and the others. However, Euratom was to prove disappointing in practice as member states continued to pursue national interests and showed little interest in cooperative projects. Its role in the process of European integration has ultimately been negligible.

THE COMMUNITY TAKES SHAPE, 1958–69

The 1960s were dominated by three factors: the mainly unspectacular but continuous efforts to operationalise the contents of the Treaty of Rome; the attempts by De Gaulle to push the Community away from the model of integration set out in that Treaty; and the emergence of the widening-versus-deepening dilemma as Britain (and others) repeatedly sought to join the Community. The first two of these are dealt with in this section and the third will be examined in the conclusion. In fact, the progress made towards implementing the programme laid out in the Treaty of Rome varied significantly across policy areas and the Community's achievements during the 1960s are best described as somewhat mixed. However, the Six did get off to a flying start, helped by the early years of the EEC coinciding with a period of high rates of economic growth (which was one of the reasons for increased British interest) and a large increase in trade and business activity in anticipation of the creation of a common market.[29] This favourable environment allowed the EEC to move forward quickly with establishing its most essential element, the customs union. It was agreed to accelerate the programme of tariff cuts in 1960 and the customs union was achieved on 1 July 1968, eighteen months ahead of schedule.

Substantial progress was also made towards the creation of the common agricultural policy, although at some cost (see below), and the European Investment Bank began operations. Competition policy was a little more muted, in that direct policy development was absent, but much essential background work was carried out.[30] Little progress was made in the fields of energy and transport – for example, in 1963, efforts to initiate a Community transport policy were described as 'a dismal story of false starts, of politically inept Commission proposals, of persistent Council inaction, [and] of divided government views'.[31] Social policy did not fare much better and, indeed, provided a good example of the consequences of inadequate Treaty provision.[32] More positively, the Community did quickly establish an international identity that attracted a big response: many non-member states established diplomatic relations with the Community, a number sought associate or full EEC membership, and the newly independent former colonies of the members states replaced the Part IV Association arrangements of the Rome Treaty with the Yaoundé Convention.

However, against the backdrop of these developments, a serious and fundamental disagreement was developing which would lead to a crisis in 1965. De Gaulle had returned to power in France shortly after the Treaty of Rome was signed, and had initially gone along with it because it favoured French farmers and was conducive to Franco-German *rapprochement*. However, his vision of Europe was based on his preference for an intergovernmental or confederal framework (a 'Europe des Patries'), which actually had some similarities (but also differences) with the Atlanticist version espoused by the British. De Gaulle's position was, therefore, completely at odds with the supranational vision of the Commission (and many of the architects of the Treaty). In 1962 he made the first (and lesser) of his two attempts to 'hijack' the Community by presenting a French plan for political union which would have involved radical changes.

The 'Fouchet Plan', named after the French ambassador to Denmark who chaired the committee that produced it in late 1961, can perhaps be described with some accuracy as De Gaulle's intergovernmental version of the EPC. It was the culmination of two years of activity during which De Gaulle had pursued his vision of political union through various channels. He had secured agreement for regular meetings of the Six's foreign ministers in late 1959 (of which there were three in 1960). He had then sought to develop his favoured method of cooperation – summitry – first, by holding bilateral summit meetings in early 1961, with Macmillan and then Adenauer; and second, by instigating the first EEC summit meetings in Paris in February 1961 and then in Bonn in July. However, it was in the Fouchet Plan that De Gaulle's design for Europe was made most explicit. This was no less than a draft treaty for a 'union of states', with five main elements:

- regular meetings of heads of state and/or foreign ministers;
- decision-making on the basis of unanimity;
- a permanent secretariat (in Paris) drawn from member states' foreign offices (and hence clearly intergovernmental and not supranational);
- permanent intergovernmental committees in the fields of: foreign affairs, defence, commerce, and cultural affairs;
- a European assembly, whose members would be appointed by the governments of member states, and which could ask questions but played no role at all in the decision-making process.

The Fouchet Plan attracted little enthusiasm outside France. The rest of the EEC felt that the defence arrangements did not sit well within NATO and the Atlantic Alliance and, indeed, were potentially conflictual; they objected to the attempt to undermine the existing level of supranationality, and to the French determination to exclude the British (who, by then, were actively pursuing membership of the Community) from the negotiations. The fact that these points of objection were probably considered to be advantages by the French is indicative of the distance between France and her partners. Consequently, it was not surprising that, despite successive drafts of the Fouchet Plan, agreement could not be reached.

The 1965 or 'empty chair' crisis exposed the rift between the French and the other five even more starkly, and its outcome – the Luxembourg Compromise – marked a major turning point in the development of the European Union. The fundamental issue was that, in 1966, in accordance with the Rome Treaty timetable, the EEC was due to move from taking its decisions predominantly by unanimous agreement to taking most of them by majority voting. This effectively forced De Gaulle's hand and he felt compelled to make a stand. In fact, the immediate cause of French wrath was a 'package' proposed by the Commission to the Council which linked three elements:

- the completion of the financial arrangements for the CAP (which the French wanted);
- a switch in the method of financing the Community, from direct national contributions to a system of 'own resources', which would redsignate the bulk of the tariff revenue from the common external tariff 'belonging' to the Community (which the Commission wanted);
- an increase in the powers of the Parliament, particularly with regard to budgetary matters (which the Parliament and the Netherlands wanted).

It had become the standard practice of the Commission to try and broker 'package deals', often incorporating quite unrelated elements (although there actually were linkages in this case).[33] The objective was to encourage agreement by sugaring an unpalatable policy for any member state by offering compensation elsewhere in the 'package'; and, up to 1965, this strategy largely worked. However, on this occasion the French were unwilling to compromise: they wanted the CAP financing but refused to accept the rest, and they boycotted the Council for seven months (hence the empty chair) and effectively brought the Community to a halt.

By early 1966 it was clear that the situation had to be resolved. Obviously the Five were becoming increasingly concerned about the future viability of the Community, but there were also pressures on De Gaulle as his domestic popularity began to wane. However, compromise remained elusive, and at a meeting of the member states in Luxembourg in January 1966, to which the Commission was not invited, the French and the other five essentially agreed to differ. The Luxembourg Compromise stated that:

> Where, in the case of decisions which may be taken by majority vote ... very important interests of one or more partners are at stake ... the Council will endeavour ... to reach solutions which can be adopted by all the members of the Council ... the French delegation considers that where very important interests are at stake the discussion must be continued until unanimous agreement is reached.'[34]

This became interpreted as giving the right of national veto to a member state if it felt that a vital national interest (never defined) was threatened, and, in practice, amounted to a victory for France, as the need for unanimity in the Council was maintained.

As the 1960s drew to a close there were two other significant events in the Community. The first of these was that the three communities created in the 1950s – the ECSC, EEC and Euratom – were merged in July 1967 to form the 'European Communities', which became commonly referred to in the singular.[35] The three had always shared the Assembly/Parliament and the Court of Justice, but from mid-1967 they also had a common Council of Ministers and Commission (High Authority). The second was the very first attempt to reform the CAP, in the shape of the Mansholt Plan, named after the then Agricultural Commissioner, which appeared in 1968.[36] This sought to address the rising cost of the CAP through increasing farm incomes by structural reform of the agricultural sector. There were too many small, inefficient farms and too much disguised unemployment in agriculture; rationalisation was required on a massive scale to create farms of an economically viable size. The Mansholt Plan would have substantially reduced the amount of land under cultivation and halved the numbers working in agriculture by 1980. Not surprisingly, it was far more than the member states could take; it earned Mansholt the nickname 'peasant killer', and led to very little, although some half-hearted, minor structural reforms were introduced in the early 1970s. Effectively, however, the Mansholt Plan was ignored.[37] Meanwhile the most vociferous critic of the CAP waited in the wings.

BRITAIN, EFTA AND THE EUROPEAN COMMUNITY

The British had initially expected negotiations for the EEC to fail, just as those for the EDC (and EPC) had done, and waited in the wings to offer a watered down, intergovernmental escape route in the shape of an industrial free trade area. However, the EEC was successfully created and Britain was left with the European Free Trade Association (EFTA) – the 'Outer Seven' to the Community's 'Inner Six' – with the intergovernmentally inclined Scandinavian and Alpine Europeans. This division of Europe between countries who support some degree of supranationality and those who favour cooperation on mainly intergovernmental lines continues today. It was the fundamental reason for the opt-outs from the Maastricht Treaty of Britain and Denmark, both founder members of EFTA. It is why the Community of Twelve wished to get the Maastricht Treaty (and various other measures) agreed before it admitted Austria, Sweden and Finland, two founder members and one subsequent member of EFTA, respectively.

In fact, British reluctance to participate in the process of European integration was based on rather more than a preference for intergovernmental cooperation. Britain had not suffered economic devastation on anything like the same scale as continental Europe during the war, and had never been occupied. Indeed, she had emerged victorious and, therefore, feared neither Germany nor her own superpower allies. The British also had a very particular view of their position in the world, in which they saw Europe as only one of three legs of their foreign policy.[38] The others were the 'special relationship' with the Americans, and the Commonwealth, and it was not possible to emphasise one leg too much at the expense of the others. Consequently, whilst Britain could encourage and, indeed, play a limited role in European integration, she could not get too deeply involved. However, it quickly became apparent that this was based on an inflated and outdated assessment of Britain's importance, as Britain experienced continued economic weakness, accompanied by sterling and balance of payments crises and, in the 1960s, growth rates much lower than those of the Six. Britain's political decline was in some ways steeper and was clearly indicated by the Suez débâcle, the abandonment of the independent British nuclear deterrent ('Blue Streak'), and Britain's exclusion from the first of the two superpower summits in 1961. Moreover, the non-European legs of Britain's foreign policy triangle were becoming much weaker: much of the Commonwealth was in the process of a rather messy and embarrassing move to independence,[39] and the Americans increasingly preferred a more balanced relationship with western

Europe as a whole. Finally, it became obvious that EFTA was only of limited value.[40] There seemed little alternative to EC membership and so, eventually, on 31 July 1961, the British Prime Minister Harold Macmillan announced Britain's intention to apply for membership.[41]

The first ministerial conference between Britain and the Six was in October 1961; the negotiations were inevitably dominated by agricultural matters and dragged on for over a year until they were halted by the French in January 1963.[42] The French negotiators became increasingly tough in late 1962, and the Nassau Pact, by which Macmillan agreed to buy Polaris missiles from the Americans, was the immediate catalyst for De Gaulle's veto of Britain's application for membership, delivered at a press conference on 14 January 1963. While there remain some doubts as to whether the veto was inevitable,[43] the rationale for it is clear enough. De Gaulle had two concerns: that Britain did not share the objectives of the Six; and that she would act as a 'Trojan horse' for American interests in Europe. Whilst the logic of the latter is perhaps debatable, this is not true of the former: it is quite clear that the decision to apply was a defensive reaction stemming from 'a gradual official realization of the danger that the EEC might become an economic and political embarrassment to Britain'.[44] De Gaulle was thus quite right to the extent that his veto of British entry was based on a mistrust of Britain's motives and the belief that its application in no way reflected a conversion to the views of the Six. A third reason for the French action was that Britain was perceived to be a potential rival for leadership within the Community in a way that Germany, because of recent history, could not be for some time. The effect of the veto on British entry was that the simultaneous membership bids of Denmark, Norway and Ireland[45] were withdrawn. France's five partners were unhappy but felt they had little option but to carry on without British participation in the Community.

In 1961–3 the Labour Party had been divided over Community membership but with a majority against. This was reflected at the October 1962 Party Conference, where five 'safeguards' (or conditions that the Party required to be fulfilled before it could support membership) were adopted:

- a satisfactory solution for the Commonwealth;
- a satisfactory solution for remaining members of EFTA;
- guarantees for British agriculture;
- freedom to pursue an independent foreign policy;
- freedom to engage in autonomous domestic planning.

However, by 1967, after three years in government, the Party had officially changed its mind and its policy.[46] The first experience of government since 1951 had brought home to the Labour Party the extent to which Britain's position in the world had declined, and what its remaining options were. More specifically, the 'safeguards' had mostly become less relevant. The Commonwealth had become a burden and EFTA clearly had limitations, and the Labour government had tried planning (in the shape of the National Plan in 1966) and found it lacking. In fact, from an economic perspective, membership of the European Community was growing more attractive in the face of the continued parlous state of the economy, typified by successive sterling crises, comparatively low rates of economic growth and the realisation that

Britain's economic prosperity was beginning to lag behind that of France and Germany in absolute terms.

On 11 May 1967 Britain applied for membership of the Community for the second time, and Denmark, Norway and Ireland followed again. This time the background and the approach were radically different. There was little domestic opposition and few conditions were imposed. A systematic attempt was made to win over the five and to pressurise De Gaulle, and the British contribution to science and technology was emphasised; in fact, there was talk of a European Technological Community, which would help Europe compete with the Americans. The Commission produced a favourable 'opinion' on the British application in September but on 22 November, superficially prompted by the sterling crisis and the devaluation of the pound (with the implication of a weak British economy), De Gaulle delivered his second veto, at a press conference, for much the same reasons as the first and with much the same effect. On this occasion the British applications (and others) remained on the table, although it was clear that their acceptance would have to wait for the demise of De Gaulle. They did not have to wait too long.

WIDENING, DEEPENING AND THE HAGUE SUMMIT: A NEW AGENDA FOR A NEW DECADE?

At the end of the EU's (EEC's) first decade a debate began as to whether or not there was such a thing as a 'widening-versus-deepening' dilemma;[47] in other words, was it the case that enlarging (widening) the EEC would conflict with more integration (deepening)? There was (and is) certainly plenty of scope for incompatibility in general terms in that a very large EC may become paralysed and incapable of taking the necessary decisions to integrate further. In addition to this potential 'gridlock', a larger, more heterogeneous EC makes it more difficult to complete economic and monetary union; indeed, widening could potentially have a negative impact on a range of existing policies, most obviously the CAP and the CFSP. In addition to the problems caused by economic divergence of new members, there is the more fundamental dilemma of the impact of new members who are 'politically divergent' (in the sense of not concurring with the federalist ambitions of the EU's founding fathers); such countries may deliberately seek to hold back deepening.

On the basis of the existence of the widening-versus-deepening dilemma, De Gaulle's blocking of Britain may be considered wise and well-founded in that the UK would have certainly sought to fashion the EC in an image different from that of the architects of the Treaty of Rome. In fact, if one accepts the historical argument that Britain has always acted ruthlessly to break up any excessive build-up of power on the European mainland, then interpreting British intentions as more destructive than constructive was not unreasonable. Obviously, in reality, De Gaulle's motivations for vetoing British accession were probably as ignoble as those behind Britain's efforts to join the EEC. However, the main result in this context is not tainted by any of this: in holding off potential new members (that is, not widening), the EEC gave itself the time, space and energy to engage in its first phase of deepening. Similarly, negotiating association agreements with Greece (1961) and Turkey (1963) and offering full membership only in the distant future also facilitated deepening.

However, this all began to change at the Hague summit – in effect the first meeting of the European Council – in December 1969. Shortly after his veto of the second British application to join the Community, the tide began to turn against De Gaulle domestically and he lost power in 1968. His successor, Georges Pompidou, although he too had a strong preference for intergovernmentalism over supranationality,[48] proved to be much more amenable to developing the Community further. Indeed, it was the French who proposed that a meeting of heads of state should be convened, and the ensuing summit was to mark a turning point in the history of the European Community and a renewal of the 'Community spirit'. The Hague summit was concerned with the completion, deepening and enlargement of the Community and, specifically, agreed (or set in motion steps that led to agreement of) the following:

- the financing of the CAP;
- the reactivation of applications for membership of Britain, Ireland, Denmark and Norway;
- the objective of economic and monetary union;
- the establishment of regular discussions between foreign ministers;
- measures relating to a whole range of minor issues, including technological cooperation, development aid, social policy and the creation of a European university.

Thus the Community took the decision to widen and deepen simultaneously – apparently there was no conflict. Unfortunately, while other causal factors were obviously also at work, subsequent history suggests there was a problem, as this agenda went on to preoccupy the EC for much longer than the immediate future.

NOTES

1. A. Briand, 'Memorandum on the Organisation of a Regime of Federal Union', *International Conciliation*, Special Bulletin (June 1930), pp. 327–53. This was actually the first formal proposal for European union made by a European government in the twentieth century but was vague and ill-defined and not well received outside France. Similar ideas are also presented in a contemporary book by the former French Premier, see E. Herriot, *The United States of Europe* (London: Harrap, 1930).
2. It is interesting to note that the membership of the pan-European Community included Konrad Adenauer, Georges Pompidou and Carlos Sforza.
3. Quoted in A. Boyd and F. Boyd (eds), *Western Community* (London: Hutchinson, 1948), p. 18.
4. See R. C. Mowatt, *Creating the European Community* (London: Blandford, 1973), pp. 38–42.
5. United States Department of State, *Foreign Relations of the United States* (hereafter *FRUS*), vol. III (Washington, DC, 1949), p. 134.
6. Max Beloff, *The United States and the Unity of Europe* (London: Faber, 1963), p. 14.
7. This was extended to become the Organisation for Economic Cooperation and Development (OECD) in 1961.

8. Mowatt, *Creating the European Community*, p. 28.

9. In addition to the obvious security concerns, the French feared that reversing the decline in German production would lead to over-production of steel in western Europe and consequent problems for (less competitive) French producers, which would damage France's prospects for economic recovery. See D. Acheson, *Present at the Creation* (London: Hamilton, 1970), p. 339 and FRUS, vol. III (1950), pp. 697–701.

10. Robert Schuman, 'Declaration of 9 May 1950', reproduced in P. Fointaine, *Europe – A Fresh Start: The Schuman Declaration, 1950–90* (Luxembourg: Commission of the European Communities, 1990).

11. The European Economic Community (EEC) and European Atomic Energy Community (EAEC), or Euratom, were created by two separate Treaties of Rome in 1957.

12. Schuman, 'Declaration of 9 May 1950', p. 46.

13. Ibid., p. 45.

14. R. Pryce, *The Politics of the European Community* (London: Butterworth, 1973), p. 6.

15. See, for example, D. Mitrany, *A Working Peace System* (London: Oxford University Press for the RIIA, 1943).

16. For a brief discussion see D. W. Urwin, *The Community of Europe: A History of European Integration since 1945*, 2nd edn (London: Longman, 1995), pp. 58–9.

17. Technically the motion was not concerned with the ratification of the Treaty but with whether or not its ratification, should be discussed, but rejection of this obviously implied no ratification, and hence the EDC failed, and with it the EPC.

18. In addition, Germany agreed never to produce atomic, chemical or biological weapons, and Britain stationed troops in mainland Europe and made a long-term commitment to European defence. All this paved the way for the eventual agreement to Germany's reinstatement as a full sovereign power, and its membership of NATO in 1955.

19. In December 1952, in a letter from the Dutch Foreign Minister to the other five, a common market and further economic integration were proposed. This was endorsed at a meeting in February 1954 and sent to panels of experts for further examination. See Mowatt, *Creating the European Community*, pp. 128–30.

20. Text of the Messina Resolution is in Keesings Research Report, *The European Communities: Establishment and Growth* (London: Keesings Publications, 1975), pp. 9–12.

21. M. Camps, *Britain and the European Community, 1955–63* (London: Oxford University Press), p. 49.

22. Common usage of the expression 'Treaty of Rome' refers to the treaty which created the EEC (and not the treaty creating Euratom); this practice will be continued here, although strictly speaking it is ambiguous.

23. This consists principally of Article 237, which allows 'any European state' to apply to join; a specification of the relationship with former colonies of member states ('Part IV Association', which was to be developed under a succession of names – Yaoundé then Lomé and now Cotonou); provision for 'association' of non-member states; and the common commercial policy, although this is also an integral part of the customs union (and hence the common market).

24. For example, compare the structure of ASEAN, widely regarded as the second most successful attempt to develop regional integration.

25. France, Italy and Germany had 4 votes each, Belgium and Holland 2 each, and Luxembourg 1; a qualified majority required 12 votes.

26. See, for example, W. Pickles, 'Political Power in the European Community', in C. A. Cosgrove and K. J. Twitchett (eds), *The New International Actors* (London: Macmillan, 1970), pp. 201–21.

27. See, for example, D. Coombes, *Politics and Bureaucracy in the European Community: A Portrait of the Commission* (London: Allen & Unwin, 1970).

28. For example, see *Resolution and Joint Declaration of the Action Committee for the United States of Europe*, 18 January 1959, p. 1: 'the [achievement] that could and should be most rapidly carried out concerns atomic energy'.

29. See, for example, J. Pinder 'Implications for the Operation of the Firm', *Journal of Common Market Studies*, vol. 1, no. 1 (January 1963), p. 41.

30. H. von der Groeben, *The European Community: The Formative Years* (Brussels: Commission of the ECs, 1987), p. 61.

31. L. Lindberg, *The Political Dynamics of European Economic Integration* (Stanford: Stanford University Press, 1963) p. 143.

32. Von der Groeben, *The European Community*, p. 66.

33. The CAP financial arrangements would increase Community spending, which implied a need for more, or 'own', resources, which in turn implied the need for democratic control, which logically should come from the Parliament.

34. Reproduced in J. Lambert, 'The Constitutional Crisis, 1965–66', *Journal of Common Market Studies*, vol. 4, no. 3 (May 1966), p. 226.

35. This practice has been adopted throughout this chapter. On many occasions the term 'Community' clearly refers specifically to one of the three Communities but, where necessary, it has also been used to refer implicitly to all three.

36. *Bulletin of the European Communities*, Supplement no. 1, January 1969.

37. Interestingly, after his retirement, Mansholt radically changed his views and became converted to the argument that, although inefficient in some respects, small farming units were preferable because they kept people in employment in situations where alternative work might not be available, and also because they caused less ecological damage. See *The Common Agricultural Policy: Some New Thinking from Dr. Sicco Mansholt*, pamphlet published by the Soil Association (August 1979).

38. This is the 'three spheres of influence' argument as elaborated in Winston Churchill's Speech at Zurich on 19 September 1946 – reproduced in A. Boyd and F. Boyd (eds), *Western Union* (London: Hutchinson, 1948) – and arguing that Britain had three important bilateral relationships, with Europe, America and the Commmonwealth, respectively, and could not run the risk of over-emphasising one of them as this might undermine the other two.

39. Moreover, on the economic front, 1961 was the first year in which British exports to Europe were greater than those to the Commonwealth. (This compares dramatically with the situation at the end of the Second World War, when the former were only between a quarter and a third of the latter.)

40. In truth it had never amounted to much: the combined population of the six other members – Austria, Denmark, Norway, Portugal, Sweden and Switzerland – and hence the size of the market to which Britain had free access, was little more than that of Britain by itself. Although three other very small countries subsequently joined – Liechtenstein, Finland and Iceland – there was also a steady stream of departures to join the Community: Britain and Denmark in 1973, Portugal in 1986 and Austria, Sweden and Finland in 1995.

41. House of Commons Debates, 5th series, vol. 645, col. 928 ff.

42. The story of the first British application is told in S. George, *An Awkward Partner* (Oxford: Oxford University Press, 1990), pp. 28–35; S. George, *Britain and European Integration since 1945* (Oxford: Basil Blackwell, 1991), pp. 43–6, and J. W. Young, *Britain and European Unity, 1945–92* (London: Macmillan, 1993), pp. 76–85.

43. Young, *Britain and European Unity*, p. 84.

44. George, *An Awkward Partner*, p. 32.

45. The remaining members of EFTA had sought an associate status with the Community, being unwilling to seek full membership, for political reasons.

46. This was not to be the last change of mind. Labour Party ambivalence towards the Community was to continue for fifteen years, with a tendency towards grudging acceptance whilst in power and opposition when not. It was only in the early 1980s that the possibility of withdrawal from the Community was officially abandoned.

47. For a comprehensive introduction, see Helen S. Wallace, *Widening and Deepening: The European Community and the New Agenda* (London: Royal Institute of International Affairs, 1989).

48. See, for example, H. Simonian, *The Privileged Partnership: Franco-German Relations in the European Community, 1969–84* (Oxford: Clarendon Press, 1985), p. 35.

The European Community, 1970–85: Turbulence, Europessimism and Eurosclerosis – Widening at a Cost

INTRODUCTION

The next fifteen years were to be the most difficult period in the EC's history. To a significant extent this was due to problems relating to absorbing Britain, and to a lesser extent Denmark – the 'awkward partner' and one of the 'reluctant Europeans'.[1] Widening and deepening did not take place simultaneously, and while the 1973 enlargement was clearly not the only reason why integration slowed down, it was a source of constant interruption and disruption to the daily business of Brussels. The main casualty of this period was what had already become the holy grail of the supporters of European integration – economic and monetary union. There were some apparent steps forward:

- the implementation of the European political cooperation procedure (EPC);
- the new partnership with former colonies – the Lomé Convention;
- the creation of the regional fund;
- the first direct election of the European Parliament;
- the accession of Greece;
- the adoption of a new system of direct funding for the EC ('own resources');
- the creation of a new common fisheries policy (CFP).

However, all of these developments can be interpreted negatively and, to some extent, related to the adverse aspects of widening:

- EPC was never particularly successful and its first application – the Cyprus crisis in 1974 – was a near complete failure despite the close involvement of a full EC member (Britain) and despite (or perhaps better, because of) that of two associate EC members with full membership aspirations (Greece and Turkey);[2]

- The Lomé Convention, partly forced on the EC by the accession of the UK, has never lived up to expectations.
- The regional fund essentially failed in terms of its original purpose, which was to provide a positive income stream to the British to offset their large net EC contribution via the agricultural fund.
- The first significant act of the directly elected European Parliament was to reject the EC budget and provoke a crisis.
- The Greek application for membership prompted the first ever negative *avis* ('opinion') from the Commission, which was overruled by the Council, but susequent events have arguably justified the former's reluctance to admit Greece at that time.
- The adoption of a new system of direct funding for the EC ('own resources') was one of the issues that provoked the budgetary crisis.
- The common fisheries policy proved to be difficult to create and was a second source of dispute and acrimony between Britain and the rest.

It would clearly be possible to put a more positive 'spin' on developments in the period but, nevertheless, it is indisputable that these were troubled times and that much of the trouble stemmed from the 1973 enlargement.

However, there were obviously other factors behind the malaise that afflicted the EC at this time besides widening-induced indigestion. For a large part of the period (covered by this chapter) the European Union, like much of the rest of the world, suffered from economic recession. The economic growth of the 1960s could not be sustained and negotiating the sharing out of the fruits of economic growth was clearly much easier than distributing the cutbacks and losses during periods of retrenchment. The disarray was typified by the European reaction to the 1973 oil crisis: the EC had been moving (very) gradually towards some kind of energy policy with security of supplies as its central objective, and the OPEC decision to raise prices in late 1973 might have been expected to act as a catalyst for the policy. Unfortunately, a situation that surely demanded a common response met with quite the opposite. The British and French sought bilateral arrangements with Iran and Saudi Arabia respectively, and the Netherlands found its supplies completely cut off by OPEC. The cooperation that did occur was through the International Energy Agency and not the EU. Indeed, the latter has struggled to create an energy policy ever since, with very limited success.

Nevertheless, the purpose of this chapter is also to highlight those areas where some progress was made in the 1970–85 period, notwithstanding the negative effects of widening on the development of the European Community, highlighted above. However, before analysing the positive side of policy development, the examination of the 1973 enlargement needs to be completed. There is a tale to be told about the process of this enlargement itself and it is to that story that we now turn.

ENLARGING THE EUROPEAN COMMUNITY: BIGGER AND BETTER OR WIDER AND WEAKER?

The beginning of the 1970s was dominated by the accession negotiations with Britain, Ireland, Denmark and Norway. To a great extent the entry bids of the three smaller countries stood or fell with that of Britain, since they were largely following Britain because of strong economic linkages with the British market. Indeed, they pursued Community membership with varying degrees of underlying enthusiasm ranging from the Irish, who saw it as a means of diversifying their trade partners, through the doubtful Danes to the increasingly (and, ultimately, too) sceptical Norwegians. The French remained far from enthusiastic about British accession, with Pompidou harbouring doubts similar to those of De Gaulle. However, in the face of an increasingly assertive and confident (West) Germany, France began to perceive Britain as a potential ally. More pragmatically, the French saw withdrawing their opposition to British membership of the EC as a bankable concession that could be traded off for the agreement of a new system of financing the CAP. Finally, the obvious Europeanism of Edward Heath and the fact that he was even prepared to distance himself from the USA[3] was clearly helpful.

It was perhaps fitting that Britain should finally progress to EC membership in January 1973 under the government of Edward Heath,[4] although the support of the general public was far from certain with an April 1970 Gallup poll indicating that nearly three-fifths of the electorate did not even approve of the application for membership.[5] It was not surprising, therefore, that the negotiations, which began in mid-1970 and lasted for almost exactly a year, required a Heath–Pompidou summit in May 1971[6] to regenerate momentum – the acquiescence of the French remained critical – and had to deal with a number of contentious issues, most notably:[7]

- *The length of the transition period.* Eventually it was agreed that this should be five years for both agricultural and industrial goods.
- *Agriculture.* Essentially, the Heath government accepted that higher food prices were an unavoidable cost of EC entry but sought to minimise the impact, in the short term, by phasing in the CAP as slowly as possible, and in the long term, by negotiating a satisfactory budgetary arrangement.
- *The UK contribution to the Community budget.* The agreement for the transitional period was that Britain should pay 8.64 per cent of the EC budget in 1973, rising to 18.92 per cent in 1977, with limits on further increases in 1978 and 1979; this fell somewhere between the British proposal of a maximum of 15 per cent and the Commission's two scenarios (21.5 per cent and 20–25 per cent). However, there was no agreement about the permanent arrangement to apply from 1980 and so, implicitly, this meant that the Community's recently agreed 'own resource' system (see below) would apply.[8]
- *The Commonwealth countries.* Some joined the Lomé Convention, others accepted less generous bilateral arrangements or were included in the EU's GSP (Generalised System of Preferences), and specific special arrangements were made in some cases, such as the Caribbean (sugar) and New Zealand (dairy produce).
- *Sterling.* This particularly concerned the French, who, on the one hand, regarded sterling's international role as potentially a burden that might have to be shared by France and the rest of the Community in the event of a run on sterling,[9] and on the other (somewhat contradictorily), saw it as a source of advantage to the British, who could finance balance of payments deficits by simply issuing more sterling (which, of course, potentially exacerbated the first problem). However, the matter

was resolved quickly and amicably at the Heath–Pompidou summit and effectively disappeared from the agenda.

- *Fisheries.* At the very same time as they were negotiating the first enlargement, the existing EC members agreed a common fisheries policy which included free and equal access to each others' waters. This was widely perceived as a cynical attempt to gain advantage over the four applicant countries, which all had extensive fishing industries. It was not acceptable and special arrangements had to be made for the three countries that eventually joined; and, indeed, the fisheries issue was an important factor in the Norwegian decision not to join.

All these issues related to the EEC (since membership of the ECSC and Euratom raised only minor problems) and, although they were resolved, in some cases the resolution was superficial and the issues subsequently re-emerged as major problems. Indeed, it was the economic aspects of EC entry that dominated the debate in the UK,[10] and the political aspirations of the EC barely featured at all.

Formal political positions in the House of Commons took the traditional line. Notwithstanding that it was formally the (reactivated) 1967 application of the then Labour government on which the negotiations were based, the Labour Party in opposition opposed the terms of entry (and actually voted against accession).[11] Moreover, in its manifesto for the October 1974 election, it pledged to 'renegotiate' membership. In the event, this proved to be a rather perfunctory re-examination of the main points of contention of the British membership bid. Few concessions of real substance were obtained and, in particular, the agreement for budget rebates agreed at Dublin in 1975 was wholly inadequate, as subsequent events in the early 1980s were to show.[12] Indeed, the Labour Party's volte-face was largely due to the realisation that many of its concerns were unfounded. The manifesto listed objectives in the following seven areas:[13]

- agriculture;
- the Community budget;
- economic and monetary union;
- regional, industrial and fiscal policies;
- capital movements;
- the economic interests of the Commonwealth and developing countries;
- the harmonisation of VAT.

On the basis of this 'renegotiation' the government recommended the continuation of British membership of the Community, even though the Cabinet was split and could only vote 16–7 in favour.

The House of Commons vote was of similar proportions (396 votes to 170),[14] as was the popular vote in the referendum, with 67.2 per cent voting in favour of membership. To what extent this reflected an underlying belief in the value of continued EC membership and to what extent it reflected the impact of a well orchestrated and much better funded 'yes' campaign is perhaps debatable. Moreover, the referendum did not close the debate: opposition to involvement with the EC has continued (and still continues) in both the major British political parties.[15]

Meanwhile, Ireland and Denmark had also joined the EC in 1973. Their negotiations had proceeded in parallel with those of Britain. For the Irish, despite the constraint of neutrality, there was little option but to follow the British; some 70 per cent of Irish exports were to Britain and EC membership was not only essential but also desirable because it provided an excellent opportunity to reduce this dependence on Britain. In the referendum in 1972, 83 per cent voted in favour of joining the Community. The passage to EC membership proved more difficult for the Danes. The economic logic of membership was inescapable: Denmark had a substantial agricultural sector that would clearly benefit from the CAP, and with one of the two main Danish export markets (Germany) already within the Community and the other (Britain) about to join, remaining outside could have been economically catastrophic; but there were other considerations. In particular there were Denmark's Nordic ties and its preference for intergovernmental rather than supranational cooperation. Also, the Norwegian 'no', which was delivered the week before the Danish referendum, was not encouraging. In the end, however, economic logic won the day and there was a clear majority in favour of accession in the Danish referendum although, at 63 per cent, the popular vote endorsing EC membership was the lowest of the three new members.

Norway proved to be even more difficult with 53 per cent eventually voting against accession in the referendum. In a configuration that was to repeat itself twenty-three years later, concerns about agriculture, fisheries and the (then fledgling) oil industry swung the balance against EC entry. Moreover, the preceding campaign[16] tore the country apart and effectively made EC membership a taboo subject in political circles for fifteen years. Two governments fell, old parties divided and new ones were created. Norway, like the remainder of EFTA, was eventually content with an agreement to create an industrial free trade area to cover the sixteen countries of the EC and EFTA.

The 1970s also ended with the EC in the throes of negotiating an enlargement; specifically, the first phase of the second (Mediterranean) enlargement of the EC, which culminated in the accession of Greece in 1981. This has been widely interpreted as a mixed blessing on both the economic and political front. Uniquely, a broadly negative Commission opinion[17] on the Greek membership bid was overturned in the Council of Ministers for political reasons: the need to provide support for (restored) democracy in Greece was judged to override all other considerations. Nevertheless, the Commission's misgivings were soon proved to be well-founded as the Greeks effectively sought to renegotiate the economic conditions of their accession in 1982[18] and went on to play a frequently rather maverick role in the EPC procedure. Indeed, the Greeks, along with the British and the Danes, have become widely regarded as among the least enthusiastic EC members and those most likely to cause 'difficulties' for the process of European integration. Once again, widening and deepening appeared to be uncomfortable bedfellows.

ECONOMIC AND MONETARY UNION: THE SNAKE, THE TUNNEL AND THE EUROPEAN MONETARY SYSTEM

Whilst widening did successfully proceed in the early 1970s (albeit with three, not four, new members), the main item on the 'deepening' agenda – economic and monetary union (EMU) – did not, although it was reactivated in a less ambitious form at the end of the decade. Of course, the EC did have fixed exchange rates (prior to 1973) through participation in the IMF system but the inadequacy of this was made apparent: first, by the French devaluation and German revaluation in 1969, which led to arbitrary changes in French and German agricultural prices and, to offset these, the creation of the representative (green) currency system; and, second, the temporary collapse of the IMF system in 1971 (and subsequent permanent collapse in 1973). Consequently, the first step to implement the formal commitment at the Hague summit was taken by creating the Werner Committee.

The Werner Report advocated economic and monetary union (EMU) by 1980, to be achieved in three stages although only the first of these, the 'snake' (in the tunnel), was outlined in detail.[19] However, whilst the meaning of monetary union was clear enough (free capital movement, fixed exchange rates or a single currency, common monetary policy), economic union was a variable and controversial concept.

The vagueness about economic union and the subsequent stages of 'EMU 1980' reflected an ongoing debate between the 'monetarists' (France, Belgium, Luxembourg and the Commission), who argued that monetary union should be implemented immediately by fixing exchange rates and that this would compel member states to pursue complementary macroeconomic policies and hence economic union would quickly follow, and the 'economists' (Germany and the Netherlands), who asserted that some degree of movement towards economic union (economic convergence) should be pursued first, as, without it, fixing exchange rates (monetary union) was not sustainable. In the event, the 'monetarists' won the argument to the extent that it was principally the 'monetarist' elements of the Werner Report that were eventually adopted. However, subsequent events have arguably supported the view of the 'economists'.

The first stage involved the narrowing of permitted intra-Community exchange rate fluctuations and the establishment of a medium-term financial assistance facility (to help those countries with weaker currencies to stay in the system). The reduced exchange rate fluctuation was to take the form of an agreement to limit the degree of fluctuation between Community currencies to a band of 1.2 per cent of their central parities (the 'snake'), which was to operate within the wider band of 1.5 ($\pm$0.75) per cent against the US dollar (the 'tunnel').[20] Unfortunately, an international monetary crisis arose before the system could begin. A feature of this was a loss of confidence in the dollar and a consequent flow of funds into Europe; but this was a flow mainly into the deutschmark (and, to some extent, the Dutch guilder), which put severe pressure on intra-Community exchange rates and forced those two currencies to revalue. EMU had to be temporarily abandoned. The essential problem was that the worldwide system of fixed exchange rates established after 1945 was entering its death throes.

Following the Smithsonian Agreement, which restored the IMF system with revised central rates for the major currencies and wider bands (the revised 'tunnel') around the central parity – 4.5 ($\pm$2.25) per cent – the 'snake' was finally launched on 24 April 1972, also with a wider band of 2.25 per cent (but which was still obviously narrower than that around the dollar). The 'snake' initially contained only the six EC member states but the three applicant countries joined after a week. Sterling came under strong pressure very quickly and Britain and Ireland[21] were forced to leave the system within eight weeks. The Danes also left in June although they re-joined in October. The Italian lira departed in February 1973 and then in March the IMF system of fixed exchange rates collapsed completely. This meant that the 'tunnel' disappeared. However, the 'snake' continued but with some flexibility, which allowed the Germans to revalue; the 'snake' also admitted two associate members (Norway and Sweden).

The 'snake' had thus weathered the storm of this international monetary crisis but within its first year had been reduced to a membership of two-thirds of EC member states and did not include the currencies of two of the 'big four' countries of the Community. The system did not look like the first stage of economic and monetary union. This was effectively recognised at the December 1974 Paris summit, by which time the franc had also left (January 1974) and the currencies of the Netherlands, Norway and Germany (again) had been revalued.[22] The system did carry on and, indeed, the French did re-join (at the old parity) in 1975, only to leave again in 1976. However, adjustments of central rates became commonplace and the 'snake' degenerated into a mere deutschmark bloc or zone. Thus its membership consisted of the deutschmark and the currencies of a number of smaller countries, some of which were not even members of the EC, but which found it desirable to be linked to the German currency, mainly because of trade links with Germany.

The attraction of the 'snake' was clearly the link with Germany (with its highly credible anti-inflationary stance) and not EMU. The 'snake' had failed completely and the aspirations of achieving EMU in Europe had faded with it. There were a number of reasons for this but essentially they fall into two categories: internal and external. The latter were largely beyond the EC's control (although not the former), and the principal factor was the collapse of the international system of fixed exchange rates. The situation was aggravated by the emergence of high and divergent inflation rates[23] in the early 1970s and the oil crisis from late 1973. The early to mid-1970s was a wholly inauspicious period in which to attempt a narrowing of exchange rate fluctuations. However, it was not merely these external factors but also the inadequate response of the Community in dealing with them which led to the demise of the 'snake'. Arguably the fundamental deficiency was the lack of (internal) political will to pursue EMU. Whenever short-term national interests clashed with the pursuit of EMU, member state governments favoured the former. France was typical – into EMU (1972) and out (1974), in again (1975) and out again (1976) – treating membership of the 'snake' as an optional addition to its national policy; there was never any question of giving EMU priority.

In the face of this abject failure it is perhaps surprising that EMU did not disappear from the agenda completely in the late 1970s. In fact, not only did it not disappear but the 'snake' was replaced by a successor: the European Monetary System (EMS). The full story of its creation has been told elsewhere[24] but, in short:

- The arguments for (and the proponents of) economic and monetary union had not disappeared; they continued much the same as before, as did their belief that EMU was an essential, inevitable staging post on the road to a fully integrated Europe and, therefore, the sooner it was reached the better.
- The experience of the 1970s could, if anything, be interpreted as strengthening the case for EMU. Much had been learnt about the practicalities of narrowing

exchange rate fluctuations, and the extent of the commitments needed to achieve EMU had been made painfully clear.

- At the same time, EMS was much less ambitious (and therefore more realistic) than the Werner Report's grand design. The immediate objective was not a first stage towards EMU, but rather a 'zone of monetary stability'.
- The external situation, although far from calm, with floating exchange rates and another oil shock in 1979, was still more propitious than it had been in the early 1970s when just about the worst possible configuration of external economic circumstances occurred.
- Internal circumstances were also better to the extent that there was a sense in which EMS represented a modest and attainable objective with a degree of clear internal political backing. Credit is frequently given to the then Commission President, Roy Jenkins,[25] for relaunching economic and monetary integration, but, in fact, it was reconstructed firmly on the back of the Franco-German understanding between Giscard d'Estaing and Schmidt; consequently, it was much more likely to be backed by a strong internal political will to succeed.

The European Monetary System was agreed at the Bremen and Brussels summits in 1978 and came into effect on 13 March 1979. It had five main elements:

- *The European Currency Unit.* This was a basket currency, built up of snippets of each EC member state's currency. It served as a means of settlement between Community monetary authorities and as a divergence indicator.[26]
- *The Exchange Rate Mechanism (ERM).* If a country's currency deviated by more than three-quarters[27] of its permitted ($\pm$2.25 per cent) margin of fluctuation against the ECU then it was deemed to have crossed its divergence indicator and there was a presumption that some corrective action would be taken. However, as was the case with the 'snake' it was the bilateral parity grid that really mattered: every EMS currency had a central rate against every other and could only fluctuate by $\pm$2.25 per cent[28] around this; if it went beyond, then it had to be brought back within the prescribed limits, otherwise it dropped out of the system.
- *The European Monetary Fund.* This was supposed to be created after two years. In fact, this did not happen, and the European Monetary Cooperation Fund carried on with a somewhat extended role.
- *Credit facilities.* These were intended to assist currencies with temporary problems and to discourage speculation.
- *Special measures.* These consisted of cheap loans to help less prosperous members (of the exchange rate mechanism) – that is, Italy and Ireland (and Britain, had it joined).

Although it became a member of the EMS (like all EC member states), Britain did not join the exchange rate mechanism (ERM). This was essentially because of the implied loss of sovereignty and, specifically, a reluctance to accept externally imposed discipline on economic policy, although the precise nature of the argument differed according to the political party in power. The Labour government, in place at the time of the inception of EMS, was concerned with the UK's tendency to relatively high inflation and was unwilling to accept the prospect that it might have to deflate the economy, thereby aggravating unemployment, in order to stay within the ERM or, alternatively, accept a decline in competitiveness, which would ultimately have the same effect. The Conservative government, which replaced it in 1979, wished to pursue control of the money supply as the centrepiece of its economic policy, and targeting the money supply was incompatible with an exchange rate target. In the event, membership of the ERM proved to be relatively flexible in the first five years as there were a number of changes in central rates and the system was very much an adjustable (or, for some currencies, very nearly a crawling) peg rather than a fixed system.[29]

POLITICAL COOPERATION AND DECISION MAKING

The disappointing progress made towards the principal economic objective of the 1970s was matched by similarly modest developments on the political front. However, the political rhetoric still continued and, indeed, scaled new heights with the publication of two documents concerned with the future course that European integration should take:

- *The Tindemans Report* on European Community was commissioned by the December 1974 Paris summit and appeared in early 1976.[30] It was a combination of an elaboration of the general framework for integration, and specific proposals. The latter included a common foreign and defence policy, the relaunch of EMU, and more European social, regional and industrial policies. However, there were two radical proposals: first, there was a clearly federal institutional framework with a supranational executive independent of national governments, account-able to an elected and bicameral parliament; and secondly, the report raised the possibility of a two-tier Community to encourage movement towards European Community at the speed of the fastest rather than the slowest in the 'convoy'. In the event, the Tindemans Report was never really seriously discussed,[31] although it appeared on the agenda of several summits; it was too radical and lacked a timetable, although, in fact, the 1991 Intergovernmental Conference covered much the same ground with a degree of success.
- *The Draft Treaty of European Community* was prepared by a Parliamentary Committee under the chairmanship of the late Altiero Spinelli and was over-whelmingly approved by the European Parliament in February 1984. In essence the Draft Treaty sought to reverse the drift towards intergovernmentalism by increasing the powers of the Commission and the Parliament and reducing those of the Council. However, the Draft Treaty was never going to be taken up by the member states and, ultimately, amounted to no more than a contribution to the debate.

The problem for the authors and advocates of the ideas of the Tindemans Report and the Parliament's Draft Treaty was that, on balance, in terms of deepening, the EC was static or even moving backwards politically. The most significant political and institutional development in this period was the formal recognition of the role of the summit meetings of heads of state – the creation of the 'European Council'; and this was arguably a step towards intergovernmentalism.[32] In essence, two roles emerged for summits: the first (and their preferred role) was to set the agenda and direction of the Community; secondly (and largely by default), summits are the fora which settle those disagreements that are so politically sensitive that they cannot be agreed at lower levels – for example, the British budgetary dispute (see below).[33] Thus, to a significant degree, the European Council has usurped the role of the Commission as the initiator of EC policy.

The European Parliament

The other principal institutional development was the first direct election of the European Parliament in 1979. On the face of it this marked a significant step forward as the Parliament of appointed part-time members metamorphosed into one of directly elected full-time members. However, the turnout in the elections was disappointing in some countries and the French and Danish national parliaments made it clear that there was no presumption that direct elections implied an extension of the European Parliament's powers. Indeed, with the exception of budgetary matters (see below), business carried on much as it had done before direct elections and the Parliament had to wait until the Single European Act before its powers were significantly enhanced.

Economic and Political Cooperation

The notable advance in political integration should have been the establishment of the European Political Cooperation (EPC) procedure but EPC proved difficult to implement. Various claims have been made about its impact – the coordination of member states' positions in the UN, the joint imposition of economic sanctions on Rhodesia (after 1975), Iran (1980), the Soviet Union and Poland (1981), and progress in the Euro-Arab dialogue and some development of an independent (of the US) policy towards Latin America have all been put forward as EPC successes – but such policy developments are relatively superficial and probably would have taken place anyway. It is very easy to mistake acting on the coincidence of national interests for EPC-induced cooperation, and to attribute causal linkages where there are none. Moreover, in some cases, the responses through EPC were strained and limited,[34] and on a number of occasions EPC clearly failed, particularly:[35]

- the 1974 Cyprus crisis following the Turkish intervention(s): this was the first real test of the EPC procedure and, after some initial promise, the EC failed to establish a common position – essentially, it just fell in line behind the US and the UN;[36]
- the very long delay in reacting to the Russian invasion of Afghanistan (in 1980);
- the very limited response to the shooting down of a South Korean aircraft by the Russians in 1983.

It is clear from the above catalogue that EPC had a somewhat chequered history in its initial fifteen years. Whilst, on the one hand, it could still be interpreted as marking the first tentative steps towards political integration, on the other hand it could be seen as no more than mutually advantageous intergovernmental political cooperation between economic partners; indeed, EPC was not dissimilar to the Fouchet Plan put forward by De Gaulle. This argument can be applied to developments in general in the political sphere in the 1970–85 period: the progress made was largely at the expense of the Commission and supranationality, and biased towards intergovernmentalism; it was a step towards greater European cooperation rather than European integration.

DEEPENING IN THE FACE OF ADVERSITY: A MORE POSITIVE INTERPRETATION OF DEVELOPMENTS, 1970–85

Although it would only be a heavily blinkered Euro-enthusiast who did not see the efforts to achieve the primary deepening objectives of the Hague summit (EMU and EPC) as essentially ending in failure, this is not so obviously true of the various secondary developments. It is possible to interpret the policy development that did take place in the 1970–85 much more positively than was done in the introduction to this chapter; indeed, the widening of the EC to include the UK can be considered as having acted as a catalyst in some policy areas. The first of these was regional policy, and advancement here was related directly to the accession of Britain. The decision to press forward with EMU created a need for some kind of regional fund to cushion its effects on less prosperous regions and, indeed, this was recognised in the Werner Report. The final push, which led to the establishment of the European Regional Development Fund (ERDF), was provided by the British,[37] who saw such a fund as a means of compensating them for their relatively small share of agricultural expenditure. In fact, they were allocated 28 per cent of the ERDF but the fund amounted to only 1.3 billion units of account over its first three years (1975–7) – the British had wanted 3 billion; this was only 5 per cent of the total budget, compared with the more than 70 per cent allocated to CAP spending over the same period. However, the initially temporary ERDF became permanent and progressively larger, although the British share declined after the Mediterranean enlargement in the 1980s.

The Lomé Convention

A second major development – the Lomé Convention – was also directly related to Britain joining the Community. British accession raised the problem of how to accommodate the former British colonies; indeed, a satisfactory arrangement for the Commonwealth was one of the conditions set by Britain in its accession negotiations. The original EC Six already had an arrangement with their former colonies – the Yaoundé Agreement – which was due to expire in 1975. It was decided that its successor should also include appropriate members of the British Commonwealth. The resulting Lomé Convention covered 46 countries – known collectively as the ACP (African, Caribbean and Pacific) countries – and was hailed as a breakthrough in North–South relations, replacing a colonial relationship with partnership. It was innovatory in a number of ways, most notably through the creation of a stabilisation fund ('STABEX'), which sought to compensate ACP countries for unanticipated falls in export earnings. The reality of Lomé has fallen well short of its aspirations[38] but it has to be conceded that, not only has the 'membership' of the ACP grown to more than seventy, but the relationship still continues, not least of all because of the wishes of the ACP.

The Common Fisheries Policy

Thirdly – after a difficult start in the early 1970s – another enlargement-related policy development was the creation of the Common Fisheries Policy (CFP). This had been a major point of contention between the original Six and the three new members who joined in 1973 (and Norway). The latter, with much more substantial fishing interests (and waters) than the Six, felt that the agreement immediately before they joined, of a CFP which embodied the principle of free and equal access to each others' fishing grounds, was unacceptable. The disagreement was resolved by granting the new members a variety of exclusions and exceptions for a ten-year period. This meant that the CFP had to be renegotiated in 1983. The need to do so was made even greater by the adoption in the mid-1970s, by all major fishing nations, of much extended fishing limits off their coasts of up to 200 miles. This created vast tracts of fishing waters 'belonging' to EC member states, notably the 'Community fishpond', consisting of most of the North Sea. These had to be managed and the need for a coherent CFP became critical. The debate and negotiations were protracted and acrimonious but eventually a new (twenty-year) CFP emerged in 1983 which consisted of:

- the principle of free access for all EC fishermen to all EC waters, but with some exceptions;
- a modified version of the marketing measures of the original CFP;
- a system of conservation and management of stocks, notably the establishment of scientifically determined, annual total allowable catches (TACs), which are then divided into national quotas;
- structural policies to assist regions highly dependent on the fisheries industry;
- various agreements with third countries, negotiated at Community level.

The CFP has perhaps ultimately failed to deliver; it has suffered from the same 'too little, too late' approach to policy as the common agricultural policy, and the fishing industry has been permanently in crisis. However, at its inception it appeared to be a model policy, showing how common problems could be addressed, to the potential advantage of all, and at a relatively low cost.[39]

Industrial Policy

A fourth area of significant EC activity (not covered in the introduction) was industrial policy. This initially seemed an unlikely area for meaningful progress. The Colonna Report[40] in 1970 tried to establish a very broad framework for industrial policy but was essentially ignored by the member states. However, drawing on its wider powers with respect to the steel industry,[41] the Commission was able to develop the much narrower role of mitigating the effects of the decline of the 'traditional' industries within Europe, not only steel but also, to a lesser extent, textiles and shipbuilding. Having established its credentials, it then sought to make a more positive contribution by championing the cause of new 'high-technology' industries. Following the success of 'Eureka' and, particularly, 'ESPRIT', which dealt with new, high-technology products in general, and information technology, respectively, the EC was able to move to a genuine industrial policy. This consisted of the 'First Framework Programme' (1984–7), which sought to integrate all Community assistance for research and development into a single coherent system. The current 'Framework Programme' accounts for nearly 4 per cent of the total EC budget (more than half the expenditure on 'Internal Policies').

However, even when viewed from as positive and optimistic a perspective as possible, these four developments were only modest 'successes' at best and the 1970–85 period was undoubtedly characterised by growing gloom and pessimism. In the early 1980s, the EC reached rock bottom when its efforts to reform its budget backfired badly; widening (the accession of Britain) really did seem to be conflicting directly with deepening (the adoption of the 'own resource' system for the budget). It is to this crisis which we now turn.

CRISIS IN THE COMMUNITY: BUDGETARY PROBLEMS AND THE REFORM OF THE COMMON AGRICULTURAL POLICY

The Community was originally financed by direct contributions from member states but it was always envisaged that it would eventually be funded by its 'own resources'. In part this intention reflected a desire to extend integration further, but it also had a certain logic since it was difficult to assign the proceeds of the common external tariff accurately. It was eventually agreed to adopt the 'own resource' system in 1970 but it was not fully implemented until 1980. At this stage, there were three 'own resources':

- the proceeds of the common external tariff (customs duties);
- agricultural levies, consisting primarily of the (variable) import duties levied on agricultural imports but also including sugar and isoglucose levies, which are a kind of production tax on EC sugar producers to contribute to the cost of the EC sugar regime;
- up to 1 per cent of VAT, levied on the common assessment base.[42]

Unfortunately, this apparently logical step forwards had a strongly adverse impact on one particular member state.

At the same time, the EC budget was coming under growing pressure because of the demands of the unreformed common agricultural policy (CAP). It is not possible to dwell too much on the latter here but the deficiencies of the CAP have been extensively catalogued elsewhere.[43] The main points relate to EC prices set well above world levels, which led not only to dear food for EC consumers, but also to excessive food production, creating surpluses which were expensive to store and to dispose of, leading to a situation in which two-thirds of the EC budget was spent on agricultural price support. The issues of CAP reform and budgetary problems were thus inextricably linked. Indeed, the need for reform of the CAP was recognised virtually from its inception and an unsuccessful attempt to introduce reform had been made as early as the late 1960s in the shape of the Mansholt Plan. The Commission subsequently went on to produce a whole range of documents, which had no more effect than the Mansholt Plan, including *The 1975 Stocktaking*, *The 1978 Reflections, Reflections on the CAP* (1980), *The Report on the Mandate* (1981) and *Guidelines for European Agriculture* (1982). The net result was that in the early 1980s the Community entered a period of crisis, with its budget paralysed by the intro-duction of the 'own resource' system on the receipts side, and excessive spending on the CAP on the expenditure side.

However, it was not until the budgetary pressures became uncontainable that serious CAP reform could begin; indeed, this has been a general feature of CAP reform. There were in fact three serious budgetary problems that emerged in the early 1980s:

- intra-EC institutional disputes over the control of the budget (principally between the Council and the Parliament);
- the issue of budgetary imbalances (particularly the net contribution of Britain);
- the tendency of EC expenditure (mainly on the CAP) to exceed EC revenue, thereby effectively causing the EC to run out of resources.

After the Parliament had delayed the adoption of the 1980 budget by six months, and further inter-institutional wrangles in 1982, a shortfall in the 1983 budget was only averted by the device of suspending (and thereby postponing) some agricultural payments. By mid-1984, EC budgetary arrangements were on the verge of chaos with the 1983, 1984 and 1985 budgets all causing problems: the Parliament was blocking Britain's 1983 rebate in an attempt to force budgetary reform, most member states were opposing the Commission's request for a loan to cover the imminent shortfall in the 1984 budget, and the Commission's preliminary draft budget for 1985 actually anticipated an illegal deficit. These difficulties led to the first major budgetary reforms, agreed at the Fontainebleau summit in June 1984 (and discussed below).

The intra-EC institutionary struggle to control the Community purse strings (principally between the Council and the Parliament) dated back to 1975 when the Parliament was given the last word on non-compulsory EC expenditure, that is, expenditure not covered by the Treaty of Rome. The disagreements continued throughout much of the 1980s (with occasional truces), until the introduction of multi-annual financial perspectives from 1988. The second problem – budgetary imbalances – mainly concerned Britain and stemmed from the original accession terms in 1973 and the total inadequacy of the 'Dublin Amendment', agreed as part of the Labour government's 'renegotiation', which was supposed to have addressed the problem. The problem was not so much that Britain was paying too much into the EC budget since its contributions were not radically out of line with its share of the total EC GDP,[44] but rather, that it was receiving a disproportionately low share of EC expenditures, which were heavily biased towards agriculture (and the UK had a relatively small agricultural sector). Thus, in 1979, Britain, one of the poorest EC members, was one of only two (very substantial) net contributors, along with (West) Germany. While Mrs Thatcher's demand for a £1 billion refund may have been a crude line of negotiation, it was not an unjustified request.

The third, and from a Community point of view, arguably the major problem of the budget in the early 1980s was that the EC was running out of money. Reducing expenditure was difficult (the CAP was highly resistant to reform), if not impossible, because the Community was increasing the scope and the range of its non-agricultural activities and this expansion required additional resources. This left increasing Community revenue as the most practical option. The EC ran out of funds in 1983, when it had to suspend (and postpone) some agricultural payments to balance the budget. This brought the crisis to a head and led to the first major attempt at reform, at the Fontainebleau summit in June 1984 where the following were agreed:

- The ceiling on VAT contributions was raised from 1 to 1.4 per cent from 1986 (with the prospect of a further rise to 1.6 per cent at a later date).
- The British rebate was set at two-thirds of the difference between its VAT payments to the Community and its share of expenditure (to be paid by an automatic downward adjustment in its VAT payments the following year).
- One-off measures were agreed to deal with the shortfalls in the 1984 and 1985 budgets.
- The agreement at the preceding (March 1984) summit on financial discipline was confirmed; this included the requirement that CAP expenditure should grow at a slower rate than the 'own resource' base, which implied a declining share of total expenditure on agriculture.

The summit brought a kind of temporary relief but permanent solutions were not far behind. The transformation of the Community in the mid-1980s was both dramatic and unanticipated. The second phase of the first Mediterranean enlargement – the accession of Spain and Portugal in 1986 – lay immediately ahead but the decade after Fointainebleau in 1984 was to be a period in which the EC switched its focus back to deepening, with a vengeance, and widening was pushed back as the EC sought to get the essential components of further (and substantial) deepening into the *acquis communautaire* (and therefore non-negotiable to new members) before it embarked on a further expansion of its membership.

NOTES

1. These rather apt descriptions of the UK and Denmark were coined by S. George, *Britain in the European Community: An Awkward Partner* (Oxford: Oxford University Press, 1994); and T. Miljan, *The Reluctant Europeans* (London: C. Hurst, 1977), respectively.
2. See J. Redmond, *The Next Mediterranean Enlargement of the European Community: Turkey, Cyprus and Malta* (Aldershot: Dartmouth, 1993), for a full account of this.
3. J. W. Young, *Britain and European Unity, 1945–1992* (Basingstoke: Macmillan, 1993), pp. 107–8.
4. Heath's credentials in this respect are summarised in George, *An Awkward Partner*, p. 49.
5. S. Z. Young, *Terms of Entry: Britain's Negotiations with the European Community, 1970–72* (London: Heinemann, 1973), p. 19.
6. For an account of this meeting, see U. Kitzinger, *Diplomacy and Persuasion: How Britain Joined the Common Market* (London: Thames & Hudson, 1973), pp. 119–25.
7. The terms of entry are outlined in HMSO, *The United Kingdom and the European Communities* (Cm 4715, July 1971). For a detailed account of both the outcome and the negotiations, see Kitzinger, *Diplomacy and Persuasion*.

8. The dire consequences of this for the net British position were well known from an early stage. See, for example, the *Economist*, 18 May 1974.

9. Article 108 of the Treaty of Rome (EEC) provides for mutual assistance from other member states to Community members experiencing balance of payments difficulties.

10. A flavour of this is provided by the extracts published in Section 5, 'Growth and the British Economy', in J. Barber and B. Reed (eds), *European Community: Vision and Reality* (London: Croom Helm, 1973).

11. The vote in the Commons was 356 in favour and 244 against. There were significant numbers of defectors on both sides, with 39 Conservatives voting 'no' and 69 Labour MPs voting 'yes'. The vote in the House of Lords was much more decisive with 451 in favour and only 58 against.

12. The 'Dublin Amendment' is summarised in D. Swann, *The Economics of the Common Market*, 4th edn (Harmondsworth: Penguin, 1978), ch. 1, Appendix I, pp. 53–4. A more detailed analysis is provided by J. R. Dodsworth, 'European Community Financing: An Analysis of the Dublin Amendment', *Journal of Common Market Studies*, 1975/76. Essentially, the agreement set a number of conditions before repayments could be made that were so stringent that it was never to be triggered, and, in any case, it related only to gross (i.e. rather than net) contributions and was subject to a maximum repayment of ECU 250 million.

13. The objectives and the outcome of the 'renegotiation' are outlined in HMSO, *Membership of the European Community: Report on Renegotiation* (Cmnd 6003, March 1975).

14. Of course the 'government victory' was achieved because of the votes of the Conservative and Liberal opposition, since more Labour MPs actually voted against membership (145) than in favour (137).

15. To take an example from both parties: for a short time in the early 1980s the left wing of the Labour Party actually managed to get into the Labour Party programme a commitment to withdraw from the EC; and in early 1995, a number of Conservative MPs had the Party Whip withdrawn over the matter of the Party's European policy even though this reduced the (then Conservative) government's small majority to dangerous proportions.

16. This is described in F. Nicholson and R. East, *From Six to Twelve: The Enlargement of the European Communities* (Harlow, Essex: Longman, 1987), pp. 126–8.

17. Commission of the ECs 'Opinion on the Greek Application for Membership', *Bulletin of the ECs*, Supplement 2/76 (1976).

18. Greek demands were set out in the Greek Memorandum of March 1982, which is reproduced in Nicholson and East, *From Six to Twelve*, pp. 195–200.

19. The 'snake' was the narrower band within which intra-EMU members' exchange rates were permitted to fluctuate and this was located within the wider band of fluctuation allowed under the international system for exchange rates against the currencies of non-EMU member currencies (the 'tunnel').

20. This had been reduced from the standard IMF band of 2 (± 1) per cent around the dollar for participants in the European Monetary Agreement, which replaced the European Payments Community in 1958.

21. At this time Britain and Ireland had a currency union. It was not until March 1979, when the Irish decided to join the European Monetary System and Britain did not, that the British and Irish pounds became separate currencies.

22. It is true that the European Monetary Cooperation Fund (EMCOF) had been created in April 1973 but this had only a minimal role and in no way resembled even an embryonic European central bank.

23. This put upward pressure on the currencies of countries with relatively low inflation (like Germany) and corresponding downward pressure on those with high inflation (countries such as Britain and Italy).

24. For example, see P. Ludlow, *The Making of the European Monetary System* (London: Butterworths, 1982).

25. Most famously, see the speech reproduced as R. Jenkins, 'European Monetary Union', *Lloyds Bank Review*, no. 127 (1978), pp. 1–14.

26. It also had a substantial unofficial role as a denominator of private transactions.

27. This was actually always less than 75 per cent, and, in fact, varied depending on the currency. This was because national currencies also formed part of the ECU but with differing weights, and consequently, as they fluctuated, they pulled the ECU with them to some extent; the larger the weight of the currency, the more it pulled the ECU, and so an adjustment was made to compensate for this, otherwise the countries with larger weights would have an unfair advantage.

28. Wider bands of ± 6 per cent were offered to the 'weaker' economies of Britain, Ireland and Italy. Only Italy opted for these as Britain declined to join the ERM and Ireland chose the normal, narrower band.

29. The subsequent history of the EMS (after 1985) is taken up in the next chapter.

30. Commission of the ECs, 'European Union', *Bulletin of the European Communities*, Supplement 1/76 (January 1976). A useful summary and analysis is provided by M. Holland, *European Community Integration* (London: Pinter Publishers, 1993), pp. 60–8.

31. This was also true of a subsequent report that was commissioned by the national leaders – the Report of the 'Three Wise Men' – which appeared in 1979 with conclusions along similar lines to those of Tindemans. For more detail, see Commission of the ECs, *Thirteenth General Report on the Activities of the European Communities (1979)*, ch. 1, paragraph 8, p. 23.

32. The decision to have regular summits three times a year (reduced to two in 1985) was taken at the Paris summit in December 1974.

33. For a definitive analysis of the role and functions of summits, see S. Bulmer and W. Wessels, *The European Council* (Basingstoke: Macmillan, 1987).

34. There were two cases in 1982 involving the imposition of economic sanctions on Argentina and Israel, after their respective invasions of the Falklands and the Lebanon; and two more examples in 1986, relating to sanctions on South Africa, and on Syria in reaction to its alleged involvement in terrorism.

35. D. Swann, *The Economics of the Common Market*, 7th edn (London: Penguin, 1992), p. 69.

36. The EC's response is analysed in detail in Redmond, *The Next Mediterranean Enlargement*, pp. 74–7.

37. The creation of the ERDF is described in George, *An Awkward Partner*, pp. 66–9; and, more fully, in R. B. Talbot, *The European Community's Regional Fund* (Oxford: Oxford University Press, 1977).

38. See, for example, J. Ravenhill, *Collective Clientism: The Lomé Convention and North–South Relations* (Columbia, NY: Columbia University Press, 1985).

39. The story of the creation of the CFP is told in M. Wise, *The Common Fisheries Policy of the EC* (London: Methuen, 1984); M. Leigh, *European Integration and the CFP* (London: Croom Helm, 1983); and J. Farnell and J. Elles, *In Search of a CFP* (Aldershot: Gower, 1984). A shorter, more recent account which also analyses some of the subsequent problems experienced with the policy is provided by J. Redmond, 'The CFP of the EC – a Genuine Crisis or Business as Usual?' *European Environment*, 1/3 (June 1991). For more detail, see R. Long and P. Curran, *Enforcing the CFP* (London: Fishing News Books, 2000).

40. Commission of the ECs, *Memorandum on Industrial Policy in the Community* (1970).

41. These stemmed from the Treaty of Paris, which established the ECSC.

42. This is not a percentage of the total VAT levied but a percentage of the total value of goods and services on which VAT is levied (that is, the common assessment base). Thus, for example, a country with a VAT rate of 20 per cent retains 19 per cent and gives (up to) 1 per cent to the Community, and similarly, a country with a rate of 10 per cent retains 9 per cent and gives (up to) 1 per cent. Consequently, no member state can reduce its contribution to the EC's 'own resources' by reducing its VAT rate, since the 1 per cent is a percentage of the common assessment base and is not related to the actual amount of VAT collected or the rate at which it is levied.

43. For example, see any textbook on the economics of the EC, and for a more detailed analysis, see (amongst others) R. Fennell, *The Common Agricultural Policy* (Oxford: Clarendon Press, 1997); W. Grant, *The Common Agricultural Policy* (Basingstoke: Palgrave Macmillan, 2001); and R. Ackrill, *The Common Agricultural Policy* (Sheffield: Continuum, 2000).

44. However, there were some lesser problems on the revenue side: Britain tended to import more from outside the Community than other member states and consequently paid a larger proportion of customs duties and agricultural levies, and also, as a country with high consumption and low investment and a tendency to import more than it exports, Britain had a relatively large VAT base (and hence paid more VAT).

chapter 1

The European Community, 1985–92: from Community to Union – Deepening Dominates while Widening Waits

INTRODUCTION

There was a remarkable transformation in the European Community in the mid-1980s. It is not absolutely clear why exactly this '*relance*' took place except that perhaps the Community had reached rock bottom and had nowhere else to go but upwards. The answer probably lies in a combination of political and economic factors:[1]

• On the political side there was unease about the policies (and reliability) of the Americans, stemming from Reagan's rather aggressive style of diplomacy, which led to fears of an arms race and renewed cold war between the two superpowers.

• More importantly, on the economic side, the deep recession of the early 1980s, the comparative economic decline of Europe, its failure to create jobs at the rate the US seemed able to do, renewed fears about technological backwardness and dependency in Europe, all combined to concentrate European (Community) minds. European industry began to adopt an increasingly European perception and strategy[2] and began to see the fragmentation of the European economy as a major problem. There was also a growing consensus in favour of supply-side policies, economic deregulation and budgetary discipline. The combination of all these factors created an irresistible pressure for change and led to two major steps forward in the field of industrial policy: the establishment of the first Framework Programme for EC research and development policies, and the single market programme (SMP); the latter was to be seized upon by proponents of European integration in general, as a flagship for their cause, and was, therefore, to develop into much more than a mere component of industrial policy.

This astonishing change of gear was facilitated by the fact that there seemed to be no further widening possibilities beyond Spain and Portugal, who were set to join in

1986. The Spanish accession negotiations, in particular, had not been easy but they were over, and the EC was free to focus on deepening – which it did with spectacular success. If there was a conflict between widening and deepening – and the events described in the previous chapter rather suggest that there may have been – then it no longer mattered. Of course, the situation was to change dramatically by the early 1990s, with the number of countries applying for membership in double figures, but by then the Community had acquired a sense of purpose and a head of steam that made it determined to sideline any further enlargement until it had its deepening (or at least an irreversible commitment to it) firmly in place; in practice, this meant ensuring that either key policies were created in embryo (such as the Common Foreign and Security Policy) or their creation was timetabled in detail (EMU), so that new members would have to accept them as a part of the *acquis communautaire*, thereby making it impossible for widening to undermine deepening.

The centrepiece of this reawakening was the single market programme (SMP), to be completed by 31 December 1992. This soon became much more than simply finishing off the common market: it was about relaunching the idea of European integration after fifteen years of virtual stagnation, and it was about reviving the economic fortunes of Europe in a much broader sense, through the artifice of further integration. The SMP – '1992' – became a target, a symbol and, indeed, an advertisement (almost to the point of being a propaganda vehicle) for the Community. The adoption of the SMP was a catalyst for a new phase of European integration which, together with the collapse of the Soviet empire, was to transform the agenda of the Community and of the wider Europe. Although few could have predicted or expected it in 1985, the European Community was about to enter into the most significant period for European integration since that immediately preceding the signing of the Treaty of Rome. However, before this could be done the Community had to get its financial affairs in order.

UNFINISHED BUSINESS: REFORMING THE BUDGET AND THE COMMON AGRICULTURAL POLICY

If the SMP were to have the intended effect and revitalise Europe, then the EC had to resolve the two related problems that had been the source of so much internal EC conflict in the early 1980s – the budget disputes and the reform of the CAP. The Fontainebleau summit provided only a temporary respite and budgetary shortfalls in 1985 and 1986 had to be made up by additional contributions as agricultural surpluses continued to mount. An anticipated deficit of ECU 6 billion in 1987 concentrated minds, and a Commission plan – what became known as the 'Delors I' package – was put forward and formed the basis of discussion (and, ultimately, agreement). However, the debate dragged on and agreement was not reached on the reform of the CAP and the future financing of the EC – the one could not be agreed without the other – until a special EC summit was held in Brussels in February 1988. The main elements of the budget deal were as follows:

- a five-year (1988-92) 'financial perspective', which set out guidelines for the total budget and its main sub-categories for each of the five years;

- an overall ceiling for expenditure, progressively rising from 1.15 per cent of Community GNP in 1988 to 1.2 per cent in 1992;
- a shift in the composition of expenditure away from the CAP – the growth of spending on agriculture was limited to a maximum of 74 per cent of the growth rate of the EC's GNP – to the structural funds (principally the Regional and Social Funds), which were to double in size by 1993 and thereby increase their share of the budget to 30 per cent;
- a fourth 'own resource', which was added in the shape of a percentage of each country's share of the EC's GNP – the remaining three sources of revenue (agricultural levies, customs duties and VAT) were to continue as before, with the VAT contribution to remain at a maximum of 1.4 per cent;
- the British rebate, which was to continue, in a slightly modified form, at the rate agreed at Fontainebleau.

Shortly after the Brussels summit, an Inter-institutional Agreement was reached between the Commission, Council and Parliament, designed to facilitate improvements in budgetary procedures.

The overall package was a major step forward. At a stroke it pre-empted further disagreement amongst EC institutions since the size of the overall budget and its main constituents became pre-determined, the shortfall in revenue was made good and the British budgetary rebate was renewed on a permanent, mutually acceptable basis. The most fundamental effect of the reform was that it freed the Community to focus on new initiatives. The other main consequence was allied to this last point: the introduction of the fourth 'own resource', based on GNP, created a degree of progressivity into the EC budget. There still remained the same random distributional effects on the expenditure side, which were as likely to be regressive as progressive (as the British had found out to their cost), but these too were being mitigated by the shift, away from agricultural spending, to the structural funds. The budget was thus redesigned so as to be more likely to cause redistribution from the richer to the poorer member states. Indeed, the three poorest members – Greece, Ireland and Portugal – became the major beneficiaries (in terms of net receipts as a percentage of GNP) and the two major contributors (Germany and Britain) were joined by most of the other richer states (provoking complaints of the kind made by the British in the early 1980s and condemned at that time as '*anti-communautaire*' by those same countries). Finally, there was one other positive point: the GNP-based resource introduced an element of flexibility into the budget which would allow a technically (if not always politically) easy solution to any problem of future shortfalls.

At the same summit in Brussels in 1988, after the modest start made with dairy quotas in 1984, the reform of the CAP began in earnest. The limitation on agriculture's share of the budget has already been mentioned but this was allied with the introduction of 'stabilisers'. These brought to a halt the system of open-ended price support which had been a central feature of the CAP since its creation. From now on, full price support would only be provided up to a certain level of production; 'stabilisers' amounted to production quotas and the CAP had finally been capped. The other main element of the reform was the introduction of a Community-funded set-aside scheme, whereby farmers would be encouraged to take some of their land out of production. It is, of course, important to set the 1988 package in context because both the size of the 'quotas' and the levels of guaranteed prices remained generously high, but a real start had finally been made.

The very success of the Delors I package meant that there was less pressure to negotiate a successor, because budget crises had been effectively kept off the agenda. Nevertheless, the ambitious Maastricht agenda (discussed below) arguably meant that the absence of disputes over the budget had become even more critical in the 1990s. Eventually, agreement on a successor – Delors II – was reached at the Edinburgh summit;[3] its main elements were:

- a seven-year financial perspective (1993–99), with guidelines as before;
- an overall ceiling for expenditure, progressively rising from 1.2 per cent of Community GNP in 1993 to 1.27 per cent in 1999;
- a further shift in the composition of expenditure, along the same lines as Delors I, with agriculture set to fall to 46 per cent of the total budget in 1999 and structural operations to increase to 35 per cent;
- a continuation of the British rebate;
- the same four 'own resources' but with the VAT rate to be reduced from 1.4 to 1 per cent by 1999.

Thus, in general, Delors II was similar to Delors I: it made budgetary disputes unlikely, it continued the shift of expenditure from the CAP to structural operations and, once again, it alleviated inequity by shifting further away from the regressive VAT component of 'own resources' (effectively implying an increase in the progressive GNP-based resource).

As in 1988, the CAP was also further reformed, although the linkage was less direct and less essential (as the principle of open-ended price support had already been abandoned). This does not mean that agreement was reached easily – it took five drafts by the Portuguese presidency alone, before the reform was agreed in mid-1992. The main elements were as follows:

- a 29 per cent decrease in the price of cereals over three years;
- a 5 per cent decrease in the price of butter over two years (the price of skimmed milk powder remained unchanged) and continued dairy quotas;
- a 15 per cent decrease in the price of beef over three years;
- various accompanying measures to promote environmental protection, afforestation of agricultural land, and early retirement for older farmers.

In general, prices were moved much closer to world levels, and, although the reforms did not go as far as the Commission's original proposals, they were much more radical than earlier efforts: the large price cuts and the shift in emphasis from price support to direct income supplements laid the ground for transforming the CAP into a much improved policy.

BACK TO DEEPENING: THE SINGLE EUROPEAN ACT (SEA) AND THE SINGLE EUROPEAN MARKET

The beginnings of the EC's revival were rather muted and are to be found in the agreement at the Fontainebleau summit to set up an *ad hoc* committee of 'personal representatives' of government heads under the chairmanship of James Dooge, leader of the Irish Senate. (The Irish assumed the EC presidency in the second half of 1984.) The Dooge Committee eventually reported to the Milan summit in June 1985 and made a number of rather familiar proposals to reform the EC's institutional structure, but these seemed likely to go the same way as the Tindemans Report on European Union. However, the proposal for an intergovernmental conference (IGC) to discuss further measures was endorsed, and the IGC eventually came up with a document[4] that had as its main element the completion of the single (common) market – which won the support of the British and the Danes, who had opposed the IGC in the first place. However, it had much potential for extension, and the institutional reforms clearly took the EC nearer to the edge of the slippery slope of federalism.[5]

Ultimately, it was a rather modest document although it still represented a major achievement in the light of the state of the Community in the early 1980s. It lacked a dominant central focus but rather was something of a pot pourri, which sought to tidy up the Treaty basis of the Community by putting a number of EC activities on a more formal basis, and to press forward by initiating progress in a number of new areas and modifying the decision-making process to facilitate this. More specifically:

- The completion of the internal market became a formal EC objective.
- A number of areas in which the EC was already active – the environment, research and development, and regional policy – were formally incorporated into the EEC Treaty.
- The EPC procedure and the European Council (summits), which had always operated outside the Treaties, were given a legal basis (although not by Treaty incorporation).
- The Parliament's powers were enhanced by introducing a second reading for policy legislation in ten of the areas concerned with the creation of the single market, and by the introduction of the 'assent procedure', which required its approval (by an absolute majority) of the accession of new members to the EC, and of association agreements with third countries.
- The use of (qualified) majority voting in the Council was extended to cover two-thirds of the single market measures (although unanimity was still required for the more contentious areas, notably taxation, free movement of people, and employees' rights and interests).
- The workload of the Court of Justice was eased with the creation of a junior appendage – the Court of First Instance – to deal with cases in a few specific areas.

Thus, on the face of it, the SEA was ultimately rather a modest document but, nevertheless, it was to lead to much more than its somewhat meagre contents suggested.

The flagship of the SEA, and indeed of the EC, soon became the Single Market Programme (SMP), which was detailed in the 1985 Cockfield White Paper,[6] although it effectively amounted to finishing off the programme set out in the Treaty of Rome. The fundamental core of the EEC had been a customs union, to be extended into a common market by the free movement of factors of production. However, though tariff barriers had been removed, the development of non-tariff barriers meant that trade was still impeded, whilst the majority of the measures required to establish the common market had simply not been taken. The White Paper sought to complete this original task and create a single market within which the four freedoms (of movement) – of goods, services, capital and people – would apply. Three types of non-tariff barriers were identified:

- *Physical barriers.* These existed at customs posts and related to goods (import controls and documentation, veterinary and plant health controls, etc.) and people (passports, immigration controls, baggage searches, etc.).
- *Technical barriers.* These impeded all four freedoms. The essential element for goods was the differing technical standards which prevailed in different member states. Negotiating Europe-wide standards had proved very difficult and so the SMP introduced a new system where only essential requirements had to be agreed collectively, and anything beyond this was subject to the principle of mutual recognition – thus if a product was acceptable in one EC member state then it was also acceptable in all the others. This speeded progress up considerably. Other areas covered related to free movement of labour and the professions, a common market for services (particularly transport and financial services), the liberalisation of capital movements, harmonisation of company law, and rules on intellectual and industrial property rights and public procurement (the purchase of goods and services by governments and the public sector); the latter was particularly important as it accounts for about 15 per cent of Community GDP.
- *Fiscal barriers.* Indirect taxation obviously creates significant distortions. Consequently, the approximation of VAT rates and excise duties was considered an essential component of the SMP.

In many ways, the White Paper was a remarkable document because not only did it describe some 300 measures that were necessary to complete the single market but, in an annex, it laid out a detailed timetable indicating the dates by which each of the measures should be proposed by the Commission and adopted by the Council; the target date for completion was 31 December 1992. It was the adoption of the White Paper, with its target date, which gave the SMP its impetus: '1992' became the codeword for the essential deepening of the EC.

In general, the benefits to be had from creating a single market are indicated in the standard theory of customs union.[7] However, the Commission commissioned a series of studies to assess the impact of the SMP more precisely, and the results were summarised in the Cecchini Report.[8] The Cecchini Report was in two parts: the first identified the costs of not having a single market (the costs of 'non-Europe'), and the second tried to estimate the benefits of its creation, using two approaches. The microeconomic estimates considered the impact of removing non-tariff barriers on individual actors in the EC economy, that is consumers, companies and governments. The end result was a welfare gain of 4.3–6.4 per cent of (1988) EC GDP and the Report focused on the mid-point – 5.3 per cent, or over ECU 200 billion – as an appropriate summary statistic.[9]

The macroeconomic estimates made use of macroeconomic models, specifically those of the OECD (INTERLINK) and the Commission itself (HERMES) – and came up with an average gain of 4.5 per cent of Community GDP over the medium term.[10] The micro- and macroeconomic estimates were of the same order of magnitude, which implied that some kind of confidence could be attached to them, and also the Report asserted that the gains could be even greater because these were what Cecchini called the 'raw' benefits, which could be improved by 'accompanying measures'. Essentially, one effect of the 'raw' benefits was to improve the public budgetary balance by a value of 2.2 per cent of Community GDP. The Cecchini Report postulated that this could be used to stimulate the economy further, and after exploring various scenarios settled on the most plausible, which indicated an improvement of 7 per cent in the EC's GDP and the creation of 5 million jobs in the medium term.[11] However, realisation of these gains required[12] a firm and watchful EC competition policy, a reasonably even distribution of the benefits, and convergent and prudent (non-inflationary) member-state economic policies; and EC governments had to be seen to be implementing the SMP efficiently and irreversibly in order to ensure its credibility.[13]

In addition to these caveats, the Cecchini Report attracted a number of criticisms,[14] which implied that it might have been overstating the benefits, notably:

- the programme was incomplete and did not go far enough;
- a large proportion of the benefits stemmed from economies of scale (the cost savings to be generated by larger production runs), implying that European firms were too small but many economists would dispute this;
- the redistributive effects of the SMP were largely ignored and, implicitly, the transitional costs (such as unemployment) were assumed to be negligible;
- allied to this was the argument that the SMP (and the Cecchini Report) neglected the 'social dimension' (which had to be created subsequently), and was for business and not for people;
- the external impact of the SMP was ignored, and in fact there was only one, rather threatening reference to this in the entire Cockfield White Paper,[15] which might lead to retaliation that would undermine the benefits of the SMP.

At this point it is only fair to observe that one study[16] actually found much greater benefits – of up to 35 per cent of GDP – but this was based on a theoretical basis that few economists would find acceptable and is not supported by any other estimates. Consequently, there remained a strong case for arguing that the benefits as calculated by the Cecchini Report were overstated. The obvious question then becomes: Why was so much fuss made about '1992'? The answer is probably twofold: first, the effects were still positive and non-negligible (if smaller than the official estimates); second, the real importance of the SMP was its psychological effect – it reinvented the Community and set it on an upswing, the like of which had not been seen since the 1950s. The importance of the SMP was not so much in itself but in the way that it prepared the ground for something much greater: the (Maastricht) Treaty of European Union.

THE MAASTRICHT TREATY AND EUROPEAN UNION

Thus there were two internally generated forces driving the European Community towards further integration in the late 1980s: the SEA, with its inbuilt dynamic which encouraged further development, and the SMP, which highlighted the absence of (and therefore the need for) accompanying monetary and social measures. To these should be added a potent external factor which Delors has called 'the acceleration of history'[17] – that is, the events in eastern Europe from 1988 onwards: the 1989 revolutions which led to the collapse of communism, the reunification of Germany in 1990 and the collapse of the Soviet Union in 1991. This created pressures for further development of the EC through a number of channels:

- Most simply, the Community had to respond, and equally important, had to have the structures to respond to events in eastern Europe.
- Reunification reawakened old fears about Germany and many saw reinforcement of the Community as the best way of coping with the new Germany.
- The switch from an East–West focus to new security concerns in south-eastern Europe and the Gulf revealed deficiencies in the Community's ability to respond, and laid bare the inadequacy of its procedures for political cooperation.
- Finally, dramatic change in Europe became almost normal for a few years, and this created pressure for change in the Community and also a climate in which even quite ambitious development of the EC did not seem extraordinary.

The eventual outcome of all this renewed momentum was two intergovernmental conferences (IGCs), on economic union and political union, which were initiated at the Strasbourg (December 1989) and Dublin (June 1990) summits, respectively. The IGCs revealed the wide range of opinion across member states, ranging from the ultra-supranational and federal Italians, whose main fear (along with the Spanish) was relegation to the second division of economic and monetary union (EMU), to the minimalist British with their (ultimately successful) obsession with avoiding the 'F-word': federalism. The French, with their reservations about political union, and the Germans, with a very fixed view of EMU (involving an independent European central bank charged with maintaining price stability), were somewhere in between. The smaller countries, though less influential, shared various combinations of the concerns of the larger countries.

There was an early debate about the form the final outcome should take: on the one hand, there was the 'tree with branches' model favoured by the more federal elements, while on the other, there was the 'three pillars' approach, which gave some scope for intergovernmentalism; ultimately, pragmatism won the day and the latter prevailed. The negotiations[18] dragged on throughout 1991 but proceedings were eventually brought to a successful conclusion when the Treaty of European Union (TEU) was signed at Maastricht in December. Ultimately the agreement owed much to the negotiating skills of the Dutch presidency and, more fundamentally, to the fact that all the member states, and, indeed, the EC institutions (the Parliament rather more so than the Commission), were able to claim victory on some issues. Thus, in the usual way, heads of state were able to return to the electorates and put their own nationalistic and self-serving gloss on the outcome of the summit. The TEU which they agreed had three main elements or 'pillars':

- *the new European Community*, which built on existing EC treaties (the ECSC, EEC and Euratom Treaties and the SEA) and included economic and monetary union;

- *foreign policy and defence cooperation*, which essentially developed the European Political Cooperation (EPC) procedure, and remained intergovernmental;
- *the justice and home affairs pillar*, which covered police and judicial cooperation, immigration policy and asylum, and was also intergovernmental.

Together these three components constituted the 'European Union'.

There was one final feature of importance – the British 'opt outs'. The first of these gave Britain the right to determine if and when it joined the third stage of economic and monetary union (and remains in place). It is more properly described as the right to opt out or in. However, the second opt out was precisely that: Britain chose not to participate in the social chapter of the TEU, although this was abandoned following the election of a Labour government shortly afterwards.

There was a range of institutional reforms in the TEU. In the first place, various reforms introduced by the SEA were extended: notably the use of qualified majority voting in the Council; the areas covered by the cooperation procedure (whereby the Parliament has two readings and the right to table amendments in some of the areas where the Council takes decisions by majority vote); and the assent procedure (whereby an absolute majority in a Parliamentary vote is required before a measure is finally approved). Secondly, the Parliament's powers were extended in a number of relatively minor ways. It now formally has the right to set up committees of inquiry, appoints an ombudsman, and is consulted on the appointment of the Commission, which is then subject to a vote of confidence in the Parliament. Thirdly, a new procedure – co-decision making – was introduced in a limited number of fields.[19] This is identical to the cooperation procedure except that whereas, under the latter, Council can reject the Parliament's amendments at second reading if they are unanimous, under co-decision a conciliation committee has to be convened, and if a compromise does not emerge then the Parliament can, as a last resort, reject the legislation. This is clearly a negative power and, indeed, the British government referred to it as the 'negative assent procedure' (finding the term 'co-decision' distasteful). Nevertheless, it does represent a new departure in EU decision-making procedures.

However, the main areas for deepening were (economically) economic and monetary union (taken up below), and (politically) the Common Foreign and Security Policy (CFSP). The latter was to take the form of 'common positions' and 'joint actions' and cover 'all questions relating to the security of the Union, including the eventual framing of a common defence policy, which might in time lead to a common defence.'[20] The elaboration and implementation of any actions with defence implications were to be undertaken by the revitalised Western European Union (WEU).

Finally, there are four other elements of the TEU that merit attention:

- *The establishment of a Committee of the Regions, 'with advisory status'*.[21] This created a direct channel through which regional representatives can participate in the EU's decision-making process.
- *The Cohesion Fund* (increasing in size to ECU 2.6 billion per annum by 1999). This was created to finance 'projects in the fields of environment and trans-European networks in the area of transport infrastructure',[22] in the poorer regions, thereby offsetting the inevitable worsening of regional imbalances that the EMU would entail.

- *The concept of common citizenship of the European Union.*[23] This was modest in content, involving extensions of electoral rights throughout the Union, the sharing of consular services outside the EU and so on, but was highly symbolic.
- *The principle of subsidiarity enshrined in the TEU.*[24] In general this requires policy decisions to be taken at the appropriate level, be it local, regional, national or European.

However, there are differing interpretations of the impact and purpose of subsidiarity, with the British seeing it as a way of restricting the powers of the Commission whilst the Germans view it as a means of protecting the constitutional position of the Länder. In fact, the Commission did become more circumspect in its policy proposals for a while, but, in the long run, subsidiarity seems more likely to strengthen the argument for taking decisions at European level.

The Treaty of European Union was thus a complex document which managed to include both federal and intergovernmental elements. The negotiations were difficult and the ratification of the Treaty was not much easier as it became increasingly clear that the enthusiasm of governments for extending European integration was running considerably ahead of popular opinion. The result was that several countries had difficulties in ratifying the TEU,[25] which consequently did not come into effect until November 1993, eleven months late.

Nevertheless, the TEU remains a 'historic' agreement, although an unfinished one; it did incorporate some decisions but was, in many ways, better considered as an agenda or framework, as a great deal was left to be determined at subsequent intergovernmental conferences. For example, much of the policy development – such as the CFSP – amounted only to principles and procedures and the detail was to be fleshed out by practice. In other areas – notably justice and home affairs – ongoing problems were not fully resolved at Maastricht. Finally, one interesting effect of the TEU is clear: it moved Europe closer towards a multi-speed EU. Such an arrangement was incorporated into the Treaty through only partial membership of EMU and the British and Danish opt outs.[26] The TEU may eventually be regarded as a significant turning point, although perhaps not quite in the way that its more enthusiastically federalist architects would have wished.

FROM EMS TO ECONOMIC AND MONETARY UNION

The centrepiece of the first pillar – the new European Community – of the TEU was undoubtedly economic and monetary union (EMU). Of course, this is by no means a new ambition and the previous chapter described the unsuccessful effort to achieve this in the 1970s. It is perhaps useful to define what precisely EMU is, which turns out to be rather more straightforward for monetary union than for economic union. There is common agreement that the former consists of a single currency or permanently and irrevocably fixed exchange rates,[27] a European central bank implementing a common European monetary policy, the pooling of reserves, and free capital movement. Economic union is more controversial: at one extreme lies the view of economic liberals, who would see it as little more than a single market with market forces essentially left to get on with it; at the other end of the spectrum, there are those who are committed to strongly interventionist government policies, who would regard economic union as being much more and requiring a whole range of common policies. The version of EMU espoused by the TEU lies somewhere in between, and a reasonable approximation is provided by the Delors Report, which describes economic union in terms of four basic elements: the single market, competition policy, structural and regional policies, and macroeconomic policy coordination (including budgetary matters).[28] However, this issue of definition is rarely explicitly addressed even in the academic literature. The tendency is to refer to economic and monetary union but actually to focus much more on monetary than economic union, and what follows here will reflect that practice.

The EMU provisions grew out of the EMS, which was the much more modest successor – seeking merely to create 'a zone of monetary stability' – that emerged from the ashes of the rather grandiose EMU 1980 project. EMS operations began in 1979 and have been progressively more stable, culminating in effectively fixed exchange rates in the five years preceding the crisis in September 1992. Indeed, to the surprise of many, in the period 1979–92 the EMS was generally considered a qualified success. Currencies in the exchange rate mechanism (ERM) were more stable after than before 1979, and also compared with non-ERM currencies since 1979,[29] and the realignments that did take place were carried out smoothly and efficiently. More controversially, EMS arguably provided a more efficient framework for reducing inflationary expectations (because of the linkage with Germany). It was partly on the back of this success that the Committee on Monetary Union was established at the Hanover summit, under the chairmanship of Jacques Delors, to draw up a plan for economic and monetary union. Another factor was the feeling of many that a single currency was a logical consequence of a single market.[30] The resulting Delors Report,[31] echoing the strategy of the 1970s, proposed a three-stage approach to EMU: in Stage I all member states would join the ERM; Stage II would involve the creation of a European Central Bank and its gradual acquisition of monetary competencies; and Stage III would see the transfer of full economic and monetary authority to the EC, and the irrevocable fixing of exchange rates (and subsequently a single currency).

At the Madrid summit in June 1989 it was agreed to proceed to the first stage of EMU on 1 July 1990, but it was decided that the subsequent stages needed further consideration and the IGC on EMU was set up at the Strasbourg summit in December 1989. The EMU section of the TEU that emerged was essentially based on German conditions and a French timetable. There were five convergence criteria that member states had to fulfil before they could participate in the third and final stage:

- *price stability*: the inflation rate should be no more than 1.5 per cent above the average of the three EC countries with the lowest price rises;
- *interest rates*: long-term interest rates should be no more than 2 per cent above the average of the three EC countries with the lowest rates;
- *deficits*: national budget deficits should be less than 3 per cent of GDP;
- *debts*: the public debt ratio must not exceed 60 per cent of GDP;
- *currency stability*: a national currency must not have devalued within the previous two years and must have remained within the 'normal fluctuation margins'[32] of the ERM during the same period.

Stage II of EMU was to begin on 1 January 1994 with the creation of the Frankfurt-based European Monetary Institute (EMI), which was to pave the way for the final stage. Also during Stage II, national central banks were to be granted their independence and governments were to avoid excessive budgetary deficits. Finally, if a majority of member states fulfilled the convergence criteria, then a special Council, meeting before the end of 1996, could agree to move to Stage III on 1 January 1997 (with only those states participating). If no majority existed, then Stage III would begin, with those states that were ready (even if they comprised a minority), on 1 January 1999.[33]

Thus the EC seemed at last to be set fair on a course to economic and monetary union. Somewhat ironically, at the time of the Maastricht summit, only two member states actually fulfilled all five conditions for participation in the final stage of EMU and this 'group' did not include Germany (because of the inflationary and budgetary impacts of reunification). However, things were to get even worse as the ERM all but collapsed in 1992–3. There was a lull before this storm when the first stage of EMU seemed to be moving towards completion as first Spain (June 1989), then Britain (October 1990) and finally Portugal (April 1992) joined. The British volte-face had been a long time coming and the decision came, in a sense, from the fact that Britain had run out of reasons not to join, rather than from any sense of genuine enthusiasm. The superiority of an exchange rate target over a monetary target, particularly if the former was connected to the deutschmark, was becoming more widely accepted and many of the barriers to sterling's involvement (such as Britain's position as an oil exporter) simply seemed less important. However, British scepticism remained and there was some question as to whether the pound had entered the ERM at too high a rate.

The storm broke in September 1992. There was no single trigger but a combination of factors, notably economic recession in Europe, high German interest rates, falling American interest rates and a stagnant US economy, and political uncertainties stemming from problems over the ratification of the TEU. The ERM's Nordic satellites were the first targets: the Finns were forced to float their currency in early September and the Swedes only maintained their peg by raising overnight lending rates to draconian levels (and were ultimately forced to abandon their link in November). The Italians devalued by 7 per cent on 13 September but were then, along with the British, forced to leave the system altogether on 'Black Wednesday' (15 September); on the same day the Spanish devalued by 5 per cent. Moreover, the British departure was acrimonious: it was accompanied by accusations that the Germans had been more willing to support the franc than the pound and that remarks made by the Bundesbank President had been unhelpful. The Spanish, Portuguese and Irish introduced exchange controls (in violation of the single market rules) but they could not stave off the inevitable: the peseta (again) and the escudo devalued by 6 per cent in November and the punt by 10 per cent in January 1993.

The malaise continued. In May the peseta and the escudo devalued again (by 8 per cent and 6.5 per cent respectively). Then in the middle of the year, as the French cut interest rates to try to alleviate their recession whilst the Germans showed little inclination to cut theirs, matters came to a head and the ERM virtually collapsed at the end of July. The possibility of the deutschmark leaving the ERM was discussed, but the eventual decision was to continue but with the fluctuation bands widened from ± 2.25 to ± 15 per cent. Thus, in late 1993, as the TEU finally came into effect, its economic centrepiece was shrouded in uncertainty and the Treaty seemed to be not just an agenda but a rather ambitious one.

LIMITING WIDENING AND PRIORITISING DEEPENING?

Enlargement did not entirely cease during this period of revitalised integration; Spain and Portugal were admitted in 1986. These countries were similar to Greece in that they were relatively poor Mediterranean states which had just emerged from periods of military dictatorship, but they were to prove much less problematic and more *communautaire* than the Greeks had been. However, the actual negotiations were more arduous because many of the problems were addressed in detail rather than being put off until later (as had happened in the Greek case). The motivation for accepting the Iberian applications had been political – supporting the return to democracy – but the problems were mainly economic. On the EC side delays were caused by French insistence that the problems of the last enlargement (notably the British budgetary dispute) should be resolved before the Community embarked on the next one. On the side of the applicants, the problems were due to the challenge to the Common Fisheries Policy presented by the sheer size of the Iberian fleet; the potential impact on French and Italian farmers of absorbing Iberian agriculture; and the effect of adding to the overcapacity in the steel and textile sectors by incorporating the Iberian producers. All of these problems applied to both Spain and Portugal to some extent but it was the former which raised the major concerns because of its size. Indeed, the Portuguese accession was clearly delayed by being linked to that of Spain.

However, the beginnings of the Iberian enlargement had preceded the *relance* of the EC, and Spanish and Portuguese accession were relatively straightforward. Matters became much more complicated from the late 1980s, as the events triggered by the SEA and the collapse of the Soviet bloc led to a deluge of membership applications, some of them from the most unlikely places, which were to raise the importance of the issue of further enlargement to a critical level. The principal single catalyst for this increased interest in the EC was the SMP, which raised the profile of the Community and caused fears of a 'Fortress Europe'. The effect of this was to make many countries around the world re-examine their relationship with the EC, and those that were eligible have virtually all applied to join or signalled an intention to do so. The collapse of the Soviet empire clearly also opened up new possibilities and there was a growing feeling that the EC and 'Europe' were increasingly considered to be the same thing, and that non-membership of the former implied exclusion from the latter.

Three groups of would-be EC members had emerged by the early 1990s:

- the countries of EFTA;
- the central and eastern European countries (CEECs) which had formerly been Soviet satellites or republics;
- a diverse trio of northern Mediterranean countries.

The first formal applicant was Turkey (1987), followed by Austria (1989), Cyprus and Malta (1990), Sweden (1991), and Finland, Switzerland and Norway (1992), with

Poland and Hungary (1994) and eight of the other CEECs not far behind. However, the existing EC membership was anxious to focus on deepening, and sought to deflect further enlargement and enable deepening to take place by two means. The first was by getting either the essential components of deepening in place, or a commitment to their realisation in place, before any more countries joined; this made the new policies part of the *acquis communautaire*, which had to be adopted in its totality by new members. Thus the Commission initially announced (on behalf of the EC) that any further enlargement negotiations had to wait until the SMP was completed; to the SMP was added the ratification of the TEU and agreement of the Delors II budget package, which covered the 1993–9 period.

The second strategy of the EC was to offer applicants some alternative to full membership in the short run (and possibly beyond). The member states of EFTA were offered a place in the European Economic Area (EEA), which was an arrangement whereby the EFTA countries could participate in the single market (and various related EC policies) without actually joining the EC; at the time of its inception this was what both the EC and EFTA appeared to want. The eastern, central and southern European applicants were offered some form of association. Association is a relationship created but not defined in detail by the Treaty of Rome, which may or may not include a reference to eventual membership and is often regarded as a step in that direction anyway, or at least the acceptance of a country's eligibility for membership. It has been defined by practice and basically consists of a customs union or free trade area, some EC financial assistance, an institutional framework and some economic (and more latterly political and cultural) cooperation.[34] The fundamental problem with all these alternatives is that politically they failed to satisfy the aspirations of the applicant countries, which saw these arrangements as a form of second-class citizenship; and economically they potentially offered the pain of membership (competition from the existing EC members) without the gains (guaranteed access to the EC market,[35] participation in EC decision-making and access to structural-fund monies).

In the face of such strong pressures, the newly renamed European Union could not hold off the applicant states for long, and indeed, to a significant extent did not want to; expansion offered numerous advantages to existing members, as well as being considered politically essential. In the past the Community/Union had struggled to enlarge and develop new policies simultaneously but after 1992 it had little choice but to try. The next chapter examines the last ten years of the European Union, a period during which it has sought to widen and deepen simultaneously. Widening has been driven by the growing dominance (and attractiveness) of the EU in Europe, and deepening has been driven by the Maastricht agenda. The key question is whether the EU can now manage the trick of expanding its membership without diluting its purpose.

NOTES

1. L. Tsoukalis, *The New European Economy*, 2nd edn (Oxford: Oxford University Press, 1993), pp. 47–55.

2. For example, see W. Dekker, *Europe – 1990* (Eindhoven: Phillips, 1980). This was a report published by the President of Phillips, calling for a programme to create a single market for Europe.
3. For a detailed analysis, see M. Shackleton, 'The Delors II Budget Package', *Journal of Common Market Studies*, The European Community in 1992 – Annual Review of Activities, vol. 31 (August 1993).
4. For further analysis of the IGC and the SEA, see J. Lodge, 'The Single European Act: Towards a New Euro-Dynamism', *Journal of Common Market Studies*, vol. XXIV, no. 3 (March 1986); J. W. De Zwann, 'The Single European Act: Conclusion of a Unique Document', *Common Market Law Review*, vol. 23 (1986); and A. Moravcsik, 'Negotiating the SEA: National Interest and Conventional Statecraft in the European Community', *International Organisation*, vol. 45 (Winter 1991).
5. The Italians felt it did not go far enough, the Danes and the Greeks thought it went too far and there was a last-minute constitutional problem in Ireland, which had to be resolved.
6. Commission of the ECs, *Completing the Internal Market: White Paper from the Commission to the European Council* (Luxembourg, June 1985). This was produced under the auspices of Lord Cockfield, the then senior British Commissioner; consequently he is widely regarded as, in some sense, the architect of the SMP and so the White Paper often bears his name.
7. See, for example, D. Swann, *The Economics of the Common Market*, 7th edn (London: Penguin, 1992); and A. M. El-Agraa, *The Economic of the European Community*, 4th edn (London: Harvester Wheatsheaf, 1994).
8. P. Cecchini, *The European Challenge, 1992: The Benefits of a Single Market* (Aldershot: Wildwood House, 1988) is the popular version and is the one referred to here, as it is the most readily accessible. A more technical summary is provided by M. Emerson, 'The Economics of 1992', *European Economy*, no. 35 (1988). The full findings are summarised in sixteen volumes as: Commission of the ECs, *Research on the 'Cost on Non-Europe'* (Luxembourg, 1988). The Cecchini Report remains the only fully comprehensive study of the effects of the SMP, with the partial exception of J. Pelkmans and L. A. Winters, *Europe's Domestic Market* (London: RIIA/Routledge, 1988).
9. Cecchini, *The European Challenge*, p. 83.
10. Ibid., p. 97.
11. Ibid., table 10.2, p. 101.
12. Ibid., pp. 104–6.
13. See A. B. Philip, *Implementing the European Internal Market: Problems and Prospects* (London: RIIA, Discussion Paper no. 5, 1988).
14. For example, see B. Burkitt and M. Baimbridge, *What 1992 Really Means: Single Market or Double Cross* (Bradford: British Anti-Common Market Campaign, 1988); and T. Cutler, C. Haslem, J. Williams and K. Williams, *1992 – The Struggle for Europe* (Oxford: Berg, 1988).
15. Commission of the ECs, *Completing the Internal Market*, paragraph 19, p. 8, states that 'the commercial identity of the Community must be consolidated so that our trading partners will not be given the benefit of a wider market without themselves making similar concessions'.
16. R. E. Baldwin, 'The Growth Effects of 1992', *Economic Policy*, no. 9 (1989).
17. Jacques Delors, Speech at the College of Europe, Bruges, 20 October 1989.

18. A useful summary of the negotiations is provided by A. Duff, J. Pinder and R. Pryce (eds), *Maastricht and Beyond* (London: Routledge, 1994), ch. 3.
19. These are: internal market rules, free circulation of workers, rights of establishment, general environment programmes, education and training, trans-European networks, health, consumer protection, the research and development framework programme, and culture. In all but the last two categories, decisions in the Council are taken by qualified majority.
20. Treaty of European Union, Title V, Article J.4.
21. Ibid., Title II, Articles 198a, 198b and 198c.
22. Ibid., Title XIV, Article 130d.
23. Ibid., Title II, Articles 8a to 8e inclusive.
24. Ibid., Title II, Article 3b.
25. France, Britain and Germany all had difficulties, and the Danes needed two opt outs (of the third stage of EMU and of deliberations and actions under the CFSP which have defence implications) and a second referendum. A comprehensive account of the problems is provided by Duff, Pinder and Pryce (eds), *Maastricht and Beyond*, ch. 4.
26. Mention should also be made of the Schengen Agreement, which became effective, after much delay, in late March 1995. This allowed free movement of people in a passport-free zone, but only covered seven of the fifteen EU member states originally.
27. In principle, either of these will do since it is the ending of intra-union exchange rate fluctuations that is critical. In practice, however, there are important differences, particularly with regard to credibility and confidence.
28. Committee for the Study of Economic and Monetary Union, *Report on Economic and Monetary Union in the European Community* (Luxembourg: Office for the Official Publications of the ECs, 1989), section 3, paragraph 25, p. 20.
29. See, for example, H. Ungerer, O. Evans and P. Nyberg, 'The European Monetary System – Recent Developments', *International Monetary Fund Occasional Paper*, no. 48 (1986); and A. A. Weber, 'EMU and Asymmetrics and Adjustment problems in the EMS – some Empirical Evidence', *European Economy*, special edition, no. 1 (1991).
30. Indeed, this view was encouraged by the Commission, which produced what might almost be described as a 'Cecchini Report for EMU' in the shape of: Commission of the ECs, 'One Market, One Money', *European Economy*, no. 44 (October 1990).
31. Committee for the Study of Economic and Monetary Union, *Report on Economic and Monetary Union*.
32. Treaty of European Union, Protocol on the convergence criteria referred to in Article 109j of the Treaty establishing the European Community, Article 3. The ± 2.25 per cent margins that prevailed at the time of the Maastricht summit were not specified and thus 'normal' can presumably be equally applied to the ± 15 per cent bands that became applicable from August 1993.
33. In fact the widely held view that this was the latest date by which EMU must begin is not technically correct. The 1 January 1999 start date was to become applicable only if the Council failed to set a start date for EMU by the end of 1997 (Treaty of European Union, Title II, Article 109j, paragraph 4). There was nothing to stop the Council from deciding in 1997 to set a date later than the beginning of 1999. Indeed, given the performance of the ERM since 1992, this may have begun to look like a desirable option.

34. For a useful analysis of association and the EEA, see D. Phinnemore, *Association: Stepping Stone or Alternative to EU Membership?* (Sheffield: Sheffield University Press, 1999)
35. This is because all EC agreements with third countries include safeguard clauses which allow the EC to restrict imports in certain (often ill-defined) circumstances.

The European Union, 1993–2003: Deepening and Widening?

AN AMBITIOUS AGENDA?

The year '1992' already had a special place within the EU as the target date for the completion of its single market – the Union's original primary objective. However, '1992' went on to acquire an even greater significance as the year that marks the beginning of the most intensive phase of European integration since the period following the end of the Second World War. This astonishing burst of activity has culminated in two momentous steps in the opening years of the new millennium – the creation of a single currency, the Euro, in 2002 and agreement to admit ten new members to the Union in 2004. There is no doubt that both these developments are politically driven. The familiar pattern of a primarily politically motivated policy leading to extensive and potentially adverse economic consequences is repeating itself yet again. However, the stakes involved are much higher this time and failure could be catastrophic for the Union. In particular, the EU has found itself compelled to try to deepen and widen at the same time. The debate is no longer seemingly about whether the EU pursues deepening or widening but rather how it coordinates its efforts to achieve them both simultaneously.

Unfortunately, it is not so easy simply to abolish this central dilemma: the potential conflict between widening and deepening remains, and whilst, if political motivation leads to political flexibility and concessions, that may make the problem less acute, there remain areas of conflict where the differences (and difficulties) are entrenched too deeply. There are four (inter-related) basic areas of conflict and all of these need attention if simultaneous deepening and widening is to be achieved:

- Financial: enlargement to include new poorer members may be costly to the EU, and more specifically, will divert funds away from internal policies (deepening) into (the costs of) widening.
- Institutional: the Rome Treaty institutional framework was designed for six members and then stretched with increasing difficulty as the EU doubled in size by 1986; the current list of prospective members will lead to a further doubling,

and without changes, further deepening could be held back by institutional gridlock as the institutions find that what works with six members does not work with 25 or more.

- (Individual) Policies: the development of some individual policies (such as environmental policy and the common agricultural policy) may be inhibited by new members as the EU is forced to take account of more views.
- Ultimate Objectives: it is by no means certain that all (or even any) of the prospective new members will share the objectives of the Union's founding fathers; indeed, just as future enlargement will bring more economic divergence, it is also likely to bring greater 'political divergence'.

In addition, the conflict is made potentially greater because of the extent of deepening and widening that is envisaged. Both quantitatively and qualitatively, the next enlargement is on an unprecedented scale: the number of countries is comparatively huge and the relative economic weakness and political frailty of the prospective members exacerbates the dilemma – there is a rich diversity amongst the states about to join the EU and most are either small or micro-states. At the same time the EU is engaged in the most ambitious phase of its internal development since the 1950s, with economic and monetary union at the centre but also more deepening on a whole range of fronts.

The task ahead of the EU is therefore a difficult one but also an unavoidable one. The EU had to enlarge to the east because the newly independent countries there would not be denied entry to the Union, and the Mediterranean applicants could not be ignored indefinitely; enlargement had become politically inevitable. However, whilst the pressure for widening was largely external in origin, the push for deepening was internally driven. A hard core of EU member states (including Germany[1] and France) had become convinced that the move towards EMU could be delayed no longer and were determined to go for it even if it meant leaving some members behind and introducing differential integration. In the mid-1990s the EU therefore found itself with an extensive and potentially conflicting agenda but one from which it could not escape.

The rest of this chapter groups EU developments into three categories. The next two sections deal with widening (in 1995 and forthcoming) and deepening (primarily economic and monetary union but also the common foreign and security policy and the proposed European Constitution). The fourth section looks at other significant policy developments – which in some cases may be linked to either deepening (for example, employment policy) or widening (institutional reform). The penultimate section returns to the 'widening versus deepening' debate and discusses the proposed European Constitution, and the final section considers how the EU might be assessed as an international organisation.

MORE ENLARGEMENT: 1995[2] AND BEYOND

The volte-face of the EFTAns was remarkable but not really surprising, although, of course, not all of them were able to brush aside their long-standing objections to joining the EU. The Norwegians, as in 1970–1, actually negotiated accession terms but these were rejected in a referendum with a similar result to that of 1970–1, and for similar reasons (to do with fish, oil and the environment mainly);[3] Iceland and Switzerland did not get even that far: the former through fears of being totally dominated on account of its smallness, and through a desire to protect its fishing grounds; the latter because of the peculiarities of its system of democracy and various concerns relating to agriculture, foreign ownership of Swiss land and property, the environment, and its neutrality.[4] But Austria, Sweden and Finland were prepared to go all the way, driven by fears of exclusion from the single market, and the existing EU membership was happy to accept these relatively rich, Western democracies, which were – along with the USA, Japan and the rest of western Europe, the European Union's only important trading partners.[5] It was debatable to what extent these new members – particularly Sweden[6] – had abandoned their preference for intergovernmental cooperation in favour of an approach more in keeping with the vision of Europe of the EU's founding fathers; their motivation was arguably based on more negative factors. However, what is certain is that 1995 witnessed the last enlargement by the 'classical method'[7] whereby new members were simply tacked on to the EU and nothing changed internally very much except that the numbers got bigger. Post-1995 enlargement was going to have to be 'adaptive'[8] – in short, the EU would have to change itself.

However, it was the end of the cold war and collapse of the Soviet bloc that really brought enlargement to centre-stage. While the former Communist states were keen to pursue NATO membership as an insurance policy against any vestigial Russian hegemonial ambitions, the real prize was membership of the EU, which, they believed, would bring in its wake several economic benefits: trade, investment, financial stability, and employment opportunities, as well as more intangible but still important gains including a much clearer European identity and some support for progress towards becoming strong and secure democracies. There were also potential economic and political benefits for the existing members of the EU. Just as completing the single market led to gains stemming from increased opportunities for trade, and economies of scale in production, so extending the single market into eastern Europe should generate similar gains for both current and new EU members. Other possible benefits included a more powerful EU voice on the world stage and more effective cooperation to deal with common threats such as environmental pollution and organised crime.

Whilst the post-1995 enlargement brought with it large potential benefits, these were matched by the possibility of substantial costs for the EU. These were described in the context of the 'widening versus deepening' dilemma at the beginning of this chapter (under four headings), but can be re-stated in more general and extensive terms.[9]

Financial issues have been at the centre of the enlargement debate. In addition to the opportunity cost of diverting funds into eastern Europe, identified in the context of the widening and deepening debate, there are much bigger issues. The financial implications of widening are potentially strongly adverse as all thirteen of the current aspiring EU members are poorer than the EU average, in some cases by a considerable margin, and would anticipate being net beneficiaries from the EU budget. Also, the large agricultural sectors of the prospective members are potentially extremely costly. Particular countries like Poland and Romania cause obvious concerns but dependence on agriculture is common to most of the applicant countries: in the mid-1990s, on average 22.5 per cent of their total workforce were employed in agriculture and contributed 8.6 per cent of their total gross value added, compared with 5.3 per cent and 2.4 per cent (respectively) for the EU.

Institutional difficulties are inevitable as the Rome Treaty structures, designed for six and stretched for fifteen, finally reach breaking point. The main issues relate to numbers in the Commission and Parliament, and voting weights in the Council, as well as potential paralysis in decision making.

Specific policies will have to adapt to accommodate such a large influx of new members. This is not merely to do with the possibility that new policies or further development of old policies will be inhibited (deepening), but existing policies may go backwards ('shallowing') because they become unworkable in their present (integrated) form.

The central policy or philosophy of the EU – supranational integration – may also be threatened and a growing number of members join solely to gain economic and political advantages with no accompanying 'vision' of Europe. The ultimate question is whether the new members will 'go native' and take on the characteristics of the current membership of the EU 'club', or whether the 'club' will have to change to accommodate the new members.

Nor is it all good news on the respective members' side of the fence. There has been a backlash in public opinion as it has become increasingly clear that EU accession will not necessarily lead to immediate improvements. Indeed, unpopular internal policies will continue to be necessary to make EU membership work in their favour. The economic sickness will continue: the EU provides additional treatment and not a miracle cure. Even more fundamentally, there are those who question whether the policies being encouraged and pursued to facilitate EU accession necessarily coincide with the policies that will best transform the economies of the former Communist states.[10]

For its part, the EU has not been enthusiastic about further enlargement and has repeatedly sought to slow down the process. It eventually took its first major step in 1993 when it laid down eight criteria that had to be met by new members.[11] Some of these were very precise (such as being a democracy and adopting the *acquis communautaire*) but others were sufficiently vague (a functioning market economy and an adequate administrative system, for example) to give much scope for interpretation. At the same time, the EU began to negotiate a range of ever-closer agreements with the applicant countries – trade agreements, 'Europe agreements', accession partnerships and so on – designed to bring the applicants gradually closer to the EU and facilitate full membership when it eventually came. In addition, starting with the PHARE (Poland and Hungary Assistance for Restructuring their Economies) programme in 1989, the EU provided financial support through various schemes to assist with economic reconstruction, environmental protection, transport and agricultural development. However, the most important requirement for the aspiring members was the need for them to adopt the *acquis communautaire* – effectively the common law of the Union, a body of detailed rules divided into over thirty chapters and covering free movement of goods, people, services and capital, company law, competition policy, agriculture, fisheries, transport, taxation, economic and monetary union, statistics, social policy and employment, energy, industrial policy, small and medium-sized business undertakings, science and research, education and training, telecommunications and information technologies, culture and audiovisual policy, regional policy, environment, consumers and health protection, justice and home affairs, customs union, external relations, common foreign and security policy, financial control, financial and budgetary provisions, and institutions.

Four years of negotiations were to take place before the Copenhagen European Council meeting in December 2002 was finally able to agree terms of accession. The first major milestone in this process was the adoption by the European Commission of 'Agenda 2000' in 1997. This was the Commission's response to a request from the December 1995 meeting of the European Council, in Madrid, to prepare an assessment of the candidates' applications for membership and a detailed analysis of what enlargement might mean for the EU. As with most of the important EU documents during the enlargement process, Agenda 2000 provided a single framework that addressed widening as well as deepening issues, but so far as the candidates were concerned, it recommended that negotiations should commence with six countries: Poland, Hungary, the Czech Republic, Cyprus, Estonia and Slovenia. The Luxembourg European Council of December 1997 accepted this, while at the same time making it clear that 'enlargement is a comprehensive, inclusive and ongoing process, which will take place in stages; each of the applicant states will proceed at its own rate, depending on its degree of preparedness'. What this meant in practice was that other candidates would not be ignored, while the six could not necessarily expect to make identical progress towards membership since each application would be negotiated separately.

A detailed pre-accession strategy was also worked out, involving greater assistance, with funding going to two priority areas: reinforcement of candidates' judicial and administrative capacities (30% of total funding) and assistance toward their adoption and application of the *acquis* (70%). Each of the favoured six was to sign an Association Agreement with the EU, covering trade-related issues, political dialogue, legal reform and other areas of cooperation. Accession Partnerships would identify the priorities to be attended to in each candidate's preparations. The Luxembourg meeting also decided to set up a European Conference, a multilateral forum in which all candidates, including Turkey, would meet existing members to discuss a wide range of issues. This met for the first time in March 1998 at the same time as formal negotiations between the EU and the six commenced, and a broader accession process got under way with all ten central European candidates and Cyprus. (Malta, which had frozen its application in 1996, reactivated it in October 1998, enabling it to join in this process.) The Helsinki Council meeting of December 1999 decided that five more countries could be included in the negotiations: Lithuania, Latvia, Bulgaria, Romania, and the Slovak Republic.

In February 2001, the Treaty of Nice was signed, amending the existing treaties, and setting out the changes that would need to be made to the EU's own institutions if enlargement was not to stifle decision making within the Union. Only the detailed negotiations over the thirty areas of the *acquis* with individual candidates remained, with each candidate having different concerns that needed to be discussed: Poland wanted a delay of several years before foreigners could buy land, Latvia wanted concessions relating to its right to hunt bears and lynxes, several wanted some delays before full implementation of the EU's requirements on the environment. The complexity of these negotiations is clear from the fact that the eventual Treaty of Accession, signed on 16 April 2003, is more than 6000 pages in length.

Several possible hitches had to be overcome before that point: Ireland's referendum on the Nice Treaty, in June 2001, rejected the Treaty, which would have in effect killed off enlargement had not this vote been overturned in a second referendum in October 2002. The same month saw an EU decision that ten candidates: Cyprus, the Czech Republic, Estonia, Hungary, Latvia, Lithuania, Malta, Poland, the Slovak Republic and Slovenia would be ready for membership by May 2004 (thus enabling their citizens to vote in the EU parliamentary elections scheduled for June 2004). A brief alarm was raised early in 2003 when French President Chirac fiercely criticised several candidates for backing the US–British policy on Iraq, hinting at one point that he might call for a French referendum on enlargement.

Two further new members, Bulgaria and Romania, are currently scheduled for possible admission in 2006. Croatia formally applied for membership at the beginning of 2003, and will probably be followed by other Balkan countries. Much greater controversy surrounds the admission of another candidate, Turkey, which in fact first applied to join as long ago as 1987. As a relatively poor state with a population of 62 million, Turkey's accession would pose considerable economic problems for the Union, but these are not the principal obstacles to Turkey's membership. One long-running issue is whether, despite major reforms in recent years, Turkey yet meets EU requirements in terms of human rights and its justice system, particularly with regard to its Kurdish minority. Of potentially greater significance is Turkey's Islamic identity. Some, including Britain, and also the United States, which has strongly supported Turkey's campaign for admission to the EU, see Turkey's accession as helping to build bridges between the West and the Islamic world, as well as deflecting any tendencies in Turkey towards religious extremism. Others are afraid of adverse consequences for the Union's own cultural homogeneity and also worry about potential social unrest if Turks have unrestricted rights of migration to western Europe. Turkey itself has made clear its increasing irritation at the EU's seeming inability to reach a final decision on this issue, which is likely to be one of the largest confronting the EU in the next five years.

However, whilst the EU will have to deal with difficult cases like Turkey at some point, in the immediate future it will have its hands full absorbing ten new members. It is impossible to predict the effect that such an influx of new members all at once will have, but it is clear that the EU will change in a number of ways:

- It will become much bigger as an organisation, and to change direction will be less easy and take more time.
- It will be a poorer organisation with more poor members.
- It will become an organisation in which most members are small states.
- Its geographical centre will shift to the north-east, thereby making its peripheral Atlantic and Mediterranean members even more peripheral.

Thus the EU will become more unwieldy and probably less predictable. Nevertheless, it could also emerge after a few years as immensely powerful and rich. But what of deepening? The last ten years have seen substantial progress and it is to an examination of this process that we now turn.

DEEPENING THE UNION

The latest stage of widening has occasioned intense debate about the future of the Union and in particular the prospects of maintaining the remarkable momentum of the EU since 1986 towards the 'ever closer union' promised by the Treaty of Rome. While some saw enlargement as a chance to slow down any progress towards a more centralised federal Europe, given that eastern European states which had only relatively recently won control over their own affairs were seen as more likely to emphasise the intergovernmental aspects of the Union's decision making, others were equally determined to continue 'deepening' the EU, even if this meant accepting the prospect of differential integration – a multi-tier or multi-speed Europe. Hence, at the same time as the EU moved towards doubling its membership (again), it also took several major steps towards the goal of a more fully integrated community. It was not to be sidetracked from the Maastricht agenda, and, in particular, there was a determination to realise economic and monetary union (EMU).

The Euro

EMU's chequered history has been described in previous chapters; however, what is of primary interest in evaluating the likely success of efforts to achieve EMU at the turn of the century is not how the EU got to the point of agreeing to adopt a single currency in 1999 but, rather, what had changed since the days of the 'snake' in the 1970s and the 'EMS' in the 1980s to make EMU more feasible. In fact, there were at least three significant differences: first, previous efforts had provided useful practical experience and had given the idea a degree of momentum, and also the Commission's attempt to popularise the (rather dubious) argument that a single market needed a single currency[12] had achieved some success. Secondly, the political will to prioritise the (European) objective of EMU at the expense of domestic objectives, often missing in the past, was quite clearly in place in the late 1990s; whilst the general populations of EU member states may have had serious misgivings, the political elites were mainly in favour of EMU and, perhaps rather arrogantly, saw public opinion as lagging behind. Finally, the lessons from the past that economic convergence had to precede and facilitate monetary integration and could not be enforced by it afterwards had been learnt and put into operation (albeit not entirely adequately) by the Maastricht convergence criteria. In the 1990s EMU was a policy whose time had come; even the near-collapse of the EMS in 1992–3 did little to halt its momentum.

While there are clear advantages in having a single EU currency in terms of reduced transaction costs, economies of pooling reserves and (especially) facilitating internal EU trade, these are only worth having if they are not offset by the loss of the exchange rate as a policy weapon.[13] However, if (as many believe) EU member states cannot pursue independent monetary policies, then there is little to lose and much to gain by participating in EMU. On the other hand, if exchange rate policy does have a significant effect even if only in the short run, then EMU becomes problematic unless all participants have very similar economic cycles. EMU means one monetary policy for all, and if member states are at different points in their economic cycle then they may require different monetary policies. A related argument concerns the possibility of asymmetric shocks: if EU members react differently to a given external event – such as an increase in oil prices or an East Asian financial crisis – then they need different monetary policies, and a single policy across the EU will not do. Thus, in strictly economic terms, there are good arguments on both sides of the EMU debate. However, in reality EMU is widely perceived as preparing the way for political union and is therefore seen as a political project for which economic sacrifices may be required.

Maastricht had set in motion a clear pathway towards a common currency, for which the name 'Euro' was devised at the 1995 European Council meeting in Madrid. Potential members had to meet the five convergence criteria (relating to inflation, currency stability, interest rates, governmental budget deficits and long-term debt) before they could be deemed fit to participate, and the 1998 European Council eventually agreed that eleven members were ready – all except Greece, Sweden, and the two countries that had opted out of the third stage of EMU, Britain and Denmark. At the same time the European Central Bank (ECB) was established at Frankfurt with the principal task of using its power to set interest rates to maintain price stability. The Euro was effectively launched as an electronic currency on 1 January 1999, when exchange rates amongst the eleven were fixed irrevocably. Since then, the Danish position has been confirmed by a referendum in 2000 in which 53 per cent of the people voting rejected Euro membership, Britain continues to sit on the fence (see below), and in 2001 the decision was taken to permit Greece to join, notwithstanding widespread misgivings about its readiness. As other countries, including France and Italy, had only managed to meet the membership criteria by a certain amount of creative accountancy, it was not surprising that doubts in financial markets about its viability led the 'electronic Euro' to fall significantly below the rate in relation to the dollar that had been set in 1999, with falls continuing after the first Euro coins and notes were issued and the old currencies withdrawn, early in 2002. During 2003 the Euro stabilised and indeed picked up significantly against the dollar.

The British position continues to be 'wait and see'; the packaging (the 'five economic tests'[14]) is different from the last time – that is, when the EMS was launched (Thatcher's 'when the time is right') – but the message stays the same. Britain's efforts to participate in previous arrangements – the 'snake' (1973) and EMS (1992) – have been brief and spectacular failures. If the UK's experience of fixed exchange rate systems in the twentieth century generally – the return to gold (1925–31), the restoration of the pound after the Second World War (1949) and the (lost) battle to avoid devaluation in the 1960s (1964–7) – are also remembered, then British reluctance to get involved in EMU is understandable. The policy was confirmed in June 2003 when the government completed a new assessment of the five economic tests,[15] which are:

- Are UK economic cycles and structures convergent with those of the members of EMU so that Britain could live comfortably with EMU's 'one interest rate fits all' policy?
- Is there sufficient flexibility in EMU to deal with any problems?
- Would membership of EMU encourage and improve the conditions for firms making long-term decisions to invest in Britain?

- What will be the impact of joining EMU on the UK's financial services industry, particularly the City of London?
- Will EMU membership enhance growth and stability in the UK and, therefore, lead to more jobs?

The government concluded:

> since 1997 the UK has made real progress towards meeting the five economic tests. But, on balance, though the potential benefits of increased investment, trade, a boost to financial services, growth and jobs are clear, we cannot at this point in time conclude that there is sustainable and durable convergence or sufficient flexibility to cope with any potential difficulties within the euro area. So . . . a clear and unambiguous case for UK membership of EMU has not at the present time been made and a decision to join now would not be in the national economic interest.[16]

The British position is thus clear, although it has to be said that it is based on a spurious precision: the five tests are neither exact nor quantifiable, and the decision comes down to personal judgement.

Only time – possibly a decade or more – will determine whether the adoption of the Euro was a reckless gamble or a decisive step towards building a stronger identity for the EU as a powerful actor on the world stage. Two broad scenarios have been advanced for the future of the common currency. In the first, particularly if Britain eventually chooses to join, the Euro will become a rival to the dollar as a reserve and trading currency. Given that one of the few major chinks in the armour of American hyperpower is its huge external deficit, which is dependent on the rest of the world feeling it has little choice but to purchase dollars, a highly successful Euro would be an important weapon for those Europeans – and others – who see the dominating issue of this century as the need to balance American power. The EU, even without developing as a military rival to the United States, which many see as unnecessary and dangerous, would have been able to act as a serious constraint on the United States' ability to do as it chooses.

In the second scenario, the long-term viability of the Euro would come increasingly into question, particularly if there was no substantial improvement in the German economy. Germans were not asked their opinion in a referendum about the Euro, and most evidence is that they would probably have voted *nein*. The ECB's remit is to guard against inflation, not to engage in larger macroeconomic management, such as aiding in expansionary policies to combat unemployment. Its view on the latter is that Germany needs to engage in substantial restructuring of its economy, but this would be electorally unpopular in the short term as it would almost certainly contribute to unemployment and worsening welfare standards. The Euro, and its supra-national overseers in the ECB, would be portrayed as the villains of the piece, with the deutschmark seen, nostalgically, as at the heart of the golden age of German economic power. The ensuing tensions would be too much for the Eurozone, which would fall apart in acrimony, jeopardising the entire European enterprise.

Common Foreign and Security Policy

The major economic element of deepening – which dominated the first pillar of the Maastricht Treaty – was economic and monetary union. The principal political element of deepening makes up the second pillar – the Common Foreign and Security Policy (CFSP) – and it is to this that we now turn. The European Political Cooperation (EPC) framework established in 1970 had acted to a marginal extent as a coordinator of European foreign policies where there were clear common interests – most effectively in fostering a Euro-Arab dialogue. There was also a marked increase in diplomatic intercourse during this period, but less so amongst defence personnel, who continued to interact mainly within the NATO framework. However, the dramatic changes in Europe that accompanied the end of the cold war sharply exposed the limitations of EPC and its successors. Several problems constantly reappeared over the decade and a half since 1989:

- There exists a permanent tension between the 'Atlanticist' tendencies of Britain and others who stress the importance of retaining a strong American security commitment to Europe and the 'Europeanists', led by the French, who want to develop a much more powerful independent security identity. This tension is aggravated by the United States itself, which has frequently expressed misgivings about the possibility of an EU military arm emerging outside the NATO framework, as summarised in Secretary of State Madeleine Albright's '3 Ds': no decoupling (from NATO), no duplication, and no discrimination (e.g. against the American arms industry).
- There has been a large gap between the rhetoric of the Europeanists and their willingness to commit substantial sums to defence spending at a time when most (including the USA) were hoping to obtain a substantial 'peace dividend' from the end of cold war tensions.
- Ireland, Sweden, Austria and Finland all have traditional policies of neutrality which constrain their ability to participate in a military alliance.
- Because foreign and defence policies concern matters perceived as vital national interests, states are unwilling to permit qualified majority voting and abandon their vetoes. Yet all the members of the EU, because of their different geopolitical circumstances, have widely varying priorities with a subsequently higher probability that almost any potential common policy might encounter a veto from at least one state. Greece, for example, consistently refused to permit the EU to recognise the former Yugoslav Republic of Macedonia.
- Common defence policies require standardisation of equipment and ideally a single, harmonised defence industry as well as similar standards of training and expertise amongst defence personnel. Despite agreements, such as the letter of intent signed by the six states with the most important defence industries in 1998, progress towards consolidating the industry has proved elusive, while there are also vast differences in training and levels of skill amongst European forces.

Problems of this kind were most sharply visible in the numerous crises in Yugoslavia, the Middle East and Afghanistan during this period, with the intense divisions in Europe over the 2003 Anglo-American attack on Iraq bringing matters to a head. However, headline events of this kind do not tell the whole story about the post-Maastricht attempt to develop a Common Foreign and Security Policy (CFSP). There were, first, several institutional developments. The Treaty of Amsterdam created the new position of High Representative for the CFSP, who would simultaneously hold the post of Secretary-General of the Council. A very high-profile appointee to this office, Javier Solana, former Secretary-General of NATO, ensured that this would not be seen merely as a sop to integrationists, although Solana has reportedly encountered numerous difficulties in his efforts to make the position a meaningful one. The Secretary-General, together with the European Commissioner for External Affairs and the Foreign Minister of the state currently providing the Presidency of the Council make up the 'troika' which represents the EU in its external relations. Amsterdam also introduced the concept of a 'common strategy' – to be adopted unanimously by the European Council in 'areas where member states have major common interests'. Significantly, this was singled out for particular criticism by Javier Solana in 2001.

Further institutional developments were to establish a Political and Security Committee (COPS, in its French acronym), which the 2000 Nice Council envisaged as having a central role in coordinating policy, and to initiate Council of Defence Ministers meetings. Most significantly, the decision was taken to establish an EU Rapid Reaction Force of 60,000 to deal at short notice with peacekeeping, humanitarian intervention and other emergencies. There are considerable doubts about the realistic prospects for this force, although an important symbolic step was taken on 31 March 2003, when a 320-strong force wearing the EU emblem took over the command of the NATO mission in Macedonia.

It is too early to tell whether such institutional developments will have a major impact on the progress of the CFSP, although the complex mix of national, intergovernmental and embryonic Community elements in CFSP decision making does not at first sight seem promising. In some respects the more interesting developments over the last few years have been taking place at more informal levels, as diplomatic interaction amongst EU defence and foreign affairs officials has steadily increased. In areas like trade and relations with the third world there is already a degree of EU coordination. One event that was seen as highly significant at the time was the meeting at St Malo in December 1998 between the French and British leaders. Britain had been the strongest and most consistent opponent of any kind of significant EU role in the defence field and even the fact that it was prepared to discuss such matters was seen as a breakthrough, as was its limited acknowledgement of the possibility of a degree of European defence autonomy. In fact, the St Malo meeting is best seen as the culmination of a long period of slowly improving Franco-British relations in defence and other areas since Maastricht.

The sobering experience of European inadequacies during the 1999 Kosovo crisis produced further limited progress, including the Rapid Reaction Force proposal, and, as Stanley Hoffmann very cautiously puts it, 'a kind of embryonic European identity emerged within limits' . The sharp divisions within Europe over the 2002–3 Iraq crisis were unquestionably a major setback to the CFSP but not necessarily an irretrievable one as Britain sought to mend fences with its European partners, while the leading anti-war states similarly sought to adjust pragmatically to the initial Anglo-American victory in the Iraq war.

It would be possible to include a range of other policies here under the 'deepening' heading but these are better taken up in the next section because deepening is essentially driven by EMU on the economic front and the CFSP on the political front. These are the two 'big ideas' of the EU as it moves into the new millennium, and both of them are ambitious and drag a whole range of other policy developments in their wake. However, neither of them are clear-cut winners and, in fact, both have been tried before and failed. Similarly to widening, the EU is pursuing deepening on a scale way beyond anything ever tried in the past. If organisations are like bicycles and need to move forward to prevent the rider from falling off, then the EU is currently racing ahead in top gear; the problem is that a high-speed crash is a much more dangerous way of falling off a bicycle and it is much more difficult to remount afterwards.

OTHER POLICIES: CONSOLIDATION AND DEVELOPMENT

The European Community/Union that the UK joined in 1973 amounted to little more than a partially complete single market, agriculture and external trade policies and lots of aspirations. The organisation that Malta, Cyprus and eight CEECs are joining some thirty years later is much more extensive and complex.[17] Many policy areas continue to deepen at a steady and unspectacular rate – social policy and the research and development framework programme are two examples. These policies are ignored in this short survey section. Instead, the focus will be on policies that relate specifically to widening or to the principal elements of deepening (EMU and the CFSP), and on policies which develop in ways that constitute a specific change in direction, or are in new areas. The former group covers institutional changes and financial/budgetary developments (incorporating the structural funds and CAP reform); the latter consists of employment, fisheries and competition policies and the new Cotonou (formerly Lomé) Agreement.

Institutional Reform
The first group of policy areas were addressed by the 'Agenda 2000' document and/or the Nice IGC/summit. Institutional reform is an extremely difficult issue for the EU; indeed, the Amsterdam IGC/summit was supposed to address this matter but failed.[18] The fundamental problem is that the EU's institutional structure is essentially based on a fragile compromise between large and small EU member states whereby small states are given greater representation than their size merits, but not to the extent that they can block measures that are supported by most of the larger states acting in unison. The relatively modest modifications to the voting weights in the Council introduced to take account of the 1995 enlargement were extremely controversial and required a special meeting to resolve the differences between Britain and the rest.[19] The institutional reforms required for the 2004 enlargement required an IGC and several years but were eventually agreed at Nice in December 2000. The key decisions were:

- From 2005 members will be limited to a single Commissioner each up to a maximum of 26; beyond that point there will be fewer Commissioners than member states.
- The use of QMV (qualified majority voting) was extended to cover most of the Council's business, and voting weights were agreed for new members and slightly adjusted for existing members.
- The total number of MEPs was capped at 732.

Clearly the intention is to streamline procedures so that the efficiency of decision making is not impaired. Unfortunately, since MEPs will each represent an even larger number of citizens and some member states will not have a Commissioner, it might be considered that the increased efficiency is at the expense of democratic legitimacy. This may not matter too much if the decision-making power continues to reside in the Council of Ministers where every member has a representative, but the extended use of QMV and growing role of the European Parliament continually undermines and erodes the ability of even the larger member states to control the direction of the Union. In international organisations, this is unusual, to say the least.

Structural Funds and the CAP

Meanwhile, efforts to reform the structural funds (SFs) and, in particular, the common agricultural policy (CAP) have continued. The main concern about the SFs was that they would be simply overwhelmed by the demands of the incoming CEECs. The easy solution of just increasing the size of the pot is neither desirable (as there are other priorities) nor feasible; at a time when member states are trying to control their expenditure so that they can participate in EMU, they are clearly not prepared to pay more into the structural funds. Fortunately, the early estimates of the costs of extending the SFs to the CEECs were basically alarmist and the levels of transfers implicitly assumed were simply far beyond what the CEECs could realistically absorb. More appropriate assumptions bring the transfers down to manageable levels and consequently the SFs have only needed modest reforms.

However, the reform of the CAP has continued. The majority of EU member states have never embraced CAP reform with any enthusiasm. Reform has always been driven by budgetary constraints and external factors, notably pressure from the Americans and other agricultural exporters through the GATT/WTO. This has continued to be the case in recent years. In the first half of the 1990s the CAP was reformed as a consequence of the Uruguay Round. From the later 1990s onwards it has been budgetary pressure due to concerns about the cost of extending the CAP to eastern Europe that has compelled continuing reform. The process has involved a slow and (politically) painful shift away from open-ended price support for all producers, to more targeted, income-related rather than production-related subsidies. In June 2003, EU farm ministers agreed to decouple the vast majority of farm subsidies from the volume of production entirely.[20] The net result of these developments in the SFs and agriculture has been that the EU budget has continued to cause few practical problems. Consequently, it has been possible to progress fairly smoothly from the 1988–92 (Delors I) and 1993–9 (Delors II) financial perspectives to a third one for the 2000–6 period, and to keep projected expenditure within the desired limits.

Finally, we turn to four policy areas where there have been significant developments in recent years.

Employment Policy

The EU has always been implicitly concerned with promoting employment (and reducing unemployment) but it is only in the last ten years that it has moved to try and develop a specific and active policy. The first major step was a White Paper in 1993[21] which sought to establish a medium-term strategy for the EU. It was a discussion of the possibilities rather than a policy proposal as such but it did spawn the concept of trans-European networks (TENs), some of which have now materialised, although there have been financial problems. Subsequent measures have included a chapter on employment in the Amsterdam Treaty, a special summit on employment in Luxembourg in 1997 (with little concrete result), and the introduction of National Employment Plans and EU Guidelines for Employment, which are intended to encourage consistency in, and coordination of, national employment policies. However, despite a great deal of debate and seemingly a reference to it at every European Council since 1992, EU employment policy is open to the criticism that it is all talk and no action; indeed, while all the significant policy levers remain at member-state level this will continue to be the case. On the other hand, all EU policies begin as talk, and, particularly as the EU moves towards fuller economic and monetary union, employment policy may well be given teeth. It would not be the first EU policy to develop in this way.

Common Fisheries Policy

A new common fisheries policy (CFP) was introduced at the beginning of 2003. A number of changes were made to the previous CFP, which had run since 1982. In particular, a more long-term framework is to be created to replace the current system which is based on annual fishing quotas and related measures. This should facilitate planning beyond the short term and lead to better conservation of fish stocks. Better monitoring and policing methods are to be introduced to reduce overfishing, to enforce the CFP's rules more comprehensively and consistently, and to ensure that all fishermen. Finally, a number of relatively modest new measures have been introduced to try to reduce the number of active vessels. The Commission has promised more measures in the future – and they will be needed. Whilst the previous CFP did prevent a free-for-all in the North Sea, it did little to eliminate the two fundamental problems of the fishing industry – overcapacity and overfishing, leading to the depletion of the fish stocks. There are still too many boats chasing too few fish and there is not yet enough in the new CFP to suggest that much will change.

Competition Policy

As part of its efforts to modernise competition policy, the Commission is continuing to pursue its rather radical proposal[22] to abolish the system whereby restrictive practices and abuses of dominant positions (monopolistic behaviour) have to be notified to, and authorised directly by, the Commission itself. Instead these would be dealt with by national courts, thereby leaving the Commission free to focus on the bigger cases and general policy issues.

Former Colonies

The new millennium marked the end of the Lomé Convention – or more precisely, the fourth trade and aid agreement of that name between the EU and its former colonies – to be replaced by the Cotonou Agreement, a twenty-year agreement with five-yearly reviews of the financial protocol. There was no repeat of the rhetoric of 'partnership' that accompanied the launch of Lomé in 1975. The ACP countries (former colonies) were well aware of their downward slide in the pecking order of

EU priorities and accepted the fairly modest agreement as being the best they could hope for. The EU did, however, make some changes: the new agreement marginally improves the EU–ACP trade framework, introduces political dialogue, explicitly addresses corruption, adopts poverty reduction as its main objective, promotes participatory approaches (involving, for example, the private sector and trade unions) and uses programming to disburse funds with decentralised (to local level) administrative and, to some extent, financial responsibilities. It is likely that many of these changes are designed for the benefit of the EU as much as the ACP countries, and the EU's bottom line (the value of trade concessions and EU aid) is much the same.

Much of this chapter has focused on the 'big' policy areas but, as indicated above, there is a great deal of activity in the EU at all levels; the Union really is deepening in a very comprehensive way.

CONCLUSION (I): WIDENING, DEEPENING AND THE EUROPEAN CONSTITUTION

The European Union is now a mature and much sought-after organisation. It has embarked on an extremely ambitious course involving simultaneous widening (enlargement to the east and south) and deepening (economic and monetary union, and closer cooperation across a whole range of policy areas). It is possible that an extreme outcome may occur: either the EU may actually pull it off and make it all the way to a full economic union of most of Europe in double-quick time; or the EU may fail spectacularly, implode and have to start again from a much lower base with fewer members. However, there is a more probable scenario in the middle ground – the EU could follow the path of 'differential integration' or 'flexibility'. Clearly, this is viewed as an increasingly probable way forward within the Union as the Amsterdam Treaty of 1997 had allowed for the possibility of 'closer cooperation' to enable certain member states to work together on specific developments, even when not all members wished to; this carried various strict conditions that limited its practical scope. However, it was taken further at Nice where it was agreed to remove the right of each member effectively to veto the launch of enhanced cooperation, with the only proviso being agreement by at least eight states, while retaining the right of other states to join in when they wished.

Several possible scenarios can be identified:

- a *'multispeed' Europe* is where all member states pursue the same objectives but some achieve them later than others because of economic weakness or political disposition;
- a *'multi-tier' or 'multi-layer' Europe, or a 'Europe of concentric circles'*, is where there is a 'hard core' of member states on a kind of fast track, surrounded by a 'soft core' of members who have only agreed to pursue a (common) subset of the objectives of the 'hard core'; beyond them there could also be a succession of 'softer cores' with progressively more limited agendas;
- a *'Europe à la carte' or 'Europe of opt outs'* is where every member has its own agenda and participates only in those policies in which it wants to take part.

These various expressions are frequently discussed very loosely, but clearly there are important differences amongst them. The alternative to all three is for the EU to continue to integrate 'en bloc' – a 'single speed' Europe – but if widening and deepening do prove to be incompatible then the possibility of a 'multispeed' or 'multitier' compromise becomes increasingly likely.

Notwithstanding its huge current agenda, the EU has built up a head of steam and is intent on pressing on even further. In December 2001 the European Council decided to convene a European Convention, headed by Valéry Giscard D' Estaing, with the task of producing a draft constitution for the EU by mid-2003. The Convention was to concentrate on ways of reforming the Union with a view to simplifying its procedures and institutions, making it more accessible to the people of Europe and preparing the way for a much larger EU from 2004, as well as responding to other global changes. It has been attended by controversy from the start. Its preliminary draft constitution in 2002 alarmed anti-federalists by ruminating about the possibility of using 'the United States of Europe' as a name for the Union, and also referring to 'certain common competences on a federal level'. This, however, was little more than a formal acknowledgement of the fact that the EU does, in reality, already possess some federal elements. More controversial were its proposals to reduce the number of Commissioners to 13, who would be assisted by 12 'Councillors' from the states which did not have a Commissioner, and to appoint a President of the EU Council for a 30-month term, renewable once, who would be assisted by a Directorate, an executive bureau which would prepare the agenda for Council meetings. At the same time, Council decisions would mostly be made on the basis of a simple majority, provided that the majority contained three-fifths of the population of the EU. There was also to be a European Foreign Minister, a weapons procurement agency and increased defence cooperation.

The combined effect of these proposals would be to weaken the power of the Commission, which rested significantly on its role as the initiator of EU policy proposals (a significant part of this would pass to the Council Directorate), at the same time as weakening the power of small states, who would lose out from the proposals to reduce the size of the Commission and increase the emphasis on population size in Council votes. Giscard himself, when he presented his proposals, clearly foreshadowed an essentially administrative role for the Commission when he referred to a Europe 'in which you have all the administration of the single market handled by the Commission [and] all the action of the states acting jointly being inspired and led by the Council and its chairman'. The European Parliament also saw its limited powers being potentially eroded by a proposal for a grandiosely labelled 'Congress of the Peoples of Europe', which would include representatives of national parliaments, although this was to have a mainly ceremonial role. Therefore it was not surprising that the European Council failed to reach agreement to adopt the draft Constitution at the end of 2003, and the debate continued into 2004.

Exercises like the European Convention and documents like the European Constitution occur every few years in the EU, and frequently provide a springboard for a significant advance in the development of the Union. As the EU continues to debate the current version of the European Constitution, it is difficult to believe that the Union can take on even more ambitious commitments. However, in the light of events in Europe since the mid-1980s, almost anything seems possible. A phrase used by Jacques Delors in a slightly different context twenty years ago may be appropriate again: are we about to witness another 'acceleration in history' in Europe?

CONCLUSION (II): THE EUROPEAN UNION AS AN INTERNATIONAL ORGANISATION

The character and purpose of a regional organisation can perhaps best be judged by examining two factors: its relationship with the outside world, and its own internal structure. Unfortunately, in both regards, the European Union lacks clarity. With regard to the first of these, it is clear that the EU does have an external policy, notably:

- the EU has a trade (or trade and aid) agreement with virtually all parts of the world, including association agreements, the Cotonou Agreement and, of course, the EEA;
- the EU has negotiated as a group in the GATT talks, most recently the Uruguay Round, and in the four-yearly UNCTAD meetings;
- the EU member states have worked as a unit in the CSCE (even though separate EU representation was not allowed), and, to some extent, at the UN (although with much less coherence);
- the EU has had a seat at Western economic summits since 1975;
- the EPC procedure, subsequently replaced by the CFSP, has led to a range of EU joint statements and actions (although there have been failures).

However, whilst the economic element is fairly well defined, this is not true of the political identity projected by the EU. Moreover, even the economic aspect is muddied by the fact that member states continue to act separately in their own right (alongside EU actions). The internal structure of the EU is, in some ways, even more difficult to define because it is obviously a highly contentious issue. The uneasy compromise between the 'federalists' and the 'intergovernmentalists' may be strained to breaking point by the pursuit of the current agenda, and the EU's internal structure is therefore ambiguous.

Thus, as international organisations go, the European Union remains something of an enigma. It is a curious mix of the supranational and the intergovernmental, which incorporates both elements with a degree of the former (the 'European Community'), and others which are clearly run along the lines of the latter (the CFSP and Home Affairs). This uniqueness is reflected in the EU's budget, which is radically different from those of other international organisations in that the overwhelming majority of it – 95 per cent – is spent not on administration, but on actual policies. Futhermore the EU is not a 'finished' organisation. It was created in an evolutionary form and continues to evolve. However, there is significant disagreement amongst its members as to the direction that this evolution should take and over what the final form of the organisation should be. This is much more marked than in other organisations. Finally there is the question as to whether the EU is a role model for regional integration elsewhere. There have indeed been many imitators but none have been very successful. Arguably the EU is a product of a unique time and unique circumstances, and is, and will continue to remain, outside the behaviourial norms of other international organisations. Perhaps it is not an organisation at all, but really is a superstate in the making. Only time will tell.

NOTES

1. For an indication of the firmness of the German position, see W. Schäuble and K. Lamers, *Reflections on European Policy*, reproduced in K. Lamers, *A German Agenda for European Union* (London: Federal Trust and the Konrad Adenauer Stifung, 1994).
2. A comprehensive account of the 1995 enlargement is to be found in J. Redmond (ed.), *The 1995 Enlargement of the European Union* (Aldershot: Ashgate, 1997).
3. For a detailed account of the Norwegian case, see C. Archer, 'Norway: the One that Got Away', in Redmond (ed.), *The 1995 Enlargement of the European Union*, ch. 7.
4. See J. Redmond (ed.), *Prospective Europeans: New Members for the European Community* (Hemel Hempstead: Harvester Wheatsheaf, 1994), for chapters dealing with Iceland and Switzerland in detail.
5. A feature of EU trade is that whereas the EU is an important trading partner for virtually every country in the world, the only countries that are similarly important to the EU are the USA, Japan and the countries in western Europe that are or have been part of EFTA; indeed, prior to 1995 EFTA's share of EU external trade was slightly greater than that of the USA and Japan combined. This has implications for the bargaining strength of the EU and its willingness to give concessions to its trading partners.
6. See L. Miles, *Sweden and European Integration* (Aldershot: Ashgate, 1997).
7. See C. Preston, 'Obstacles to EU Enlargement: the Classical Community Method and the Prospects for a Wider Europe', *Journal of Common Market Studies*, 33, no. 3 (September 1995).
8. For an explanation of the concept of 'adaptive' enlargement and a comparison with 'classical' enlargement, see J. Redmond and G. Rosenthal (eds), *The Expanding European Union: Past, Present and Future* (Boulder, CO: Lynne Rienner, 1998), Introduction.
9. For a detailed analysis see S. Croft et al., *The Enlargement of Europe* (Manchester: University of Manchester Press, 1999) pp. 68–83.
10. For example, see Wendy L. Fuevell, 'Between Transformation and Accession in Central Eastern Europe: Contradictions and Complementarity: an Assessment of the Implications of the EU Enlargement Criteria for the Politico-economic Transformation in the Czech Republic, Hungary, Poland and Slovakia' (unpublished doctoral thesis, University of Birmingham, 1999).
11. For a fuller description and analysis, see Croft et al., *The Enlargement of Europe*, pp. 61–2.
12. See European Commission, 'One Market, One Money', *European Economy*, no. 44 (October 1990).
13. Useful accounts of the arguments for and against EMU are to be found in M. Crawford, *One Money for Europe? The Economics and Politics of EMU* (New York: St Martin's Press, 1996); and D. Currie, *The Pros and Cons of EMU* (London: HM Treasury, 1997).
14. For useful and accessible explanations of the five tests, see Commentary, 'UK Membership of the Single Currency: an Assessment of the Five Economic Tests', *European Access*, no. 6 (December 1997); and B. Harrison, 'An Assessment of the Chancellor's Five Economic Tests for UK Entry into the EMU', *British Economy Survey*, vol. 27, no. 2 (Spring 1998).

15. HM Treasury, *UK Membership of the Single Currency: an Assessment of the Five Economic Tests* (London, 2003, Cm 5776).

16. Ibid., Executive Summary, p. 6.

17. A comprehensive account of developments in the European Union is provided by the Commission's *General Report on the Activities of the EU*, which is an annual publication. A more critical alternative is provided by the Annual Review of the *Journal of Common Market Studies*.

18. For a detailed discussion of the problems and the possibilities, see Croft et al., *The Enlargement of Europe*, pp. 68–71.

19. Essentially Britain, initially supported by Spain, sought to hold the minimum number of votes required to block a proposal in the Council at the pre-enlargement stage.

20. There is a vast literature on the CAP and its reform, and any current textbook on the EU would have a chapter on the CAP which would make a good starting point. Alternatively, the following might be consulted: J. Rollo, 'Reform of the CAP: the Beginning of the End or the End of the Beginning', *World Today*, January 1992; Commentary, 'Agenda 2000: CAP Reform Proposals', *European Access*, no. 5 (October 1997); A. Swinbank, 'EU Agriculture: Agenda 2000 and the WTO Commitments', *The World Economy*, January 1999; R. W. Ackrill, 'CAP Reform 1999: a Crisis in the Making', *Journal of Common Market Studies*, vol. 38, no. (2 June 2000); S. Goodman, 'CAP Reforms: the Rural Development Policy', *British Economy Survey*, vol. 29, no. 2 (Spring 2000), pp. 29–32; S. Tangermann and A. Banse (eds), *Central and Eastern European Agriculture in an Expanding European Union* (London: Cabi Publishing, 2000); A. Landau, 'The Agricultural Negotiations in the WTO', *Journal of Common Market Studies*, vol. 39, no. 1 (March 2001).

21. European Commission, *Growth, Competitiveness and Employment: The Challenges and Ways Forward into the 21st Century* (Brussels, 1993, COM (93) 700 final December).

22. European Commission, *White Paper on the Modernisation of the Rules Implementing Articles 85 and 86 of the EC Treaty* (Brussels, 1999, COM (99) 101 final April).

12

The New Regionalism

Attempting to find an objective definition of an international 'region' is a fruitless exercise because there is no unproblematic means of distinguishing one group of states from another by geographical, cultural, economic or other grounds. For example, is the 'natural' regional home of the United States in the Americas, the Pacific or the Atlantic? What are the boundaries of 'Europe' or 'Asia' or 'South-East Asia'? Which states are influenced by what are sometimes termed 'Asian values'? In practice, the only common elements in the overwhelming majority of regional organisations are that it is possible to draw an unbroken line around them on a map and their members perceive themselves as linked together in one or more ways.[1] What is beyond dispute is that such organisations have proliferated in number, with most of the world now participating in more than one hundred regional arrangements.[2] In this chapter we discuss the factors behind the resurgence of interest in regionalism in the 1990s, consider developments in the three major regions outside Europe and analyse the problems encountered by the new regionalism as well as its future prospects.

EUROPEAN DEVELOPMENTS OUTSIDE THE EU

Apart from the remarkable developments in the EU discussed in the previous chapter, Europe enjoyed an upsurge of regional organisation in several other contexts during the 1990s. The long moribund Western European Union (WEU) appeared to enjoy a new lease of life when the Maastricht Treaty gave it responsibility for developing a common EU security policy. However, the ongoing fragmentation of former Yugoslavia rather cruelly exposed the limitations of this aspect of the EU, and, although the WEU did increase its staff to more than 50, this could hardly be seen as a serious move towards its assumption of the role envisaged by Maastricht.[3] Other European developments related mainly to the collapse of communism in Eastern Europe. The Council of Europe, which has become increasingly focused on its human rights role, increased its membership from the original 18 when it was set up in 1949, to 41. It also strengthened its provisions for the legal protection of human rights in 1998 by merging its two main organs, the Commission and the Court, into a single institution combining the powers of both, and by appointing full-time judges to the Court, rather than relying on part-time judges as previously. This was a response to the growing importance of the Council in European jurisprudence: in 1981 the Commission received 404 applications for it to consider various human rights cases; this rose to 2032 in 1993, and 4750 in 1997. In 2001 the Court received no fewer than 13,858 applications, leading to calls that it concentrate on cases raising fundamental issues.[4] In 1995 the Conference on Security and Cooperation in Europe (CSCE), which had played a significant role in monitoring the 1957 Helsinki Accords, became the Organisation for Security and Cooperation in Europe (OSCE), with 55 members. As such it had an important consultative purpose with regard to Pan-European security issues while also, through its Office of Democratic Institutions and Human Rights (ODIHR), assisting the transition to democracy and the rule of law throughout the former Soviet bloc.

A plethora of new organisations also appeared in Eastern Europe and the former Soviet Union. In some cases these were envisaged as transitional arrangements, pending (and preparing the way for) accession to the EU. This was clearly true of the various institutions established by the Visegrad Four (Poland, Hungary, Czech Republic and Slovakia), such as the Central European Free Trade Area (CEFTA). Although cooperation amongst these states was at first made difficult by their competing to be the favourite contender for EU entry, the EU's own advice that accession would take some years to bring about and that they would be considered as a group rather than individually was instrumental in returning them to a more collaborative path, although trade within the group remained at a relatively low level. Much the same may be said of attempts to form subregional groupings between east and west European states, such as the Pentagonale, later renamed the Central European Initiative (CEI), which envisaged cooperation across several areas including telecoms and transport.[5]

Another post-cold war organisation, the Black Sea Economic Cooperation Scheme (BSECS), established in 1992 by eleven countries following a Turkish initiative, was less a preparation for EU membership (since for all except the existing EU member, Greece, and possibly Turkey, this was a fairly distant prospect) than a response to the challenge posed by deepening European integration and the need for a security dialogue over emerging issues in Central Asia and elsewhere. Its more ambitious aims of promoting greater harmonisation of policies in various areas made little progress, although trade within BSECS did increase.[6] The Commonwealth of Independent States (CIS) was envisaged as a means of managing the break-up of the former Soviet Union with the minimum disruption, while building upon the existing economic and security networks amongst the 12 members. However, the CIS region remains one of the world's leading sources of tension and real or potential conflict.

THE NEW REGIONALISM

Just as they had been in the 1960s, it is clear that European developments were a major influence on the creation of new regional organisations, from relatively small subregional groupings such as the Maghreb in the Arab world or MERCOSUR in Latin America to larger groupings such as APEC in Asia and the Pacific. Deepening integration in the EU, together with the prospect of enlargement, aroused apprehensions among its external trade partners that they might find themselves facing sharply reduced trade with Europe. Not counting trade within the EU itself, the Union accounts for around 20 per cent of total world trade, so even a relatively small shift from extra-European to intra-European trade could have serious repercussions. But the new impetus to regionalism also stemmed from larger considerations, including the desire for greater bargaining power in multilateral fora such as the WTO, and the fact that the world's remaining superpower, the United States, began to show an interest in both sponsoring regionalism and participating in the process itself.

Most fundamentally, the new regionalism may be seen as a response to the increasing impact of globalisation and the related shift in politico-economic orthodoxies over the past few decades. Globalisation is a multifaceted set of processes, primarily involving the emergence of global financial markets exchanging ever vaster sums with increasing speed of movement, and of global actors, such as transnational corporations and the owners of huge media empires, whose power and wealth may exceed that of many governments. Although neither the concept of globalisation, nor its consequences, are unproblematic,[7] there is general agreement that globalisation weakens the power and even the legitimacy of the state by undermining its claim to be able to provide various collective goods, such as security against external threats. Globalisation is also seen as the bearer of an all-devouring global culture, variously labelled as one of modernity, capitalism, westernisation or, most simply, Americanisation. As such, it may threaten more traditional national and regional cultural identities.

The new regionalism is a response to globalisation in three distinct but interrelated ways. The first is essentially defensive, with regionalism seen as a way of emphasising and protecting local cultures and, more importantly, local enterprise. In this respect it has been argued that, whereas the first post-war wave of regionalism was mainly driven by governments and national bureaucracies, the second was much more of a 'bottom–up' process, resulting from pressure from various local interest groups anxious to protect themselves from external competition.[8] Governments, in turn, have seen in regionalism a means of maintaining their political authority.[9] Secondly, new regionalism stems not only from protectionist impulses but from competitive ones. It is seen as conferring enhanced bargaining power in global negotiations, while providing a more secure opportunity for commercial amalgamations to take place at the regional level with a view to building up the capacity to compete in global markets. Finally, globalisation has been accompanied by a breakdown of traditional socialist and 'Third Worldist' ideologies emphasising state control of industry and economic self-reliance, and their displacement by the perceived need to restructure national economies in line with neoliberal economic doctrines. Governments have, in some cases, found it easier to promote such structural adjustment if at the same time it has been accompanied by and taken place within a context of regionalisation.[10]

Apart from the question of the causes of the new regionalism, analysts have focused on three main problems:

- Will regionalisation promote the welfare of the majority of people in participating countries?
- Will it promote regional security?
- Will it harmonise with or work against multilateral trade liberalisation, which most economists see as crucial to a global improvement in economic welfare?

Inevitably there are many differences of opinion over all three issues. This is in part because there are many differences among regional organisations: some are essentially free trade areas; some customs unions, imposing a common external tariff; others envisage much wider integration, including the free movement of labour. Some are heavily institutionalised, such as the EU; others much less so, such as ASEAN. Some contain mostly highly developed, industrialised states, others mainly poor primary producers. Some see themselves as helping to promote multilateralism by simplifying WTO bargaining, others have a more protectionist flavour. A further complicating factor in recent years has been deteriorating economic conditions, first in Asia then more widely in Latin America and the main Western economies. This has inevitably had an adverse effect on moves away from protectionist policies and, more generally, on regionalism itself. Even in the European Union states have backed away from strict enforcement of the rules designed to ensure economic stability following the launch of the Euro in 2002.

As long ago as 1950, Jacob Viner argued that the welfare effects of customs unions, both regionally and globally, depend on whether they are essentially trade-creating or trade-diverting and that it was, in practice, impossible to assess this except by considering individual cases.[11] Much the same may be said of regionalism's contribution to security, particularly as security problems today tend to be concerned less with inter-state tensions than with intra-state conflicts or with transnational issues such as criminal activities, including drug and people smuggling. While regional organisations may help to create 'security communities' with well established routines of conflict resolution, they may also, by creating losers as well as winners and by opening borders to criminals as well as to legitimate business transactions, exacerbate other sources of insecurity. Once again, few, if any, generalisations may be made about all organisations and it is necessary to examine the particular organisations, a task to which we now turn.

AFRICA

There have been ambitious proposals for Pan-African and subregional organisations in the continent since the idea of a United States of Africa was first promulgated at the beginning of the twentieth century.[12] Notwithstanding repeated setbacks and failures, most African states remain committed to regionalism as part of the solution to their profound and growing economic, political and social problems. For example, both the principal Pan-African institution, the Organisation of African Unity (OAU), and the most important subregional institution, the Economic Community of West African States (ECOWAS), have engaged in far-reaching restructuring processes since the late 1990s.

The immediate aftermath of independence for most African states in the late 1950s and early 1960s did not immediately produce a particularly encouraging climate for regionalism. Divisions emerged between Anglophone and Francophone states, between radicals and moderates, and between neighbours now able to dispute the generally artificial borders they had been bequeathed by European colonialism. Finally, the tension caused by the outbreak of the Congo crisis in 1960 seemed for a time to push African states into various subregional groupings rather than a single all-embracing entity. During 1961 and 1962, three such groupings were created, known as the Casablanca, Brazaville and Monrovia groups.[13] However, in 1963 the decision was taken to merge such existing groups into a single institution, the OAU. Earlier ideas promoted by Ghana's President Nkrumah to work towards an African superstate with its own army, parliament and government were soon abandoned in favour of a more pragmatic conception of a loose association of sovereign authorities.

The Organisation of African Unity

The OAU differed from other regional structures in that its principal aims were neither collective security nor the pursuit of regional integration. Rather, it represented an attempt to lay down some general principles – such as sovereign equality, non-interference in internal affairs, territorial integrity, condemnation of political assassination and subversion, the peaceful settlement of disputes, and dedication to the emancipation of the remaining colonial territories in the continent – that were to govern relations among African states and help towards developing a sense of collective identity. An additional important role was to work towards the liberation of the remaining African countries governed by white minority regimes, to which end the OAU set up a committee in 1963, charging it to provide moral and material support for the liberation movements and to act diplomatically both to secure international legitimisation of armed struggle in the UN and elsewhere and to isolate the minority regimes.[14] In this objective it achieved some success. It helped to shape the response of those external powers which supported the liberation struggles or wished to give humanitarian aid by indicating which struggles and movements it regarded as legitimate.[15] It also succeeded in making the cause of the liberation of Southern Africa an international issue by repeated pressure at the UN.

In other areas the OAU enjoyed, at best, only limited success. It was able to assist in bringing about a peaceful settlement in a conflict between two of its members, Algeria and Morocco, that broke out in 1963, but other conflicts proved more intractable. For instance, in 1964 serious fighting broke out between Ethiopia and Somalia over Somalia's irredentist claims in Ethiopia. Although there were periods of truce in this conflict, occasionally arranged through OAU auspices, fighting persisted and sometimes intensified. Much the same was true of the bitter conflict between Rwanda and Burundi from 1966, where refugees from both sides were accused of subversive activities across the border. This was a classic post-colonial situation, resulting from borders which cut across tribal areas, where the OAU could do little other than organise temporary ceasefires.[16]

OAU mediation was of some help in resolving a dispute between Gabon and Equatorial Guinea in 1972 but of limited value in Chad in 1981–3. In general, however, there was considerable resistance to permitting OAU involvement in internal conflicts, although these produced some of the most serious crises in the region. Thus, hundreds of thousands of lives were lost in Uganda, Sudan, Rwanda and Burundi with the OAU able to do little but stand by and watch. In some respects the OAU was presented with an even more difficult problem in the 1967–70 Nigerian civil war, because here the OAU itself became a factor, albeit a minor one, in the conflict.[17] Initially the federal government of Nigeria was adamant in refusing to permit the OAU even to discuss the war because it felt that this might go some way towards legitimising the breakaway state of Biafra as an independent entity, while the Biafran leadership was equally intent upon encouraging OAU involvement. But here too, many thousands were being killed and the crisis was receiving worldwide press attention, so the OAU would have laid itself open to considerable ridicule if it had simply ignored the Nigerian situation. In the event, it established a Consultative Committee on Nigeria but this, in line with general OAU policy, declared after its first visit to Nigeria that 'any solution of the Nigerian crisis must be in the context of preserving the unity and territorial integrity of Nigeria'.[18] Acceptance of the break-up of an existing African state had been seen by all as opening a Pandora's Box of cataclysmic proportions and the OAU felt it had no option in this case but to reaffirm this principle. But this put it in the position of having to support one side in the civil war, which inevitably damaged its chances of mediating. By 1969, the Biafran side refused to accept any OAU role, while the federal government, in contrast, insisted that it would only accept mediation from the OAU.

During the cold war period, African states shared one common cause – the ending of apartheid in South Africa – and were also, to some extent, able to maintain the superpowers' interest in their affairs by taking advantage of their competition for influence. By the 1990s both factors had vanished, and at the same time the range and extremity of the problems facing Africa had significantly increased. The 1980s had witnessed falling per capita incomes, lower per capita food production and a smaller share for the region in the world market for exports.[19] Internal order was collapsing in an increasing number of countries. Aids and drought combined to exacerbate an already desperate situation in many states. Corrupt and incompetent governments and sporadic interference from outside made matters even worse. Moreover, Africa was clearly in danger of being the major loser from the process of regionalisation taking place elsewhere. A few attempts were made in the 1990s to remedy this last problem. The OAU established a Mechanism for Conflict Prevention, Management and Resolution, in 1993, but despite rhetorical support for shifting greater responsibility for peacekeeping to regional organisations, the major powers were unwilling to provide the necessary underpinning and support that would have been required to enable the OAU to undertake a more substantial role.[20]

Similarly, moves towards economic integration, notably the coming into force in 1993 of the African Economic Community (AEC), established in the 1991 Abuja Treaty, had achieved relatively little ten years on. The AEC, which was seen as the economic wing of the OAU, envisaged progressing over a 34-year period towards a full economic union, through six stages, the first involving a strengthening of existing subregional economic communities and establishing new ones where they did not exist. However, a 1999 review of progress concluded that there were doubts as to whether even this relatively modest first stage objective had been achieved. One inherent problem in the region is that there is considerable room to doubt whether

African countries, generally poor primary producers facing, in some cases, considerable geographical barriers between them, are natural trading partners.

By the end of the century the OAU had adopted some 20 treaties and agreed hundreds more communiqués and declarations.[21] It is hard to resist the conclusion that these brought little more than words to bear in confronting Africa's increasingly desperate situation. At one time African leaders had been able to blame their countries' problems on the legacy of colonialism and continuing neo-imperialist practices by the Western powers. While both charges had some measure of validity, they came to be seen by the major Western powers and the IGOs they dominated, such as the World Bank, as little more than an alibi for bad governance by the African states themselves. It was in this spirit that a number of leading African states agreed in 2001 to an initiative known as the New Partnership for Africa's Development (NEPAD), a comprehensive programme designed to address Africa's increasing marginalisation in the face of globalisation. At the heart of this programme was an agreement by the African leaders to embark upon internal reforms designed to promote good governance, and also to establish a regional mechanism for conflict prevention, management and resolution, in return for a fresh commitment by the developed world to assist Africa in these endeavours: a commitment that was made by the Group of Eight at their June 2002 meeting. The NEPAD programme involved replacing the OAU with a new organisation entitled the African Union (AU), which also came into being in 2002.

The African Union

The AU constitution envisages a much more ambitious organisation than its predecessor, with far-reaching powers to intervene in the event of 'grave circumstances' such as war crimes or genocide in a member state, together with a common defence policy and a strong emphasis on democracy, human rights and the rule of law. Its institutions would include not only an Assembly of heads of state and government, a Permanent Representatives Committee and a secretariat, to be termed the Commission, but an elected parliament, a court of justice and an Economic, Social and Cultural Council that would give strong representation to civil society groups.[22]

Scepticism about the AU was not confined to the more cynical elements of the Western media. Many African NGOs thought it unlikely that the new organisation would succeed in forcing some governments away from deeply entrenched corruption, while others were also apprehensive about the degree to which NEPAD would simply push Africa further along an IMF/World Bank path of structural adjustment that they believed had contributed more to Africa's problems than it had solved.[23] The Libyan leader Colonel Gaddafi, who had taken the lead in promoting the AU, which he saw as a potential means of extending Libyan influence in the continent, also favoured maintaining traditional anti-Western rhetoric in the new organisation, rather than making it a vehicle for partnership with the West, as envisaged in NEPAD.[24] If, however, the more ambitious aspects of the AU represent a triumph of hope over experience, the organisation may also constitute the continent's last chance of breaking out of its vicious circle of inexorable decline.

ECOWAS

Several subregional organisations have also been established in Africa, including the Arab Maghreb Union and the Southern African Development Community. By far the largest of these is the Economic Community of West African States (ECOWAS), comprising 16 states with a combined population of nearly 200 million, including both Francophone and Anglophone countries. This was established in 1975 with the aim of progressing fairly rapidly to a free trade area and eventually to full economic union. It achieved a few successes, including doubling trade within the subregion – but only from a very low base of 3 per cent of total trade – and it was able to finance a few joint projects such as road-building.[25] In general, however, its achievements are a huge distance from the optimistic rhetoric that attended its formation. West Africa has been amongst the world's most unstable regions and ECOWAS has had virtually no impact on its members' economic and security problems. It did become involved in the internal conflicts of Liberia and Sierra Leone through its peacekeeping force, the Economic Community Monitoring Group (ECOMOG), but this aroused apprehensions, particularly in Francophone Africa, about Nigeria's hegemonic ambitions in the region. In the event, UN involvement was required to bring about a settlement of both conflicts, but in 2002 Nigeria and Ghana called for further military integration and enhancement of the region's peacekeeping capabilities.

An ECOWAS executive report in 2000 addressed in frank terms the reasons for the organisation's failure to achieve any of its goals. Among other factors, it identified political instability and bad governance, poor infrastructure compounded by lack of political will and bad economic policies, the failure to involve civil society and the private sector, and the existence of too many organisations, as well as failings of the organisations themselves.[26] Sadly such a list could be applied to most other African regionalist ventures. It was hardly surprising that, when civil war broke out in the Ivory Coast in 2002, initial ECOWAS offers of assistance were rebuffed by the government.

ASIA

Asian regionalism in the twenty years after the Second World War was limited and to some extent externally promoted, as in the case of the South-East Asia Treaty Organisation (SEATO), a strategic alliance formed between Pakistan, Thailand and the Philippines together with the United States and other Western powers, in 1954. In the Indian sub-continent, prospects for regionalism were limited by the continuing hostility between India and Pakistan, although both states, together with the smaller states of the subregion, were able to come together to form the South Asian Association for Regional Cooperation (SAARC) in 1985. This set itself fairly broad and general goals of promoting welfare and economic, social and cultural collaboration, but, realistically in the circumstances, excluded 'bilateral and contentious issues' from consideration. While the Indo-Pakistani confrontation continues, only modest achievements may be expected of SAARC, although it has made progress in reducing some tariffs, and at the beginning of 2002, despite very high tension including the threat of nuclear war between the regional superpowers, was able to request a draft treaty framework for a free trade area to be achieved by the end of the year.[27]

ASEAN

South-east Asia was to witness one of the more promising experiments in regional organisation outside Europe in the form of the Association of South-East Asian Nations (ASEAN), created by the Bangkok Declaration in 1967. Indonesia, Malaysia, the Philippines, Singapore and Thailand were the founding members, Brunei (1984), Vietnam (1995), Laos and Myanmar (1997), and Cambodia (1999), joining much later. ASEAN was formed during a period of regional tension caused by the Vietnam War and the period of political upheaval and extremism in China known as the Cultural Revolution. ASEAN thus originated as a response to various external threats and deliberately avoided setting up more than the most minimal institutional structures or defining its economic goals in other than the vaguest and most flexible terms.

The first eight years of its existence saw little more than 'symbolic' achievements.[28] This largely reflected its reactive and negative foundations. Unlike the EU, which from its early years had a shared vision of a politically and economically integrated region, ASEAN had been essentially an attempt to ward off external threats, particularly from Communism, by showing solidarity. It was this common thread of anti-Communism which brought about the first major development of ASEAN when the collapse of the (non-Communist) governments in Cambodia and South Vietnam led to fears of Communist-led revolutionary activities within ASEAN, and to the Bali summit in early 1976 at which it was decided to press ahead with ASEAN cooperation on virtually all fronts. Two major documents were signed. A Treaty of Amity and Cooperation called for mutual respect and non-interference in each others' internal affairs and the peaceful settlement of disputes. A Declaration of Concord called for cooperation in economic development and the establishment of a 'Zone of Peace, Freedom and Stability' (ZOPFAN). The main emphasis was on economic cooperation, particularly intra-ASEAN trade liberalisation and the development of large-scale ASEAN industrial projects. However, in 1979, only minimal tariff reductions could be decided in a Preferential Trading Arrangements (PTA) agreement. Intra-ASEAN trade has remained at under 20 per cent and only two of the projected five large-scale industrial projects agreed at Bali actually materialised. There are many reasons for this, including lingering animosities amongst the ASEAN members and the considerable differences in levels of economic development and national wealth: Singapore's per capita GDP is 100 times that of Cambodia and Vietnam. But the main factor is a general lack of will in ASEAN to shift away from existing protectionist attitudes in some of the larger states.[29]

During the 1980s and early 1990s most ASEAN members enjoyed economic growth rates of around 6 per cent. They also experienced a period that was relatively free of the kinds of security issues that had dominated the 1950s and 1960s. This led some to proclaim the existence of an 'ASEAN way' to economic prosperity and political stability that was based on 'Asian values'. ASEAN was able to bask in the reflected glory of its members' high rates of economic growth and to claim that ASEAN's very flexibility, vagueness of purpose and lack of strong institutions were themselves attributes of the 'ASEAN way'. A similar emphasis on informality underlay several other regional and subregional initiatives during the 1980s and early 1990s, as well as inter-regional forums. One of these, inspired by ASEAN, was the ASEAN Regional Forum (ARF), established in 1994 and with a current membership of 23, including the 10 ASEAN states, the United States, the EU (acting as a single member), Russia, Japan, Australia, New Zealand, India, China and, unusually, North Korea. It is, essentially, a security dialogue with an ASEAN-like emphasis on decision making through consensus formation, and on confidence-building measures rather than direct cooperation, with recent discussions having focused on peacekeeping, piracy, disaster relief, transnational crime and terrorism. Many potential disputes remain just below the surface among some of these dialogue partners, especially between China and several, if not most, of the other members of ARF, and a clear, if unspoken, ASEAN objective in ARF is to encourage China to seek peaceful settlements of these conflicts.

An Australian initiative that might also be considered an exemplar of the 'ASEAN way' was the formation of Asia Pacific Economic Cooperation (APEC) in 1989. This includes Australia, Brunei, Canada, Chile, China, Taiwan, Hong Kong, Indonesia, Japan, Korea, Malaysia, Mexico, New Zealand, Papua New Guinea, the Philippines, Singapore, Thailand and the United States. The ASEAN states were at first uneasy about the possibility of such a group being dominated by its English-speaking members and in 1990 formed, with the other Asian members of APEC, the East Asian Economic Caucus (EAEC), to counter this possibility. APEC was initially conceived primarily as a forum for economic dialogue, but the United States decided in 1993 to press for trade and investment liberalisation within APEC. The target of full liberalisation by 2020 was set in 1994, although – in line with 'the ASEAN way' – there was considerable ambiguity about precisely how this target was to be met and even about what it meant in practice.[30] APEC functioned primarily as a networking framework for private as well as public sectors, with the former dominating, in the view of one author, but with the state performing a 'key coordinating and legitimizing role'.[31] However, others have argued that the value of APEC came into severe question amongst its Asian members following the economic collapse in South-east Asia in 1997, with the American push for freer trade particularly disliked.[32]

Driven in part by New Regionalist dynamics and imperatives, ASEAN itself began to shift towards a clearer programme of objectives together with greater institutionalisation during the early 1990s. At the fourth ASEAN summit, at Kuala Lumpur in January 1992, there were two significant economic agreements, although both were much watered down versions of the original proposals. The first of these was the 'Framework Agreement on Enhancing ASEAN Economic Cooperation'. This had its origins in a Philippine proposal for a wide-ranging but ill-defined ASEAN economic treaty. It binds ASEAN members to strengthen cooperation in specific sectors, including trade, industry, transport, communications, finance and banking. It also allows for subregional growth areas both within ASEAN and between non-ASEAN states, such as Singapore's growth triangle linking Singapore, Johor (Malaysia) and Riau province (Indonesia). The Agreement allows two or more ASEAN members to initiate economic cooperation amongst themselves and not to have to wait until all members are ready.

The second measure agreed at Kuala Lumpur was the creation of an ASEAN free trade area (AFTA), initially over a 15-year period ending in 2008, later amended to just ten years. The essence of AFTA is a commitment that tariffs on all goods with a 40 per cent or more ASEAN content are scheduled to fall to 0–5 per cent. However, in recognition of the considerable differences in levels of development within ASEAN, members were to cut tariffs at different speeds. In subsequent years this programme was expanded to include non-tariff barriers and quantitative restrictions and extended to trade in services, and the possibility of creating a free investment area was also discussed.[33] The Agreement allows for excluding products under three circumstances: 'temporary exclusion', where tariff reductions may be delayed for a short period to protect local industry; 'sensitive agricultural products', which have a deadline of 2010 before tariffs are to be reduced; and 'general exceptions', where a state believes issues of national security, public morals, the protection of human, animal and plant life, or articles of high cultural value are involved. At present, 8660 items fall under the first of these categories, 829 under the second and 360 under the third. However, tariff reductions for non-excluded items have continued in accordance with the agreed timetable, notwithstanding the severe blow to economic confidence in the region delivered by the 1997 economic crisis. Since the Agreement involved clear legal commitments that went far beyond the earlier loose and flexible arrangements to which ASEAN was accustomed, it was also decided to take the (for ASEAN) revolutionary step of promoting the Secretariat to a more prominent position with the task of monitoring the Agreement.[34]

ASEAN has, from the start, faced some obvious problems, many of which have been exacerbated by enlargement. Its membership embraces two of the world's richer states, Brunei and Singapore, as well as several of its poorest; politically the range extends from more or less functioning democracies to the secretive dictatorship of Myanmar; culturally there are significant numbers of Muslims, Christians, Buddhists, Hindus and Communists. Such differences, at the very least, tend to cast doubt on assertions about 'Asian values' and the 'ASEAN way'. If the region has so far avoided the extremes of state collapse and internal violence that are increasingly common in Africa, that success has been tested to the limits in Indonesia. In general, ASEAN has been unable to act collectively in the face of severe problems, such as the economic crisis, the serious toxic smog that enveloped Indonesia in 1997–8, the 1997 coup d'état in Cambodia, the Indonesian army's murderous rampage when it was obliged to leave East Timor in 1999, and the continuing repressions of the Myanmar government. In recent years, individual ASEAN members, if not yet the organisation as such, have moved marginally away from the tacit agreement that ASEAN members should not criticise each others' internal affairs.[35] However, an attempt by Thailand and the Philippines in 1998 to replace the strict ASEAN principle of non-intervention with a new formula of 'flexible engagement', which, in essence, would permit constructive criticism of a country's human rights record, met with failure as a much weaker formulation – 'enhanced interaction' – was adopted.[36]

Even that area which, at least until 1997, seemed to provide the clearest evidence of ASEAN's success – economic growth – has come into question in recent years, with some seeing free trade as essentially a Western agenda and some calling for greater financial rather than commercial integration, given that the crisis was severely exacerbated by lack of liquidity and banking deficiencies. Japan has also promoted the idea of greater monetary integration.[37] Yet, for the moment, free trade appears as one of ASEAN's clear success stories and one that is likely to be built upon in the next few years. The November 2002 ASEAN summit agreed in principle to a comprehensive economic partnership between Japan and ASEAN, including trade and also financial services, information technology and human resources, while the same meeting concluded a framework for developing a free trade area with China.[38]

Both of these, if they are translated into concrete measures, would represent major achievements for the organisation: genuine triumphs, perhaps, for the 'ASEAN way'.

THE AMERICAS

The regionalist architecture in the Americas ranges from one all-embracing organisation, the Organisation of American States (OAS), to numerous subregional organisations and, most recently, a significant free trade area initiative, the North American Free Trade Area (NAFTA). It is no exaggeration to say that the history of the OAS and more generally of regional integration in Latin America is largely identical with the history of US policies there and the Latin American response. But alongside this central theme (and to some extent an aspect of it) has emerged another: the search for a distinct Latin American identity. In the last fifteen years the Americas have also been leading exemplars of the new regionalism.

Tensions between US objectives in the hemisphere and Latin American aspirations for their own region may be seen as part of a more fundamental conflict between two sets of ideas, which one author terms 'unilateralism' and 'multilateralism'.[39] The most famous early expression of the 'unilateralist' idea was the Monroe Doctrine of 1823, in which President Monroe declared a US special interest in the hemisphere as a whole and a determination to exclude European influence from it. At about the same time as Monroe's statement, Simon Bolivar was proposing one version of the multilateralist idea: a union of the former Spanish colonies of South America.[40] The other version of multilateralism was the concept of Pan-American union, which first appeared in the 1880s and which was the origin of the present-day OAS.

Pan-Americanism was first promoted by the United States at the first International Conference of American States, in 1889, whose aims were to promote arbitration as a means of settling disputes and also to develop economic relations among the countries concerned. This was also the aim of the first regional organisation to be established, the International Union of American States (1890), whose purpose was to collect and disseminate commercial information.[41] However, as the main meeting place for all of the states of the Americas, the International Union's four-yearly or five-yearly conferences also provided a forum for the expression of Latin American opposition to the US assumption of a general right of intervention in Latin American affairs. Indeed, pressure from its southern neighbours was great enough for the United States formally to accept the principle of non-intervention at two Pan-American conferences, in 1933 and 1936.[42] A period of substantial cooperation followed, which reached a peak during the Second World War, and the desire to continue this after the war gave a major impetus to the formation of the OAS.[43] The Latin American countries were also anxious to place their special relationship with the United States on a distinctive organisational basis in order to prevent that relationship from being subordinated to America's global interests in the newly formed UN. It was, to a great extent, the efforts of the Latin American states at the San Francisco Conference which resulted in Articles 51, 52 and 53 of the UN Charter, encouraging regional organisations to have a substantial role in the settlement of local disputes.

The OAS

The OAS Charter reflected the varied concerns of its members. For example, the principle of non-intervention is firmly enshrined in Articles 15 to 20. These prohibit not only military intervention but 'any other form of interference or attempted threat against the personality of the State or against its political, economic and cultural elements'. This is a clear, if indirect, statement of the widespread Latin American fear of becoming dependencies of the United States in ways other than the normal political ones. Equally, however, US concerns are reflected in various affirmations of the principles of representative democracy and individual liberty. In other respects the Charter was a sweeping proclamation of a great range of supposedly shared values and beliefs which are virtually meaningless as guides to action – the statements, for instance, that 'the education of peoples should be directed towards justice, freedom and peace', or that 'the spiritual unity of the continent is based on respect for the cultural values of the American countries and requires their close cooperation for the high purpose of civilisation'.

During the first twenty years of its existence the OAS demonstrated a modest success in peacekeeping and peaceful settlement, and some 40 disputes were resolved by its machinery.[44] It employed the full range of techniques and instruments available to international organisations for these purposes, including fact-finding missions, behind the scenes diplomacy by the OAS Secretary-General, mediation, diplomatic pressure and, in the 1960 Dominican case, economic sanctions. Disputes where the OAS helped to reduce tension included conflicts between Costa Rica and Nicaragua (1948–9), the Dominican Republic and Haiti (1949–50), Cuba and Guatemala (1950), Costa Rica and Nicaragua (1955–6), Honduras and Nicaragua (1957), Panama and Cuba (1959), the Dominican Republic and Haiti (1963–5), El Salvador and Honduras (1969), Costa Rica and Nicaragua (1977), Peru and Ecuador (1981), Colombia and Venezuela (1988), and Trinidad and Venezuela (1989). It also supervised the ceasefire arrangements in Nicaragua following the end of the civil war there in 1989, and was similarly involved in internal conflicts in Suriname (1991) and Haiti (1992). However, the United States ignored the OAS when it intervened in Panama in 1989. Several of the earlier disputes were resolved partly through the efforts of the Inter-American Peace Committee, which had been created by the OAS for this purpose, but in 1956 the powers of this body were severely curtailed when it was decided that it could not send an investigative mission to the location of a dispute unless both sides invited it to do so. OAS peacekeeping and peacebuilding efforts have probably been most successful where the organisation was offering, in essence, a way out with minimum loss of face for two sides who did not really wish to raise the level of tension between them. However, it has undoubtedly played a useful, if sometimes modest, part in such areas as confidence building, reducing tension, and peace maintenance.

The OAS was significantly affected from the outset by the United States' cold war agenda. It was, for example, employed on a number of occasions by Washington to help legitimise interventions against leftist regimes in the region, as in the case of Guatemala in 1954, when the government was overthrown by an invading force of US-supported exiles, or the Dominican Republic in 1965, when a revolutionary group seemed likely to gain power there. The United States' greatest concern, however, was with the Communist regime of Fidel Castro in Cuba. The United States was unable to obtain support from the other American countries for a joint intervention, but in January 1962 it secured OAS agreement to economic sanctions against Cuba for the latter's activities in support of guerrillas in Venezuela. The OAS also declared that 'adherence by any member of the OAS to Marxism–Leninism is incompatible with the Inter-American system' and that 'this incompatibility excludes the present government of Cuba from participation in the Inter-American system'.[45] Further diplomatic and economic sanctions against Cuba were voted in 1964 and 1967, although several OAS members did not vote for sanctions, and Mexico refused to impose them.

The end of the cold war provoked a re-evaluation by the United States of its own future role and interests in the region. In June 1990 George Bush launched the Enterprise for the Americas Initiative (EAI), which proposed writing off part of the debt owed to US agencies, steps to increase foreign investment, and the eventual creation of a free trade area covering the whole of the hemisphere.[46] In 1991 the Organisation passed Resolution 1080 pledging defence and promotion of representative democracy and human rights in the region, and stated a firm resolve to stimulate the process of renewal of the OAS to make it more effective and useful. Resolution 1080 has been invoked four times, in relation to Haiti (1991), when it led to an embargo on the country; Peru (1992), when diplomatic pressure enabled the OAS to monitor elections there; Guatemala (1993), when the OAS issued a condemnation of the suspension of constitutional democracy; and Paraguay (1996), when the Organisation gave its backing to the President when he was threatened by a military takeover. The OAS has also sent more than thirty electoral observation missions since 1990.[47] A Charter amendment was agreed in 1992 empowering the OAS General Assembly, by a two-thirds vote, to exclude any member state whose democratically constituted government was overthrown by force. In 1996 the OAS set up the Inter-American Convention against Corruption – the first region to establish such an institution. Steps were also taken in 1997 to strengthen the Inter-American Court of Human Rights by giving it greater financial and administrative freedom from the Organisation as a whole.[48] The chief significance of such developments is that they implied a clear shift away from a strict application of the principle of non-intervention, hitherto the cornerstone of the OAS.

South America has made rather less progress in its pursuit of economic development: an item on the OAS agenda from the start. Inevitably the region's striving for development has been inextricably entangled with its ambiguous relationship with the United States – both necessary supporter and potential exploiter. This ambiguity was present in President Kennedy's Alliance for Progress scheme, launched in 1961. This was an ambitious two-year programme whose objectives included not only accelerated economic growth but internal political, social and economic reforms, but with US assistance linked to its general anti-Communist policies in the region.

It was a sense of dissatisfaction with the economic dimension of the OAS that underlay the 1967 revisions of the Charter. These raised the status of the OAS Economic and Social Council and incorporated, as an ultimate objective, the economic integration of Latin America. They also replaced the virtually moribund Inter-American Conference with a General Assembly, which was to meet annually and whose powers were enhanced. The more confrontational atmosphere in the third world during the 1970s led some Latin American states to propose sweeping changes in the OAS Charter, by which it would enunciate the principle of 'collective economic security' and sanctions against 'economic aggression'. Understandably, perhaps, Washington resisted such demands.

Subregionalism

The cold war period also witnessed several regional and subregional attempts to promote free trade and broader economic integration. In the first wave of regionalism these included the eleven-member Latin American Free Trade Association (LAFTA), formed in 1960 but replaced by the Latin American Integration Association (LAIA) in 1980, the five-member Andean Pact, formed in 1969, the five-member Organisation of Central American States (ODECA), formed in 1951 and followed by the Central American Common Market (CACM) in 1960.

These institutions had only limited success. Although CACM initially experienced substantial growth in trade, its progress was interrupted in 1969 by the war between two of its members, El Salvador and Honduras. Moreover, the two poorest countries, Honduras and Nicaragua, gained less than the others from the grouping, an outcome which caused much dissension. In the case of LAFTA, intra-regional foreign trade grew after its establishment but only to around 10 per cent of the region's total trade. As with CACM, the rigid and conservative attitudes of the state-owned companies tended to provide foreign-owned multinational corporations with the greatest opportunities and, in both cases, there was an inequitable distribution of benefits between richer and poorer members. The Andean Group attempted to avoid some of these problems, with its stated aims including a reduction of economic inequalities amongst its members, and with preferential treatment for Bolivia and Ecuador actually specified in its Agreement. However, Chile's belief that the Group had adopted too restrictive a code for foreign investment led to her withdrawal in 1976. In general, all of these organisations suffered from intrinsic structural weaknesses, in that the economies of their members were competitive rather than complementary, a problem exacerbated by the fact that in many cases there were severe geographical barriers to trade. Moreover, the region still tended to cling to centralist and protectionist attitudes that inhibited trade, a predisposition made worse by the debt crisis of 1982, which led to a new round of protectionism.

The Americas were in the vanguard of the new regionalism. By 1992, South America's share of total world exports had fallen from 12 per cent in 1950 to only 3.6 per cent.[49] Regionalist ventures elsewhere gave rise to (possibly unjustified) fears that Latin America would lose out even more unless it joined in the process. Initiatives from the late 1980s included the November 1988 Treaty on Integration, Cooperation and Development, between Brazil and Argentina, eventually followed by the Treaty of Asunción in March 1991, which created the Common Market of the South (MERCOSUR), which also included Paraguay and Uruguay as members; the Group of Three, formed by Colombia, Mexico and Venezuela in 1989, which was followed by the Caracas Agreement of 1993, extending membership to Costa Rica, El Salvador, Guatemala, Honduras, Nicaragua and Panama; and the North American Free Trade Agreement (NAFTA), formed in 1994 between Canada, Mexico and the United States. There were also attempts to breathe new life into the existing subregional arrangements, as with the re-branding of the Andean Pact as the Andean Community, in 1996.

MERCOSUR

Of these the most significant initiatives were MERCOSUR and NAFTA. MERCOSUR came into force on 1 January 1995. It had four main ingredients: liberalisation of trade amongst its members and, by negotiated agreement, with other states and regional organisations; the creation of a customs union with a common external tariff, by six-monthly stages until 2006; coordination of economic policies; and cooperation in certain specific sectors. Various exceptions were also included to protect vulnerable industries, especially in the smaller countries. Unlike earlier efforts at regional integration in the continent, the institutional structure envisaged for MERCOSUR was fairly minimal.[50] It should be noted also that MERCOSUR was envisaged as a response to the neoliberal agenda being promoted by the major Western countries and the institutions dominated by them, such as the World Bank. Hence, it started life with a commitment to 'open regionalism' within the overall context and rules of the World Trade Organisation, rather than as a protectionist device.[51] For example, total trade between the EU and MERCOSUR doubled in value between 1990 and 1997.[52]

The MERCOSUR countries enjoyed a dramatic growth in their intra-regional trade, with its share of total exports increasing from 8 to 21 per cent between 1991 and 1996, and increasing more slowly thereafter.[53] More limited progress occurred in other areas such as industrial cooperation. There were some inherent tensions, mostly deriving from the fact that Brazil, with 79 per cent of the organization's total population and 71 per cent of its GDP, dwarfed the other members, including its long-time rival, Argentina. This hindered closer and more rapid integration and also tended to prevent efforts at political and security cooperation, as did the fact that Argentina was in favour of the US project of a Free Trade Area of the Americas (FTAA), proposed by President Clinton in 1994, while Brazil was not. However, the two sides were able to reach agreement in 1996 on strengthening their political cooperation, particularly so far as support for democratisation was concerned, and in the Rio Declaration of 1997, MERCOSUR was declared to be a 'strategic alliance'.[54] This, however, had little more than rhetorical significance: Argentina refused to support Brazil on one crucial issue, its campaign to be made a permanent member of the UN Security Council.

Periods of economic crisis tend to put the greatest strain on free trade areas and both Brazil and Argentina experienced severe economic downturns and negative economic growth in 2000–2, with Brazil's public debt rising to 240 billion dollars and Argentina actually defaulting on international commercial debt. There was also anxiety amongst some foreign investors over the election of a leftist President in Brazil in October 2002, although he was quick to state that rebuilding MERCOSUR was 'the main priority of our foreign policy', and to call for coordinated agricultural and industrial policies, together with the creation of a regional Development Bank.[55] However, he also expressed strong reservations about the United States' FTAA project. Although the EU has shown itself still supportive of MERCOSUR, the organisation's future is probably dependent on a significant upturn in the global economy.

NAFTA

NAFTA may be seen essentially as an extension, to Mexico, of the Canada–US Free Trade Agreement of 1988, since its provisions are identical except for trade in energy being excluded, in deference to Mexican sensitivities about their oil industry.[56] As its name implies, NAFTA's focus is very much on trade rather than broader economic integration, although its provisions for the removal of barriers between the three countries also apply to investment, and there is also an emphasis on the protection of intellectual property rights. Its Secretariat is essentially a coordinating body with responsibility for overseeing NAFTA's complex trade dispute settlement procedures, which oblige disputes that cannot be settled by mediation or conciliation to go before a panel of private-sector experts, whose decisions are binding. NAFTA was and remains controversial. Some have criticised it as being driven essentially by American industrial concerns to exploit a cheaper labour market, and one that is less subject to environmental constraints.[57] But more recently, pressure has grown in the United States itself to amend the Treaty in various ways, including agricultural tariffs, which were being gradually eliminated, against the wishes of powerful lobbies on both sides of the border. However, there can be little dispute that NAFTA was established primarily in response to a US agenda that included increasing its own trade, creating an organisation that assisted its negotiating strength *vis à vis* the EU, and dealing with the problem of illegal immigration from Mexico.[58]

NOTES

1. Even this limited definition does not always work, as in the case of the non-contiguous European Free Trade Area.
2. Wilfred J. Ethier, 'The New Regionalism', *Economic Journal*, vol. 108, July (1998), p. 1149.
3. Hilaire McCoubrey and Justin Morris, *Regional Peacekeeping in the Post-Cold War Era* (The Hague: Kluwer Law International, 2000), p. 78.
4. Facts gleaned from the Council of Europe's website.
5. The original five Pentagonale members were Hungary, Yugoslavia, Czechoslovakia, Austria and Italy. The 1992 relaunch as the CEI added Poland and some of the states of former Yugoslavia. Ian Kearns, 'Subregionalism in Central Europe', in Glen Hook and Ian Kearns, *Subregionalism and World Order* (Basingstoke: Macmillan, 1999), pp. 21–7.
6. Gerasimos Konidaris, 'The Black Sea Economic Cooperation Scheme', in Hook and Kearns, *Subregionalism and World Order*, pp. 41–52.
7. David Armstrong, 'Globalization and the Social State', *Review of International Studies*, vol. 24 (1998), pp. 461–78.
8. Percy S. Mistry, 'The New Regionalism: Impediment or Spur to Future Multilateralism', in Bjorn Hettne et al. (eds), *Globalism and the New Regionalism* (Basingstoke: Macmillan, 1999), p. 123.
9. Mario Telo (ed.), *European Union and New Regionalism* (Aldershot: Ashgate, 2001), p. 7.
10. Edward D. Mansfield and Helen V. Milner, 'The New Wave of Regionalism', in Paul F. Diehl (ed.), *The Politics of Global Governance: International Organizations in an Interdependent World* (Boulder, CO: Lynne Rienner, 2001), pp. 328–30.
11. Jacob Viner, 'The Customs Union Issue', cited in Diehl, *The Politics of Global Governance*, pp. 316–17. See also Alan Winters, 'Regionalism and the Next Round', in

J. J. Schott (ed.), *Launching New Global Trade Talks: An Action Agenda* (Washington, DC: Institute for International Economics, 1999), pp. 47–60.

12. I. Wallerstein, *Africa: The Politics of Unity* (New York: Random House, 1967).

13. I. Wallerstein, 'The Early Years of the OAU', *International Organization* (Autumn 1966), p. 775.

14. L. T. Kapungu, 'The OAU's support for the Liberation of Southern Africa', in Y. El-Ayouty (ed.), *The Organization of African Unity after Ten Years* (New York: Praeger, 1976), p. 136.

15. M. Wolfers, *Politics in the Organization of African Unity* (London: Methuen, 1976), p. 189.

16. B. D. Meyers, 'Intraregional Conflict Management by the OAU', *International Organization*, Summer 1974, pp. 358–9.

17. For details of the OAU's response to the Biafran crisis, see Z. Cervenka, 'The OAU and the Nigerian Civil War', in Y. El-Ayouty (ed.), *The Organization of African Unity after Ten Years*, pp. 152–73.

18. Ibid.

19. Adebayo Adedeji, 'Africa in the Nineties: a Decade for Socio-Economic Recovery and Transformation or Another Lost Decade?', 1989 Foundation Lecture to the Nigerian Institute of International Affairs (NIIA, 1991), p. 7.

20. A. LeRoy Bennett and James K. Oliver, *International Organizations: Principles and Issues* (Upper Saddle River, NJ: Prentice-Hall International, 2002), p. 255.

21. A. Abass and M. A. Baderin, 'Towards Effective Collective Security and Human Rights Protection in Africa: an Assessment of the Constitutive Act of the New African Union', *Netherlands International Law Review*, vol. XLIX, no. 1 (2002), p. 3.

22. AU and NEPAD websites. See also 'African Union: a Dream under Construction', *Africa Recovery*, UN Department of Public Information, vol. 16, no. 1 (April 2002).

23. Ibid.

24. *The Times*, 9 July 2002.

25. S. Riley, 'West African Subregionalism: the Case of the Economic Community of West African States (ECOWAS)', in Glen Hook and Ian Kearns, *Subregionalism and World Order*, pp. 63–83.

26. ECOWAS website.

27. SAARC website.

28. J. Wong, 'ASEAN's Experience in Regional Economic Cooperation', *Asian Development Review*, 3 (1985), p. 83.

29. M. T. Yeung, N. Perdikis and W. A. Kerr, *Regional Trading Blocs in the Global Economy: The EU and ASEAN* (Cheltenham: Edward Elgar, 1999), p. 53.

30. J. A. Frankel, *Regional Trading Blocs in the World Economic System* (Washington, DC: Institute for International Economics, 1996), p. 265.

31. J. A. Camilleri, 'Regionalism and Globalism in Asia Pacific', in M. Tehranian (ed.), *Asian Peace: Security and Governance in the Asia-Pacific Region* (London: I. B. Tauris, 1999) p. 59.

32. H. Dieter and R. Higgott, *Explaining Alternative Theories of Economic Regionalism: From Trade to Finance in Asian Cooperation*, CSGR Working Paper 89/02, January 2002, University of Warwick, p. 3.

33. www.us-asean.org/afta.htm.

34. Jeannie Henderson, *Reassessing ASEAN*, Adelphi Paper 328 (London, 1999), p. 23.

35. Ibid., p. 53.
36. Ibid., pp. 49–51.
37. H. Dieter and R. Higgott, *Explaining Alternative Theories*, provide a detailed discussion of this point.
38. *The Yomiuri 'Shimbun' Online*, 20 Oct. 02.
39. G. Pope Atkins, *Latin America in the International Political System* (New York: Free Press, 1977), p. 308.
40. M. Margaret Ball, *The OAS in Transition* (Durham, NC: Duke University Press, 1969), p. 5.
41. G. Connell-Smith, *The Inter-American System* (London: Oxford University Press, 1966) p. 15.
42. Pope Atkins, *Latin America*, pp. 322–5.
43. Bryce Wood, 'The Organization of American States', in *The Yearbook of World Affairs, 1979* (London: Time Books, 1979), p. 150.
44. Viron P. Vaky and Heraldo Munoz, *The Future of the Organization of American States* (New York: Twentieth-Century Fund Press, 1993), p. 10.
45. Pope Atkins, *Latin America*, p. 332.
46. P. Calvert (ed.), *Political and Economic Encyclopaedia of South America and the Caribbean* (Longman: Harlow, 1991), p. 12.
47. www.oas.org, February 2000.
48. C. R. Thomas, 'The Organization of American States in its 50th Year', *INTERAMER*, no. 65 (Washington, DC, 1998), pp. 65–6.
49. W. Mattli, *The Logic of Regional Integration* (New York: Cambridge University Press, 1999), p. 155.
50. F. M. Abbott, *Law and Policy of Regional Integration: The NAFTA and Western Hemispheric Integration in the World Trade Organization System* (Dordrecht, Boston, London: Kluwer, 1995), p. 176.
51. P. Cammack, 'MERCOSUR: from Domestic Concerns to Regional Influence', in Hook and Kearns, *Subregionalism and World Order*, p. 96.
52. J. Dauster, 'MERCOSUR and the EU: Prospects for an Inter-Regional Association', *European Foreign Affairs Review*, 3 (1998), pp. 447–8.
53. L. V. Pereira, 'Toward the Common Market of the South: Mercosur's Origins, Evolution and Challenges', in R. Roett (ed.), *MERCOSUR: Regional Integration and World Markets* (Boulder, CO: Lynne Rienner, 1999), p. 7. See also M. H. Ferrari, *The MERCOSUR Codes* (London: British Institute of International and Comparative Law, 2000), p. xxv.
54. M. Hirst, 'Mercosur's Complex Political Agenda', in Roett, *MERCOSUR: Regional Integration and World Markets*, pp. 38–42.
55. MERCO Press, 29 October 2002.
56. J. Frankel, *Regional Trading Blocs*, p. 258.
57. Abbott, *Law and Policy of Regional Integration*, p. 6.
58. Ibid., pp. 16–20.

13

Towards Global Governance?

INTRODUCTION

Most of the IGOs considered to this point conform to a particular pattern or template. They have been formed by sovereign states to provide cooperative solutions to various international problems but without transforming or even significantly affecting the foundation stone of the contemporary international system, namely the fact that the sovereign state itself is the sole location and source of legitimate political authority. Most fundamentally, IGOs have been required to respect the central corollary of sovereignty: the principle of non-intervention in a state's internal affairs. The main exception to this model is the European Union, whose members have pooled a limited measure of sovereign power in the common institutions of the Union, but even in that case, states retain the capacity to withdraw from the Union should they choose to do so, leaving ultimate authority in the hands of the states.

During the last few decades, and with increasing emphasis since the end of the cold war, the claim has been advanced that a structure of global governance has been emerging alongside (and partly as a consequence of) the globalisation of international economic relations. Some see this as presaging the end of the state, or at least its substantial demise; others envisage a 'neomedieval' order in which authority is dispersed among many agents: states, markets, transnational corporations, IGOs and nongovernmental organisations (NGOs). There are also varying opinions about the extent of global governance: some restrict it to the trade and financial sectors, others discern elements of governance in issue areas such as the environment, security, human rights, and communications. This chapter will examine some of those areas where particular roles have been attributed to IGOs, after first considering some more general aspects of global governance.

The term 'global governance' is intended by all who use it to denote a broader, looser conception of political authority than either 'world government' or 'international governance' encapsulates. Whatever else they disagree about, analysts of global governance concur on that one central point. 'Government' is seen as requiring executive agencies with generally accepted legitimacy and with coercive capacities to enforce compliance with their edicts: a combination of characteristics which is absent at the inter-state level. 'Governance' is a more complex and less concrete phenomenon. One of the best brief definitions of the term is offered by Keohane and Nye: 'By governance we mean the processes and institutions, both formal and informal, that guide and restrain the collective activities of a group.'[1] The 'group' in this case is any interlinked network in some specific issue area that operates globally. Both the members of the network and the agencies of governance may include actors other than states, such as transnational corporations and nongovernmental organisations.

Global governance, in this understanding of the term, may simply emerge without conscious management as an outcome of some structural facet of international relations, such as a balance of power in the security field or the workings of a market in international economics. Such unmanaged instances of global governance, however, are not what has provoked the very large recent literature on the phenomenon, which has focused to a great extent on governance that exhibits some measure of institutionalisation. Institutions in this context may be formal structures, like the World Trade Organisation (WTO) or the International Monetary Fund (IMF), or they may be more informal, such as the array of collaborative intergovernmental groupings, private-sector associations, and domestic laws of leading states, all of which contribute to the regulation of global finance.[2] But whether formal or informal, institutionalised global governance will be characterised by: (i) the existence of a normative foundation or a shared understanding of desired objectives and standards of conduct relevant to the specific subject of governance; (ii) agreed rules that seek to give juridical shape to and operationalise the normative foundation; and (iii) a regulatory structure to monitor and enforce compliance with and determine changes to the rules and to resolve disputes. In this chapter we are primarily concerned with formal global governance, particularly in the areas of international economic relations and human rights.

INTERNATIONAL ECONOMIC ORDER

A vast number of national, intergovernmental and private-sector agencies as well as market regulatory structures are involved to some extent with global economic governance. Here, four of the most important are considered – the IMF, the World Bank, the WTO and the Group of Seven (G7), which became the Group of Eight (G8) when Russia became a member in 1997–8.

The IMF

The Great Depression of the 1930s, which was exacerbated by competitive and self-defeating devaluations and protectionist policies, had demonstrated the need for an international economic regime that would both provide stability, especially with regard to exchange rates, and promote trade. The Bretton Woods conference of 1944 was given the task of addressing these needs, and its deliberations laid down the foundations of the post-war economic order for the next 25 years.

Bretton Woods created two new IGOs: the IMF and the International Bank for Reconstruction and Development (IBRD) or World Bank. The overall aim of the regime presided over by the IMF was to create a stable and predictable international monetary system that would avoid the competitive devaluations that had characterised the pre-war era. It was to have three main features. First, it was to promote stability, primarily through a regime of fixed exchange rates, in which states agreed to intervene to buy or sell each others' currencies, with the aim of preventing sharp fluctuations. Secondly, the members of the IMF all paid a subscription, which was then used to provide short-term credits to countries experiencing balance of payments difficulties. This credit was not to be given automatically but was to be linked to the imposition of a set of policy changes that were intended to encourage financial discipline in the recipient state. Thirdly, and most importantly, the regime rested upon the assumption by the United States of international economic hegemony. Most critically, the United States committed itself to exchange gold for dollars at any time at a fixed value of $35 per ounce. In practice this meant that countries tended to hold reserves in interest-bearing dollars rather than gold. The United States also undertook the responsibility of maintaining international liquidity through Marshall Aid, and by its preparedness to run balance of payments deficits.

The system worked well enough while the United States enjoyed unchallenged economic dominance. However, serious problems began to emerge in the 1960s. In part these stemmed from the fact that enormous financial power was beginning to build up outside the control of governments, as international banks and multinational corporations accumulated huge financial assets, thus creating a global market in money outside the Bretton Woods regime. Another set of problems was associated with the increasing inability of the United States to continue to play the role it had assumed after the war. Japanese and European economic power had grown beyond its initial dependence on the United States, and those states were becoming resentful of what they perceived as an American ability to abuse its favoured position by increasing expenditure on domestic policies and on the Vietnam War without bearing the normal political cost of unpopular tax increases.

One of the problems with an international economic regime that depends critically on the hegemony of a single state is that the hegemon may feel constrained to take actions for essentially domestic reasons that have serious consequences for the entire global economy. This was the case in 1971 when President Nixon severed the link between gold and the dollar and took other steps designed to improve the US economic situation. This 'Nixon shock' marked the effective end of the Bretton Woods regime but not of the IMF, although, following a revision of its articles of agreement in 1978, it abandoned its emphasis on fixed exchange rates. Moreover, although it arranged large loans for the troubled British and Italian economies in the 1970s, the organisation increasingly focused on lending to the third world and, after the end of the cold war, also to the economies undergoing transition from communism in eastern Europe. In this context, with its membership and capital increasing to 183 and $300 billion respectively,[3] its functions came increasingly to justify the term 'global governance', especially when combined with the work of the World Bank, the G7 and the WTO. We shall return to this point after briefly considering the latter three institutions.

The World Bank

The World Bank was originally established to assist the post-war recovery of Europe, but by the 1960s was concentrating exclusively on aiding development in the third world by providing low-interest loans to support major investment projects. Like the IMF, it is funded by member subscriptions, but also by bond flotations on the international financial market and interest on its loans. Both organisations have weighted voting systems, with the United States having voting power in the IMF of 17.11% of total votes, as against Japan's 6.14%, Germany's 6%, Britain and France's 4.95% and Argentina's 0.99%.[4] World Bank voting rights are broadly similar. American influence within the two organisations is further enhanced by the fact that both are housed in the same building in Washington.

The World Bank Agreement explicitly requires the organisation's officials not to be 'influenced in their decisions by the political character of the member or members concerned. Only economic considerations shall be relevant to their decisions ...'.[5] In practice, however, this stipulation has proved impossible to adhere to with any rigour, partly because of the inherent inseparability of economic and political factors and partly because of the impact of American policies. For example, when Robert McNamara became president of the Bank in 1968, he shifted its priorities to some degree away from support for large-scale infrastructural and industrial projects towards dealing with what were perceived to be the underlying causes of poverty in the poorest economies. Inevitably, this took the Bank into politically sensitive areas such as population control and education.[6] More directly, when legislation in the US Congress in 1977 instructed the government to take account of human rights considerations as well as aid recipients' support for international terrorist aircraft hijacking this automatically had an impact on the Bank's decisions. But the greatest controversy has surrounded the increasing tendency by the IMF and World Bank in the last two decades to tie loans to 'structural adjustment' policies, often linked with political conditions revolving around the development of 'good governance' in the recipient states.

Structural adjustment policies derive from the neoliberal perspective that came increasingly to dominate economic thinking in the 1980s and 1990s, particularly with the demise of alternatives such as Eastern European state socialism or Japanese state-guided capitalism. The main tenets of neoliberalism are a firm belief in the efficacy of market forces and hence in the necessity of deregulation and privatisation in economies based on some variant of state control or intervention, and a stress on trade-led growth rather than protectionism. These views form the basis of the 'Washington consensus' over economic policy, so-called because they are shared (and collectively reinforced) by the many governmental, private-sector and intergovernmental economists who are Washington-based.[7] 'Good governance' involves the development of more transparent and accountable political institutions, ending corrupt practices and human rights abuses, and promoting democracy and the rule of law. Both 'good governance' and structural adjustment policies tend to be accompanied by an emphasis on efficient and professional management practices, and hence the transfer of a degree of power from political to technocratic and bureaucratic groups.

In 2002 the organisations had loans and credits outstanding to 88 countries for a total of $88 billion, in most cases explicitly tied to such conditions. They had also developed surveillance and monitoring mechanisms designed, in the words of the IMF website, to 'persuade members to follow policies that are in their own best interest and avoid disruptions in the economies of other members'. Surveillance should not be 'limited to macroeconomic policies but touch on all policies that significantly affect the macroeconomic performance of a country, which, depending on circumstances, may include labor and environmental policies and the economic aspects of governance'. Some criticisms of the IMF–World Bank approach are considered shortly, but at this point it should simply be noted that it fulfils the criteria for global governance listed earlier, given that neoliberalism and good governance both embody powerful normative assumptions as well as convictions about the 'scientific' nature of their central propositions.

The WTO

The third of the major agencies of global economic governance, the WTO, reflects the same economic orthodoxy and has also encountered strong criticism. Bretton Woods had considered establishing an institution like the WTO but the US Congress rejected this, which left only the much weaker regime of the General Agreement on Tariffs and Trade (GATT). This was, in essence, a set of principles, mainly non-discrimination and reciprocity in trade, that provided an agreed framework within which more detailed negotiations could take place. The regime worked adequately in the area for which it was originally designed: the reduction of tariff barriers against manufacturing exports. A number of 'rounds' of negotiations, sponsored by the US, progressively reduced such tariffs to relatively insignificant levels. But several significant problems remained, including a wide range of protectionist devices known as 'non-tariff barriers', such as systematic border delays, preferential government procurement strategies and the use of a wide range of rules and regulations in areas like health and national standards that were designed to make it difficult, if not impossible, for imports to compete effectively with domestic alternatives.[8]

Another set of problems concerned trade in items that had not been included in the original GATT. For example, trade in commercial services such as insurance, data processing and telecommunications was not subject to the GATT regime but only to various specific and limited regimes that had emerged in a random fashion over the years. The significance of this omission may be deduced from the fact that trade in services grew by about 15 per cent per year during 1982–92, as against an annual growth of less than 10 per cent in merchandise exports. The most constant source of irritation – to the present day – was government protection of the agricultural sector. Because agriculture is subject to sharp fluctuations of production and income and because all countries regard it as a vital interest that they should be able to feed their people, agriculture has always received some degree of protection.

All of these issues were the subject of the most comprehensive series of trade negotiations to date: the Uruguay Round, which ran from 1987 to 1993. After much heated debate the negotiations produced agreement on a wide range of issues – so wide, in fact, that the text of the main agreement was more than 400 pages long, with over 20,000 pages of supplementary agreements and specific commitments by countries. Chief highlights were the incorporation into the GATT of trade in services, and trade-related aspects of investment and intellectual property; relatively modest commitments to liberalise trade in agriculture by reducing export subsidies and other measures; the phasing out of many existing quotas on textiles; subjecting government procurement activities to further regulation and liberalisation; improving dispute settlement procedures; and establishing the WTO to take the place of the GATT.

The WTO is essentially a more institutionalised GATT, with a broader range of responsibilities and more powers in the event of disputes. Of all the organisations charged with economic global governance, it has probably incurred the greatest hostility from anti-globalisation protestors, for reasons considered shortly. However, there is little in its essential features to explain why, for example, one anti-globalisation movement, the International Forum on Globalisation (IFG), should declare that the WTO 'is among the most powerful and one of the most secretive international bodies on earth. It is rapidly assuming the role of world government, as 134 nation states, including the United States, have ceded to its vast authority and power.'[9] In fact the (now 148) WTO members reach agreement by consensus in the two main WTO organs, the Ministerial Council, which meets at least every two years, and the General Council, which is the effective governing body of the organisation on a day-to-day basis. The Secretariat, with a staff of only about 550 and a budget of around $100 million, has far less real influence than, for example, the EU Commission or even the UN Secretariat, having mainly administrative and technical duties.

A highly controversial aspect of the WTO is its dispute settlement procedures. Under the GATT regime, disputes were settled essentially through diplomatic processes. The WTO system involves compulsory submission to a juridical panel, if diplomacy is ineffective, with sanctions against states refusing to accept the panel's findings. Only a 'negative' or 'reverse' consensus (a unanimous vote *against* adopting the findings of a panel, or Appellate Body) can prevent a report being adopted. This is the opposite of the GATT procedure, which required a unanimous vote *in favour* of a report for it to be adopted, enabling the losing state in a dispute to block the report.[10] However, it should be noted that WTO sanctions mainly consist of permitting injured parties in a dispute to take retaliatory measures: a sanction whose effectiveness depends essentially on the commercial power of the sanctioning state. The first seven years of the WTO saw 250 cases submitted to the disputes procedure, as against only 300 cases in the entire life of the GATT, from 1947 to 1994, and it is chiefly in this respect that the WTO can lay claim to some global governance capacity. In addition, given that the system covers a much wider range than GATT, it has had a more extensive and substantial impact on domestic legislation, since WTO rules have required states to make sometimes far-reaching amendments to their own laws in order to conform with WTO standards.[11]

The Group of Seven/Eight

One of many complaints that are sometimes heard about international economic governance is that the system as a whole lacks coherence.[12] If there is an agency charged with overall coordination of the system, it is the Group of Eight (G8), to which we now turn.[13] This began in 1973 as informal meetings of the leaders and finance ministers of the USA, Britain, France, Germany and Japan, with Italy and Canada being admitted later. The collapse of the Bretton Woods system had been followed by a quadrupling of the price of oil and there was a clear need for some sort of collective response to the developing global economic crisis from the major powers.

Initially the G7 summits were intended to provide little more than an opportunity for the world's leaders to discuss their common problems and, it was hoped, to help prevent a 1930s-style rush to competitive and self-defeating protectionism. The

original conception was for leaders to meet informally, without their advisers present, and with the world's press also kept at a distance. Inevitably meetings became
more formal, more of a public event and more thoroughly prepared in advance by
technical experts. It also proved impossible to restrict the content of the meetings to
economic matters and the pattern of G7/8 summits since the Birmingham summit of
1998 has been for Finance Ministers (not including Russia, which is not regarded by
the others as having the same economic weight) and Foreign Ministers to meet
before the main summit meeting. Indeed the summit meetings themselves have, in
the last ten years or so, been less concerned with global economic governance than
with a wide range of other issues, including development, security, terrorism, human
rights, transnational crime, drugs, the environment and education, as well as specific
current trouble-spots. Of these, the problems of developing countries, especially
in Africa, have been a major concern of summits since the mid-1990s. Efforts have
also been made to open up the summits to participation from non-G8 actors.
A small number of African leaders have been invited to recent summits, such as the
2002 Canadian meeting, while the UN Secretary-General and administrative heads
of other international economic institutions have also attended. Since the 2000
Okinawa summit, the presence of civil society representatives has been given formal
acknowledgement in the shape of a centre for NGO activities.

In its role as the chief coordinating agency of global governance, the G7/8 has
enjoyed, at best, only limited success. This is, in part, due to the complexities of
global economic management in the post-Bretton Woods era. At first the summits
tended to specify economic tasks, such as reflation or curbing public expenditure for
each member, in the belief that this would permit balanced economic growth within
the G7 as a whole. This approach was not without its problems. The most successful
of the earlier meetings is generally judged to have been the Bonn summit of 1978,
when West Germany and Japan agreed to reflate their economies in return for
American commitments to tighten fiscal policy to reduce inflation, and take action
to reduce oil imports. However, the Germans came later to believe that they had
been pushed into policies that exacerbated their own inflation without having any
long-term impact on resolving world economic problems. The summit also illustrated the dangers of macroeconomic policy in an uncertain world, since it was
followed a year later by the Iranian revolution and a further sharp increase in oil
prices which helped to spark the inflation and subsequent recession of the 1980s.
It was also becoming clear that international financial movements were increasingly
subject to their own imperatives, in particular short-term speculative motives. Given
that by the mid-1980s the global total of international financial exchanges, at around
$60 trillion, was many times greater than the total exchange of goods and services, at
around $4 trillion, this meant that the impact of the G7 economies, even when their
leaders were able to agree concerted action, was strictly limited.

From 1985 until the early 1990s, the dominating issue was how to deal with
Mikhail Gorbachev's revolutionary approach to East–West affairs, and from 1989,
how to respond to the rapidly changing European scene as the cold war ended and
the Soviet empire collapsed. Here too, the impact of the G7 was not always conducive
to the Soviet Union's making a stable transition to democracy and capitalism.
Gorbachev's pleas to the G7 in 1991 for a substantial aid package brought him little
more than patronising advice about his lack of understanding of the workings of

market economies, and the fact that his failure to secure aid occurred in such a public arena was one element in his own downfall and the collapse of the Soviet Union over the next year. While these were not necessarily unwelcome events in the West, they had not been deliberately planned outcomes of the summit and brought a less desirable element of additional instability to European affairs. Since then the summits have attracted increasing criticism and have become a leading target of 'anti-globalisation' protests, notably at Genoa in 2001, when one person died and many more were injured.

Paradoxically, opposition to the G7 has mounted at about the same rate as its real influence has diminished. Some summits have had a significant impact on events – helping to break the logjam in the Uruguay Round, initiating schemes for debt relief for the poorest nations, and securing agreement to initiate the new trade round at Doha in 2001, for example. The exchange of information and views at the summits is also of great value. But for several reasons, including a shift in economic orthodoxy away from Keynesian managerial notions, disagreements among the G7 leaders, the highly technical nature of many contemporary financial problems and the increasing unwieldiness of the summits themselves as their agendas and participants have both grown, the G7 has found itself less and less able to function as the central agency of global governance.

CRITIQUES OF GLOBAL ECONOMIC GOVERNANCE

The four institutions considered here have all incurred vociferous criticism from many different points on the political spectrum. The critics sometimes represent fundamentally opposed viewpoints: right-wing Americans argue that US sovereignty is under assault, while anti-capitalists argue that the system works essentially as a means of ensuring American domination. Moreover, some represent various kinds of special interests, ranging from protectionist lobbies to environmental activists. However, there is also a growing body of critical academic opinion, including 'whistle-blowing' by former insiders, such as the Nobel Prize winning former chief economist at the World Bank, Joseph Stiglitz.[14] The most frequently advanced criticisms of the structure of global economic governance are as follows.

- *The organisations are, in effect, instruments of powerful transnational corporations and international banking conglomerates.* For example, governments rely upon their leading traders for advice on WTO negotiations.
- *The structure is systematically weighted against the third world.* For example, poorer countries lack the resources to engage in the kind of detailed research and planning characteristic of major Western delegations in WTO negotiations. Voting in the IMF and World Bank is dominated by the richest countries, and the poorer countries have relatively little access to the G7/8.
- *It lacks democratic accountability.* None of the officials in any of the organisations is elected, and their proceedings are not open to democratic scrutiny.
- *It is insufficiently sensitive to (and may in fact work against) environmental concerns.* For example, some of the major projects funded by the World Bank, such as dams,

have caused serious ecological damage. Some WTO disputes panels have reached decisions opposing legislation designed to prevent environmental decay or preserve endangered species.

- *The structural adjustment conditions imposed on developing countries inflict more harm than good* and increase the dependence of developing countries on the powerful northern economies. Stiglitz was especially critical of the austerity programmes imposed by the IMF and World Bank on East Asian economies in the wake of the 1997 economic crisis there, which, he argued, had made the situation worse. Similar points have been made in respect of reform programmes imposed on Latin American states and Russia.
- *Global economic governance undermines national sovereignty.* This is a charge levelled by many countries: including powerful states such as the USA.
- *It lacks transparency.* The anti-globalisation movement has inevitably attracted more than its fair share of conspiracy theorists but some of Stiglitz's more recent comments provide some backing for such views, while others have argued that the fact that the institutions tend to draw their experts from a narrow group of Western technocrats encourages an exclusive and secretive culture.[15]
- *It is inefficient.* There are, it is argued, too many agencies involved in global economic governance with too little coordination among them, and the agencies tend to impose a 'one size fits all', neoliberal blueprint, which does not allow for sufficient flexibility to suit different circumstances.
- *It promotes inequality* within as well as between societies. Globalisation as such is believed to favour the richest sectors of society at the expense of the poorer by, for example, providing opportunities for high profits for a few by cutting labour costs for the many. In so far as the organisations are associated with such processes, they share the responsibility for these adverse effects.
- *It damages human rights*, particularly labour rights. Privatisation and deregulation policies – both crucial aspects of structural adjustment – tend to increase unemployment and also reduce the power of organised labour.

Most of these criticisms have some force, although the organisations themselves have been quick to respond with arguments that increased trade does bring benefits to all, that no country is obliged to accept IMF/World Bank aid, that WTO membership is not imposed on any state but rather has been urgently sought by most states, that ultimate power remains in the hands of governments, that structural adjustment policies have produced the required benefits – for example in South Korea[16] –and that the organisations have attempted to meet the criticisms that they are unaccountable, undemocratic and secretive by various reforms. Moreover, since 1987, when it admitted deficiencies in this respect, the World Bank has taken much greater account of environmental concerns.[17]

What is clear is that all four institutions have taken an increasing interest in the problems of developing countries. Indeed, in so far as they do indeed constitute a structure of global governance, this structure has tended more and more to take the form of governance of the poorest countries by the richest, rather than a system that applies equally to all. This is not without benefits for the poorer countries, who receive aid, technical assistance and advice on political, social and economic reform. However, they have been obliged to adapt to an agenda determined almost entirely in the richer economies and which, inevitably, will reflect the thinking – if not the selfish interests – of those economies. Furthermore, the agenda has expanded continuously to embrace many non-economic aspects of the domestic policies of the poorer states. Here, too, this can bring benefits in the shape of good, or at least better, governance in the poorer countries. But if there is a degree of global economic governance, at least so far as the poorer countries are concerned, this has developed in an unplanned, *ad hoc* fashion and with the agents of global governance not accountable for failures of structural adjustment or responsible for its victims or for the social unrest to which it may give rise. In other words, 'governance' may, in the international context, involve power without the responsibility that 'government' domestically carries in all but the most dictatorial of societies.

HUMAN RIGHTS

Traditionally, international law is concerned solely with the rights and duties of states in their relations with each other. The sovereignty of states – the guiding doctrine of contemporary international society – has in particular precluded the international community from any responsibility for the rights of individuals or from any role with regard to a state's treatment of its own citizens. In a formal sense, individuals were only accorded a personality in international law by virtue of their membership of a state. The UN Charter's Article 2.7 enshrines the principle that states alone are responsible for matters falling within their domestic jurisdiction.

There have always been some exceptions to the general rule of no international involvement in human rights questions. In the nineteenth century the practice of slavery was outlawed as a result of international pressure. Similarly, there were European interventions against Turkish mistreatment of Christian subjects of the Ottoman empire. Some even argued that 'humanitarian interventions' were in fact permitted under international law, an assertion that has been frequently reiterated in recent years in support of several such interventions by the UN, NATO or the United States.[18] But only since 1945 have much more extensive claims been advanced for the right of the international community to concern itself with the protection of human rights. This changed attitude was prompted most immediately by the atrocities committed by the fascist powers before and during the Second World War. Early evidence of a new international approach to human rights came with the UN Charter, which contained seven specific references to human rights. Since then, and with increasing force since the end of the cold war, several developments have contributed to the emergence of a multifaceted international human rights regime, comprising both global and regional arrangements and ranging in authority from documents with little more than declaratory significance to substantial and influential institutions. Some of the latter contain provisions that merit their inclusion under the broad heading 'global governance'.

Obstacles

Four key obstacles have hindered the development of a meaningful regime for the international protection of human rights, from the first faltering steps after the

Second World War to the present day. The first is that state sovereignty remains the cornerstone of the international system and no state has shown the least enthusiasm for altering this in any fundamental way. This is not simply a matter of a rogues' conspiracy to guard their privileges, although, clearly, the more dictatorial the leader, the less he is likely to wish to see any externally imposed rules that impinge upon his freedom to do as he pleases within his own domain. But at the other end of the spectrum, the hard-won freedoms and rights of individuals in those few states where such things exist depend upon strong internal institutions, especially those underpinning the rule of law, and until the rest of the world can catch up in this respect, such communities are unlikely to abandon their own distinct and effective sovereign polities in return for some unproven and improbable cosmopolitan order.

Secondly, the concept of 'universal' rights has always encountered problems. This is partly for reasons relating to 'cultural relativism': the argument that each society has its own distinctive conception of rights in line with its own distinctive culture. Saudi Arabia, for example, refused to sign the Universal Declaration of Human Rights in 1948 because it could not accept one implication of the principle of freedom of religion: the right to change one's religion, which the Saudis saw as the crime of apostasy.[19] The Soviets claimed that economic rights, such as the right to work, were more important than the traditional Western emphasis on the rights of the individual against the state. Similarly, several third world states have emphasised the rights of the community over the individual and have argued that for very poor states the imperative of development – and the right to subsistence – overrides individual rights. Most recently, states such as Malaysia and Indonesia have asserted the existence of 'Asian values', which also stress the community rather than the individual. Asian states were primarily responsible for the insertion of a clause in the declaration of the 1993 UN World Conference at Vienna to the effect that a global human rights regime must take account of 'the significance of national and regional peculiarities and various historical, cultural and religious backgrounds'.[20] Even within Western states there are different views of the application of the 'right to life' in the context of capital punishment or abortion. The extent of this problem may be illustrated by the fact that more than thirty states from all regions entered reservations of various kinds when they signed the UN Covenant on Civil and Political Rights.[21]

Thirdly, states have used human rights as a weapon against their political enemies while ignoring violations by their allies. The United States sought to embarrass the Soviet Union by drawing attention to political prisoners there, and one factor behind the 1951 UN Refugee Convention was the fact that most refugees at that time were likely to be fleeing the Soviet bloc, thus enabling Washington to score easy propaganda points. The Soviets responded in kind by publicising racist practices and laws in the United States. Similarly, African states made South African apartheid a major target of UN criticism from the 1960s, while ignoring gross human rights violations in Uganda and other black African states.

Finally, enforcing an international human rights system poses unique problems. The major powers are unlikely ever to incur more than criticism, while sanctions, including the use of force, may be imposed against weaker culprits. States with powerful friends will enjoy more protection than those without such support. Monitoring and punishing violations effectively may impose huge costs, both financially and in terms of the lives of soldiers risked, and there are serious limitations to the willingness of richer states to bear such costs.

The UN and Human Rights

The most universal and comprehensive, but probably the least effective part of the human rights regime is that deriving from the various bodies of the UN. The central UN body is the Human Rights Commission, which operates under the auspices of the Economic and Social Council and whose first task was to draw up the Universal Declaration. This represented the first attempt to arrive at an agreed international definition of rights, and contains 30 articles which are mainly concerned with setting out traditional civil and political rights such as equality before the law, freedom from arbitrary arrest, and freedom of peaceful assembly. Article 28 is interesting in that it states the right of all to 'a social and international order in which the rights and freedoms set out in this Declaration can be realised'. This clearly articulates the principle that individual rights within states are to some extent dependent on the nature of the system of relations among states. Apart from the Declaration, the Commission has also been responsible for drawing up several conventions on specific aspects of human rights, such as racial discrimination, torture, the rights of women and the rights of the child. Each of these has its own supervisory committee. Two key legal documents are the two UN Covenants, one on civil and political rights, the other on economic, social and cultural rights, the separate treatment of these two areas reflecting a divergence of opinion as to which was the more important. Although the Covenants – which have more legal force than the Declaration – were drawn up in the 1950s, they were not agreed by the General Assembly until 1966 and did not come into force until 1976.

During its first 20 years, the UN contented itself primarily with laying down numerous norms in the human rights area, its relative inactivity partly a reflection of deep political divisions. In its second 20 years it gradually acquired a slightly greater assertiveness in relation to human rights, as in 1974 when a special sub-Commission was established to look into 'situations which reveal a consistent pattern of gross violations of human rights', and 1982 when a special rapporteur on summary or arbitrary executions was appointed.[22] The last years of the cold war saw renewed efforts to strengthen the UN's human rights regime. In particular, a more extensive system for monitoring states' observance of their international human rights obligations was developed, greater publicity was given to serious violations of rights in a number of cases, more effective means of investigating and fact-finding were established, and human rights were a significant factor in several of the UN's peacekeeping missions.[23] A further development came in 1993 when the UN established the post of Commissioner for Human Rights, the second occupant of which was the former Irish politician Mary Robinson, who gave the post a relatively high profile.

However, the UN has not proved a suitable base for an effective human rights regime for several reasons. Its agencies are poorly funded and on occasion have even incurred charges of incompetence, bureaucratisation and corruption. More fundamentally, the UN system is weighted against criticism of its members, let alone taking significant action against them for their domestic misdeeds. For example, the Human Rights Committee (HRC) has the role under the Civil and Political Rights Covenant of responding to five-yearly reports submitted by UN members, and also of hearing petitions from individuals against their states when the states concerned have signed an Optional Protocol permitting the Committee to receive such reports. In practice, even when states have signed the Optional Protocol, the HRC's powers are constrained by its lack of resources, by the emphasis in the Covenant on amicable diplomacy and conciliation, by the fact that it cannot impose sanctions, and by the fact that its eighteen elected members seldom all come from states characterised by high levels of human rights observance.[24]

All of the major regional organisations have strengthened their human rights provisions in recent years, including the most successful IGO in this regard, the Council of Europe, as indicated in the previous chapter. As the Council, which was set up in 1949 with 18 members, including Turkey, now embraces most of the former Communist European states, this may be seen as a significant human rights regime. But in so far as *global* rather than *regional* governance in the human rights area is concerned, the most significant recent development has been the decision to create an international criminal court (ICC).

The International Criminal Court

In general, the international community has resisted the notion of creating global juridical agencies vested with the authority to exercise jurisdiction and determine sanctions against individual wrongdoers. There are several reasons for this, of which the most important is the state monopoly over the making, implementation and enforcement of law that is inherent in the principle of sovereignty. The League of Nations, for example, considered but rejected the idea of setting up an international court to deal with terrorists.[25] The League's Permanent Court of International Justice and its successor, the International Court of Justice, are closer to arbitration courts, hearing cases brought voluntarily to them by states in contention, than to municipal courts exercising compulsory jurisdiction against violators of the law.

In cases where an offence had some distinct 'international' component, most notably piracy, which was seen as an offence against all civilised nations, an alternative principle of 'universal jurisdiction' developed. This was the idea that certain categories of crime could be tried by any state that apprehended the miscreant or, if not, that the state had a duty to extradite the accused individual to another state that would put him or her on trial. The principle sometimes cited in such cases is that of *jus cogens*, which expresses the idea that there are certain fundamental norms that cannot be overridden by other legal obligations, such as those entered into in treaties. The principle was extended to cover the slave trade in the nineteenth century and aerial hijacking, hostage-taking and apartheid in the 1970s. The 1984 Convention against torture also incorporated the principle, and although the 1948 Convention against genocide stipulates punishment either in the territory where the act was committed or 'by such other international penal tribunal as may have jurisdiction', practice since then, particularly with regard to former Nazi war criminals, has in effect embraced the universal jurisdiction principle.

In a number of important cases attempts have been made to extend the universal jurisdiction principle to other 'crimes against humanity'. In the 1980 Filartiga case, the family (then domiciled in the USA) of a man who had been tortured and killed in Paraguay, citing an American Statute dating back to 1789, was able to secure a judgement against a Paraguayan official visiting New York.[26] In 1998, in a case of enormous political and symbolic importance, the former Chilean dictator General Pinochet was held in London while British courts debated a request for his extradition to Spain for crimes against humanity. After deliberating over various complex legal issues, it was decided to extradite him, but in the end he was permitted to return to Chile on medical grounds. Since a major part of Pinochet's case rested on his claim to sovereign immunity, this case made significant inroads into the doctrine of sovereignty itself.

The concept of universal jurisdiction contains elements of global governance, since it assumes the existence of globally applicable norms. However, the enforcement of such norms is left in the hands of states rather than international institutions tasked with that purpose and, in practice, is frequently subject to numerous political considerations. The creation of the ICC marked an important step towards true global governance in the human rights area. After the Second World War, the Nuremberg and Tokyo war crimes tribunals convicted a number of Germans and Japanese for war crimes, conspiracy to wage aggressive war, crimes against peace and crimes against humanity. Although the horrendous nature of the offences involved was enough for criticisms of the tribunals that were voiced at the time to be disregarded, a number of misgivings about the trials remained, notably that they represented merely the justice of the victors, whose own wartime conduct would not necessarily stand up to close scrutiny; that they violated the principle that punishment could only be exacted in respect of acts that were clearly established as criminal at the time of the offence ('no retroactive justice'); that the Nuremberg hearings were flawed by strict judicial standards because they took place in a mood of vengeance; and that the use of capital punishment was mistaken.

Such doubts, combined with the effects of the cold war, prevented any further developments in international criminal jurisdiction until 1993, when the International Criminal Tribunal for the Former Yugoslavia was set up by the UN Security Council, followed a year later by a similar tribunal for Rwanda, in the wake of numerous atrocities committed by all sides as Yugoslavia disintegrated, and the massacre of a million Tutsis in Rwanda. These tribunals were to apply existing humanitarian law, including the Geneva Conventions and the Genocide Convention. After a very slow start when the Yugoslav Tribunal was hampered by lack of funds, procedural difficulties and some obstruction from the British and French, who were concerned that the Tribunal might hamper their diplomatic efforts to secure peace, it began to bring an increasing number of accused individuals to the Hague, most notably the former Yugoslav President, Slobodan Milosevic, whose trial began in 2002. Although the Tribunal mainly heard cases against Serbs, there were some trials of Croats and it also examined (but rejected) the case for arraigning NATO soldiers for their bombing campaign in Kosovo in 1999. The Rwanda Tribunal was rather less successful, bringing only a relatively small number of the many thousands who had been involved in the genocidal massacre of Tutsis to trial.

The relative success of the Yugoslav Tribunal was one factor behind the decision to proceed with the creation of the ICC, which was voted for by 120 states in 1998 and achieved the necessary ratifications to come into force in 2002. However, two of the seven states which voted against it were Security Council Permanent members, China and the USA – along with Israel, Iraq, Libya, Yemen and Qatar. This raised some doubts as to the likely effectiveness of the ICC, particularly as the USA continued to distance itself from any possibility that its own servicemen and political leaders might ever be held to account in an international court. In August 2002, America even went so far as to pass legislation entitling it to 'rescue' US personnel detained by the ICC – conjuring up the bizarre prospect of an American invasion of the Hague.

Partly because of earlier American objections, the ICC contains numerous provisions designed to limit its powers. Its remit is 'the most serious crimes of international concern', specifically genocide, crimes against humanity, war crimes and the crime of aggression – although its efficacy in the last case is weakened by the fact that the UN, despite fifty years of deliberations, has been unable to arrive at an agreed definition of 'aggression'. Its Statutes do not permit capital punishment and there are specific provisions in them against retroactive justice: two of the issues that caused misgivings about the Nuremberg Tribunals. The Court is essentially complementary to national jurisdictions rather than a substitute for them, which means that any state with a reasonably effective and impartial legal system is unlikely to find its citizens arraigned. Alleged crimes may be referred to it by states, the Security Council, or its own Prosecutor, but Article 17 of its Statutes contains a proviso that is potentially open to a fairly broad interpretation, to the effect that a case is inadmissible if it 'has been investigated by a State which has jurisdiction over it and the State has decided not to prosecute the person concerned, unless the decision resulted from the unwillingness or inability of the State genuinely to prosecute'. There are also procedures aimed at preventing cases brought for frivolous or politically motivated reasons, as well as permitting states to argue that disclosure of certain information might be harmful to their national security interests.

The ICC commenced activity in 2003 and at this stage it is impossible to tell what kind of impact – if any – it will have upon events. It is in part designed as a deterrent and it is in the nature of deterrents that it is impossible to determine with any accuracy their precise impact if the action being deterred does not happen. It is also clear that the ICC – like the agencies of global economic governance – is far more likely to be utilised in the case of conflicts involving small third world states than against its more powerful members, such as Russia or Britain. However, the Court still qualifies as an instrument of global governance – if a weak one. Its juridical proceedings will be under the control of its own independent lawyers, and although states retain a power of oversight through an Assembly, decisions in this may be taken on the basis of a two-thirds majority, with no individual state having a right of veto. Yet, for all the reasons outlined here, human rights remain the most intractable of possible subjects of global governance. The ICC, together with the occasional willingness of the UN or NATO to engage in 'humanitarian interventions', represents little more than a tentative step towards a preparedness to prevent or punish the very worst cases of inhumanity, rather than the foundation stone of a comprehensive and effective system for the international protection of human rights.

TOWARDS GLOBAL GOVERNANCE?

The Nuclear Non-proliferation Treaty

Elements of global governance, as defined here, may be found in several other areas of international relations. For example, the Nuclear Non-Proliferation Treaty

(NPT) of 1968 distinguishes between nuclear weapons states (NWS) and non-nuclear weapons states (NNWS), and commits the former:

> not to transfer to any recipient whatsoever nuclear weapons or other nuclear devices directly or indirectly; and not in any way to assist, encourage, or induce any non-nuclear weapon state to manufacture or otherwise acquire nuclear weapons or other nuclear explosive devices, or control over such weapons or explosive devices.[27]

The task of enforcing compliance with the NPT rests with the International Atomic Energy Authority (IAEA), formed in 1956, and to a lesser extent with the Nuclear Suppliers Group (NSG), set up in 1974 by exporters of materials for civil nuclear programmes. The IAEA has the right to inspect and monitor states' use of nuclear technology, and the obligation to report its findings to the Security Council. The NSG has undertaken a wider range of responsibilities over nuclear-related exports than the NPT and has a range of diplomatic and commercial sanctions at its disposal. However, the NPT ultimately rests upon the voluntary acquiescence of states in its regime. Three nuclear states, India, Pakistan and Israel, together with Cuba, have not signed the treaty; two others, Iran and North Korea, have sought to acquire a nuclear capability; while the collapse of the Soviet Union has left open the possibility of other 'rogue states' and possibly even terrorist groups (who of course would not be signatories of the Treaty) acquiring nuclear weapons.

The environment

Similar problems occur in other areas of would-be global governance. For example, the environment is thought by many to be the classic case requiring management by global rather than national or even regional authorities, since environmental problems observe no territorial boundaries, making international cooperation to deal with problems that affect all, essential. Yet the international political system retains all of those features – notably the principle of sovereignty and the incentive to cheat or be a free-rider on international agreements if cost–benefit calculations indicate advantages in so doing – that make cooperation difficult. Hence, for every partial success in environmental governance, it is easy to point to several failures.

The contrasting fortunes of international efforts to deal with two distinct problems, the depletion of the ozone layer and global warming, illustrate this. Some similar issues were involved in each case. For example, one issue that had been central in all environmental debates since the first major international conference at Stockholm in 1972 was the fact that the wealthier states were asking the developing countries to take actions to curb pollution when their own wealth had been partly founded on the technology that caused the pollution. A related question concerned the fact that the more environmentally friendly technology was owned by corporations based in the richer countries, which therefore stood to profit greatly at the expense of the poorer countries if international measures were adopted that required the use of such technology. There were also scientific uncertainties about the degree to which each problem was being exacerbated by human factors, and about what the exact consequences were likely to be. Finally, all of the problems inherent in global governance – which agencies were to be charged with responsibility for it, how great should their powers be, how were principles of democracy to be reconciled with both efficiency and the realities of power, and how was state and corporate compliance to be monitored and enforced – were present in all of the environmental negotiations.

The ozone layer in the atmosphere reduces the amount of ultraviolet radiation that reaches the earth's surface and therefore helps prevent the risk of skin cancer and other health problems. The possible contribution of certain chemicals, especially chlorofluorocarbons (CFCs), which are used in refrigeration and air conditioning, to depleting the ozone layer had been speculated about for some time when the UN Environmental Programme (UNEP), which had been set up after the 1972 Stockholm Conference, called for international negotiations to reduce CFC emission. As the scientific evidence on these matters became increasingly clear, states were able to agree to a treaty in Vienna in 1985, and a more important Protocol to the treaty in Montreal in 1987, together with amendments at various conferences since then. These required states to phase out their production of CFCs, and included a financial mechanism, the Global Environment Facility (GEF), designed to compensate developing countries, which were, for the most part, initially reluctant to participate in the agreement.[28] Another innovation was to introduce voting rules in the GEF that, in effect, require a two-thirds majority of both developing and developed countries for decisions about the transfer of resources. Although the potential substitutes for CFCs were relatively expensive, taxes imposed by states on CFCs made it more cost-effective for industry to switch to the substitutes.[29] By 2002 the CFC problem had effectively been eliminated.

One of the principles that has governed environmental negotiations since the Stockholm Conference has been what was later termed 'common but differentiated responsibility': namely that although all have environmental obligations, poorer countries are entitled, on grounds of basic fairness, to the free transfer of the most modern technology, financial compensation for introducing measures to reduce pollution that might harm their own economic development, and even to exemption from some measures. This principle was fundamental to the agreements reached at the 1992 UN Conference on Environment and Development (UNCED) in Rio de Janeiro, and the 1997 Kyoto Protocol, whose main concern was with the problem of global warming. The first conference produced a Framework Convention on Climate Change (FCCC) that was designed to deal with the problem of the contribution made by human-produced carbon in 'greenhouse gases', such as automobile emissions, to global warming. The Kyoto Protocol added teeth to the Convention by requiring states to reduce emissions of greenhouse gases by agreed percentages, with states not meeting their targets effectively 'fined', and also a complex system by which parties to the Protocol could transfer to, or acquire from, other parties 'emission reduction units' – in other words states could 'trade' their permitted emission capacities. 'Sinks', which absorb greenhouse gases naturally, such as forests, could also count towards a state's target reduction. Developing countries had no reduction requirement but projects to reduce emissions in poorer countries that were funded by developed countries would count towards the developed country's target.

The exemption of developing countries from the Protocol was the major factor cited by the US Senate when it expressed its opposition to the Protocol in 1997 in the Byrd–Hagel Resolution, which also claimed that the Protocol's current provisions would damage the US economy. Similar points were made by President George W. Bush's administration, which singled out the exemption of India and China for particular criticism. Although the Protocol is close to receiving the required number of ratifications for it to enter into effect, the absence of the United States, responsible for some 36% of total greenhouse gas emissions, must cast doubt upon the prospects for a sufficient global reduction in emissions, especially as some argue that as much as a 60% reduction is required by 2012, as against the Protocol's target of around 5%.[30]

There are several reasons for the much greater success of the ozone layer agreements compared with the Kyoto Protocol. First, there is far more consensus about the human contribution to depletion of the ozone layer, and also about its adverse consequences, than about the causes and consequences of global warming. Secondly, very powerful special economic interests see themselves as potentially threatened by the requirement to reduce greenhouse gases, which was much less the case with CFCs. Thirdly, it would be far harder to monitor and enforce compliance with the Kyoto Protocol than it was with the ozone layer agreements. Finally, not all accept the particular conception of fairness that underlies the 'common but differentiated responsibilities' principle, or the implication that governments in developed countries should engage in significant intervention in the economic activities of their private sectors.

The Law of the Sea

This last factor was also a significant element in the Reagan administration's rejection of the deep seabed mining provisions of the Third UN Convention on the Law of the Sea in 1982, which similarly had various provisions designed to favour developing countries, including production ceilings on seabed mining production, which were designed to protect existing producers; the transfer of seabed mining technology to developing countries; as well as provisions for the proposed Seabed Mining Authority to have its own mining company and levy taxes on other companies, all primarily in the interests of poorer countries. The Reagan administration saw such provisions as conflicting with its own free market convictions, as well as setting up an IGO with, potentially, too much freedom from state control. Considerations of this kind, as well as those already discussed earlier in this chapter, are likely to act as major constraints on the development of global governance. While the international system may not display the propensity to inter-state violence in pursuit of separate national interests that was so characteristic of earlier periods, it is still, in its essentials, based upon state sovereignty, albeit a sovereignty operating within an increasingly complex and widespread structure of constraints.

NOTES

1. R. O. Keohane and J. S. Nye, Jr, 'Introduction', in J. S. Nye, Jr and J. Donahue (eds), *Governance in a Globalizing World* (Washington, DC: Brookings Institution Press, 2000), p. 12.
2. Jan Aart Scholte, 'Governing Global Finance', *CSGR Working Paper*, no. 88/02 (University of Warwick, 2002), pp. 8–13.
3. Ibid., pp. 5–7.
4. IMF website.

5. F. L. Kirgis, Jr, *International Organizations in their Legal Setting* (St Paul, MN: West Publishing, 1993), p. 570.
6. R. A. Isaak, *International Political Economy: Managing World Economic Change* (Englewood Cliffs, NJ: Prentice Hall, 1991), pp. 199–200.
7. Paul Langley, *World Financial Orders* (London and New York: Routlege, 2002), pp. 126–31. See also R. Higgott, 'Economic Globalization and Global Governance: Towards a Post-Washington Consensus?' in V. Rittberger (ed.), *Global Governance and the United Nations System* (Tokyo: United Nations University, 2001), pp. 127–57.
8. J. J. Schott, assisted by J. W. Burman, *The Uruguay Round: An Assessment* (Washington, DC: Institute for International Economics, 1994).
9. IFG Website, viewed 19 November 2002.
10. Gilbert Gagné, 'International Trade Rules and States', in R. A. Higgott et al. (eds), *Non-state Actors and Authority in the Global System* (London and New York: Routledge, 1999), pp. 229–30.
11. Gary P. Sampson, 'Overview', in Gary P. Sampson (ed.), *The Role of the World Trade Organization in Global Governance* (Tokyo: United Nations University Press, 2001), p. 3.
12. For example, P. Sutherland, J. Sewell and D. Weiner, 'Challenges Facing the WTO and Policies to Address Global Governance', in Sampson, *The Role of the World Trade Organization*, pp. 101–9.
13. The discussion of the G8 that follows is based in part upon J. D. Armstrong, 'The Group of Seven Summits', in D. H. Dunn, *Diplomacy at the Highest Level: The Evolution of International Summitry* (Basingstoke: Macmillan, 1996), pp. 41–52.
14. Joseph Stiglitz, *Globalization and its Discontents* (New York: Allen Lane, 2002).
15. Scholte, 'Governing Global Finance', p. 18.
16. A point made by the former Managing Director of the IMF, Michel Candessus, in response to criticism of him by Stiglitz, *Nouvel Observateur*, 12 September 2002. See www.globalpolicy.org for the full article.
17. Marc Williams, 'The World Bank, the World Trade Organisation and the Environmental Social Movement', in Higgott et al., *Non-State Actors*, pp. 241–54.
18. M. S. McDougal, *Human Rights and World Public Order* (New Haven and London: Yale University Press, 1980), pp. 238–46.
19. Geoffrey Robertson, *Crimes against Humanity: The Struggle for Global Justice* (London: Allen Lane, 2002), p. 29.
20. Ibid., pp. 74–5.
21. United Nations, *Human Rights: Status of International Instruments* (New York: United Nations Publications, 1987), pp. 4–18.
22. General Assembly Document, A/10235, 7 October 1975, pp. 12–13; and J. Donnelly, *International Human Rights* (Boulder, CO: Westview, 1993), p. 62.
23. D. P. Forsythe, *The Internationalization of Human Rights* (Lexington, MA: Lexington Books, 1991), pp. 55–86.
24. See Robertson, *Crimes against Humanity*, pp. 47–59, for a strong critique of the Human Rights Commission. A more favourable account may be found in Dominic McGoldrick, *The Human Rights Committee: Its Role in the Development of the International Covenant on Civil and Political Rights* (Oxford: Clarendon Press, 1991).
25. Robertson, *Crimes against Humanity*, p. 346.
26. Mark Gibney, 'On the Need for an International Civil Court', *Fletcher Forum of World Affairs*, vol. 26:2 (Summer–Fall 2002), p. 50.

27. NPT, in J. Simpson (ed.), *Nuclear Non-proliferation: An Agenda for the 1990s* (Cambridge: Cambridge University Press, 1987), pp. 215–21.
28. E. R. DeSombre, *The Global Environment and World Politics* (London and New York: Continuum, 2002), p. 112.
29. Ibid., p. 106.
30. *Guardian*, 10 December 2002.

chapter 14

The Emergence of Global Civil Society

The term 'civil society' has been employed in several distinct ways in political thought. John Locke used it interchangeably with 'political society', which he imagined as an association based on the rule of law and formed by men in a state of nature to protect their property, which he saw as consisting of life and liberty as well as 'estate'.[1] Locke, however, was very clear that such civil societies excluded absolutist forms of government, while later writers, with the same aim of finding a theoretical foundation for resisting oppressive state power, tended to define civil society as a zone of social activity existing apart from the state. Hegel saw moral superiority and purpose as residing in the state rather than in civil society and Marx equated civil society with 'bourgeois society', or the social relations emanating from capitalism. Both thus problematised the term and made it more ambiguous in its connotations than more contemporary theorists, who returned to the notion of civil society as a zone of private social interaction that prevents the state from undermining individual freedom. David Held's definition provides a succinct and relatively uncontroversial rendering of the modern understanding of the term:

> Civil society constitutes those areas of social life – the domestic world, the economic sphere, cultural activities and political interaction – which are organized by private or voluntary arrangements between individuals and groups outside the *direct* control of the state.[2]

The concept of a *global* civil society is of much more recent coinage, emerging in the 1990s alongside its conceptual partners, globalisation and global governance. Although used primarily to refer to NGOs which operate internationally, it has also been employed to refer to social movements, global advocacy networks and sometimes even transnational corporations. There is, perhaps inevitably, an even greater looseness and flexibility in the use of the term in international relations than in the context of the individual state, but it is possible to distinguish three broad interpretations of the role of global civil society, as elaborated in most writings on the subject. Although distinct, these are not mutually exclusive and we shall begin by considering each in turn.

GLOBAL CIVIL SOCIETY AS A PARTNER IN GLOBAL GOVERNANCE

Kofi Annan, the UN Secretary-General, is one of the greatest enthusiasts for an expanded role for global civil society in global governance. In 1999 he argued:

> We have entered an era of ever-greater partnership and there are few limits to what civil society can achieve ... it is clear that there is a new diplomacy where NGOs, international organizations and governments can come together to pursue their interests.[3]

He expanded on this a year later in his Millennium Report:

> Formal institutional arrangements may often lack the scope, speed and informational capacity to keep up with the rapidly changing global agenda. Mobilizing the skills and other resources of diverse global actors, therefore, may increasingly involve forming loose and temporary global policy networks that cut across national, institutional and disciplinary lines. The UN is well situated to nurture such informal 'coalitions for change' across our various areas of responsibility.[4]

Cynics might argue that the Secretary-General, and his predecessor, who had made similar points in 1994, were doing little more than seeking to compensate for the diminishing resources their organization was receiving from governments, by speaking to an alternative constituency of non-state actors which would both be more willing than governments to work within a UN framework and also provide much needed material assistance and expertise. While such considerations might have been a factor in the UN's turn to NGOs, the reality is that several IGOs have come to rely on the non-state sector for various kinds of support. Moreover, the role of this sector in international affairs dates back much further than the recent UN financial crisis.

The first World Congress of International Associations took place in Brussels in 1910, with 132 International Nongovernmental Organisations (INGOs) represented. This may be seen as the earliest evidence of INGOs perceiving themselves as, in certain respects, a single force on the international stage. At first some INGOs were given the right to attend and speak (but not vote) at some committees of the League of Nations, but they had effectively lost this right by 1939.[5] However, Article 71 of the UN Charter gave the Economic and Social Council (ECOSOC) the capacity to 'make suitable arrangements for consultation with non-governmental organizations which are concerned with matters within its competence'. Following some governmental concern about the possible abuse of this right, an ECOSOC resolution in 1968 spelt out at some length the principles that were to govern NGO access to ECOSOC and its subsidiary organs, namely, that a qualifying NGO 'shall be of representative character and of recognised international standing'; it should also be representative of a substantial number of people, be democratically accountable, and have transparent funding arrangements.[6]

Other IGOs began to allocate informal and sometimes formal roles to NGOs from the 1980s onwards. Following its establishment of the NGO–World Bank Committee in 1982 and the formation of an NGO Working Group on the World Bank in 1984, the Bank has held regular meetings with the NGO community.[7] In a directive in 1989 the Bank attempted to define NGOs in a way that clearly implied their possession of quasi-governance functions in the provision of welfare, describing NGOs as

> groups and institutions that are entirely or largely independent of government and that have primarily humanitarian or co-operative rather than commercial objectives; they are private organizations that pursue activities to relieve suffering, provide basic social services, or undertake community development,

adding – almost as an afterthought – that 'they also include citizens' groups that raise awareness and influence policies'.[8] The Bank has sometimes included NGOs on its missions to specific countries and it collaborates with the leading anti-corruption NGO, Transparency International, in its own work against corruption.[9] It has also incorporated many NGO environmental concerns in its policy-making.

Sceptical voices argue that the Bank's apparent openness to civil society influence is superficial and intended mainly to deflect or tame opposition to its work.[10] However, such critiques may reflect more fundamental ideological disagreement with the Bank's commitment to liberal capitalist principles – in other words, whatever the Bank did would not be sufficient to satisfy some of its critics while it retained its essential nature. There can be little doubt that it has led the way in providing greater access to global civil society in a manner that many other IGOs have emulated. Partly because of an increasing sense that it may be able to bring real influence to bear on world affairs, the civil society community has both grown hugely in numbers and attempted to organise its own affairs more effectively. In 2002, the Second World Social Forum, held in Brazil, attracted 68,000 participants from 131 countries.[11]

So far as their actual involvement in global governance is concerned, the first key role of NGOs is in the setting of normative standards and translating these into an international policy agenda. For example, NGOs were mainly responsible both for formulating the concept of sustainable development and for ensuring that it entered the international discourse at major world gatherings. The growth of NGOs is shown in Figure 14.1. Several specific issues have been identified by NGOs, then targeted for sustained international pressure with the objective of bringing about new international legal instruments. The 1984 Convention Against Torture, for example, was largely a product of a long-term campaign by Amnesty International and other NGOs.[12] NGOs were also influential in bringing about the International Criminal Court, improving international standards relating to the exploitation of children, and identifying and publicising numerous environmental issues, including global warming, the protection of endangered species, and the dangers of various proposals to build dams.

One notable achievement was the 1997 treaty banning antipersonnel landmines, which was the main outcome of the International Campaign to Ban Landmines, which won the Nobel Peace Prize in the same year. The Campaign was unusual in that it was a loose network of more than a thousand NGOs from many countries, together with supporters in IGOs and some governments, most notably Canada, whose Foreign Minister, Lloyd Axworthy, called an International Strategy Conference on landmines in 1996, announced at the Conference that he intended to

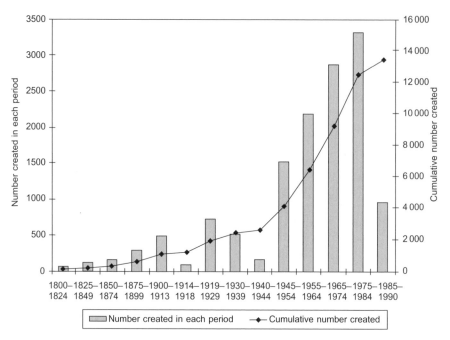

Figure 14.1   The rise in the number of nongovernmental organisations (NGOs),
1800–1900

Source: Union of International Associations, *The Yearbook of International Organizations*, 27th edn, *1990–1991* (Munich, New York, London, Paris: K. G. Saur, 1990), pp. 1666–8.

promote a landmines treaty a year later, and challenged the Campaign to work to secure governmental support.[13] Axworthy was later to speak of global civil society in terms that gave it an explicit role in governance: 'One can no longer relegate NGOs to simple advisory or advocacy roles in this process. They are now part of the way decisions have to be made.'[14] Networks of this kind – termed by some 'global public policy networks'[15] – have been greatly facilitated by the internet and are seen by some as heralding, in the words of the UNDP's 1999 Human Development Report:

> the emergence of a new, much less formal structure of global governance, where governments and partners in civil society, the private sector and others are forming functional coalitions across geographical borders and traditional political lines to move public policy in ways that meet the aspirations of a global citizenry. ... These coalitions use the convening power and the consensus-building, standard setting and implementing roles of the UN, the Bretton Woods institutions and international organizations, but their key strength is that they are bigger than any of us and give new expression to the UN Charter's 'We the peoples.'[16]

A related NGO role involves monitoring states' observance of various international instruments. The best established instance of this is the widely accepted function of the ICRC in relation to the laws of war, in particular the Geneva

Conventions. However, the ICRC owes its high level of acceptability by states in part to the ICRC's traditional discretion and refusal to publicise the many violations of which it becomes aware. Other NGOs, which do not enjoy the ICRC's privileged position, rely on 'naming and shaming' governments, a policy whose success is likely to vary directly with the degree of openness and democracy in the state concerned. In the human rights field, Amnesty, Human Rights Watch and the International Committee of Jurists are particularly prominent in this variant of the monitoring function.[17] The environment – the classic instance of a policy area that transcends national territorial boundaries and so is particularly susceptible to action at the global level – is another area where global civil society plays a major monitoring role. While this takes place primarily through 'naming and shaming' activities, there are some instances where INGOs have been allocated a formal or semi-formal role, such as the responsibility of the International Bureau for Whaling Statistics for monitoring whaling fleets' compliance with their allocated quotas.[18] In some cases both standard setting and monitoring occur within the context of a 'global public policy network', comprising actors from the public sector (IGOs as well as states), business and commerce, and global civil society. The World Commission on Dams, whose task is to 'undertake a global review of the development effectiveness of large dams and to develop internationally acceptable criteria and guidelines for future decision-making on dams', is a good example of such a network.[19]

Finally, some IGOs allocate specific monitoring roles to global civil society – most notably the World Bank, through its Inspection Panel, which was established in 1994. The Panel, whose three members are not Bank employees, is empowered to hear and investigate claims from NGOs and other civil society groups who believe they are, or might be, adversely affected by Bank projects. In some cases negative findings by the Panel have halted the relevant project or caused it to be amended, but it should be noted that this has been the cause of considerable controversy, and that in other cases the Bank's Board has restricted the activities of the Panel. One problem for the Bank – which is responsible primarily to governments – is that some complaints can have highly political motives. For example, a claim filed with the Panel in 1999 by the International Campaign for Tibet, for investigation of the China Western Poverty Reduction Project, touched very sensitive nerves with the Chinese government. However, the Panel's relative success was sufficient for it to be emulated by the Asian Development Bank and the Inter-American Development Bank.[20]

NGOs have also played even more direct parts in global governance, including sharing in the implementation of some programmes and even, in some instances, having specific tasks effectively subcontracted to them by governments and IGOs.[21] This may take many forms: for example, the World Bank frequently includes NGO representatives on its missions to individual countries.[22] But by far the largest NGO role is in delivering development assistance generally, and particularly during humanitarian emergencies. This is, in part, a simple consequence of significant reductions in foreign aid provided by governments, which fell from 0.33 per cent of the combined GDP of the developed countries in 1988 to 0.24 per cent in 1998.[23] Since the number and severity of complex humanitarian emergencies arising from civil conflict and state failure has increased sharply since the end of the cold war, this has necessitated an ever greater response from global civil society. Such emergencies have been defined by Andrew S. Natsios as having five common characteristics:

the deterioration or complete collapse of central government authority; ethnic or religious conflict and widespread human rights abuses; episodic food insecurity, frequently deteriorating into mass starvation; macroeconomic collapse involving hyperinflation, massive unemployment and net decreases in GNP; and mass population movements of displaced people and refugees escaping conflict or searching for food.[24]

This suggests a further principal reason for the increasing role of NGOs in such work: it requires a range of skills and technical expertise – from medical care to road building – as well as a degree of local knowledge that is unlikely to be found in a single agency, governmental or otherwise, but may be found in a group of the major INGOs, such as Oxfam, Médicins Sans Frontières and Catholic Relief Services. The leading humanitarian INGOs have organised themselves into various partnerships (InterAction, in the USA; the International Council of Voluntary Agencies, in Europe) in order to enable them to respond more effectively to emergencies. Here, as in other aspects of global civil society, the Internet has played an important part in such coordination.[25]

Direct involvement in global governance of this kind has not been without sometimes serious problems. Some see dangers in NGOs being drawn too closely into quasi-governmental roles, both through providing an excuse for inaction by wealthy states, and through compromising their other function of helping to hold governments and IGOs to account. The relationship between IGOs and NGOs is not always easy, given their different relations with governments and the fact that they are frequently competing for the same resources.[26] Considerable controversy has surrounded the roles of NGOs (and also IGOs) when they attempt to bring humanitarian aid in situations of internal conflict. As one critic argues, UN and NGO resources in a number of African conflicts have become 'part of a complex economy of warfare between rival clans', with aid helping to keep conflicts going rather than to resolve them.[27] However, as the American experience in Somalia demonstrated, even when intervention in such crises is backed by far more substantial power than is at the disposal of the UN or NGOs, major problems can arise and complete impartiality is close to impossible.

LEGITIMATION OF GLOBAL GOVERNANCE

The literature on global civil society places a considerable emphasis on a second major role: helping to legitimise global governance, in particular through filling the 'democratic deficit' that is often seen as an inherent problem in IGOs. Globalisation is perceived as giving rise to two distinct types of problem so far as accountable, democratic governance is concerned. First, national governments are finding that they are increasingly affected by developments at a global level yet the agencies of such developments – markets and transnational corporations – operate without any kind of democratic accountability. Secondly, power in various areas is passing from governments to IGOs such as the WTO, which are likewise not elected or otherwise directly accountable. The former UN Secretary-General Boutros Boutros-Ghali saw the participation of NGOs in UN and other IGO activity as having an important 'democratizing potential',[28] while both academic observers and activists have seen the growth of global civil society as playing several roles on the international stage equivalent to those played by national groups in states, including enabling public participation in global governance, promoting debate, disseminating information, bringing an element of accountability to IGO activities and helping to legitimise IGO decisions in the eyes of the public.

As long ago as 1954, one of the earliest theorists of international organisation, David Mitrany, saw Article 71 of the UN Charter as having this potential:

> When the drafters of the Charter ... in Article 71 brought private international organizations into a formal relationship within the constitutional organs of the UN, they were ashamed merely to have taken over and given a regular form to what had been a hesitant practice in the working of the League of Nations. In fact they did much more. Whether knowingly or not, they took an important step toward a possible modern solution to the problem of democratic representation.[29]

Mitrany's ideas about particular clusters of democratic practices and institutions developing in the context of specific functional areas of international activity relate to his overall functionalist perspective on international organisation. To some extent they anticipate more recent debates about the possibilities for 'cosmopolitan democracy', whose leading advocate, David Held, argues:

> The idea of a democratic order can no longer be simply defended as an idea suitable to a particular closed political community or nation state. We are compelled to recognize that we live in a complex interconnected world where the extent, intensity and impact of issues (economic, political or environmental) raises questions about where those issues are most appropriately addressed. Deliberative and decision-making centres beyond national territories are appropriately situated when those significantly affected by a public matter constitute a cross-border or transnational grouping, when 'lower' levels of decision-making cannot manage and discharge satisfactorily transnational or international policy questions, and when the principle of democratic legitimacy can only be properly redeemed in a transnational context.[30]

One of the central contentions of such arguments is that specific transnational issues (such as the environment) give rise to specific transnational constituencies of affected groups and individuals who can no longer be defined in terms of traditional democratic notions of universal suffrage within a determinate territory. Democratic legitimacy in such circumstances may derive less from having directly elected representatives in each issue area than from the more varied activities of global civil society. The Commission on Global Governance (an international group of eminent persons) similarly called for the establishment of a Forum of Civil Society, which it saw as more likely to meet the need not just for greater but for more genuine public participation in global governance than the more traditionally grounded idea of a world assembly of parliamentarians.[31] Some academic observers have also seen global civil society's capacity to mobilise public opinion behind specific agendas as offering a more authentic basis for democratic legitimation than frequently discredited governments. Non-state actors often enjoy closer and more intimate access to local levels of public opinion, while many contemporary issues, which are 'long-range, open-ended and diffuse in their need for attention' are not always susceptible to resolution through traditional, centralised modes of decision making.[32]

NGOs and social movements, unsurprisingly, concur with such ideas and have increasingly organised themselves into functional, regional and other groupings in order to strengthen what they perceive as their input to global democracy. In one such meeting, in Manila in 1995 of more than eighty NGO networks, one paper written for the meeting stated:

> In the long run, we have to invent the infrastructure so citizens can participate effectively in the democratic management of the global system. In the next decade, NGOs and their networks are one of the important precursors of an accountable global civil society. They are one of the few actors who try to articulate the global public interest.[33]

Other NGO spokespersons have pointed to the apparent paradox that what they term 'global citizen participation' is on the increase at the same time as participation in more conventional national political activities is declining, and cynicism and disillusionment with traditional political processes rising.[34] The argument here is that the essence of authentic democracy is citizens' participation in decision making, and that this is more likely to be found in the workings of global civil society, even if these may appear to have little in common with such traditional characteristics of democracy as regular elections and delegated authority.

GLOBAL CIVIL SOCIETY AS A SITE OF GLOBAL RESISTANCE

The two functions of global civil society discussed to this point allocate roles to NGOs, advocacy networks and social movements that, in essence, enable them to underpin global governance and make it more accountable and legitimate. Others, focusing on different kinds of activity that still fall under the broad umbrella of 'global civil society', point to a very different role: resisting and if possible overthrowing what are seen as the oppressive and exploitative features of globalisation. Such interpretations are clearly sharply divergent from views of global civil society as comprising major business enterprises as well as NGOs and advocacy networks, and are fundamentally hostile to proposals from Kofi Annan and others for 'global compacts' or 'trisectoral alliances' between states, IGOs and transnational corporations, to work together to achieve improvements in global welfare and human rights.

Anti-capitalist movements of various kinds are as old as capitalism itself, and to the extent that globalisation may be regarded as the latest stage of capitalism, protests against it may be seen as the most recent example of those. Some of its specific criticisms have been briefly mentioned in the previous chapter but at their heart is a perception of globalisation as one of the root causes of numerous evils, including environmental damage, an increasing gap between the richest and poorest countries, growing third world indebtedness, deteriorating conditions of labour (especially for women), worsening public services, and the impoverishment of various sectors of third world economies (such as coffee growers) whose products bring substantial profits for Western transnational companies.

Anti-globalisation protesters cover a range of viewpoints, from those wishing to see radical reform of institutions like the World Bank and IMF to anarchists wanting to bring about the collapse of the entire capitalist system, but most share an ideological antipathy to the kinds of neoliberal economic doctrines that became the dominant orthodoxy during the 1980s. These called for structural adjustment of national economies to make them more open to trade, less controlled by the state and more privately owned, in the belief that such reforms would in the long run create more jobs, lower prices, make companies more competitive and give poorer countries greater access to foreign capital and advanced technology. However, they also required countries to impose various financial disciplines designed to curtail inflation and free up labour markets, whose short-term effects frequently included higher prices and unemployment. The anti-globalisation movement saw such effects as inherent in capitalism itself, rather than a temporary by-product of attempts to liberalise economies, as they were perceived by advocates of neoliberal adjustment policies.

To the extent that structural adjustment programmes (SAPs) were associated with the IMF and World Bank, those organisations became targets of anti-globalisation protests. During the late 1980s, many countries in Latin America and Africa experienced violent riots against SAPs, with several hundred casualties in one case, the 'IMF riots' in Venezuela in 1989.[35] However, although clearly related to each other, these involved essentially national movements protesting about the consequences of specific national policies, rather than a global phenomenon. During the 1990s groups began to emerge, especially in Canada and Mexico, that were opposed to such products of globalisation as the formation of NAFTA, while the demonstrations against the presence of the Indonesian President Suharto at the 1997 APEC conference in Vancouver clearly showed the potential of such international gatherings for gaining worldwide publicity. The large-scale demonstrations against the 1999 meeting in Seattle of the WTO, which had the open intention of forcing the meeting to be abandoned, are generally seen as the first real instance of the new phenomenon of a movement against globalisation as such, whose members are not primarily the victims of structural adjustment policies but often middle-class individuals from Western countries, and whose targets are international gatherings, especially of organisations seen as symbolising or implementing globalisation. Later demonstrations took place at Washington, Prague, Florence and elsewhere, with one protester killed by police at Genoa in July 2001.

One frequently commented-upon irony of the anti-globalisation movement is that it is itself very much a product of globalisation. More specifically, it is a movement that not only makes very intensive use of the Internet to spread information about forthcoming demonstrations and the alleged evil-doings of IGOs and transnational corporations, but in a very real sense is itself a 'virtual movement' that exists in cyberspace, rather than in some more territorially-bounded form. There are, indeed, numerous organised coalitions of activists, such as Direct Action Network, Alliance for Global Justice, Global Action and (founded in 1994 on the fiftieth anniversary of the Bretton Woods Conference) 50 Years is Enough – the US Network for Global Economic Justice. Some of these have established office addresses but by far the greatest part of their work is carried out via the Internet. This makes them susceptible to some of the excesses and eccentricities of the cyber-community as well as making use of its undoubted value as a site for the free (and rapid) flow of information. Indeed, the very freedom of the Internet and the possibility of communicating one's views to a wide audience attracts the holders of bizarre and extreme opinions as well as those with more thoughtful and soundly based views. For example, the anti-globalisation movement has more than its share of conspiracy theorists who believe that globalisation is in effect a secret plot by some fifty of the world's richest men to take over even more of the world's resources than they currently own. There are also individuals who believe that violence is the only method of achieving fundamental political change, as well as an array of representatives of various fringe religions.

It is difficult at this stage to assess the significance of the anti-globalisation movement. Greater police preparedness and also a growing tendency to remove the sites of important international meetings away from places where they can be easily accessed by protesters will inevitably reduce its capacity to cause major disruption at such gatherings, still less to cause them to be abandoned. However, to the more radical leftists, who are probably the most experienced and strongly motivated of the demonstrators, such moves merely serve to reinforce their own propaganda lines: that the police are agents of international capitalism and that the world's leaders have no real contact with the people they are supposed to serve.

Ultimately, the impact of the movement will depend on the degree to which its concerns resonate with those of the wider community. This, however, is a matter not just of public support for the specific issue being raised by the activists, but of the degree to which some of their tactics also alienate people, and the extent to which their actions result in some engagement with more conventional political processes. For example, the Zapatista uprising in the Mexican state of Chiapas in the early 1990s was seen by some analysts as a forerunner of the wider anti-globalisation movement.[36] The uprising was a response by the indigenous peoples of Chiapas to a series of developments that had inflicted serious economic damage upon them, but its larger significance derived from the fact that the leaders of the uprising identified NAFTA and IMF structural adjustment policies as the chief culprits, and also because they made extensive use of the Internet from the beginning to publicise their cause, in return winning support from within Mexico but also globally, as other social movements and NGOs took up their cause. Yet although the Internet clearly helped to internationalise the Zapatistas' cause, and to prevent the government from any expectation that it could simply violently repress the movement, one observer argues that the presentation of the Zapatista cause in anti-liberal terms, together with 'the tendency of some members of the transnational network to view the actions of the Mexican government and the international community in conspiratorial terms', cost the Zapatistas potential support in policy circles in the US and also with influential sections of the Mexican elite that might otherwise have been sympathetic to their cause.[37]

The fact that the anti-globalisation movement is so diverse in its membership, objectives and tactics is both a source of strength and a significant constraint on its prospects of achieving more success than it already has. Its strengths are that it brings together a wide range of individuals who, despite many different perspectives and separate interests, share a conviction that there is something fundamentally wrong with globalisation which requires equally fundamental reform, if not something more drastic. This gives the movement a vitality and dynamism that single-issue net-works might lack. Its organisational diversity, ranging from well established formal transnational NGOs like Greenpeace or Friends of the Earth to networks that exist entirely through the Internet, such as People's Global Action, also gives it the poten-tial for an effective alliance between experience and enthusiasm, between adminis-trative skills and flexibility. Its tactics have been classified by one analyst into broad categories such as education and mobilisation, framing and symbolic mobilisa-tion (e.g. street theatres, 'global witnessing'), disruption, mimicking official public activity (e.g. by holding 'global people's assemblies' or conducting 'people's tribunals' against TNCs), and electronic activism.[38] Here too is a variety of modes of activism each of which is likely to prove attractive to different constituencies. Yet tactics deemed acceptable or entertaining by some will seem like unacceptable violence or foolish pranks to others, while a vague antipathy to globalisation may not be suf-ficient as a unifying factor when so many different interest groups are involved.

CRITIQUES OF GLOBAL CIVIL SOCIETY

All three variants of global civil society have encountered a range of criticisms. First, it is not difficult for any group wishing to push some narrow purpose to exploit the increasing readiness of IGOs and some governments to grant access to private-sector associations. This, at best, can waste the time of overburdened officials in the UN and elsewhere, at worst can give credibility and an international voice to groups whose views would not otherwise command much attention, or indeed would generally be regarded as repugnant. Secondly, even when civil society associations genuinely represent some issue of broad international concern, they vary greatly in their own transparency and efficiency. Jan Aart Scholte has pointed to several potential defects in this respect, including limited opportunities for members of an NGO to participate in its affairs, and opaque financial and decision-making procedures.[39] Against this is the fact the NGOs are aware of their vulnerability to this kind of criticism and have taken steps towards greater self-regulation through such devices as codes of ethics and standards of conduct.[40]

Probably the greatest area of controversy about global civil society concerns the claim that it fills the 'democratic deficit' of globalisation and enhances the inter-national legitimacy of IGOs. Several criticisms of this assertion have been advanced. NGOs and social movements are frequently drawn from very narrow sectors of the population. Their leaders are often unelected and the vast majority tend to stand for viewpoints associated with the left–liberal end of the political spectrum, which casts some doubt upon their claim to represent broad public interests. In addition, civil society remains largely a phenomenon associated with the wealthier Northern states rather than the poorer South, which provides only about 20 per cent of NGOs.[41] There are many reasons for this, ranging from the greater likelihood that states will suppress the growth of civil society in the South, to the obvious fact that the fund-ing required for local NGOs to operate internationally may be beyond the resources of most Southern NGOs. However, some have also suggested that Northern NGOs may have self-interested motives for keeping Southern NGOs in a subordinate posi-tion in so far as their own funding may partly depend upon their claim to act as intermediaries for the South: a claim that might be jeopardised if there was a stronger Southern-based transnational civil society.[42]

There are particular difficulties where the global human rights agenda is dominated by Western NGOs, which may lack sensitivity towards and understanding of the different cultures and value systems that may underlie different human rights perspectives in some third world countries. Nor does the civil society claim to embody a more authentic, participatory form of democracy than the frequently discredited and tired-looking processes of traditional constitutional democracy command universal assent. However righteous their various causes, NGOs in a strict sense represent nobody but themselves.[43]

Similarly, civil society's belief that it may act as a source of legitimacy and accountability for global governance inevitably invites questions about NGOs' own accountability. One much-cited case in this context concerns the campaign waged by Greenpeace against Shell Oil Company's attempt to scuttle the Brent Spar oil rig. Shell had received full international authorisation for this and in fact several of Greenpeace's claims about the ecological dangers were later proved to be unfounded. However, the Greenpeace campaign was having a serious impact on Shell's revenues so the company accepted the heavy cost of alternative means of disposing of the rig. Yet it had, in reality, no legal remedy against Greenpeace, not least because it would have incurred even greater international hostility and loss of revenues had it attempted to sue them.[44] Even in the highly unlikely event of a TNC forcing an NGO into bankruptcy in an effort to gain redress for an unwarranted campaign against its business operations, a similar – if not identical – organisation would swiftly appear in its place. Considerations of this kind have caused some to levy the charge of enjoying power without responsibility against some of the more influential NGOs, particularly in the environmental area. Another complaint against some of the NGOs who have privileged access to the World Bank is that they do not even accept any degree of accountability to other NGOs, who are frequently not kept fully informed about the deliberations of the World Bank–NGO Committee.[45]

Even the role of NGOs as direct participants in global governance has not been immune from criticism. Critics from one perspective have argued that NGOs are merely used by governments and IGOs to lend legitimacy to some of their activities, or as a cheap way of responding to public calls for action to be taken in the event of a humanitarian emergency. There can be little doubt that the needs of failed and fragmenting states are increasing well beyond the current capacity of IGOs and NGOs to deal with them, while assistance from Western governments has either not kept pace with the increasing demands or, in the case of some governments, has actually fallen.

As already argued, in some cases NGOs and IGOs lack the power to prevent their limited assistance from being misused or stolen or employed in ways that may unwittingly add to the crisis rather than aid in resolving it. Moreover, while relief in humanitarian emergencies may command public support and hence some governmental funding, the more complex, and often more expensive tasks of nation-building and laying down the foundations for a more secure future for developing countries may not be able to obtain the necessary support from the powerful Western governments. NGOs, in other words, may assist in bringing some short-term relief but may also help to deflect criticism that governments are not doing enough to tackle the roots of the problem.

A different kind of criticism concerns the overall culture of global civil society, in that some activists may prefer the 'gesture politics' of holding alternative conferences or conducting mock trials of TNCs simultaneously with intergovernmental negotiations, especially those concerned with the environment, rather than engaging in the duller task of attempting to influence the wording of some specific clause in an environmental treaty.[46]

Yet a balanced view would have to reach the conclusion that global civil society, in all three guises considered here, has had an increasing impact on world politics. If its more inflated claims to be the main provider of democratic legitimacy to global governance may be discounted, there can be little doubt that it has added vital dimensions of participation, information and opposition that have helped to prevent global governance from taking place on some lofty plain, far removed from the public gaze. If the deeper problems of collapsed states are not really being addressed, that is essentially a failure of governments, especially in the wealthier Western states, while it is difficult to see any purpose being served by NGOs opting out of emergency relief. And if extremists have tarnished the anti-globalisation movement, while other participants have too exaggerated a perception of the value of such activities as mock assemblies and trials, the demonstrations at Seattle and elsewhere have undeniably helped to focus attention on some very real issues in a manner that more responsible engagement in real politics might not.

NOTES

1. John Locke, *Two Treatises of Civil Government* (London: J. M. Dent, 1953), p. 159.
2. David Held, *Political Theory and the Modern State* (Cambridge: Polity, 1993), p. 6.
3. Michael Edwards, 'Civil Society and Global Governance', in Ramesh Thakur and Edward Newman (eds), *New Millennium: New Perspectives – The UN, Security and Governance* (Tokyo: United Nations University Press, 2000), p. 205.
4. Cited in W. H. Reinicke and F. Deng, *Critical Choices: The UN, Networks, and the Future of Global Governance* (Ottawa: International Development Research Centre, 2000), pp. xviii–xix.
5. Bill Seary, 'The Early History: From the Congress of Vienna to the San Francisco Conference', in P. Willetts (ed.), *'The Conscience of the World': The Influence of NGOs on the UN System* (Washington, DC: Charles Hurst, 1996), pp. 20–3.
6. For details of the ECOSOC resolution, see Appendix B to Willetts, *'The Conscience of the World'*, pp. 291–302. See also R. Wedgwood, 'Legal Personality and the Role of Non-governmental Organizations and Non-state Political Entities in the United Nations System', in R. Hofmann (ed.), *Non-State Actors as Subjects of International Law* (Berlin: Duncker and Humblot, 1999), p. 22.
7. P. Uvin and T. G. Weiss, 'The United Nations and NGOs: Global Civil Society and Institutional Change', in M. I. Glassner (ed.), *The UN at Work* (Westport and London: Praeger, 1998), p. 221.

8. Cited in A. Warleigh, 'Europeanizing Civil Society: NGOs as Agents of Political Socialization', *Journal of Common Market Studies*, vol. 39, no. 4 (November 2001), p. 622n.

9. A. M. Florini, 'Lessons Learned', in her edited book, *The Third Force: The Rise of Transnational Civil Society* (Washington, DC: Brookings Institution Press, 2000), p. 236.

10. See, for example, P. J. Nelson, *The World Bank and NGOs: The Limits of Apolitical Development* (Basingstoke: Macmillan, 1995).

11. M. Glasius, M. Kaldor and H. Anheier (eds), *Global Civil Society, 2002* (Oxford: Oxford University Press, 2002), p. 7.

12. K. Sikkink, 'Nongovernmental Organizations and Transnational Issue Networks in International Politics', in *American Society of International Law, Proceedings of 89th Annual Meeting* (New York, 1995), p. 414.

13. For a brief history of the Campaign, see Motoko Mekata, 'Building Partnerships toward a Common Goal: Experiences of the International Campaign to Ban Landmines', in A. M. Florini (ed.), *The Third Force*, pp. 143–76.

14. Address by Lloyd Axworthy to the Oslo NGO Forum on Banning Antipersonnel Landmines, 10 September 1997, cited in Mekata, 'Building Partnerships', p. 173.

15. Reinicke and Deng, *Critical Choices*, provide the most detailed discussion of such networks in the UN context.

16. Ibid., p. 91.

17. Wedgwood, 'Legal Personality', p. 24.

18. E. R. De Sombre, *The Global Environment and World Politics* (London and New York: Continuum, 2002), pp. 77–8.

19. Reinicke and Deng, *Critical Choices*, pp. 37–40.

20. World Bank website.

21. For the fullest discussion of UN practices in this area, see T. G. Weiss (ed.), *Beyond UN Subcontracting: Task Sharing with Regional Security Arrangements and Service Providing NGOs* (New York: St Martin's Press, 1998).

22. Seamus Cleary, 'The World Bank and NGOs', in Willetts, *'The Conscience of the World'*, p. 90.

23. T. W. Pogge, 'Priorities of Global Justice', in T. W. Pogge (ed.), *Global Justice* (Oxford: Blackwell Publishing, 2003), pp. 6–10.

24. A. S. Natsios, 'NGOs and the UN System in Complex Humanitarian Emergencies: Conflict or Cooperation', in P. F. Diehl (ed.), *The Politics of Global Governance: International Organizations in an Interdependent World* (Boulder, CO: Lynne Rienner, 2001), p. 389.

25. A. Iriye, *Global Community: The Role of International Organizations in the Making of the Contemporary World* (Berkeley, CA: University of California Press, 2002), p. 174.

26. Natsios, 'NGOs and the UN System', pp. 397–401.

27. J. G. Stein, 'New Challenges to Conflict Resolution: Humanitarian Nongovernmental Organizations in Complex Emergencies', in P. C. Stern and D. Druckman (eds), *International Conflict Resolution after the Cold War* (Washington, DC: National Academy Press, 2000), pp. 385–101.

28. Boutros Boutros-Ghali, 'An Agenda for Democratization' (Part 5 of his original UN document with the same title), in B. Holden (ed.), *Global Democracy: Key Debates* (London and New York: Routledge, 2000), pp. 105–24.

29. D. Mitrany, 'An Advance in Democratic Representation', cited in J. J. Lador-Lederer, *International Non-Governmental Organizations and Economic Entities: A Study in Autonomous Organization and Ius Gentium* (Leyden: Sythoff, 1963), p. 378.

30. D. Held, 'The Changing Contours of Political Community: Rethinking Democracy in the Context of Globalization', in Holden (ed.), *Global Democracy*, p. 28.

31. The Commission on Global Governance, *Our Global Neighbourhood* (Oxford: Oxford University Press, 1995), pp. 257–60.

32. Charlotte Ku, 'The Developing Role of NGOs in Global Policy and Law Making', in *Chinese Yearbook of International Law, 1994–5* (Taiwan: China Books and Periodicals, 1995), pp. 142–3.

33. D. Callahan, 'What is Global Civil Society?', *Journal*, vol. 3, no. 1 (Jan.–Feb. 1999). www.civnet.org/journal/vol3no1/ftdcall.htm.

34. M. D. de Oliveira and R. Tandon, 'The Emergence of Global Civil Society', *Issues of Democracy*, USIA Electronic Journals, vol. 1, no. 8 (1996).

35. J. Aart Scholte, ' "In the Foothills": Relations between the IMF and Civil Society', in Higgott et al., *Non-State Actors*, p. 262.

36. For a list of websites relating to the uprising, see www.eco/utexas.edu/faculty/Cleaver/zapsincyber/html.

37. C. Kumar, 'Transnational Networks and Campaigns for Democracy', in Florini (ed.), *The Third Force*, pp. 115–27.

38. J. Smith, 'Globalizing Resistance: the Battle of Seattle and the Future of Social Movements', in J. Smith and H. Johnston (eds), *Globalization and Resistance: Transnational Dimensions of Social Movements* (Oxford: Rowman and Littlefield, 2002), p. 216.

39. Jan Aart Scholte, 'Global Civil Society: Changing the World', Centre for the Study of Globalisation and Regionalisation, Working Paper no. 31/99 (May 1999), p. 30.

40. M. L. Schweitz, 'NGO Participation in International Governance: the Question of Legitimacy', *American Society of International Law Proceedings, 1995*, p. 420.

41. M. Edwards, 'Civil Society and Global Governance', p. 213.

42. See, for example, ibid., p. 211; and Warleigh, 'Europeanizing Civil Society', pp. 626–7.

43. See, for example, J. D. Brown et al., 'Globalization, NGOs, and Multisectoral Relations', in J. S. Nye, *Governance in a Globalising World* (Cambridge, MA: Brookings Institution Press, 2000), pp. 286–8.

44. Wedgwood, 'Legal Personality', pp. 31–2.

45. Seamus Cleary, 'The World Bank and NGOs', pp. 71–2.

46. J. G. Speth, 'A Post-Rio Compact', *Foreign Policy*, no. 88 (Fall 1992), p. 146.

Bibliography

CHAPTER 1 THE RISE OF THE INTERNATIONAL ORGANISATION

Armstrong, David, 'From International Community to International Organisation?', *Commonwealth and Comparative Politics*, vol. 39, no. 3 (November 2001).

Coicaud, Jean-Marc and Heiskanen, Veijo (eds), *The Legitimacy of International Organizations* (Tokyo: United Nations University Press, 2001).

Held, David and McGrew, Anthony (eds), *Governing Globalization: Power, Authority and Global Governance* (Cambridge: Polity, 2002).

Pease, Kelly-Kate S., *International Organizations: Perspectives on Governance in the Twenty-First Century* (Englewood Cliffs, NJ: Prentice Hall, 2000).

CHAPTER 2 THE LEAGUE OF NATIONS

Bendiner, Elmer, *A Time for Angels: The Tragicomic History of the League of Nations* (New York: Weidenfeld and Nicolson, 1975).

Macmillan, Margaret, *Peacemakers: Six Months that Changed the World* (London: John Murray, 2001).

Northedge, F. S., *The League of Nations: Its Life and Times, 1920–1946* (Leicester: Leicester University Press, 1986).

Walters, F. P., *A History of the League of Nations* (London: Oxford University Press, 1952).

CHAPTER 3 THE AMERICAN-LED COLD WAR UN, 1945–60

Claude, Inis, *Swords into Ploughshares* (London: Random House, 1971).

Lie, Trygve, *In the Cause of Peace: Seven Years with the United Nations* (New York: Macmillan, 1954).

Luard, Evan, *The History of the United Nations*, vol. 1: *The Years of Western Domination, 1945–1955* (London: Macmillan, 1989).

Urquhart, Brian, *Hammarskjöld* (New York: Alfred A. Knopf, 1972).

CHAPTER 4   THE THIRD WORLD UN

James, Alan, *The Politics of Peacekeeping* (London: Chatto & Windus, 1969).

Kay, David A., *The New Nations in the United Nations, 1960–67* (New York: Columbia University Press, 1970).

Luard, Evan, *The History of the United Nations*, vol. 2: *The Age of Decolonization, 1955–1965* (London: Macmillan, 1989).

Thant, U., *View from the UN* (Newton Abbot: David & Charles, 1978).

CHAPTER 5   THE UN IN CRISIS

Berridge, G. R., *Return to the UN: UN Diplomacy in Regional Conflicts* (London: Macmillan, 1991).

de Cuéllar, Javier Pérez, *Pilgrimage for Peace: A Secretary-General's Memoir* (New York: St Martin's Press, 1997).

Franck, Thomas M., *Nation against Nation: What Happened to the UN Dream and What the US can Do About It* (Oxford: Oxford University Press, 1985).

Goulding, Marrack, *Peacemonger* (London: John Murray, 2002).

CHAPTER 6   THE NEW WORLD DISORDER: THE UN AND THE MAINTENANCE OF INTERNATIONAL PEACE

Berdal, Mats, 'Lessons not Learned: the Use of Force in "Peace Operations" in the 1990s', *International Peacekeeping*, vol. 7, no. 4 (Winter 2000), pp. 55–77.

International Commission on Intervention and State Sovereignty, *The Responsibility to Protect* (Ottawa: International Development Research Centre, December 2001).

Malone, David M. and Karin Wermester, 'Boom and Bust? The Changing Nature of UN Peacekeeping', *International Peacekeeping*, vol. 7, no. 4 (Winter 2000), pp. 37–54.

Shawcross, Williams, *Deliver Us from Evil: Warlords and Peacekeeping in a World of Endless Conflict* (London: Bloomsbury, 2000).

CHAPTER 7   THE POST-COLD WAR UN

Boutros-Ghali, Boutros, *Unvanquished: A US–UN Saga* (New York: Random House, 1999).

Global Policy Centre web-page, www.globalpolicy.org.

Taylor, Paul and A. J. Groom (eds), *The United Nations at the Millennium: The Principal Organs* (London and New York: Continuum, 2000).

United Nations and UNA-USA web-pages, www.un.org and http.www.unausa.org.

CHAPTER 8   THE EUROPEAN COMMUNITY, 1945–69: ORIGINS AND BEGINNINGS

Mowatt, R. C., *Creating the European Community* (London: Blandford Press, 1973).
Thody, P., *An Historical Introduction to the European Union* (London: Routledge, 1997).
Urwin, D. W. *The Community of Europe: A History of European Integration since 1945*, 2nd edn (London: Longman, 1995).
von der Groeben, H., *The European Community: The Formative Years* (Luxembourg: Office for the Official Publications of the EU European Perspectives Series, 1987).

CHAPTER 9   THE EUROPEAN COMMUNITY, 1970–85: TURBULENCE, EUROPESSIMISM AND EUROSCLEROSIS – WIDENING AT A COST

Ludlow, P., *The Making of the European Monetary System* (London: Butterworths, 1982).
Nicholson, F. and R. East, *From Six to Twelve: The Enlargement of the European Communities* (Harlow: Longman, 1987).
Redmond, J. 'The Community Budget', in A. Griffiths (ed.), *European Community Survey* (London: Longman, 1992).
Wallace, H., *Widening and Deepening: The EC and the New European Agenda* (London: Royal Institute for International Affairs [RIIA], 1989).

CHAPTER 10   THE EUROPEAN COMMUNITY, 1985–92: FROM COMMUNITY TO UNION: DEEPENING DOMINATES WHILE WIDENING WAITS

Cecchini, P. (ed.), *The European Challenge, 1992: The Benefits of a Single Market* (Aldershot: Ashgate, 1988).
Church, C. and D. Phinnemore, *European Union and European Community: A Handbook and Commentary on the Post-Maastricht Treaties* (Hemel Hempsstead: Harvester Wheatsheaf, 1994).
Fennell, R., *The Common Agriculture Policy: Continuity and Change* (Oxford: Clarendon Press, 1997).
Monti, M. *The Single Market and Tomorrow's Europe: A Progress Report* (Luxembourg: Office for Official Publications of the EU, 1996).

CHAPTER 11   THE EUROPEAN UNION, 1993–2003: DEEPENING AND WIDENING?

Diehl, Paul F. (ed.), *The Politics of Global Governance: International Organizations in an Interdependent World* (Boulder, CO: Lynne Rienner, 2001), pp. 328–30.
Hettne, Bjorn et al. (eds), *Globalism and the New Regionalism* (Basingstoke: Macmillan, 1999).

Hook, Glen and Ian Kearns, *Subregionalism and World Order* (Basingstoke: Macmillan, 1999).

McCoubrey, Hilaire and Justin Morris, *Regional Peacekeeping in the Post-Cold War Era* (The Hague: Kluwer Law International, 2000).

CHAPTER 12   THE NEW REGIONALISM

DeSombre, E. R., *The Global Environment and World Politics* (London and New York: Continuum, 2002).

Nye, J. S. Jr. and J. Donahue (eds), *Governance in a Globalizing World* (Washington, DC: Brookings Institution Press, 2000).

Rittberger, V. (ed.), *Global Governance and the United Nations System* (Tokyo: United Nations University, 2001).

Stiglitz, Joseph, *Globalization and its Discontents* (New York: Allen Lane, 2002).

CHAPTER 13   TOWARDS GLOBAL GOVERNANCE

Florini, A. M. (ed.), *The Third Force: The Rise of Transnational Civil Society* (Washington, DC: Brookings Institution Press, 2000).

Glasius, M., M. Kaldor and H. Anheier (eds), *Global Civil Society, 2002* (Oxford: Oxford University Press, 2002).

Higgott, R. A. et al. (eds), *Non-state Actors and Authority in the Global System* (London: Routledge, 1999).

Willetts, P. (ed.), *'The Conscience of the World': The Influence of NGOs on the UN System* (Washington, DC: Charles Hurst, 1996).

Index

Page numbers in *italics* denote tables